KENYATTA

KENYATTA

By Jeremy Murray-Brown

E. P. Dutton & Co., Inc. | New York | 1973

101441

For *JOAN*

AUTHOR'S PREFACE

My interest in Jomo Kenyatta was roused when I made a film about him for the British Broadcasting Corporation. The material available seemed to me so thin and unreliable that I found myself delving ever deeper into new sources, and so was finally drawn into writing this book. I must therefore first of all express my thanks to the BBC for that initial impetus. The responsibility for this work, of course, is entirely mine.

The underlying theme of this book is provided by the clash between two great forces in history—those of British imperialism and African nationalism. Kenyatta was born into Queen Victoria's empire and lived to dine at Buckingham Palace with her great-great-granddaughter, when he was the most respected leader of independent Africa. His life story is the embodiment of a historic drama which is what makes it such a fascinating study.

It is too soon to judge what will be the final result of the clash of these two forces. Africa did not, in the words of Bernard Shaw, 'die of discouragement' through contact with Western civilization; but neither has she yet produced anything authentically new according to Toynbee's formula of challenge and response. Of Kenyatta's claim to greatness, the reader must judge.

I was born on the north-west frontier of India when it still seemed as though the sun would never set on the British Empire. My parents and grandparents believed unquestioningly in the civilizing mission and gave their working lives to its fulfilment in India. I have relatives and friends who have done, and are still doing, the same thing in Africa. I should like to think this book helped to promote understanding between those who still cherish the past and those who are looking for a new world order.

It could not have been written without the assistance of a great number of people. I have acknowledged my many debts at the end of the book and I ask forgiveness from anyone whose name appears to have been forgotten. I alone am answerable for its blemishes.

I must, however, acknowledge with warm thanks help I have received from members of the Kenyatta family, in Kenya and in England, in the use of letters and in information freely supplied. But I should make it clear that this is not, in any sense, an authorized biography and the decisions over the use of material have remained mine throughout. No portion of the manuscript has been read

[7]

prior to publication by a member of the family or by anyone acting on behalf of the President of Kenya.

I have not wished to load the text with detailed notes and these are therefore placed at the end of the book with page references, together with a list of the principal sources on which I have drawn.

East African specialists will notice that I have used African names in their commonest anglicized form. Thus I have stuck throughout to Kikuyu, Kamba, Luo, Swahili etc., rather than the correct Mu-Gikuyu, singular, A-Gikuyu, plural etc. Exceptionally I have retained the form Gikuyu for the name of the legendary founder of the tribe. The Baganda (plural, Muganda singular) speak Luganda and live in Buganda. Uganda is the European version of what the Swahili called it.

The name 'Swahili' itself derives from an Arabic word meaning 'those who live on the East African coast'. They are not strictly a tribe, but they all speak Kiswahili. Usually they are Moslems and they may or may not be of Arab descent.

There are certain words which are so much a part of everyday speech in Kenya that to put English equivalents to them strikes a false note. Most originate from Swahili, such as:

askari—an African soldier, policeman or prison warder

baraza—a meeting, from 'veranda' where the discussion took place

boma—originally a fort or stockade and so an administrative centre

posho—a day's ration of food for porters which was often included as part of their wages

safari—a journey, of any distance

shamba—the peasant holding on which the majority of Africans live, consisting of his homestead and cultivated vegetable plot, often called gardens by early writers

shauri—a discussion, affair or dispute.

Africans usually pronounce words with open syllables, i.e. each syllable must end with a vowel sound, thus: Na-i-ro-bi. Readers must imagine English words like King George spoken with two syllables each, thus: Kingi Georgi.

For simplicity I have used the word 'Kenya' throughout the early part of the book, though the country was not designated Kenya Colony until 1920. Before then it was in theory a Protectorate and called British East Africa.

My thanks are specially due to Michael Sissons, my agent, for his help and encouragement; to my friends in West Kensington for their constant support and for assistance in typing the manuscript; to my bank manager for his understanding handling of my lengthening overdraft; to Mrs Katherine Makower and Miss Antonia Raeburn for help over particular items of research; to my children for their enthusiasm in the progress of the work; to my father for making mathematical sense out of official statistics; and to my wife for her never-failing love. It is to her I dedicate this book.

Jeremy Murray-Brown
London, 1972

CONTENTS

Photographs follow pages 96, 192 and 288.

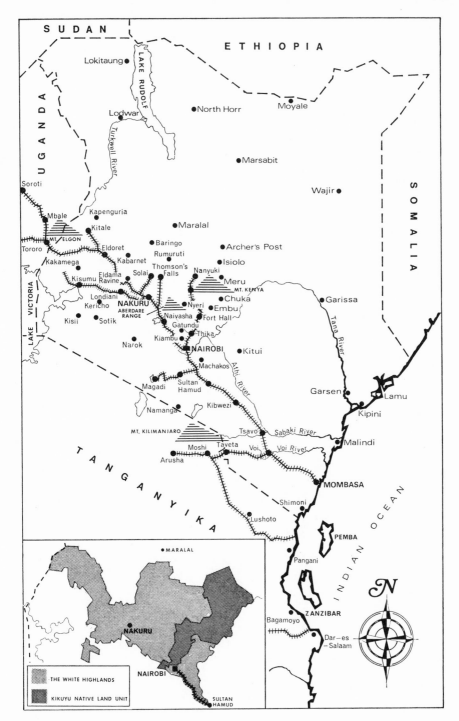

1 Kenya at the end of the colonial period
Inset shows Kikuyu Native Land Unit (dark shading) in relation to the White Highlands

Part I

CHAPTER 1

A World Outside History

There is a site in the highlands of East Africa, in what is now Kenya, which the Kikuyu people regard as the birthplace of Gikuyu, the Adam of their tribe. Four mountains stand sentinel at the corners of the horizon, the highest and most awe-inspiring being Kere-Nyaga, the Mountain of Light, whose black rock precipices and snow-covered peaks rise shimmering in the equatorial sun. To the Kikuyu they seemed like the plumage of an ostrich, and they believed the mountain was the dwelling place of their High God, Mwene-Nyaga, the Possessor of Brightness.

Their legends tell that one day Mwene-Nyaga summoned Gikuyu to his presence and showed him the world that lay within the protective girdle of the mountains. Then he gave him a wife, Mumbi, and his blessing on their descendants:

'Within these walls your sons and daughters shall roam and multiply, enjoying at the same time the beauty of the country and the fruits thereof, and always remembering that it is I who have bestowed them upon you. My blessing shall be with you and your offspring wherever you go.'[1]

According to tradition Gikuyu and Mumbi had nine daughters after whom the nine principal clans of the tribe were named, and for whom Mwene-Nyaga provided nine young men as husbands. The women were thus the original rulers of the people, but they humiliated their men and treated them cruelly. Each woman kept several husbands and killed off those who ceased to be of value. After many generations the men planned revenge. They made the women pregnant all at once and seized power from them. Thereafter they ran the tribe and kept several wives each themselves. And they changed their names. Instead of honouring the memory of Mumbi, their first mother, they called themselves after their ancestral father, Gikuyu.

But the people grew restless under the rule of those who had led the revolt against the women. These were mostly old men, as they had previously endured the worst hardship, and they had elected to serve under a supreme chief, who turned out to be a tyrant. The young warriors now suffered most, and so a further revolution took place, in which it was agreed that on reaching maturity everyone should have some say in the running of affairs. Maturity was marked by initiation through circumcision, which was established at the age of about fifteen to eighteen for boys, ten to twelve for girls. Now, every generation in turn handed over power to its successor in a peaceful ceremony, sealed with a great feast known as *Itwika,* which was held every thirty years or so. The generation which had achieved the new dispensation was given the name *Mwangi,* one who triumphs, and its successor was known as *Irongo,* one who puts things in order—for on it fell the task of building up tribal tradition. These two names were then handed on alternately to every generation that followed in order to commemorate the achievements of their original members. But great respect was still paid to the elders as they were responsible for performing the sacred ceremonies and for invoking the blessing of the High God, Mwene-Nyaga, upon all that the tribe undertook in its earthly existence.

These legends suggest a relatively late tradition, for like most African tribes the Kikuyu did not originate where they were living when they first came into contact with the outside world. But they have preserved no mythology of their more distant origins, nor did they think in terms of history. Theirs was a world which lay outside history and which saw the pattern of human life as unchanging as the stars in the sky and the seasons of nature.

In the course of time the people of East Africa have divided broadly into two distinct ways of life, represented by pastoralists and agriculturalists. The former were constantly on the move across wide, open, spaces, across deserts and plains, and were always pressing upon each other in the struggle for survival; the latter took to the more fertile and higher country where they could consolidate themselves and were better able to safeguard their future.

In the region with which this story is chiefly concerned, the dominant pastoral tribe was the Masai, a nomadic people of Nilo-Hamitic stock who herded cattle and were superbly organized for war. They effectively ruled the dry bush country which stretched from the deserts around Lake Rudolph in the north down the great Rift Valley to the wide plains of Tanganyika in the South. Eastwards they ranged to within a few miles of the coast. The Masai were not as numerous as the agricultural tribes, but their striking physique and courage, and their military organisation, gave them absolute mastery of the open country.

The agriculturalists clustered into the fertile uplands around Lake Victoria and Mount Elgon (14,178 feet), where the predominant tribes were the Bantu Luhya and the Nilotic Luo, and onto the western slopes of the Aberdares (13,120 feet) and the southern and eastern slopes of Mount Kenya (17,058 feet), the Kere-Nyaga of the Kikuyu.[2] Here lived the Kikuyu, Embu and Meru tribes, all Bantu and closely related, while a little to the east were the Kamba.

It is thought that their migrations took the Kikuyu from a primeval Bantu dispersal point in the heart of Africa eastwards past Mount Kilimanjaro (19,342 feet) to the coast, thence northwards along the coastal plain until they reached the River Tana where they turned inland following the river and so swung round until they faced south again, having reached the highlands of East Africa. Here they settled, occupying first the Murang's district, perhaps in the middle of the sixteenth century, and then fanning out north into Nyeri from the beginning of the eighteenth century and south into Kiambu from the beginning of the nineteenth.[3]

They found themselves in a region of sharp ridges succeeding one another in a seemingly endless series of waves, some as much as 500 feet in depth and extending up to twenty miles above the streams which separated them. One after another the ridges traversed the landscape which rose gradually from the plains to the mountain ranges. Above 5,000 feet where rainfall was high the countryside was then covered with natural forest—camphor on the east and south slopes, a species of giant juniper on the north and west (popularly but erroneously described as cedar). These trees gave way at 8,000 feet to bamboo, and at 9,500 feet the bamboo itself gave way to mossy heath and the winds which blew around the shoulders of the mountains.

Within the forests lived originally a race of pigmies who, according to one tradition, then disappeared into holes in the ground and lived on as a race of goblins. Anthropologists have identified these with a late Stone Age people whose underground pit dwellings have been excavated in various parts of East Africa. There was also a race of hunters called the Wandorobo. The Kikuyu system of agriculture was for each family to carve out for itself as much land as it could cultivate. In places the right to do this was secured by arrangements with the Wandorobo who, though formidable with bow and arrow, were a shy people and less organized than the Kikuyu. They gladly exchanged their territory for cattle and moved off ahead of the new-comers.

As the prosperity and numbers of the Kikuyu grew, so did their need for more land. Families simply reached out deeper into the forest, and moved to new ridges. Gradually whole areas were cleared of trees and family by family, ridge by ridge, the tribe acquired its settled ways.

The land that was obtained by these arrangements with the Wandorobo became the perpetual inheritance of the Kikuyu family concerned. It was their *githaka*. On it the head of the family built himself a hut, one for each of his wives, one for his sons and the young unmarried men, and others which served as granaries for his food stuffs. As his sons grew, took wives, built huts for *their* wives and granaries for their own foodstuffs, so the Kikuyu 'village' took shape: a cluster of round wooden huts, with thatched roofs, standing on the edge of the forest or on the slopes of the ridges and surrounded by a mass of cultivated plots. As far as the eye could see were clusters of similar huts in other plots belonging to other families, some of whom might be living by arrangement on the first family's estate as tenants, *muhoi*. But there was no sense of freehold or leasehold possession which could be exchanged or sold by individuals, and no question of rent payable on a regular basis for the right to cultivate the land.

The Kikuyu had no knowledge of the wheel or the plough or the sail, but they had fire and a relatively advanced iron technology. Their principal weapons were a spatula shaped two edged sword, known as a *simi*, a spear similar to, though shorter than, that used by the Masai, and bows and poisoned arrows. Though the Masai were their deadly enemies and effectively sealed them off from out-side influences, sections of the Kikuyu borrowed certain customs from the Masai and shared some of their myths. In some areas Kikuyu women enjoyed an immunity from attack while exchanging goods with their Masai counterparts. The Kikuyu were mostly vegetarians, meat being eaten only occasionally by men after sacrifices. Their staple crops were sweet potato and sugar cane, maize, millet, beans, yams and bananas. Many of them also specialized in bees, while their snuff was the envy of neighbours. The vicissitudes of their pilgrimage through time had endowed them with remarkable qualities. They were, in many respects, the most advanced of all the indigenous people of Kenya.

The organisation of Kikuyu society depended on two 'governing principles'.[4] The first was one of family kinship, which bound members of the tribe together in a vertical relationship stretching backwards to the generations that had died, and forwards to those who were still unborn; and the second was one of age-grades, which bound the tribe together in a complex series of horizontal relationships, and these, too, linked up with corresponding age-grades of dead and future generations.

Family kinship was based on what was known as the *mbari* or 'house' of the man who founded it, that is of the landowner, his wives and children, and grandchildren. It was a pattern which constantly reproduced itself as a family separated itself from its parent group and established its own new *mbari* on new land. But an extended kinship was maintained within a number of subclans, as at one time existed in the Scottish Highlands, and every family was identified with one of the nine clans named after Gikuyu's nine daughters. While virgin land was available the *githaka* system promoted constant expansion, but every male member of a *mbari* could at any time claim his share of the family estate, for which the senior member acted as chief trustee.

Thus family kinship, the *mbari,* was the basic social and economic unit in Kikuyu society. Each family supported itself from its own land and maintained herds of sheep and goats as the prime index of wealth, which also served for practical needs such as sacrifices and skin coverings. The more prosperous families also kept cattle. Goods such as salt, ochre for painting the body, skins, baskets and pots, knives and spears, beans and other foodstuffs, were all exchanged at markets held every four or five days at fixed locations within reach of all neighbouring ridges. Trade as such was unknown.

Tasks within the *mbari* were also prescribed by custom. The men broke up new land and planted the most important crops while the women broke up the clods the men had turned and planted lesser crops like millet, beans, cassava and sorghum. They were responsible also for all the hoeing and weeding and harvesting. Cooking, hut building, beer making—every activity was regulated according to custom. While some families specialized as smiths or trappers or wandering minstrels.

Family kinship included direct relationship with the spirits of the

family ancestors. Most tribal customs were sanctified by the inter-
cession of these spirits and in all important matters to do with the
mbari and their land, such as the building of new homesteads, planting and harvesting, the allocation of plots to members claiming
their share, their blessing had to be invoked. Thus it was vital to
avoid arousing their hostility by wrong, that is 'unclean', action or
by doing anything contrary to custom. Fear of offending the spirits
was one of the most powerful sanctions in the life of the Kikuyu, for
the spirits inhabited every glade and shadow, they dwelt in the water-
falls and under the beds of rivers, and their presence was constantly
felt about the homestead and fields. Before the hut of each family
head there often stood a fig tree in which the ancestral spirits rested;
while special groves were left throughout Kikuyuland when the
forests were cleared as sacred locations for sacrifices. For it was
through the 'scarlet thread of sacrifice' that the living found the
means of communicating with the invisible powers of the world.

The ancestral spirits moved freely in this invisible world. They
were not themselves the source of supernatural power, though they
could often release it if properly approached. But the power might
also be inadvertently disturbed and in these cases the assistance
of a professional medicine man, *mundu mugo,* was required to put
matters right. His services were also available for legitimate aims
such as winning the favor of a girl, and for arming warriors with extra
strength. But great care had always to be taken not to invite a curse.

The second governing principle of tribal life was that of age-grades
which cut right across family and clan interests and set up a different
network of loyalties throughout the tribe as a whole. Initiation into
these age-grades was by circumcision, for girls as well as boys, and
was confirmed at various stages of life by sacrifices and other ceremonies. Each age-grade had an established seniority over its successor and the various grades of eldership provided for all religious,
judicial, political and military functions. Periodically, according to
the legend of the *itwika,* power was handed over from one group of
elders to another, in exchange for handsome gifts of sheep and goats.

In effect this system of eldership was the government of the tribe.
There were no hereditary chiefs or kings, and leadership depended
on the respect of a man's contemporaries, on the number of his
wives and the size of his possessions, or on his success as a worker of
magic. It was perhaps the nearest Africa came to democratic rule in
pre-colonial days.

But the geography of Kikuyuland, its endless series of ridges cutting across the main direction of tribal movement, and the divisive tendency of the *mbari* system, for in time every clan and family had to take independent action to survive, together produced a society of intense local rivalries. Though age-grading might provide a sense of solidarity in the face of some external threat, such as attack by the Masai, its operation in pre-colonial days tended to become increasingly regional. Each ridge had its elders who jealously guarded their position against neighbouring ridges and the structure of elder- ship over the tribe as a whole remained loose, even if it existed at all.

Though this society showed remarkable resilience it contained within itself no force for change, nor did it provide its members with any opportunity for material or spiritual progress. Life for the Kikuyu took on meaning in terms of a past that was constantly reced- ing into infinity. To lose contact with this past was to risk being cut off from eternity, a fate worse than death itself. Death too was abhorrent. To touch a corpse was contaminating, and to allow a man to die in his hut was to risk fearful retribution from his spirit. As death approached, the sick and the old were taken out into the bush and left alone so that their spirits might be free to escape into the shadows when the hyenas finally despatched them.

The High God, Mwene-Nyaga, also known as *Ngai,* was a remote deity of a somewhat capricious nature. He did not concern himself with the fate of individuals, and he could be approached only through elders and the proper sacrifices on behalf of the community as a whole in times of great need. His blessing was also sought in matters affect- ing the family group, such as the birth, initiation, marriage, or death of its members. He was the Creator of all things and ultimately the source of all power. When he cracked his fingers, thunder rolled across the sky and he struck down his enemies with lightning. By implication he was thus the Creator of all men and the God of the Masai and the Kamba, who called him by the same name, *Ngai.* But he stood in a special relation towards the Kikuyu, for his principal dwelling place was Kere-Nyaga (Mount Kenya) and he had chosen the Kikuyu to be his own people, as one of their oldest texts ran: 'God has given the Kikuyu a good land, well watered and overflowing with food'.[5]

Kinship ties, age-grades, and religious worship all emphasised the corporate nature of human existence:

'A man may be considered to a strand of silk within a spider's web. No thread can hang alone; each is linked with its fellows to make a whole. Thus some threads link a man to his father, to his father's clan and to his ancestors; and others bind him to his circumcision brothers. Different ties unite him to the elders who rule the country and administer the law. All these threads come together to form a web, and that web is the Kikuyu people.'[6]

Anyone who set himself outside this pattern risked being called an evil wizard or worker of black magic. Such men conducted their trade in the dark and, if caught, were often killed, their fellow kinsmen being the first to execute judgement upon them. The destiny of the Kikuyu lay precisely in their survival as a community, as a tribe.

It must be admitted that all accounts of the Kikuyu world before the colonial period are a rationalisation of what was essentially vague and mysterious. To describe Kikuyu life in sociological terms tends to undervalue the part played by magic and what can now be seen as religious impulses in producing a harmony between human life and nature within a single created whole, in justifying the ways of God to men. For a Kikuyu of pre-colonial days to make these definitions would endanger his sense of harmony. He took the organisation of his society for granted, he asked no questions about the past or the future of his own people, and he made no distinction between material and spiritual realities. The Kikuyu cosmology was a closed and self-sufficient explanation of *all* reality, extending in space to the four mountain ranges beyond which, it was believed, the sky was supported on huge tusks of ivory, and extending in time to an infinity in which past, present and future generations were all united. The dimensions of time and space came together in the earth, and it was thus the earth which bound members of age-grades together, linked the living with the dead and the unborn, and provided the most powerful sanction of all for tradition. For an agricultural people, land was the breath of life. Without these deep rooted beliefs the Kikuyu could not have survived as a distinct people, so cut off were they in the highlands of East Africa. Yet it may well be more historical to say that it was only the experience of coming into contact with western civilisation during the colonial period which actually gave them their sense of tribal identity and discovered for them their own myths about their past.

When they first entered the forests the ancestors of the Kikuyu had no knowledge of their extent. Expansion north and west was barred by the mountains; southwards the forests stretched in a wedge for some fifty miles until the ridges gave way to the plains again. Beyond roamed the Galla and the Masai who killed anyone who ventured across their path. They had no use for the corrugated terrain of the Kikuyu.

With the cultivation of new ridges generation after generation, century after century, the Kikuyu slowly filled out this wedge. Soon after Trafalgar and Waterloo, when Britain secured her position as the greatest imperial power in the world, sections of the tribe moved into the most southerly tip of the wedge. By the end of the nineteenth century only a thin curtain of forest, no more than five miles wide, separated them from the Masai. The families which had reached the frontier faced a new crisis in their pilgrimage. At this moment history broke into their world with the arrival of men with white skins, strange and terrifying weapons, and altogether different customs.

CHAPTER 2

The Coming of the White Man

The first white man to set eyes on the snow-capped peaks of Mount Kenya was Ludwig Krapf, a German pastor working for the Church Missionary Society at Rabai, a solitary mission station situated in palm trees on a slight elevation some ten miles inland from Mombasa. The date was 3 December 1849, Europe at that time showed little interest in Africa, the Suez Canal had not been cut, and the idea that snow could be found on the Equator was ridiculed.[1]

But the reports of Krapf and his colleague Rebmann stimulated other explorers, notably Burton and Speke, to look for the source of the Nile in the mysterious hinterland about which only rumours and legend had hitherto filtered down to the coast. In Egypt the Nile rose in flood in the driest part of the year; the enigma could only be explained by supposing that the river drained its waters from the very heart of the continent. At the same time David Livingstone's journeys from the south revealed to the world the true nature of the interior of Africa and the devastating extent of the Arab slave trade. The Arabs were nominally subject to the Sultan of Muscat, who in the 1830s had moved his court to the island of Zanzibar off the East African coast and claimed jurisdiction along the coast north of the Portuguese settlements in Mozambique and over a virtually un-limited area of the interior.

It was not, until Livingstone's death in 1873 and the flood of emo-tion released by the saga of his body's last journey to the coast on the shoulders of his loyal servants to be buried in Westminster Abbey that the conscience of Europe was finally moved to take the Arab threat to the people of Africa seriously. What followed is now known as the scramble for Africa, though why it should have happened as suddenly and as completely as it did cannot easily be explained. The fact is that at the time of Livingstone's death, and apart from the Portuguese settlements and the English Cape Colonists, no European state laid serious claim to any extensive area of African soil south of the Sahara. Within a quarter of a century only Ethiopia and Liberia remained nominally free from European influence. On the maps the continent was divided up like a patchwork quilt in the different colours which represented the separate national interests of European powers.

The story of this process belongs to the wider history of European imperialism, that strange mixture of humanitarian, commercial and strategic motives which went into national ambitions in the late nineteenth century.

As far as Kenya was concerned the decisive factor was competition between British and German interests for Uganda. In 1888 the granting of a royal charter to the Imperial British East Africa Company sanctioned the appearance of the British flag on the mainland of East Africa.[2] The directors of the company were fired by Livingstone's philosophy of 'Commerce and Christianity'. They believed that Britain's imperial mission was to civilize the world through her industrial might. Commerce first (a later generation would call it 'development') and the arts of civilization would follow. None doubted it would be a Christian civilization.[3]

Before the entry of the IBEA Company no regular caravan route was known to cross the territory of what is today Kenya. The early missionaries followed Livingstone's path—up the Zambesi and Shire rivers, across to Lake Nyasa and north-westwards to Lake Tanganyika along the 'Stevenson road', so named after the Scottish businessman who floated the company to support his countrymen's missions at Livingstonia and Blantyre. From Lake Tanganyika routes branched, some westwards into the Congo, others northwards *behind* the backs of the Kikuyu to Lake Victoria whence Uganda was reached west of the Nile. Baker had come up the Nile from the north, but came nowhere near the future Kenya.

The Arabs were said to avoid the direct path inland from Mombasa for fear of the Masai, though some believed this was bluff to protect their supplies of ivory and slaves. Their regular caravan route ran from Bagamoyo, on the mainland opposite Zanzibar, due west to Tabora which was the central point from which all the great lakes could be reached.[4] But as the supply of slaves further south grew more scarce, and the search for ivory more intense, no doubt strongly armed Swahili caravans in league with the Masai would soon have struck out from Mombasa through the Kikuyu's protective forest belt if the Europeans had not forestalled them.[5] Up to this moment the Kikuyu proved they could hold their own in their territory. The reports about them which filtered down to missionaries and traders on the coast were discouraging. They acquired a reputation for xenophobia and treachery.

In consequence the first white men to attempt to reach Uganda from the East African coast aimed to skirt Kikuyuland. Their problem was one of supplies—of water and food. The natives did not easily yield food and in the dry seasons water courses were infrequent. From Mombasa, which only became a safari centre with the establishment of the IBEA Company, explorers had the option of following the coast northwards to Malindi and then striking inland along the Sabaki river, which was a lengthy detour, or of cutting directly across the burnt-up Taru plain of vicious thorn trees. After two hundred miles they reached the highlands and a friendly chief of the Kamba tribe lent his name to their depot, Machakos. Here they picked up guides before setting out across Masai territory.

The next landmark was the Ngong hills, the highest point on the plateau on the lip of the Rift Valley. In the highlands water was plentiful, though the tribes were less friendly. A clearing near the edge of the forest was used as an open market. On arrival a caravan fired its rifles in the air to attract attention. From their villages inside the forest the Kikuyu then sent out women with provisions for exchange with the goods brought by the caravan. Known as Ngongo Bagas, it became a regular resting place on the long haul to the interior.[6]

It was here that in 1883 the first European explorer to encounter the Kikuyu, a geologist called Joseph Thomson sent out to report on the terrain, found them to 'have the reputation of being the most troublesome and intractable in this region. No caravan has yet been able to penetrate into the heart of the country, so dense are the forests, and so murderous and thievish are its inhabitants.' Thomson's own experiences confirmed their reputation.

Four years later in 1887 a Hungarian, Count Teleki, was forced to shoot his way across the southern corner of Kikuyuland through being constantly harassed by the 'excitable' and 'restless' natives. He avoided them altogether on his return.

In 1890 there arrived on the scene a penniless, love-sick adventurer, Frederick Lugard. Lugard was a soldier on leave from his regiment in India who was down on his luck and trying to extricate his fortunes with some hard trekking in the bush. He had applied for service with the Italians against the Ethiopians and been rebuffed. He had then volunteered to lead an ill-assorted band of traders, hunters, missionaries, and their native hangers-on, against a force of Arabs who had cut the Stevenson Road and were holding the Scottish missions under siege. The attempt was a fiasco, though Lugard had shown personal bravery and been severely wounded for his trouble. Next, he offered to serve Rhodes. Now he was in the temporary employ of the IBEA Company with orders to reach Uganda as fast as possible to forestall the Germans under Karl Peters.

Lugard's caravan was well armed and well stocked with provisions. His instructions from the IBEA Company included the making of treaties with local chiefs wherever he could on the company's behalf and the establishment of a series of forts along his line of march. With small garrisons of men and supplies these would then become the staging posts along the regular caravan trail which the company hoped to open to Uganda.

Lugard was a controversial figure and he appeared at a decisive moment for the Kikuyu. He was a good leader of men, of an earnest uprightness of character and a sincere Christian. He did not doubt his role as an agent of Britain's mission and when he arrived in Uganda he acted with courage and firmness in a situation made impossible by sectarian quarrels between Roman Catholic and Anglican missionaries and their rival bodies of converts.

Through a career of writing as indefatigable as his trekking, Lugard went on to establish himself as one of the architects of Britain's colonial empire, with an eventual seat in the House of Lords and retirement in the Surrey hills where many an aspiring governor would come to sit at his feet.

What he said about the Kikuyu on his meeting them for the first time came to be quoted as the most authoritative assessment of the tribe at this point in its history. His object at the time was to defend his months of derring-do in the African bush against attack from critics at home.

'I lived among them for close on a month,' wrote Lugard, 'and I was more favourably impressed by them than by any tribe I had as yet met in Africa. We became the greatest of friends, and I had no hesitation in trusting myself almost alone among them, even at considerable distances from camp . . . I found them honest and straightforward; I had very little trouble of any sort among them. Some sheep were stolen from me by people from a village unfriendly to those around me, and as this was a test case, they all looked to see how the white man would stand such treatment. I had no hesitation in dealing with it in a determined manner. I imposed a fine, which, together with the sheep stolen, was to be paid within a given time, under penalty of my attacking the village. They deferred till the last moment, to see if I were in earnest, and then paid my demand which was not exorbitant. In fact, I took a great fancy to the local chief, Eiyeki, and especially to his brother Miroo. They were extremely intelligent, good mannered and *most* friendly.'

Ignoring the tribe's reputation for treachery, Lugard entered into blood-brotherhood with Waiyaki—his 'Eiyeki'—'and several other chiefs' and then reduced the treaty, thus made, to writing, the chiefs putting their marks to it.[7]

On 1 November 1890, Lugard departed for Uganda with the main body of his caravan. He left behind a junior officer, George Wilson, with orders to complete the building of the fort and the safeguarding of his supplies at a site he had chosen known as Dagoretti. With him he also left a small garrison of forty native riflemen. Wilson's nearest support was at Machakos, the supply base forty miles away across the plateau. Between Machakos and Wilson were the Masai.

Dagoretti turned out to be an impossible site. It was five miles inside the forest curtain from Ngongo Bagas, the location favoured by Lugard's employers. The stockade itself was strongly built but it was surrounded by the forest. Though this could be cleared in the immediate vicinity of the fort to give a good field of fire, it meant that water could not be reached without running the gauntlet through the 'jungle'. Collecting provisions put the defenders at the mercy of the natives. The fort only made sense if Waiyaki and his followers remained unequivocally friendly, in which case there was hardly need for one.[8]

Wilson soon ran into difficulties with the Kikuyu and was forced to abandon the fort which the Kikuyu promptly demolished.

The caravan route, however, could not be left without a station at this vital spot, the last at which supplies could be procured until Mumias was reached on the borders of Kavirondo territory at least twenty-five days' marching away. In April 1891 a strong party under Major Eric Smith set out to repair the fortunes of the white man. Smith abandoned Lugard's site altogether. Marching straight for Waiyaki's ridge, he camped in the centre of his village. On a nearby spur he erected a strong fort, complete with moat and two draw-bridges and surrounded by formidable wire and stake defences. Unlike Lugard's stockade at Dagoretti, Fort Smith—or 'Kikuyu' as travellers also called it—was in the Kikuyu cultivated areas, 'some 9 miles from the edge of the forest'.[9]

The ten years that followed Lugard's appearance amongst them turned the world of the Kikuyu upside down. A series of natural disasters accompanied the white man's arrival and was interpreted by the tribesmen as a divine judgement upon them. In succession smallpox, rinderpest, drought, and locusts, struck both Kikuyu and Masai. Some Europeans calculated that up to 50 per cent of the Kikuyu perished in certain areas.[10] Many Kikuyu families abandoned their forward areas altogether. How could they interpret God's will? Their old magic sanctions appeared powerless against the superior magic and superior weapons of the 'red stranger'. They followed the Swahili and called them Wazungu, men who always turn about, are always busy, always on the move.[11]

But although always busy with unaccountable tasks, the strangers also appeared to be preparing to stay. Did Waiyaki really understand what Lugard proposed? Was it his land anyway to offer? Or was he hoping for a suitable chance to seize the white man's magic and consolidate his own position on the outposts of Kikuyuland?

Few white men at that time appreciated the intense local rivalries of the Kikuyu, ridge against ridge, clan against clan, and the limited jurisdiction exercised in the tribe by a leader like Waiyaki. Nor did the first Europeans realize that their arrival coincided with a decisive stage in the Kikuyu move towards the no-man's-land that separated them from the Masai plains.

Waiyaki and his followers were pioneers; they were yielding to the pressures which built up deep inside Kikuyuland as the land originally cleared by their ancestors grew insufficient for the families which succeeded them. In this most southerly tip of the wedge lay the last remaining uncultivated forest. The Kikuyu reached for it at the very moment the strangers arrived. Many of these southern Kikuyu made local pacts with neighbouring Masai clans to safeguard their flanks as they moved forward. Together they raided unsuspecting ridges of their fellow Kikuyu, and so obtained further lands for themselves, in addition to extra wives and goats. Often such pacts were sealed by an exchange of women among the leaders. According to one tradition Waiyaki himself was of Masai origin and had fled from his own people because of some domestic quarrel and gained his standing with the Kikuyu through killing a noted Masai tyrant. On the frontier, survival depended on flexibility with tribal custom and a readiness to out-trick the most treacherous.

Both the Masai and the Kikuyu looked to take advantage from the white man's presence. When Major Smith arrived, the Masai took it as a signal to attack in force and Waiyaki appealed for protection. The company assisted the Kikuyu in staving them off in a pitched battle. Elsewhere the Masai were a constant menace. They interrupted the fortnightly service of mail runners along the caravan route, threatened the Kamba in the hills at Machakos, and were always likely to swoop down on the few isolated mission stations like the CMS at Rabai, or the Presbyterians at Kibwezi, or the Methodists on the Tana River. In 1892 a man soon to become famous in the administration of Kikuyuland, Francis Hall, wrote that 'they are always shot like dogs when seen'.

Hall's was the extravagant language which young men of those days used when describing their adventures. But it was representative enough of the attitude held by most of the white men who first penetrated Kikuyuland. The Africans were 'niggers' or 'kaffirs' and merited little consideration. They were clothed only in animal skins and grease, and carried weird ornaments of feathers, beads, tin, teeth, or anything else that came to hand. Their homes were foul-smelling huts which they shared with animals. Hall arrived at Fort Smith soon after there had been a spectacular showdown with Waiyaki.

Relieved of danger from the Masai through the assistance of the company's riflemen in May 1892, the Kikuyu reverted to harassing the strangers garrisoned among them. It was never clear to the Europeans which Kikuyu village was involved in these attacks; reprisals usually encountered deserted homesteads whose inhabitants had fled long before the expedition reached them. The women, children and goats were hidden, and the men either stood hurling insults from a distance or else vanished into the forests.

In August 1892 the Swahili headman of the new fort was attacked. The local Kikuyu blamed members of more distant villages, but when the Europeans succeeded in capturing one of these, a woman, she blamed Waiyaki himself, 'after a good deal of rough persuasion' as the political record has it. Waiyaki came to the fort. African tradition maintains he was summoned by the European officer in command; the political record says he came of his own accord, knowing he was suspected of treachery, to demand a hearing. A scuffle occurred and Waiyaki was badly cut about the head with his own sword. Next day he was sent under escort for trial by company officers at Mombasa, but he died of his wounds *en route* at Kibwezi and was buried there.

Hall found the Kikuyu to be 'very low class and very treacherous.

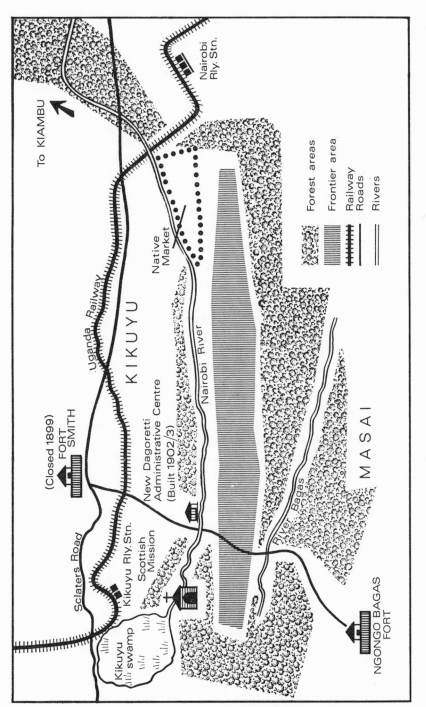

II The Kikuyu-Masai frontier at the beginning of the colonial period

Based on sketch lent by courtesy of Her Majesty's Stationery Office

To KIAMBU

FORT SMITH
(Closed 1899)

Sclaters Road

Uganda Railway

KIKUYU

Kikuyu Rly. Stn.

Kikuyu swamp

Scottish Mission

New Dagoretti Administrative Centre
(Built 1902/3)

Native Market

Nairobi River

Nairobi Rly. Stn.

MASAI

River Bagas

NGONGO BAGAS FORT

Forest areas
Frontier area
Railway
Roads
Rivers

They have continually worried the company's men ever since they arrived . . . and it is quite a common occurrence for them to cut a man up when he is out to fetch wood or water and kill him just for fun.' The method of pacification was rough, but effective. Hall went out with a European colleague and 150 armed natives from the coast.

'We burnt and destroyed everything, occasionally he or I having a long shot at some armed natives. In one place some of the men discovered a lot of goats and cattle and they took all these sharp, killing one man. We worked in two columns, he on one side of the hill and I on the other, and when we had finished met on the top. Without any rest we formed the column up, he in front with his men, then the cattle and my men as rearguard, I myself marching last. In this way I got a few long shots at the Kaffirs, for they tried to follow up on the off chance of regaining their cattle but after a few shots from me at ranges of 6 to 800 yards they soon got sick of it because I think I got two of the brutes right through.'

Because of the threat of German intervention the IBEA Company was overstretched in its attempt at full-scale penetration of Uganda. The directors faced bankruptcy and announced they would have to withdraw. In Britain public opinion was such that no government, Conservative or Liberal, could allow the British flag which Lugard had run up in Mengo, the Baganda capital, to be hauled down again. The undertakings of the company had to be honoured.[12] In 1894 Britain declared a Protectorate over Buganda, later extended to cover the whole of Uganda, and on 15 June 1895 over the remaining East African territories administered by the IBEA Company.

Meanwhile in 1890 the European powers had met in Brussels and agreed on a programme of 'development' for Africa. They would build railways in each of their areas.

Although the IBEA Company was on the verge of bankruptcy, its directors felt bound to undertake for Britain what the colonial mission required. In anticipation of government assistance they organized a railway survey party which set out in the new year of 1892. An official report by Sir Gerald Portal, the British representative in Zanzibar, followed, which, though highly critical of the company's work, decided the Protectorate government should continue with the project when the company finally went out of business.[13]

In 1895 the first rails were laid at Mombasa and for the next five years the work of building went forward. Kenya witnessed an incongruous combination of iron tracks from Birmingham and poisoned arrows, of greased spears and crude, locally-made bricks; of mules imported from Cyprus and harnesses and carts from England; of coolies specially brought over from India to do the navvying, and man-eating lions which held progress up for weeks at Tsavo; of blackwater fever and Eno's fruit salts; of wide-eyed tribes who valued iron for ornamentation on their bodies, and engines which slowly puffed their way from railhead to railhead through vast herds of game.

It was a busy time on the Kikuyu frontier which lay about midway along the route, at mile 345 according to the engineers' measurements. The survey party's caravan crossed with one of Bishop Tucker's on its way up to Uganda. In January 1893 Portal went through on his official investigation, returning in August with a party of Nubians whom he left at Fort Smith to help with cultivation. The illiterate Maltese, James Martin, was active transporting ivory on behalf of the IBEA Company. In April 1893 Hall was helping with a road to link Kibwezi with the Kedong Valley, which sappers had to blast out of the Rift escarpment.

In 1894 a free-lance missionary, Stuart Watt, arrived with his wife and five children. They had walked all the way from the coast and were only just dissuaded from entering Kikuyuland proper. He was followed by the Presbyterians from Kibwezi looking for a new site among the Kikuyu. Waiyaki's family appeared to harbour no ill-will and were ready to offer them land. Was it theirs to offer? Who was there to deny it in the tumultuous times all were living through? If nature lent a hand through famine or cattle disease, the frontier Kikuyu did not hesitate to press home their advantage over the Masai. Missionaries were known to possess strong magic which could add useful protection.

Kikuyu families quickly staked their claims in the new land on the edge of the forest, and the men at the Fort now had allies among the local people. One, named Kinyanjui, was a kind of 'safari leader' to the Europeans. On Waiyaki's removal he was promoted by the British to be the local headman from which position he steadily increased in standing until, at his death in 1929, he was recognized as a paramount chief among the Kikuyu.

In 1894 Hall took command of the station himself, and now it was the turn of the Masai to appeal for protection. Lenana and Sendeyo, two sons of a powerful Masai chief, were engaged in a bloody feud with each other, and their followers ranged across British and

German territory without taking much interest in the white man's activities. The weaker section, under Lenana, was harried by bands of Kikuyu and demoralized by the loss of up to two-thirds of their cattle through rinderpest.

They complained that the Kikuyu were carrying off their women and children and selling them to Kamba and Swahili from the coast. Hall brought a large number of them into the protection of his camp and used them as levies with Kinyanjui in his own punitive expeditions against more distant Kikuyu villages. Eventually he settled them at Ngong. (This did not deter the Masai from massacring a large Swahili caravan with Kikuyu porters returning from Eldama Ravine, a station nearer to Uganda. They caught them in the Kedong Valley, killing about 13 armed and 631 unarmed men. It was maintained later that the Masai attack was provoked by the Swahili attempting to molest their women, but before this was known a trader, Andrew Dick, undertook his own one-man reprisal raid. Throughout a long, hot day in the thorn-covered scrub he collected 200 head of cattle and disposed of over 100 warriors before his rifle jammed and the Masai speared him. Such solitary acts of courage or foolhardiness became the stuff of legend for later generations of white men.) Lenana subsequently earned respect as 'our best friend and ally among the natives'.[14] He was given a monthly subsidy and became one of the judges at the Nairobi cattle show.

In June 1895, when the Foreign Office took over the administration of East Africa, all the up-country stations came under the control of Ainsworth, promoted sub-commissioner, at Machakos, as the Kamba were then thought to be 'numerically the predominant tribe'. When Hall returned from a spell of leave in August 1896 he found conditions on the frontier almost settled: 'so many Europeans have been knocking around that the natives are quite tame and I can ride anywhere alone.' The following year activity was even greater, with the movement of an Indian Baluchi regiment up country to quell Sudanese mutineers in Uganda and with the advance operations of railway surveyors. In 1898 the railhead reached the outskirts of Kikuyuland and great inroads were made into the remaining forest areas to keep the line supplied with fuel and timber. More clearings meant more opportunities for Kikuyu settlement. In 1899 Fort Smith itself was closed and Francis Hall left to carry the British mission into the heart of the tribe where he built another fort. Here in March 1901 he died and the post was named Fort Hall after him. His grave lies in the shade of graceful jacaranda trees beside the Church of the Martyrs.

For a few more years in the Fort Hall (Murang'a) and northern (Nyeri) districts of Kikuyuland the same kind of punitive raids accompanied the business of mapping, road making and fort building. In 1902 a hut tax was introduced. Thus did Kikuyuland, like the rest of Kenya, come under British rule. The Kavirondo, Nandi, Lumbwa and Sotik tribes were brought to heel by similar methods. It did not much matter what the tax was; in some cases crocodile eggs were accepted. The important thing was a readiness to pay.

Francis Hall left his stamp on Kikuyuland. As a later political report put it: 'During those early years from 1893 onwards Mr Hall taught the Gikuyu the lesson of obedience and instilled in them an implicit faith in the promises of Government.'

Sometime towards the end of them, in a typical thatched-roof homestead shared with the sheep and goats at night, a boy was born and given the name Kamau. It is one of the commonest Kikuyu names. The world came to know him as Jomo Kenyatta.

CHAPTER 3

Kenyatta: Birth and Childhood

In those days a Kikuyu birth was not thought of as signifying the arrival of a unique personality; it was important because of the benefits it conferred on the parents and the wider family group. For the father it brought a higher grade of eldership; for the mother the justification of the price of her marriage. If it was a girl, the baby promised an increase in wealth when her time came to be married; if a boy, he would preserve continuity with the spirits of the family's ancestors, and so with the ancestors of the tribe themselves. In a sense a birth was taken for granted as part of the natural order. A man's coming into the world and his life after death were stages in a perpetual communion which stretched back to the creation of the tribe through the will of God and reached forward to all its members still to be born. The baby's life and theirs belonged to the community, as the community belonged to the soil.

There is no certainty about the exact date of Kenyatta's birth. Such records were not kept by the Kikuyu. Their memory of the near past depended not on events in an individual's life but on whatever was happening to the community at the time—a famine, a descent of locusts, or a notable battle with the Masai. Events varied from district to district, even from ridge to ridge. Particular significance was attached to anything associated with initiation ceremonies. As each age-set of initiates grew, so their relationships towards each other and the world were fixed as part of God's decree for the universe. A child entered into this cosmic order; he came from God and his destiny was known to God.

Accordingly, the year 1895 was remembered in some parts of Kikuyuland after a particular sweet-scented flower, 1896 after an obscure name for a clan, 1897 was known as the year of the sweet potato. 1898 was the year of the jigger—the burrowing flea which lays its eggs underneath a person's skin; 1899 the year when the circumcision ceremony went wrong—a dreadful omen which was followed, in 1900, by a year in which the crops failed.[1]

Though the date was unimportant, the location of a birth was remembered because of its relationship with the land. Kenyatta was born some twenty-five miles north-east of Fort Smith at a place called Ngenda, a land of sugar-cane and cattle pasture where two rivers met. True to the mystical hold which the soil possessed over the living, Ngenda was to draw him back in after years until, at Gatundu, it became the strongly-guarded home of the president of Kenya, a shrine for the Kikuyu tribe and a place of pilgrimage for many who came to honour him in his old age.

His father was known as Muigai, his mother Wambui. They were ordinary *shamba* folk—people who cultivated the soil, took additional wives as they could afford them, bred sheep and goats like everyone else. Their homestead was on a spur of land which ran down into a fork of the Thririka River. It was a pleasant site, with fine views of the sacred mountains and steep valleys falling down to the streams which wound their way between the ridges to the Masai plains.

According to Kikuyu custom every child's birth was watched carefully to ensure no offence was given to the spirits, lest disaster fell upon the family and perhaps on the tribe itself. Had the baby's feet touched the ground at the moment of birth? That called for purification. Was it born feet first? Then it must be sacrificed to the divine will. The mother either suffocated it herself or allowed the midwife to carry it out to fallow land. There she placed grass in its mouth and nostrils to stifle its cry for life and the hyenas quickly disposed of its tiny limbs. Twins were especially unlucky—a widely-held view in Africa—and were killed at once. Worst of all was for the mother to die in childbirth. The baby must carry some terrible curse to bring such evil into the homestead. Out he was placed beside his dead mother for the hyenas, and great cleansing was necessary to remove the defilement from the soil of the homestead.

But if all went well with the birth the midwife took the baby and carefully washed and oiled him. She spat a mouthful of gruel into his mouth to bless his earthly life. She carried the placenta to the family's uncultivated land and buried it with seeds and grass to bless the ever-sustaining life of the soil. The mother screamed five times to indicate a boy's arrival. Out listening in the fields the father cut five sugar-canes. His own prestige now increased and he qualified for a higher grade among the clan's elders. A sheep must be killed and a feast held. The women brewed special beer and generous quantities were spilt out on to the ground for the spirits. 'The earth is the mother whose breast gives suck to the children of the nation.'

A baby who survived the tests of birth spent his early life suspended in a goat's skin upon his mother's back as she went about her tasks in the fields and the homestead, even on the most arduous work like the daily climb from the stream with water and when she had to sling loads of firewood or sugar-cane on to her shoulders with a strap round her forehead. After two seasons she would consider him ready for the important ceremony of being born a second time, the occasion when the ancestral spirits accepted his body as their abode.

Kenyatta passed from infancy to childhood. Muigai and Wambui had another son, and he was named Kongo. There had been an older boy, also called Kongo, but he had died. The second Kongo bore the same name as Muigai's father. The ceremonies at birth were repeated; Kongo took Kenyatta's place on Wambui's back, and Kenyatta began to take an interest in what lay around him.

All children live in a world of magic, and for a Kikuyu child the spells were never broken. Experience of life did not destroy the magical environment but gave a boy increased technical skill in manipulating it. If his father was a hunter a boy learned how to make traps, or if he was a beekeeper, how to collect their honey. Smiths, charcoal burners and wandering minstrels, each possessed secrets which they passed on to their sons. A child of a warrior saw how a spear thrust could be made to heal by piercing the two lips of the wound with sharp acacia thorns and then binding stringy bark round the points in a figure of eight. Better still the needle-like fangs of a soldier ant might be held over the cut, so that its powerful jaws would grip each side and draw them together. It would never let go even when its body was twisted from its head. Children saw how fire was made by rubbing a long pencil of hard wood into a hole made in a softer block until it glowed with heat and could be fanned or blown into flames in the middle of a pile of dry bark always carried for the purpose. With practice a boy could make fire in less than a minute.

Then a boy might hide behind a bed or under the eaves of the hut to watch the special work of the doctors whose bodies were hung about with herbs and phials and horns and special instruments which a child was strictly warned not to touch. These men knew when ritual defilement had occurred or an enemy was working mischief and they could smell out the culprit. There would be cleansing to be performed or an antidote effected. If a man felt guilt he would be induced to vomit out the sin through magic herbs mixed with sheeps' excreta. More terrifying still were the wizards, strange men who lived alone and worked poison at night, who could change themselves into leopards and lie in wait for an enemy in the forest. Sometimes such men were killed, but all feared them, for they knew powerful magic.

A child must learn to recognize these forces in his surroundings, just as nature's magic produced for each tree and shrub its distinctive shape and use. The wood of the Mugago tree was so hard ants could not eat it, and so was useful for building huts. The leaves of the Muthiga, the Greenheart, had a taste of fire which cured the body of many ailments. The Mugomo fig trees were sacred and elders performed sacrifices beside them out of sight of children and women. The boy who dreamed of being a warrior paid special attention to the Murichu tree which held the secret of arrow poison. You boiled the bark and roots to a thick sticky paste which was strong enough to kill an elephant.

But it was with the family goats and sheep that a Kikuyu child spent most of his time. The Kikuyu were normally vegetarian, so the sheep and goats were not killed for food but cared for as representing the family's wealth and prestige. They were essential for buying wives and for the ceremonies which promoted a father's grade of eldership. In the life of each individual there were over a hundred occasions when a sheep was required for sacrifice.

A Kikuyu boy grew up with the animals and shared his experience of life with them. Every boy spent his childhood herding the family's flock, usually with other boys from neighbouring families. It was their first communal activity, every generation went through it in turn and it linked them all to nature. The sheep and goats helped to mediate the terrors of the magical world, for their instincts gave warning of dangers hidden from a child's eyes in the bush or the darkness of night.

Education in a Kikuyu homestead was schooling for life. Kenyatta learned to respect the elders, for nothing was more terrible than the curse of a dying father. Through songs and lullabies he absorbed into his own nature all that his mother knew of the flowers and trees and the magic of his surroundings. From her he learnt how wild and tame animals came to be separated from each other and about the greed of the hyena, the *hiti,* which played such a grim role in a man's last hours. Listening to her stories as she prepared the evening meal round the fire, maybe sweet potatoes and gruel one day, or a mixture of beans, maize and bananas the next, he picked up the traditions of his people, details of his family background and the names of his ancestors, and learnt about the ways of God and his various resting places up on the mountain peaks, and, most important, the legends of Gikuyu and Mumbi, father and mother of the tribe.

Ngenda was one of a series of ridges in what was later known as the Kiambu district of Kikuyuland, part of the southern section of the forest belt, into which clans were migrating throughout the nineteenth century. Striking out into the forest, the head of a family staked his claim to whatever he and his sons could clear and his wives could cultivate. Maybe they came to an arrangement with the Wandorobo, the aboriginal people who lived off honey and berries and game. Some Kikuyu families were said to have acquired huge estates in this way on which other members of the clan settled as tenants, each with his own *shamba*. The founder of Kenyatta's family lands at Ngenda was Muigai's grandfather, Magana. Magana means literally 'hundreds' in Kikuyu, and perhaps the name referred to the extent of his possessions.

Magana's family grew. The ridges filled out, and the clan prospered. Only twenty-five miles now separated them from the edge of the forest to the south. By the time of Kenyatta's birth there was considerable movement between Ngenda and Dagoretti. Many families followed Waiyaki. Taking advantage of the white man's arrival and the discomfiture of the Masai, the Kikuyu would leave some of their number to safeguard the lands they already cultivated, while others pushed on to the frontier. Muigai and his brother Ngengi remained on the ridge at Ngenda; Kongo and Kuria, both sons of Magana, followed the trail south. They settled on the ridge of Muthiga, not far from the site of Lugard's ill-fated stockade.

Shortly after Kenyatta's younger brother Kongo was born, his father, Muigai, died. His mother, Wambui, passed according to Kikuyu laws of inheritance to Muigai's younger brother, Ngengi. She bore him a son. The new baby carried the spirit of his dead 'father' Muigai, and was therefore named after him. Kenyatta now had two brothers, Kongo and Muigai, and on him fell the responsibilities of the eldest—the future head of the family who would one day take charge of its land and fortunes. Meanwhile Ngengi exercised the leadership of the homestead, and he was a harsh man. He stood towards his sons only as the shadow of the dead Muigai. They brought him no wealth as would daughters when they married, but instead they could always claim the rights of inheritance. For them goats must be found when the time came for *their* initiation and the purchase of *their* wives. Though tribal custom must be honoured, no natural bond of affection restrained his growing resentment at their presence.

Life for the young Kenyatta at Ngenda was hard, and his mother, Wambui, also suffered. Soon after the birth of Muigai she left Ngenda to return to her own people further north, taking her infant son with her. There she died. As soon as the news reached him, the young Kenyatta set off across country to look for her family homestead and his baby brother. He had loved Wambui deeply. Now he was alone in the world. Taking Muigai in his arms he carried him back through the bush to Ngenda, and put him in the care of Wambui's co-wives and sisters. He himself had to work the harder and undertake many chores like grinding millet which should have been women's work, while there was always herding to be done by the young boys. His childhood was over.

'The young men go, the old men stay?' asked the young Kikuyu herdboys of one another in their game of riddles. 'The ashes are poured out, the hearth stones remain', their comrades replied. Kenyatta thought of his own future and of his grandfather, Kongo son of Magana, who now lived at Muthiga twenty-five miles away. Kenyatta's generation were brought up on stories of what was happening beyond the edge of the forest. They repeated the prophecy of a famous elder called Mugo wa Kabiro who woke up one morning trembling after God had taken him on a long journey and shown him strange men like butterflies with pale skins the colour of frogs and bells on their feet. He foretold how a great iron snake would unwind itself across the land. Several boys had seen the strangers themselves. They could eat poison without taking hurt, and had been seen drinking boiling water (Eno's fruit salts).

There was one boy called Musa Gitau who had actually lived with the strangers at a place called Thogoto right on the edge of the forest. He was older than Kenyatta and his family came from the same ridge at Ngenda. They lived now near Dagoretti. One season he returned with his father's sheep and goats to their old grazing land because pasture was becoming scarce on the frontier. He told Kenyatta about the new world that was unfolding beyond the ridges, and the young herdboy, with the instincts of youth, reached the decision which was to change his future. Kenyatta left Ngenda to join his grandfather, Kongo son of Magana, at Muthiga.

He was a man of mystery, one of the workers of magic whose charms and advice were needed to help the clan in its advance into the new territory. Now he was an old man with sore legs wrapped in skin bandages. At Muthiga Kenyatta assisted his grandfather in carrying his magical equipment, and he learned something of the medicine-man's craft. But his main job, as ever, was to herd the goats. From Muthiga it was a short distance to the salt licks at Gitiba, where brackish water was mixed with earth to give the animals the saline intake necessary for their health. Gitiba was towards Ngongo Bagas, and it was an area which had seen much activity during the arrival of the white men. The railway, of which Mugo wa Kabiro had spoken, now ran across the hillsides towards some unknown destination beyond the hills. Kenyatta met people who had travelled in these iron monsters. They returned with strange tales of what they had seen:

'They talked about the big water, like a vast treeless plain, that stretched as far as eye could see and beyond that. And how they had seen large animals that spat fire and smoke come floating on the endless water, and ghastly pale people coming out of these animals' stomachs. Their dress and behaviour was different from that of the Arabs, and they seemed to keep to themselves. The stories of these marvels of the coast were told and retold, and everywhere the people heard them with gaping mouths and staring eyes.'

So Kenyatta later recalled his boyhood impressions.[2]

The herdboys had to get the goats out early, before the sun had climbed high enough into the sky to suck up the overnight dew. On clear days Kere-Nyaga's jagged form could be seen through the cold morning air. Did these mysterious strangers, they asked themselves, possess a magic that was stronger than that of Kenyatta's grandfather Kongo wa Magana? The old men were subdued. 'Against this new magic the wisdom of our ancestors is as dust blown against the rock, or as a twig carried down by a river in flood'.[3]

One day Kenyatta returned with his flock to find an unusual stirring in his grandfather's village. He ran with his friends to the chief's hut where the commotion was greatest. There stood one of the pink-faced ones. He was not angry and gesticulating, as they had been told others were, but was trying hard to be friendly. He had appeared suddenly in the village that morning, Kenyatta learned, and had asked to see the chief. Now the interview was ready, and the boy Kenyatta crowded in with his friends as close as they could to hear what the interpreter was saying.

The drum sounded its note of welcome, the elders rose to appeal to the Lord of Nature for peace, and the chief thumped the earth with his knobkerrie as he asked the visitor to explain what he wanted. Eagerly young Kenyatta listened to the words of the interpreter: 'I am God's messenger' he heard the man say, and a thrill of excitement ran through the listening Kikuyu, as the magicians and elders exchanged glances.

The stranger's name was Scott, and he came from across the stream which lay at the bottom of Muthiga ridge.[4] Hidden in the forest up there lay the houses of several strangers. The Kikuyu called it Thogoto.

The scene made a deep impression on the young herdboy. The most impressive part was what the missionary had done with his pencil and paper, those black lines and dots which carried messages for all who knew how to interpret them. This truly was white man's magic. Kenyatta had seen specially trained messengers from the white man's headquarters at Kiambu carrying the magic with them. They would visit the senior elder of a village, give him their message and then place the magic in front of him in a forked stick where it would have to be obeyed. Often the message called for the young men of the village to go down to work for the white man.

After one such visit Kenyatta stood eyeing the stick with the fluttering paper which the men had left behind. What was the secret of its power? Kenyatta questioned it. But it made no reply. He addressed it again. It remained silent. This is strange, he thought. How is it that these people bring the paper and then say that the Europeans say so and so from Kiambu? But the paper continued to flutter in the breeze. Kenyatta decided he must discover the secret of that magic for himself. He would find out what they taught at Thogoto. The date was November 1909, as the white men reckoned history, and it was a milestone in his life.[5]

CHAPTER 4

Thogoto, the Scottish Mission

The Scottish mission station of Thogoto stood at the junction of industrial Europe and the primeval jungle. More than a settler's farm or an administrative office, more than a fort or a railway even, it represented the promise of civilisation.

Its inspiration came from the Scottish missionaries who followed Livingstone's call and founded stations at Blantyre and Livingstonia on the shores of Lake Nyasa. The basis of their work was industrial training as much as pure evangelism. The same principle was adopted at the great Scottish institute at Lovedale in South Africa and at its off-shoot at Blythswood. From Lovedale and Blythswood in the south to Blantyre and Livingstonia in Nyasaland, whence they spread into Northern Rhodesia, the Scots looked to a chain of mission stations along the vertebrae of Africa, a spiritual Cape to Cairo route. In 1891, under the auspices of the IBEA Company, one of whose directors was Livingstone's son-in-law and who collectively subscribed £10,000 from their own pockets, they moved into East Africa.

Their first station was at Kibwezi, some 150 miles from Mombasa and the first location where water was plentiful after the crossing of the Taru desert. It proved a disastrous choice. Death, heartache and frustration followed hard upon each other for seven years until Thomas Watson was left as sole survivor of the original party of six Europeans. It seemed as though the missionary enterprise would die in the bush at the same time as the company which gave it birth fizzled out in insolvency.

The story of Kibwezi was a hard lesson which the Scots had to learn. They faced the same crisis as threatened the entire missionary enterprise, a crisis which was inherent in pre-colonial Africa, and which had already defeated the attempts of Jesuits to penetrate inland in the days of the Portuguese empire. Faith alone could not overcome the raw, primal barriers of Africa, the barriers to health imposed by insects and to free movement set up by natural obstacles and war-ring tribes. Faith alone could not meet the challenge of the Arabs.

The missionaries had to face the fact that from the time of Living-stone's death in 1873 until the battle of Omdurman in 1898 the power of Islam was in the ascendant in Africa. With the Koran the Arabs brought to Africa a missionary zeal every bit as fervent as the Chris-tian trader's. Islam possessed a universality and culture which stretched from the Atlantic to China. Islam was the dominating influence in North Africa, around the Sahara and in the Indian Ocean. Arab traditions entertained no sympathy for unbelievers and also licensed slavery.

Reluctantly, Livingstone's successor realized they could not do without the secular power of Europe. In seeking the protection of the British Empire the missionaries summoned not just bayonets to defend them against spears, but the total commitment of Western civilisation to develop the continent.

The identification of the missionary church with imperial power led to criticism; but in the long run it proved damaging not to the church but to the imperial idea. For a missionary church is a church committed to development. The building of hospitals and schools, the teaching of literacy and Western industrial skills, the implanting of monotheistic worship and new concepts of individual morality, these all presuppose a transformation of the closed world of tribal, village, life into the open society of urban centres and cosmopolitan intercourse. And from the seed planted by the missionaries inde-pendent native churches were to grow.

The ultimate message of the missionary was freedom, the freedom of Christ's empty tomb. It implied freedom from the ignorance of past centuries; freedom from the thraldom of malign spirits; freedom from the barriers to human progress imposed by tribal custom; free-dom from the restrictions on social and economic life placed by un-tamed natural forces. Such a liberating of men's spirits must finally lead to a demand for personal and political freedom. The missionary gospel carried with it the seeds of decay to the imperial order itself.

From Kibwezi, representatives of the mission made several ex-ploratory visits to the border ridges of southern Kikuyuland, which lay on the route of the projected railway. They wanted to position themselves in the vicinity of Lugard's old fort at Dagoretti and the appeal of a mission lying between the Kikuyu and the Masai remained strong—though in the event Thogoto scarcely touched any Masai.

In February 1898 Thomas Watson, the sole survivor of the original party which set out from Mombasa for Kibwezi seven years before, began to clear a plot near the Dagoretti ridge offered by Waiyaki's son. Medical objections forced him to move further up the hill and it was here the Thogoto mission was finally established.

At the same time famine struck the Kikuyu and thousands died. Watson brought out his bride and together they gave whatever relief they could, with special donations from Scotland. Then suddenly Watson himself fell ill. After the strains and disappointments and renewed expectations of nine years' continuous exertions, he succumbed to pneumonia and died on 4 December 1900. Within a year of her arrival his widow was left alone to continue the work of the mission.

Watson had left Kibwezi an hour after the first railway engine steamed into it. In 1899 the line reached the future Nairobi and from 1901 mission societies of all denominations prepared to enter the highlands, dividing the ridges between them and sometimes subdividing these among their own members through clashes of personalities.

From being a private missionary venture, Thogoto came under the direction of the Church of Scotland and received fresh inspiration from men with experience in Nyasaland. Watson's successor, Clement Scott, was the first white man Kenyatta saw when he came to his village in Muthiga. Believing strongly that the mission should be self-supporting, Scott bought 3,000 acres as an agricultural estate which brought new problems of management. He died in 1907 and was succeeded by Henry Edwin Scott who inaugurated a new period of growth.

The missionaries were not colonisers themselves, but they played a decisive role in the dynamics of colonisation and the history of British involvement in East and Central Africa cannot properly be understood without appreciating their importance. In essence they were Britain's response to Livingstone's challenging concept of "commerce and Christianity". At this stage in the development of British rule in Africa, the colonial philosophy was that territories which came under British protection should be made to pay their way. Exceptions were such areas as Somaliland in which Britain had a strong military or strategic interest. But in British East Africa taxes and other revenues were initially intended solely to defray the cost of administration, by which was meant, at least in the Foreign Office view, 'law and order'. No priority was given, as far as East Africa was concerned, to the exploitation of natural resources for the benefit of manufacturers or speculators in England, though the general theory of Free Trade to which Britain was still largely wedded gave a world-wide trade bias in favour of industrial Europe. Kenya, as it happened, possessed no raw materials comparable with those of the Congo, Rhodesia, or South Africa, and did not, therefore, attract the mineral prospectors or rubber concessionaires who so tarnished the colonial image elsewhere in Africa.

It was thus left to the missionaries to spearhead the advance of civilisation and so to inaugurate that process of development which is still the dominating impulse in present-day Africa. The missions were the first to introduce Western medicine and Western concepts of education to the native populations and give instruction in western industrial techniques. These mission schools were for many years the only ones available to Africans. Management of the estate at Thogoto was directed partly towards supporting the mission, and partly towards giving training in modern agricultural methods to the Africans who worked on it. The colonial administration encouraged these activities and made grants towards them, but it lacked the funds to take over sole responsibility for them, nor did the British government think of the Empire as a development agency operating primarily for the benefit of native welfare.

On the contrary the Foreign Office was at first obsessed with the need for economy and scrutinised every proposed item of expenditure recommended by its officers. Military expeditions and the establishment of forts and administrative posts in the interior of East Africa were discouraged as being an unprofitable entanglement, and the instructions from London were that all such undertakings be restricted to the minimum necessary to safeguard the railway. So niggardly was the Foreign Office the Kenya officials themselves felt the pinch. Hobley, Jackson and Ainsworth, all originally employed by the IBEA Company and taken into government service when the Protectorate was established, were kept at low salaries with poor prospects, and the territory as a whole suffered in the same way as its administrators. In 1904 the total annual revenue of the Protectorate amounted to only £109,000, of which the hut tax brought in rather less than a quarter. The main contribution came from customs dues, but there was still a regular and substantial deficit on the Protectorate's running expenses which had to be met by Foreign Office sub-

sidy. By March 1905 this was totalling some £¼ million a year, and
for the whole period of Foreign Office administration (July 1895 to
March 1905) amounted to over £1½ million.[1]

By modern standards of overseas aid, and making allowances for
the changed value of sterling, the sums involved seem almost trivial.
But East Africa was a minor sphere of British interest and such demands on the British Treasury were multiplied many times over by
the world-wide commitments of the British Empire. The Foreign
Office grant to Kenya went not into development projects but into
military expenditure. By March 1904 this had exceeded £½ million,
and it illustrates what was an important—perhaps, the most important—aspect of the British Empire, that of a peace-keeping
agency. At the beginning of the twentieth century the Pax Britannica
provided the most effective system of world order which the world
had seen, or is likely to see again, for centuries. But the economic
organisation of this system was already growing out of date as Britain,
the first nation to go through the industrial revolution, fell behind
in the changed conditions of world trade brought about by the rapid
rise of other industrial powers, notably Germany and America.

In British colonial Africa, then, rather than trade following the
flag, the reverse was the case. Well ahead of Francis Hall in entering
Kikuyuland was an adventurous Yorkshireman, John Boyes, who
established himself in the centre of the tribe as a supplier of foodstuffs to the caravans passing to and from Uganda, and as a dealer in
ivory which he collected from the Wandorobo hunters. Boyes entered
into blood brotherhood with local Kikuyu chiefs and had a small
private army drilling under a Union Jack to ensure his own safety and
enforce peace in the area in which he was operating. Francis Hall
brought these activities unceremoniously to an end by arresting Boyes
on a charge of 'dacoity' and sending him down to Mombasa for trial,
where he was acquitted. The government thereupon mounted their
own expeditions to bring 'law and order' to the furthest sections of the
Kikuyu.

In northern Kenya and in Jubaland it was two small commercial
concerns, the Boma Trading Company and the Empire Navigation
Company, that brought civilisation to these largely unexplored and
wild regions in the form of peaceful trade, and so led to the establishment of government posts in the desert oases to restrain raiders
from across the borders of Ethiopia and Somaliland. The Samburu
tribe even offered to contribute to the cost of a government station
at Marsabit to protect them.

It was indeed Kenya's financial problems that led to the policy of encouraging large scale white settlement in the highlands of East Africa, as is described in the following chapter, and so introduced a new stimulus to development which came increasingly into conflict with the missionaries. But it is worth mentioning at this point that the first settlers were not much better off than the administrators. A frequent complaint was that many of them lacked the capital or the incentives to make anything out of their stake in the continent, and in 1908 the suggestion was seriously considered of repatriating the worst off to Britain at the government's expense.[2]

There were, of course, some missionaries whose motives in coming to East Africa were escapist and less than whole-hearted; for some Italian and French Roman Catholics it seemed like a wretched exile; and there were some who after a time became settlers themselves, like Stuart Watt, the man who gave Francis Hall such a shock when he turned up with his wife and children at Fort Smith before the country was properly under control, and who then retired to the Machakos area to embark on a profitable career as a fruit farmer. But Stuart Watt and his like were free-lance evangelists with no organisation behind them and they had, perforce, to find a means of supporting themselves if they were to be of any service to the native peoples. Several members of the Scottish mission followed suit after completing their initial term of engagement. By living and working in Africa such men helped spread the Christian faith by which they lived themselves, however imperfectly. And this was true also of many of the settlers, the best of whom organized primitive schools and medical clinics for the workers and families who lived on their farms. In this, they too were following Livingstone's vision.

But for most missionaries the decision to give themselves to Africa meant great personal sacrifice, and at the least separation from friends and loved ones and lonely hours in the bush. Many paid with their lives. The first missionary grave on the coast of East Africa was that of Ludwig Krapf's wife and infant daughter, who both died within a few months of joining him at Mombasa in 1844. God bids us first build a cemetery before we build a church or dwelling place Krapf wrote home of his loss, and the grave can still be seen across the water from the old harbour of Mombasa, opposite the mellowing walls of the great Portuguese citadel, Fort Jesus. To many a missionary setting foot for the first time in the continent it was a reminder of the sacrifice required of the missionary calling. 'A queer place this,' one visitor remarked when Dr Laws showed him the graves of the ill-fated members of the Universities' Mission to Central Africa at Livingstonia, 'a queer place this, where the only places worth going to see are the graves'. 'They are the milestones of civilisation towards the region beyond,' replied Laws. Thogoto stood squarely in this tradition.

In November 1909, Kenyatta entered the formal history of the west under his tribal name of Kamau wa Ngengi (for he 'belonged' to Ngengi after the death of his father Muigai). It first appears in a list in the mission archives recording the dates when the first boys and girls came to Thogoto. Musa Gitau, Kenyatta's friend from Ngenda, arrived back himself in April 1909. He was to be an important influence on Kenyatta's future.

Thogoto was still a pioneering settlement surrounded by forest where rhino and leopard were found and from which baboons often descended to uproot preciously cultivated vegetable gardens. It was reached by a red dust track which ran along the edge of the forest from the government office at Dagoretti railway station at Kikuyu, where the line took a sharp turn to the north before descending the Rift escarpment and the road departed due west to the Kedong Valley. Midway between Dagoretti and Kikuyu the track led through a curtain of trees into a large grassy square which was dominated at one end by a rectangular building with a red corrugated iron roof, red iron supports and a red iron verandah. This was the Scottish manse, the seat of the white man's authority. It had been conveyed in ready-made sections from Britain and seemed none the worse for a period spent at the bottom of the Red Sea when the ship sank which was bringing it to East Africa. Opposite it, some three hundred yards away across the clearing, rose the newly consecrated church built of local stone and cedar wood. Behind the church, in a cluster of mud and wattle shacks, riddled with termites, lived the other members of the mission. Around were the homesteads of the Kikuyu families living on the estate—over 250 huts in all.

Beyond the clearing, in a pretty valley, flowed the Nyongara River, one of the many streams of clear water which rose in the upland forests. The railway ran along the far ridge and within sight of the manse; south and west stretched the original forest, still more than five miles thick in most parts. Thogoto was on its inner fringe, facing Kikuyuland. Tracks criss-crossed from the *shambas* and homesteads and led across the streams and ridges to the principal administrative office for the district at Kiambu, a little over twelve miles away to the north-east.

This was the scene that confronted the young Kenyatta when he arrived that November day, 1909, like any other Kikuyu herdboy described in the mission journal:

'There the boy stood, probably eleven or twelve years of age, his only clothing three wire bracelets, and a strip of cloth around his neck. Where had he come from? From a village six miles away. What did he want? He wanted to learn. Was it true or had he lost a goat while herding and feared to return home? If he was taken on as a boarder would he stay? . . . Yet here was the chance of a life, with all its wonderful possibilities, to be gained for Christ, and so a note was written, intimating to all concerned that he was to be taken on as a boarder, and given to the boy. He was then dispatched to Mrs Watson, who produced a shirt and a loin-cloth for him. He had no notion of the use of such garments, and after many attempts he got his shirt on with the buttons at the back, and finally Mrs Watson had to set another boy to dress him. That evening our small friend had a meal with the others, and after food went to church for evening prayers. Next day was Sunday. In the morning he went to church, taking his seat with a dozen other boys of the same age beside Mrs Scott at the organ, and hearing Dr Scott preach in his own language of the Saviour who had died and rose again.'[3]

To the Europeans the African herdboys seemed like shy wild animals, at once timid and curious. Some were enticed into the homes of the staff to undertake odd jobs as houseboys, cooks and gardeners. It was an exciting change from watching the sheep and goats; but they rarely stuck at it for more than a month at a time, when the urge to return to their villages 'for a rest in paint and feathers', as one missionary described them, became too strong. Angry fathers would come storming up to the manse demanding the return of their children and, as often as not, expecting to be bribed to let them stay with a gift of a blanket and tobacco. Kenyatta said his own 'father' had once done this. One man 'sold' his son to the mission in place of a fine imposed by Scott for allowing his herd to stray across the estate.

Kenyatta began life at Thogoto in this way. He washed dishes, learnt to sew, weeded in the gardens. He had relatives in the surrounding villages where he could also stay, and where the Africa of past centuries still existed, and boys still herded goats with skins over their shoulders, castor oil and red ochre on their bodies, and weird ornaments in their ears. Outside Thogoto was the old world of spears, poisoned arrows and ancient rites. Inside was growing a new order, more magical, more potent than anything the Kikuyu could imagine.

At Thogoto Kenyatta came into contact with two men who were destined to play important parts in the next twenty years of his life. The first was Arthur Ruffell Barlow, the nephew by marriage of Clement Ruffell Scott, who joined the mission at Christmas 1905, after two years on a nearby farm.

He was then nineteen and he possessed a sensitive, scholarly nature which made him withdrawn from older people. But as a young man he joined in Kikuyu dances and was one of the first Europeans to take the trouble to learn their language. Translation work remained a lifelong interest and his version of St Mark's Gospel into Kikuyu was the first New Testament writings available at Thogoto. Barlow possessed a sympathetic understanding of Kikuyu traditions which distinguished him from his more prejudiced fellow-countrymen. In the year that Kenyatta came to Thogoto he was selected to pioneer the first outstation of the mission at Tumutumu, fifty miles to the north of the slopes of Mount Kenya. He often stood in as head of the mission.

Some years older than Barlow was Scott's second recruit, John W. Arthur, who arrived at Thogoto in January 1907 as the new mission doctor. Arthur was born in 1881, the son of a Scottish evangelical businessman who took a keen interest in the overseas work of the Scottish Church, and gave generously towards its support. At the age of twelve, John Arthur decided he wanted to become a medical missionary and he passed through Glasgow Academy to Glasgow University, then one of the leading academic institutes in the world. He was a first-rate athlete and captain of the university rugby fifteen. In 1903 he graduated in medicine. He had a gentle, outward-looking character, braced by firm principles. Once convinced of the rightness of his cause he would not let himself be deflected by other arguments, though he sought compromise where these did not conflict with principle. Abstemious in his personal habits, meticulous in his methods, both as doctor and administrator, and always deeply devout, Arthur represented the finest qualities of the Scottish people. Though brought up in the imperalist atmosphere of the nineties, he was ahead of his time in his sympathetic attitude towards the native people he had come out to serve. He took over as head of the mission in 1911 and dominated affairs at Thogoto for more than a quarter of a century. More than any other white man his was the strongest influence in this formative period in the life of Kenyatta.

Within a few months of his arrival, Kenyatta fell ill. It was diagnosed as phthisis, a lung infection common among the thinly-clad Kikuyu herdboys and then attributed to the cold, damp air of the highlands. Thogoto was at an altitude of over 6,000 feet and after the rains in March pneumonia always claimed many victims.

Medical work was long-established as one of the main planks of Scottish missionary activity. When Arthur first came to Thogoto its hospital was no more than a dark and smoky thatched hut above the Nyongara River. The new Hunter Memorial Hospital, named after a benefactor of the mission and opened in January 1908, was a low single-storied building of stone, and it was here that Kenyatta was moved for treatment.[4] It consisted of hot poultices applied to his chest, which scorched the skin and left scars for the rest of his life. After a month he was released. But chest or sinus troubles continued to afflict him at intervals.

'Will our friends please remember these boys in their prayers', asked Arthur in the mission journal giving their names, 'and the medical work here, that it may be greatly used as a means of spreading Christ's Kingdom in this benighted province'?[5] In this way, from early in his life, Kenyatta received the spiritual support of Christians across the seas.

Education has become the twentieth century's philosopher's stone, a will-o'-the-wisp beckoning mankind forward to universal progress, a gospel to rival Christ's. But when the Europeans first offered to teach the children of the Kikuyu they met constant opposition. Parents were unwilling to see their boys abandon their traditional tasks around the *shambas* and were fearful of the loss in bride price which might follow if their daughters were contaminated with the strangers' magic. As a result schooling at Thogoto was desperately slow to start. It took years before the teachers were able even to record the names of children, so fearful were they of the magic of being 'written down'.

By the end of 1909 the position was slowly improving with the institution of a boarding school for sixteen boys and of industrial training schemes for a further fourteen supported by government grants.

The missionaries had to begin at the most basic level of teaching. The ages of their pupils ranged from small waifs with jigger sores and dirty bandages to young men of the warrior grades. The younger often helped teach the older. In the elementary classes, their object was to enable the boys to read Kikuyu versions of the simplest Old Testament stories. From 1908 they were able to move on to Barlow's new translation of St Mark's gospel.[6]

It took months, years even with some, to bring pupils to the stage of writing a short letter with pencil and paper. Simple arithmetic involved overcoming strong mental resistance inculcated from childhood among the Kikuyu who were brought up to believe that counting was a form of magic which usually brought evil consequences.

Life for Kenyatta and the other boys was spartan.[7] The boarders slept on hard boards and ate a monotonous but nutritional Kikuyu diet of maize and sweet potatoes, to which bits of meat were occasionally added. No matter what the weather, they rose at dawn and went to bed at dusk. For the apprentices and their teachers extra duties extended the day from 5 a.m. until 9 p.m. And at this high altitude they often had to turn out in swirling mist and rain. School routine was full and varied.

6.30 a.m.	Bell; roll call; work
8	School food
8.30	PT by Dr Arthur
8.45	Prayers
9–12	School
12–2 p.m.	Free
2–4.30	Work
4.30	Games; Drill; Boys' Brigade
5.45	School food
6.30	Prayers

There were, of course, punishments, for the Kikuyu were notorious for their sulks and the fits of rage into which they worked themselves to display their manliness. Penalties fitted the offence. Truants were denied lessons when they returned; the naughtiest boys had to stand on the table during 'break'. Untidiness lost a boy his shirt for the day, a severe punishment in the cold season. The threat of being sent to work in the fields was held over the inattentive and there were always jobs to be done around the staff houses to occupy spare minutes. Loss of food brought the unruly into line; and the ultimate sanction lay in a short length of rope at the manse.

To the Scottish men and women education was a means of producing a wholly rounded man, of training his character and Christian faith as much as his intellect. Arthur and Barlow saw in Britain's civilizing mission an obligation to bring these 'public school' values before the people they had come to serve. They were Christian zealots pursuing the best ideals of Western society at that time: order and

obedience; the team spirit; courage and self-sacrifice; pride in tradition and in the wearing of uniforms; cleanliness, punctuality and
honesty; respect for the weak, for old people and women. At Thogoto
their whole regime could be summed up in the key Scottish word:
discipline—the discipline of a community, of self, of faith based on
scripture.

Every aspect of life required discipline and contributed its measure
of moral uplift. Drill and physical jerks helped 'promote order and
obedience'. The Boys' Brigade, an early institution with uniforms
provided by well-wishers in Scotland, was 'a bracing influence'. The
first thing the boys received on returning from holidays was a good
scrubbing before they were issued with clean shirts: 'they looked
so nice, fresh and clean when we assembled for a game of football
in the afternoon'. The game itself was played for moral benefit as
much as recreational relief, or as Dr Arthur wrote 'to stiffen the
backbone of these boys by teaching them manliness, good temper
and unselfishness—qualities amongst many others which have done
so much to make a Britisher.' Prayers and hymns, vaulting horses
and parallel bars, dumb-bells, Indian clubs, competitions, Bible
stories and football, all went to turn the leisure hours of the old,
savage Adam into the purposefulness of the new Christian. And
above it all floated the Union Jack, symbol of the earthly power
which made this work for God possible. Empire Day at Thogoto
was an occasion for special celebrations.

Later generations might feel this ideal was unduly austere, taking
its model from the granite of Aberdeen rather than from the graces
of Athens. But the enormity of the gulf which separated Africa from
Western civilization at the beginning of the twentieth century
could not be bridged by half measures. Europeans who attempted
to live native style quickly went to pieces. Some missionaries who
tried this approach failed wretchedly. Many white men who let their
standards fall in the bush took to drink and self-despair, and some
became so deranged they sought refuge from the immensity of the
continent, like wild animals, in lairs under rocks or in caves. 'Going
shenzi', it was called. Sooner or later they would be found, with a toe
in the trigger of their rifles and their skulls shattered. Suicide in one
form or another ended many a white man's attempt to live according
to Africa's ways.

The missionaries were well aware of the need to look for common
ground on which to build, as Augustine had done in sixth-century
England. Barlow in particular was aware of points in the native mind

which could be turned to advantage, like the African's belief in the supernatural, and they all felt their way carefully through the complexities of tribal customs. But in the last resort no true synthesis was possible because of the total break with the past which Christianity demanded.

The missionaries also believed in the active existence of forces of evil, a belief they shared with their converts and the heathen, and they sensed these forces to be all around them in Africa, especially at times when native rites were at their height, and

'There was a curious tension everywhere: the very air seemed electric with evil, and it was as if we were compassed about and beset by unseen forces of darkness on this their own ancient vantage ground. It was a strange occult experience of which some of us were conscious.'[8]

It was the custom for churches and Sunday Schools in Scotland to 'sponsor' a child at Thogoto for £5 a year, which Arthur calculated was the cost of a boy's upkeep. In this way communities at home maintained a continuing interest in the work of their countrymen overseas. A year after his arrival at Thogoto, Kenyatta was allocated to the Sunday School of St John's (Cross) Church, Dundee, and for the next four years they supported him in their prayers and with their pennies.[9]

But his progress through the elementary grades was unremarkable and in July 1912, after completing this primary schooling, he chose to be apprenticed as a carpenter, and this is how he came to be photographed by Dr Arthur.[10] The young Kenyatta has a plane in his hands. He is wearing the thinly-striped cotton shirt of the mission boys and loose-fitting shorts. A tarbush is on the back of his head, which is poised delicately on a powerful neck. It is a strong face, and he stares at the world with a somewhat quizzical expression as though he were struggling with an interior debate.

The main object of the mission's work was evangelism, and evangelism was as slow to take effect as the offer of schooling. The first convert at Thogoto was not made until October 1907 when Clement Scott on his death-bed baptized his own houseboy, Philip Karanja. Professions of faith were infrequent when Kenyatta first came to Thogoto. It was a time of patient reaching out among the people. The greatest opposition came from the old men and women, for whom baptism could only be given if they abandoned all but one wife and swore to forgo the drinking and rituals through which their lives had been formed.

But prejudice was gradually being overcome, largely through the work of the younger Kikuyu themselves, and it was in this growing spiritual atmosphere that Kenyatta approached Christianity. At Easter 1912, with seven other boys and seven girls, all dressed in white robes, he made his vows at a solemn and moving service in the small church at Thogoto. It committed him, with "deep seriousness" according to Arthur, to spending the next two years as a catechumen, undergoing instruction every Sunday morning until ready for baptism, and to giving up tribal life.[11]

The ceremony that Easter also included the baptism of a young half-caste boy, Charles Kasaja Stokes, who had recently returned from Dundee where Mrs Watson had taken him for two years' schooling. Charles Kasaja was the son of a former CMS missionary who had married a Muganda woman and gone in for ivory trading and gunrunning on the Uganda-Congo borders until caught and shot by the Belgians. Charles was born in 1895 and never knew his father. As a small boy he came into Mrs Watson's care and she brought him up like her own son. When Charles came back from Scotland Dr Arthur told him, with that hardness with which Scotsmen often conceal kind motives, that his place in Africa was with the natives and not with the Europeans. Weeping, Charles had to find other shelter than Mrs Watson's kindly hut. Among those who befriended him was the young Kenyatta, also a lonely child. The two became good friends, and Kenyatta learnt much from him about the land across the sea where the king-emperor reigned.

Kenyatta's name rarely appears in the mission records, though it was so common that any one of a number of incidents describing a 'Kamau' might refer to him. He evidently displayed no marked intelligence or aptitude for the new skills he was learning. Had he done so he would have been selected for specialist work around the mission, as teacher or evangelist or hospital assistant, for the boys who showed promise were expected to help forward the work of the church.[12]

It may have been that his talents did not show themselves while under instruction. But perhaps the atmosphere of Thogoto was a barrier. Newly arrived Europeans had to learn vernacular phrases quickly and it was all too easy to slip into the use of imperatives: 'Fetch water! Bring firewood! Run quickly!' However innocent

in intention, this was a colonial jargon which grated on the rising
Kikuyu generation.

More patronizing was the universal use by Europeans of the word
'boy' to describe an African whatever his age. From mission records
alone it is impossible to tell how old 'boys' were. As Kenyatta's
generation grew up they came to resent more and more the European's way of addressing them. The Africans had literal minds
and were quick to detect double standards. Close your eyes when
praying, they were told, or God will not listen to you. But any child
knows better than to keep his eyes closed when something exciting is
going to happen. Peeping through their fingers they saw that the
white men often had *their* eyes open too. Years later Kenyatta was to
remember such incidents as examples of the doubts which began to
trouble him during his time at Thogoto.

The missionary influence set up strong tensions in the hearts and
minds of the young Kikuyu. Boys like Kenyatta came to Thogoto in
defiance of tribal custom and parental authority. They were a small
minority of their generation, and their adventurous spirit put them
outside the norm. Some had to endure the most savage beatings
from their parents. Three times one 10-year-old was tied up in his hut,
and three times he gnawed through his thongs to escape back to the
mission. The girls suffered terribly; and terrible too was the suffering of the mothers when they realized that a daughter was 'lost' to
the mission. 'I have no daughter! I have no daughter! My child is
dead!' wailed one mother when she saw her daughter washing in a
stream and putting on a cotton frock. With genuine anguish the
Kikuyu appealed to the missionaries to send the girls back to their
villages, as so much in their lives seemed regulated by the bride price
a daughter could fetch.

For the Kikuyu boys and girls to stand up in church and make
their professions of faith was a great leap in the dark. The scowling
faces of their fathers and mothers, perhaps framed for an instant in
the window or the door, reminded them of the curses of their ancestors. Every day they remained in the dormitory or in the households
of the missionaries cut them off from their tribe. Each vow they made
committed them more deeply to the missionary view of life and so in
the short term—which was all they could envisage—to the colonial
system. Kenyatta was one of a handful who were breaking with their
past and facing an unknown future on their own.

Kenyatta's entry into the catechumen's class and his signing on as
an apprentice carpenter were both signs of his growing maturity and

his readiness to throw off dependence on family and tribe. There were, indeed, no inducements to return to Ngenda to his 'step'-father Ngengi. His brothers now looked to him for support. Kongo, his true brother, joined him in the mission dormitory; Muigai, his half-brother, came to live for part of the year with his Dagoretti relatives. They were responsibilities which made him face the problem of his own future. The most pressing question concerned his own initiation.

Initiation was one of the most important moments in a Kikuyu boy's life. It marked his emergence from childhood into the ranks of the warriors, the first step up the ladder of eldership which in turn conferred prestige on parents. The initiate was symbolically and in a real psychological sense reborn into the full life of the community. On his successful completion of the tests of initiation depended the ending of certain sexual taboos, the establishing of rights to own land, and proof of qualities of leadership within the tightly-knit tribal structure. Initiation was a communion with the life of the tribe, a perpetuation of that vital sense of destiny which urged them forward in their pilgrimage on earth.

In the warm weather after the millet harvest in February, ridge after ridge seethed with preparations for initiation ceremonies. Boys from twelve years old upwards, girls from fifteen, were decked out in special paint and decorations and performed elaborate pre-initiatory rituals. The occasion itself was marked with feasting, drinking and dancing which continued for weeks. Often the whole course of preparatory and post-initiation events lasted for months.

The missionaries recognized the significance of the initiatory rites, of which circumcision was the outward physical symbol, and they were appalled at what they saw in them. The physical operation they considered brutal and unhygienic and in the case of girls a barbaric mutilation with permanent ill-effects. But the atmosphere in which the ceremonies were carried out seemed to them even more evil, with what they took to be the sexual innuendo of the dances and songs, the licentiousness of the old men and women and the gloating cruelty of the operators and their attendants. They taught against the practices and prayed that the people might forgo them altogether.

But for a Kikuyu boy or girl not to be circumcised was, at the time when Kenyatta was at Thogoto, unthinkable. The mission accordingly allowed their boys to enter hospital where the operation could be performed with local anaesthetics under proper medical care. Many chose this alternative. Others stole away when their turn came round and took their places in their village groups. Some returned afterwards to the mission and the Europeans always saw a change in them for the worse. If they were already baptized or in the catechumen's class they would be punished according to the rule of the church, which meant suspension from communion if they were baptized members, or a setback in their course of preparation if catechumens. Christian parents and would-be Christians who allowed their sons to undergo full tribal initiation would be similarly penalized.

With Kenyatta something exceptional took place. In 1913, presumably at the normal time of year, February, when the mission school was on holiday, the missionary teacher at Thogoto, Garrioch, collected a small group of boys who were eligible for initiation and took them down to the Nyongara stream, half a mile away. They each had their 'sponsors', or circumcision fathers, who stood behind them during the ceremony and acted as guardians on behalf of the tribe. With them came Samson Njoroge, the first Kikuyu to train as a hospital assistant. He was to be operator and he took with him a surgical knife from the hospital.

One important aspect of the initiation was for the boy not to show fear or pain. In this, at least, the small party could follow custom, and Samson took no anaesthetic with him. At the stream the boys washed themselves ceremonially and then Samson knelt on the ground in front of each and according to Kikuyu custom cut away the foreskin from each side of the top of the penis and gathered it in a bunch underneath. For a time the blood spurted freely on to the earth, symbol of the body's attachment to the soil. After their ordeal the boys trooped back to their homesteads to rest while their wounds healed. Kenyatta had asked Musa Gitau to act as his sponsor and it was to Musa's hut that he now came as to the home of a new 'father'. Musa's wife provided him with food. He was born again into full membership of the tribe. The grade was called *Mubengi,* which implied something to do with banking, and may have denoted the introduction of new economic methods among the most southerly section of the Kikuyu.[13]

Kenyatta's initiation enabled him to take his place among a recognized age-grade, though a man who had not undergone the full-scale treatment would never be regarded as a true heir to ancestral tradition. At the same time he continued with his catechumen's classes. It was a period of considerable unrest among the Kikuyu teachers and apprentices at Thogoto when they sought higher wages, better prospects, and a greater say in the way their own affairs at the mission were organized. It may have been as a consequence of these feelings that Kenyatta's group decided to undergo their tribal initiation before they were baptized and that their teacher went along with them to avoid losing them altogether.

Baptism was also a form of initiation of which the full spiritual meaning often escaped the young men who came forward. In secular terms, baptism was the hall-mark of their mission education, it gave them a diploma of respectability on which depended job prospects with Europeans and the future advancement of a baptized African's own family. He now had the opportunity of participating in the affairs of his church, which was of great attraction to young Kikuyu of ability at a time when there were few outlets in government service. The Scottish missionaries looked ultimately to the formation of a self-governing native church. Baptism gave one the right of entry into this institution.

The custom at Thogoto was for the boy or girl about to be baptized to choose a 'Christian' name, by which he or she would thereafter be known. Many opted for the great Old Testament figures like Gideon, Daniel, Joshua. Others simply chose the name of their European masters or instructors. Charles and William and George. 'Christian' names from the New Testament were always in favour, and it was to these that Kenyatta turned. He chose both John and Peter for himself, wishing to be called after Jesus's two leading disciples. But the missionaries would only allow one name. Kenyatta thereupon changed Peter into 'stone', for which there was a Biblical precedent, and added to it John. 'Johnstone', that was what he would be called. It was a small gesture of defiance at the mission rules.

So despite the irritation of the missionaries he was baptized Johnstone Kamau. The date was August 1914, and once again he made the solemn vow which bound him to his church and the Christian faith.[14]

Kenyatta had been at Thogoto for five years and had undergone two initiations. His baptism enabled him to continue in the life of the church, while his circumcision put him right with his own people. To both, however, he might also seem a turncoat; unwilling on the one hand to commit himself whole-heartedly to the discipline of the church, and separated too widely from the life of his village. As he set his face towards the adult world these conflicting loyalties tugged at his mind. He knew his tribal background could never be rediscovered according to the simple legends he had learnt from his mother

Wambui. His future in the white man's world of East Africa was equally uncertain.

After his baptism Kenyatta left the dormitory and lived for a time with friends near the mission. He had shown little promise in either his studies or his trade and the mission now asked him to sign on for a further term of apprenticeship as a mason. Masons were thought of as being a lower category of workers than carpenters, and Kenyatta refused. He had come to Thogoto to acquire the white man's magic, not technical skills. His English was poor and there was little opportunity of improving it with the missionaries; his ability to read and write appeared below average. Thogoto had little more to offer him. He turned, as did many of his generation, to the lights and bustle of a different kind of world altogether. Only a few miles away from Thogoto lay the city, Nairobi.

CHAPTER 5

Nairobi and White Settlement

Nairobi is a Masai word meaning 'cold'. An early European caravan advancing towards the Kikuyu forest belt was following the course of a stream across the Athi plains. They asked their Masai guides its name. 'Nairobi', they were told, 'the cold water'. At the point where the stream fell away from the forest's edge it lost itself in a thick papyrus swamp to which old lions retreated on hot days. The Masai grazed their cattle along its banks and had their kraals on the higher ground above it. The old caravan route passed near the papyrus swamp to reach a camping site close to the forest, the twenty-fifth from the coast. But experienced travellers tried to avoid it because of its unhealthy air. They preferred to push on to Fort Smith some four miles beyond.

Such was the original situation of Kenya's future capital city. When Kenyatta was born it lacked appeal to the eye of tourist or town planner.

On 30 May 1899, the railway reached the papyrus swamp. Beside it sappers had set up a depot for survey work.[1] The busyness of the white man, he who never stands still, was at its most impressive. To the Kikuyu who had the courage to look, the white man's camp became a live creature itself, so active were its members, and so speedily did its limbs grow.

In July 1899 the railway company transferred its headquarters to its new depot and work continued over the spectacular terrain of the Rift Valley towards Port Florence, now Kisumu, a further 250 miles to the north-west. In August the line was open to the public from Nairobi railhead to the coast. Ainsworth, the government administrator at Machakos, moved his office the forty miles across the Athi plains to the new location, and the military also made it their new headquarters. Thanks solely to the requirements of railway engineers, Nairobi was launched into the world.

Three arguments backed the construction of the railway: economic, humanitarian and strategic. The economic argument rested upon the supposed wealth of Uganda and the saving in time and transportation cost of steam locomotion over human porterage. It paid little attention to the territory which lay between the fertile belt around Lake Victoria and the coastal strip near Mombasa. The railway itself was to be 'relied upon to create almost the whole of the traffic'.[2]

The humanitarian argument was aimed against the slave trade as an end in itself, though, as a bonus, it was said that the projected line would prevent Masai raids across it against tribes to the north. In practice what defeated the Arabs was not so much an alternative commercial system as the full-scale deployment of imperial power.

Finally, the strategic argument, based on the theory of control of the Nile headwaters, soon went out of fashion. After the diplomatic harum-scarums of the Bismarckian era, in which Britain and France almost came to blows in 1898 with each side claiming the right to control the Nile at Fashoda (resolved in Britain's favour), the maritime powers were drawing closer together to confront the continental, German-speaking bloc's drive overland towards the Eastern Mediterranean. From being Britain's principal enemy in the nineteenth century Russia, in King Edward's day, became a potential ally.

No one considered in detail how a railway would directly serve the natives of East Africa. They produced no goods which could be marketed outside their own territories; their land contained no minerals for which such expensive transportation was needed; ivory was too specialized a trade to support a railway; timber was not in itself a sufficient commercial proposition, though men with timber concessions were later able to make a case for branch lines to service their mills; the natives themselves showed no desire to travel outside their tribal areas on a railway and appeared to value it only for the wire it provided for ornamentation.[3]

By 1902 the railway was open along its full length. At first it carried one train a week in each direction. Its capital cost amounted to £5½ million and it soon showed that it could run only at a loss.[4] By a process now familiar enough in Britain what was undertaken as a public service was shortly after expected to pay its way. To pay its way the railway needed customers. Where were they to be found?

Here the empire-builders had to face up to the realities of the continent into which they had 'scrambled' in the 1880s. Some, like Lugard, thought the country should be given over to surplus Indian population. Sir Harry Johnston, Lord Salisbury's lieutenant in

Uganda, went so far, in that age of epigram, to call East Africa the 'America of the Hindu'.[5] It was an idea which long persisted. The IBEA Company tried introducing Persians to improve farming methods. There was talk of bringing in Finns. Joseph Chamberlain offered it to the Jews as a permanent national home and a party of Zionists came out on a surveying expedition.[6]

None of these ideas produced customers for the railway. The only answer was to allow Europeans to settle in the highlands on the formula that only white men resident in the country would encourage natives to develop their own resources to the point of making the railway viable. The railway had been built to ease communications with Uganda; it was used to justify white settlement.[7]

Sir Harry Johnston could be relied on to find the right phrase which then passed into the mythology of colonialism. East Africa, he said, was a 'white man's country':

'In the Eastern part of the Uganda Protectorate there is a tract of country almost without parallel in tropical Africa: a region of perhaps 12,000 square miles, admirably well watered, with a fertile soil, cool and perfectly healthy climate, covered with noble forests, and, to a very great extent, uninhabited by any native race. This area lies at an altitude not less than 6,000 feet, and not more than 10,000 feet. It is as healthy for European settlers as the United Kingdom, British Columbia, or temperate South Africa . . . I am able to say decidedly that here we have a territory (now that the Uganda Railway is built) admirably suited for a white man's country, and I can say this with no thought of injustice to any native race, for the country in question is either utterly uninhabited for miles and miles, or at most its inhabitants are wandering hunters who have no settled home or whose fixed habitation is in the lands outside the healthy areas. This will be one source of profit to the United Kingdom.'[8]

The IBEA Company had set itself firmly against the alienation of native lands to outsiders. But during the period of Foreign Office administration the government was prompted by the railway authorities to acquire freehold rights to the territory a mile on either side of the proposed line. Where this passed along the floor of the Rift Valley, beside the beautiful lakes of Naivasha, Elmentaita and Nakuru, the country was devoid of all human habitation, save for wandering Masai. It was ideal ranching land.

Thus from the earliest days the principle was established that the

interests of development—what was then defined as 'public purposes'—might overrule local native interests. There was nothing
exceptional in this principle. How else could inter-tribal warfare
be brought under control unless the rights of one tribe to raid another
were curtailed? For societies which lay outside any system of inter-
community justice or morality, what universal rights were there
beyond those invoked by the missionaries?[9]

No one made this clearer nor with such freedom from cant than
Sir Charles Eliot, who became Commissioner of British East Africa
in December 1900 and is regarded as being the architect of the policy
of white settlement.

'There seems to me something exaggerated in all the talk about
"their own country" and their immemorable rights . . . By the same
reasoning does not Kikuyu belong to the Wakikuyu and Machakos to
the Wakamba? Does not all East Africa belong to the natives of East
Africa? No doubt on platforms and in reports we declare we have
no intention of depriving natives of their lands, but this has never
prevented us from taking whatever land we want for Government
purposes or from settling Europeans on land not actually occupied by
natives . . . Your Lordship has opened this Protectorate to white
immigration and colonisation, and I think it is as well that, in confidential correspondence at least, we should face the undoubted issue
—viz., that white mates black in a very few moves . . . There can
be no doubt that the Masai and many other tribes must go under. It is
a prospect which I view with equanimity and a clear conscience. I
wish to protect individual Masais . . . but I have no desire to protect
Masaidom. It is a beastly, bloody system, founded on raiding and im-
morality, disastrous to both the Masai and their neighbors. The
sooner it disappears and is unknown, except in books of anthropology, the better.'[10]

Eliot was a brilliant scholar and linguist who was only thirty-
eight when he came to East Africa. In many ways he was the antithesis
of the settler type.[11] He hated blood sports and the open-air life and
became an authority instead on the sea-slug. In his Kenya Protectorate he inherited a thinly-spread white administration and territories
which were rapidly decaying once the Arabs had the economic basis
of their lives knocked from under them. Eliot's predecessor, Hardinge, had looked to the Arabs to spearhead the new civilizing
influences of British rule—a view oddly at variance with missionary

opposition to the slave trade.[12] In administrative terms Britain had to respect legitimate Arab institutions and Mohammedan law throughout the Sultan's dominions which she was 'protecting'. But Arab society depended on slavery and British rule could only be asserted by smashing the powerful Arab interests entrenched along the mainland. By Eliot's time the Arabs' potential as developers had vanished, their once rich plantations along the coast were overgrown and their former owners lived in debt to Indian moneylenders. New civilizing forces were required if the continent was to be developed and the Protectorate made to pay its way.

To Eliot's clear mind the logic of Britain's commitment to Africa was inescapable: 'a colony should attract colonists'.[13] He estimated that in ten years white settlement would produce a profitable economy. But Eliot also saw clearly that to create reserves and isolate tribal life from the new forces which had brought Africa back into history must be self-defeating. His advocacy of white settlement was based on a policy of inter-penetration of the races, not their separate development. It was a tragedy for Kenya that this gifted and far-sighted man, who hoped to give his life to Africa, felt obliged to resign when interfered with by London.[14]

At first the term 'settler' was applied loosely by the Kikuyu to any white man who was neither a missionary nor an officer of the government wearing a lion cap-badge. Not all the newcomers intended to make long-term investments in land or to spend the rest of their lives in Africa. By 1904 there were few enough anyway—perhaps 130 only; by 1914, hardly more than 1,300. As Kenya grew, so the numbers of white men engaged in other trades outpaced the original 'settlers'.

In administrative terms they were all non-officials. The officials were the Governor's permanent civil servants who automatically voted in council in support of government—that is, their own—policy. Enough of them could always be appointed to form what was known as the official majority. This represented direct Colonial Office rule.

But the views of non-officials were also available to the Governor in determining policy. When formally admitted to a council they could vote against the government if they felt so inclined; but they would always be a minority so long as the colony was under direct Colonial Office rule. It is this group of non-officials who earned the generic name of settlers. Though the genuine settlers were only a minority they made up the most influential and most vociferous sec-

tion of the non-official community, and they were the men who had
the greatest long-term stake in the country. Often the business and the
professional community disagreed with the settlers proper, but the
latter made all the running. Unless a specific distinction is made,
therefore, the term 'settler' may be taken throughout these pages
to apply in this wider sense, as it did to the Africans themselves.[15]

In the early days the terms of settlement were imprecise and the
land survey staff overworked. Unscrupulous men could make money
quickly by speculating in the empty land, perhaps by catching a new-
comer in the bar of his hotel and selling him a vast acreage over
a couple of drinks before he had time to catch his breath. After the
Boer War hard-bitten men entered from South Africa and brought
with them the attitudes which prevailed there and the language of
kaffir and *sjambok*.[16]

The small and hard-pressed administrative staff had little time to
control the rush of activity. East Africa did not attract the highest
grade of colonial official—India and the Sudan took the cream of
university graduates. There was a 'wide open' feel to the Kenya highlands.[17] As advertised in East Africa's newspapers: 'The Land Laws
here are about the most liberal in the world'.[18] They had to be, if settlers were to be tempted to risk their savings, their families and their
lives in a continent which was spoken of as dark and savage.[19]

Later critics of the settlers were the first to admit that they were a
typical cross-section of British men and women, and that most people
would adopt the same attitudes if they were to find themselves trans-
ported from English cities and shires five thousand miles away to the
Kenya highlands. Everyone faced hard years of experiment and disaster and many were broken by them. The lot of the pioneer was
painful.

But two men were untypical. Both came to East Africa under Sir
Charles Eliot's auspices and remained to play leading roles in the
development of Kenya. The first was Hugh Cholmondeley, the third
Baron Delamere, who was born in 1870 and inherited his title at the
age of seventeen. He was a poor scholar at Eton, given to pranks and
gambling. A visit to New Zealand and Australia failed to rouse his
interest and in 1891, before he was twenty-one, he first set foot in
Africa. At once the sense of space and lack of civilization won his
heart. Entering from the coast of Somalia he made several expeditions into the interior shooting big game and making friends with the
nomadic tribes of the plains.

It was on one of these shooting expeditions that Delamere first caught sight of the Kenya highlands. He had trekked more than a thousand miles along the borders of Abyssinia and entered Kenya from the north. It was then November 1897. In December 1902, bored finally with managing his family estates in Cheshire, he sailed for Mombasa and applied for 100,000 acres of land in the Rift Valley, an area bigger than the Isle of Wight or Rutland and ten times the limit set by the administration. But Eliot was desperate to attract capital and a man like Delamere, with a title and resources, was too good a prize to turn away. On condition that he would invest at least £5,000 in it Delamere got his land on a 99-year lease and at an annual rent of £200.

Delamere gave his life to Kenya. He spent vast sums on his property and tried every scheme to improve his and his fellow settlers' prospects. At one time or another he experimented with coffee, wheat, ostriches, wattle, bark disintegration, pigs, oranges, tobacco, and all in addition to the ranching for which his land was most suited and which made him sympathetic towards the Masai. He was open-minded, courageous, outspoken and a born optimist. His vision of the future of white settlement in East Africa never faltered. His personality and rank, his flair and experience, made him the natural leader of the settler community. With Eliot he did more than any man to establish the viability of Kenya's development through white settlement.

But his hot temper also made him a wayward companion and a scourge of the administration. He entertained visiting dignitaries with a lavishness which officials could never match, while his contacts in England and access to the House of Lords gave him a standing which overawed most colonials. His style of living and the scale of his activities made the settler community suspect in the eyes of critics and provided them with ammunition in the controversies which afflicted Kenya's history.[20]

Four years Delamere's junior was Ewart Grogan, one of a family of twenty-one. Grogan was more intellectual than Delamere but equally wayward. Educated at Winchester and Cambridge, where he studied law, he was sent down for tethering a goat in his tutor's rooms. On impulse he put his future career—art or adventure—to the spin of a coin. Adventure won and Grogan set off to see the world at the time of the second Matabele rising in 1896. Railhead was then at Mafeking and Grogan joined Rhodes's columns to witness the savagery of the last real fight between the white man and the African warrior tribes. He was wounded and went on to New Zealand to convalesce. There he fell in love with a girl whose step-father turned him down for his lack of achievement.

Grogan's answer was to walk from the Cape of Good Hope to Cairo, for much of the way alone, except for a few porters. Apart from his guns and ammunition his supplies consisted of little more than quinine, permanganate of potash and three Union Jacks. It took him two-and-a-half years and he emerged a hero, to be received by the old Queen to whom he presented one of his flags. It was a staggering feat by any standards and it brought him to the attention of Cecil Rhodes, who at once cast his spell over the young Grogan. 'There, in Africa, lies your future,' Rhodes told him. 'A rich continent awaits development, but the right man must be found for the pioneering. You know, as few do, what is wanted. Give yourself to Africa, Grogan—give yourself to Africa.'[21]

Grogan collected his bride from New Zealand and, attracted by Eliot's advertisement for timber concessions of 64,000 acres, made for Kenya. But at Mombasa he found the prospects discouraging. As with Delamere, Eliot was desperate to keep the interest of the famous young man. He asked Grogan to state his own terms: 'Our future is great, and we are in need of white settlement—men like yourself—to help the new railway.' Grogan's terms included part of Mombasa's deep water frontage on which he was later able to realize a huge profit.[22]

Grogan spent the rest of his life in East Africa. He speculated in a wide range of activities, running up huge overdrafts and pulling off spectacular deals. He had a gift for epigram and with his intelligence and legal training he quickly became the spokesman for the growing number of expatriates who gathered in the bars and smoking clubs of Nairobi and grumbled about the way the country was being run. 'East Africa is the home of the leopard, the tick, the baboon and the amateur official' he once quipped. Many were the administrators who smarted under his tongue.[23]

To provoke redress over some anomaly in government, Grogan often took the law into his own hands. But on one occasion he went too far. In full view of the European and native populations of Nairobi he organized the public flogging of three Africans believed to have insulted two white women in a rickshaw. It brought him local popularity but gravely damaged the reputation of the settlers with British opinion. On instructions from London he was fined and sentenced to a month in gaol, which he spent in comfort in a private house well looked after by the ladies of Nairobi.

These two men, Delamere, the Etonian dropout, and Grogan, the Wykehamist buccaneer, were formidable characters who stamped their personalities on the new colony. After Eliot no governor proved a match for either of them. Both were fired by Rhodes and they were outspoken in their loyalties. They took for granted the belief that Britain's destiny was to develop the continent in the interests of the whole of mankind, as well as of the indigenous populations. It was what came to be known—the phrase was Lugard's—as the dual mandate. Fundamental to this outlook was the assumption that Britain's was a superior civilization. As Delamere's biographer has written:

'The idea that the interests of an assortment of barbaric, ideal-less and untutored tribesmen, clothed in sheep's fat, castor oil or rancid butter—men who smelt out witches, drank blood warm from the throats of living cattle and believed that rainfall depended on the arrangement of a goat's intestines—should be exalted above those of the educated European would have seemed to them fantastic.'[24]

By the time Kenyatta arrived at Thogoto, Kenya's future character had been decided. On 1 April 1905, the Foreign Office handed over responsibility to the Colonial Office for all Britain's East African Protectorates. A year later the Commissioner became a Governor and in 1907 he moved his headquarters to Nairobi, thereby ensuring that in the long term African, rather than Arab, influences would predominate. On 17 August 1907, a Legislative Council (known popularly as 'Legco') met for the first time in the steamy offices of the Railway Institute. Its first legislative act was to end formally the institution of slavery in the Sultan's mainland territories, a symbolic closing of one chapter of East African history.

At the end of October the same year Winston Churchill, then Colonial Under-Secretary, paid a visit to East Africa and reviewed with keen eye the fractious politics of Kenya:

'Every white man in Nairobi is a politician; and most of them are leaders of parties. One would scarcely believe it possible, that in a centre so new should be able to develop so many divergent and conflicting interests, or that a community so small should be able to give to each such vigorous and even vehement expressions. There are already in miniature all the elements of keen political and racial discord, all the materials for hot and acrimonious debate.'[25]

Liberal philosophy favoured self-government—Home Rule as it was called in Ireland. Lord Elgin, Churchill's ministerial chief, was sympathetic towards the wish of the colonists of the Transvaal and the Orange Free State to govern themselves. In East Africa, too, self government seemed the logical development of white settlement. But Churchill was shocked by much of what he saw in Kenya and later drew on his experiences to forestall settler pressure for self rule. In 1907 his vision cut through the pettiness of local men to the ennobling mission of Empire:

'In truth the problems of East Africa are the problems of the world. We see the social, racial and economic stresses which rack modern society already at work here, but in miniature . . . The British Government has it in its hands to shape the development and destiny of these new countries and their varied peoples with an authority and from an elevation far superior to that with which Cabinets can cope with the giant tangles at home. And the fact stirs the mind.'[26]

After Eliot, Kenya was not blessed with governors of vision or character. Stewart, 1904–5, was a soldier who thought in terms of punitive expeditions and strong drink; Hayes Sadler, 1905–9, knew nothing of the constitutional role which he filled, and his weakness earned him the nickname 'flannelfoot' from the settlers; Girouard, 1909–12, began with high hopes and ended with having to resign through what appeared to be a deliberate attempt to mislead his superiors at Whitehall. During his term of office the Masai were forced to move a second time from locations into which they had entered only a few years previously upon receiving solemn undertakings by all the senior British officials that they were to be their lands for ever. Girouard, it transpired, promised their land to prospective settlers, and then denied having done so.

The scandal was broken to interested parties in Britain by a government medical officer, Norman Leys, who went on to become one of the strongest critics of Britain's settler policy in Kenya.[27] In the course of the second Masai move, a legal anomaly came to light which cast further doubt on the way the British mission was being interpreted in Africa. The Masai took their case to the courts where it was held to their discomfiture that, as they were not technically *subjects* of the British Crown, but of equal sovereign status with it, they had no redress under British law.

Girouard had to his credit that his measures brought economic growth to Kenya. By the time he left, the need for a Colonial Office grant-in-aid had virtually disappeared. But it was doubtful if the benefits were felt by the Africans. The Masai, it was true, had amassed great wealth in cattle, sheep and goats.[28] But the agricultural tribes were under increasing pressure from the settlers to provide labour. In 1908 confidential revelations over the conduct of government officers in recruiting labour for work on farms shocked the Colonial Office at a time when British opinion was critical of Belgian maladministration in the Congo. 'One might almost say', minuted one official on reading the report, 'that there is no atrocity in the Congo—except mutilation—which cannot be matched in our Protectorate'[29] By 1913 an official enquiry held in Nairobi into labour practices showed that settler attitudes towards Africans had not improved. To induce Africans to leave their own *shambas* to work on European farms, the majority of witnesses urged that compulsion of some sort should be employed—by increasing native taxation, or reducing native land areas, or simply by thrashing those who refused to obey official requests for men.

The missionaries and several government officers, not to mention African witnesses, denounced these views which were symptomatic of the difficult lot of the pioneer farmers. One observer, W. McGregor Ross, found that 'the ruthlessness of some of the members of this early group of settlers' was 'almost unbelievable'. It made him, like Norman Leys, an implacable opponent of the settlers and an ally of Africans. Both were later to become closely involved with Kenyatta.[30] Flogging, withheld pay, starvation, abandonment miles from food or shelter, disease, any one or all of these might be the lot of natives working for unscrupulous adventurers trying out the farming life. One man supervised his workmen from a chair, rifle in hand, which he fired at the feet of anyone he thought was slacking.[31]

There were, of course, many good settlers who were too busy on their farms to engage in the hot-house debates of Nairobi and who genuinely cared for their African labourers. But a single incident in the neighbourhood was enough to destroy a multitude of good deeds. One settler shoots a stock thief at dusk, another fixes himself up with native concubines, a third after a binge slaps an African bystander—and there's gossip in the markets, the old men shake their heads over their beer and the young men's anger rises. This was the atmosphere in which Kenyatta's generation of Africans grew up.

Being agriculturists, the Kikuyu were the tribe most affected by the settlers as the land made available for European farms lay on the fringes of their forest boundary. As health conditions improved through Western medicines and inter-tribal fighting ceased, so the numbers of the Kikuyu increased. Families who had retreated in the years of famine and smallpox, 1897–9, now found there was no further land available on the frontiers of Kikuyuland. As a result, many came to live on European farms as squatters. In return for working for the white man they were allowed to build their own huts, cultivate their own plots and graze their own sheep and goats. Many others looked down at the city growing on the plains and sought their fortunes there.

Between the European farms and tribal Africa there existed another world, foreign to both but playing an essential part in the metabolism of development. This belonged to the Indians. The railway was built almost entirely by Indian coolies and serviced by Indian craftsmen, clerks and technicians. At one point they numbered almost 20,000. During the construction work they lived in special camps along the line of rail which acquired a sinister reputation for squalor, prostitution and vice. Africans enticed into them were regarded as corrupted and became outcasts from their villages. When the railway was completed the camps were closed and the majority of the coolies returned to India under the terms of their original contracts. A large number, however, remained in Nairobi and Mombasa and something of their reputation remained with them.[32]

The Indians stood between the economy of industrial Europe and that of primitive Africa. They were to be found wherever there was a station of the IBEA Company or an administrative post—at Machakos, Naivasha, Ravine. They did business equally with European adventurers like John Boyes and Delamere and with the Africans. Indian rupees advanced with the railway, providing a new currency for the natives in place of the cloth, beads and wire of the caravans. The administration encouraged them and were glad to close down government stores as soon as Indian shops were available.

The Indians were quick to see that Nairobi was the natural centre for European farmers. As white settlement took hold and business grew, they moved up from Mombasa and built warehouses in the bazaar.[33] They were the main contractors for all construction work; Jeevanjee and Co. were responsible for the new government station at Dagoretti, built in 1902–3, and for the first stone house in Nairobi itself.[34] Europeans described Alladina Visram's general stores as 'the Woolworth of the new territories' and found them 'an absolute boon', though they were opposed to Indians settling on the land. Indian businessmen organized the rickshaw services with African labour, forerunners of today's taxis.

The railway township began as a self-governing unit with its own doctors, police, magistrates and telegraph operators. It organized water supplies and other services with an eye only on its own needs as though its specialist nature could isolate it from the surrounding country, just as the herds of wild animals on the plains seemed undisturbed by the extraordinary monster which periodically breathed fire and steam among them. But these new economic forces quickly changed its character. In many respects Nairobi appeared more an Indian than a European township as the numbers of Indians increased, bringing with them their colourful saris and exotic spices, their turbans, sandals and gaudy decorations. By 1901 Nairobi already contained some 8,000 inhabitants.

Few visitors failed to condemn its ramshackle and unhealthy atmosphere. To Grogan it was 'that miserable scrap-heap of tin'.[35] Plague and fire were constant hazards and there was a strong attempt to move the township altogether further into the highlands. But development was too rapid and too powerful. By the time Kenyetta came to Thogoto, Nairobi's future lay-out was already fixed.[36]

From the railway station the township spread north-westwards along Government Road to where Ainsworth had his offices a little south of the papyrus swamp.[37] At first these were no more than a line of corrugated tin huts raised some three feet off the ground and with a series of tin roofs sloping down, pagoda-like, over the edge of the walls to give shade to narrow verandas. Along the road outside Ainsworth planted an avenue of blue gum trees.

Parallel to Government Road and nearer the swamp was Victoria Street, a low line of rickety wooden structures with fences in front for tethering horses. Here the Mombasa merchants hung out their boards and T. A. Wood rented the first hotel and the colourful personalities of the early days met to discuss the latest news—'Pioneer Mary' with her sword stick, McQueen the blacksmith, Boedeker the doctor, Boustead and Ridout the safari agents who fitted out the first CMS expeditions, and men and women with raffish clothes and eccentric habits like so many extras from a 'western'. Bullock carts filled with supplies for the up-country farmers and rickshaws pulled by bare-footed Africans milled about in the mud which became a stinking quagmire in the rainy seasons. The open drains running down the side of the streets would then overflow and the water from the stand pipes turn to a pea-soup colour.

Beyond Victoria Street and on the edge of the swamp lay the first Indian bazaar, which was twice destroyed by fire. A second bazaar was laid out on the south side of Government Road. Further offices, mostly of the PWD, filled out vacant plots between the railway and the commercial areas. On the far side of the railway, up the slope of the hill, lay the houses of senior railway and government officials, the club, the hospital and, at a select distance from them all, the residence of the Governor.

Disagreeable and unhealthy though the township might seem to the farmers, Nairobi was for all that *their* town. It served them, and they, the railway and the urban centre were interlocked in the powerful magnet of development. To it were attracted in growing numbers Africans, Somalis, Goans, Swahili, Arabs and Indians, all loose particles disturbed by the currents set up within the British Empire.

Nairobi was first of all a place of entertainment. At Garvey's Rooms in Government Road, on hard wooden seats, Europeans could enjoy shadow play and music-hall acts, smoking concerts and amateur theatricals. Byram Patel ran a billiard saloon. Newspapers were on sale, mail could be collected, and there were cards and other games in the hotels and clubs where whisky was only four rupees a bottle. The band of the King's African Rifles played once a week. Race meetings were held twice a year; and special fetes welcomed important visitors like Theodore Roosevelt, ex-President of the United States, out on a shooting spree.

Then, Nairobi stood for the future. Every time the farmers came in from up country there would be something new in the town. At first it was a soda-water factory, the precursor of many new industries which swelled the population and increased the demand for labour. In 1910 street lighting appeared with electricity generated from the Ruiru River, ten miles away along the road to Thika, where a rhino once got stuck in the works and plunged Nairobi into darkness. New fangled instruments were on show in the town—bicycles, motor bicycles, motor cars. On the eve of the war Lord Cranworth was running a passenger service in two five-ton lorries between Nairobi and Fort Hall. In Nairobi, all the time, there was novelty and the forward thrust of civilization.

Finally, Nairobi was the centre of government. This was where you came if you wanted to get something done, either in business or with the administration. Grogan had his house here; so did the Ali Khan. It was the place to meet people, get the low-down and discuss politics: at Wood's Hotel, where the settlers first talked about forming themselves into an association to bully the administration and explore outlets for their products; at the Norfolk Hotel, where new-comers could be buttonholed before disappearing into the blue.

In the light air and throttled atmosphere of March, before the rains broke, wild talk always circulated, of scandal, of suicide, perhaps of rebellion. At the end of June 1914 there were additional rumours of an assassination somewhere in Central Europe. Sarajevo, was it? But no one gave it a second thought as preparations went ahead for the July race meeting.

CHAPTER 6

World War I

The outbreak of war in Europe found Britain totally unprepared to defend her East African Protectorates. In the 1880s, when Bismarck pressed for colonies in Africa, Germany struck Britain as her likeliest friend in the European alliance system. The northern frontier of 'German East' was then drawn to include Mount Kilimanjaro as a gift from Queen Victoria to her nephew, the German Kaiser. When Germany's naval programme drove Britain into the Franco-Russian entente the existence of German colonies in Africa was overlooked by the strategists. In Africa the belief persisted that the colonial powers shared the same mission of civilization. The Act of Berlin in 1885 bound the signatories to the principle of neutrality in the Congo Basin. In the Brussels Convention of 1890 they all agreed not to raise native levies for military adventures in Africa against each other. In 1914, despite the overrunning of their own country, the Belgians clung to the hope that the Germans would honour that pledge to exclude hostilities from Africa. The nature of total war, hitherto unrealized on a world scale, ruled out this possibility.

Not until the very end of July 1914 did the Colonial Office flash a warning to Nairobi of the deteriorating situation in Europe. In less than a week came the news that war had broken out and on 5 August the Governor as Commander-in-Chief proclaimed a state of emergency and martial law. There were no plans for such an eventuality, no General Staff, no supplies or state of readiness of any kind. The King's African Rifles numbered only seventeen small companies, the greater part of them deployed against the Somalis in Jubaland. Their nearest port was at Kismayu, 300 miles from Mombasa by sea. Only a few men were stationed in the vicinity of Nairobi, while the vital railway to Mombasa lay unprotected only fifty miles from the frontier. The Germans had completed a railway to Moshi in 1912 and from it they could strike out in any direction they wished across the plains.

Another line ran from Dar es Salaam to Lake Tanganyika. Both Germany and Britain had access to Lake Victoria. Alerted by Berlin, the German warship *Königsberg* had put to sea from Dar es Salaam on 31 July, and she was known to be faster than British cruisers in the area.

As is their custom in all such emergencies, the British responded by improvisation and an amateur enthusiasm which caused more harm to themselves than their opponents. The territory numbered 3,248 males over twenty-one, of which 1,800 immediately enrolled as volunteers. To a man, it seemed, the settlers abandoned their farms and crowded into Nairobi with their own sporting rifles and boasting a strange assortment of dress and headgear. With quaint names and flamboyant pennants they mustered under their leaders like so many feudal companies in the Hundred Years' War: Bowker's Horse, Arnoldi's Scouts, the plateau South Africans. One was named after the Governor's daughter: Monica's Own. Eventually they were organized into the East African Mounted Rifles. The railway formed a pioneer corps. Indians enlisted in a 'Pathan' company. Delamere organized Masai scouts and carrier pigeons along the 200 miles frontier. Grogan joined the intelligence service under Meinertzhagen and advised on the Belgian frontier area. On Lake Victoria the British could count on nine vessels of various kinds and a single nine-pounder saluting gun which had no sights. Against them was a solitary German tug of forty tons which was smaller than any of the British craft but was thought to be better armed.

The first act of hostilities was the bombardment of Dar on 8 August by British cruisers, but on land the Germans were the first to move. A column with dynamite advanced quickly against the Uganda railway, Nairobi's lifeline. But the Germans made the error of using British maps which were so inaccurate the party got lost. Crazed by lack of water they were thankful to surrender when at last they were found by the railway patrols.[1]

On 8 August, at the request of the Colonial Office, the India Office in London instructed the Viceroy to send three battalions of regular troops to East Africa and to occupy Dar es Salaam. The first contingents sailed from Karachi on 19 August and in September Indian Army professionals took over from Kenya's motley crowd of volunteers. The attempt on Dar was a fiasco, repelled as much by a swarm of bees as by the Germans. Many settlers then chose to fight and die in Flanders, glad, it seemed, of the excuse to abandon the pioneer life in the bush. Others returned to their farms and struggled to save them from falling into decay as the war in Europe dragged on, and the resources of empire grew strained.

The African campaign was to continue for the duration of the European struggle. Though quickly forced to surrender in the Cameroons and South West Africa, the Germans in East Africa successfully evaded the combined British, South African, Indian, Belgian and Portuguese forces, with their African levies, for over four years. At the outbreak of war they counted on the same number of white males as were in British East Africa—including a Boer contingent who had elected to settle in German, rather than British, territory. But their isolation forced them into a mobile guerrilla type of warfare in which they were brilliantly led by their commander von Lettow Vorbeck. He was still at large when the Armistice was declared in Europe and was treated as something of a hero by the victors when at length he was persuaded it was all over.

In three respects the war in East Africa turned out to be a watershed in Kenya's history. First, the reliance on the Indian Army, combined with the strategic control of the South Africans, showed up Kenya's own weakness. With the Suez Canal closed, Mombasa could only be reached from Britain after a long voyage round the Cape of Good Hope. Kenya was at the end of the line. Wartime regulations limited cargo space in ships which called at East African ports. Though agricultural producers were much in demand and potentially could make handsome profits out of the war, the farmers of East Africa were virtually cut off. Their own essential supplies grew scarce and costs soared. Replacements of machinery and other farm equipment were virtually unobtainable. Famine struck and emergency supplies of maize and foodstuffs had to be imported from India and South Africa. The concept of a viable, self-governing white state in the African highlands was shown to be an absurdity. In the world scene East Africa had two options: an appendage to South Africa, which was the old dream of Cecil Rhodes, or a hinterland to India— Johnston's America of the Hindu. After the war these uncomfortable truths would have to be faced.

Second, the stress of a world war threw the colonists back on their own resources. Paradoxically East Africa's weakness in the imperial context gave the settlers their opportunity. With professionals from elsewhere in command of the local campaign, many Kenya residents retired to man the vital services on which the life of the territory depended. Tension soon built up between the professional soldiers who felt Kenya was not playing its part in the war effort, the colonial administration which was weakened by man-power shortage, and the settlers who felt they were getting an unfair deal out of the situation. The Governor inclined towards the settlers' point of view, feeling that as the territory was still in its pioneer stage it could ill afford to spare further key men.

The crisis gave the settlers an opportunity to exercise a form of blackmail on the colonial administration. The lead was taken by Grogan. They offered their full co-operation to the government in return for a say in the execution of policy. The outcome was altogether to the settlers' advantage. A war council was set up with strong non-official representation to which the Governor conceded the principle of election. Effectively the settlers won for themselves a measure of control over their own affairs which ran counter to the policy of the Colonial Office. The war council endorsed the electoral concession, established an economic commission which was settler dominated, and prepared the way for a soldier settlement scheme which brought a new type of settler in after the war. Over land and native labour, the two most emotive subjects in the territory's affairs, the settlers secured important legislation to the disadvantage of the Africans.

But the third aspect of the war was the most important: its impact on the Africans. Told that King George's enemies were threatening them, the natives immediately offered support. As the official history put it: 'Among the African population an ardent loyalty and alacrity to serve were equally striking. On all sides offers of help and generous gifts of cattle and foodstuffs came in from the native chiefs.' Apart from the men already enrolled in the King's African Rifles, few Africans were required to handle weapons. The great need was for native porters. Warfare in the bush and jungles of East and Central Africa depended on long supply lines through appallingly difficult terrain. They could be maintained only by a constantly moving human chain. Every territory throughout the continent was called on to provide men for this service.

Within a month of the start of hostilities, 5,000 men had been recruited. Depots were set up for the most populated tribes—at Kisumu for the Luo, Nairobi for the Kikuyu, and Mombasa for the Kamba and Swahili—and for the next four years an unending stream of men fed the troops at the front. Just how many Africans served as porters is impossible to say. In some areas 75 per cent of the male population were taken off; in all, perhaps around 75,000 each from the Kikuyu and Nyanza provinces.

The effect on African village life was devastating. Few ridges of Kikuyuland escaped the impact of recruitment into what were little more than slave gangs. Conditions in the camps and supply lines were appalling. The porters were badly fed, clothed and housed, and their ranks were decimated by the illnesses which overtook men unaccustomed to the tropical climate at low altitudes and unhygienic communal living. The official death roll was put at 23,869. Reliable observers estimated twice as many. To the number of those killed in action or from causes arising directly from the campaign must be added those who perished through diseases spread by the conditions of war. Among these the most devastating was the influenza epidemic of 1918–19 which swept through Kikuyuland and accounted for 100,000 deaths among that tribe alone.

With the upheavals caused by the war, educated Africans, that is all those with mission training, had little difficulty finding jobs in offices or on the deserted farms. Their value in these civilian roles automatically exempted them from service in the Carrier Corps. Employers relied particularly on boys from Thogoto.

When Kenyatta decided to leave the mission, Arthur declined to recommend him for employment. Perhaps he was piqued at Kenyatta's refusal to take a further apprenticeship course. But there was an allegation also, of minor dishonesty, which was reprehensible to the Scotsmen but less so to the Africans for whom the relationship between practical morality and religious belief was never so close.[2] Kenyatta was not deterred. The boy who had cared for his brothers after his mother's death and had made his own way from Ngenda to Muthiga had no inhibitions about finding a living in the European world beyond the forest boundary.

There was someone to whom the Thogoto young men could always turn. This was John Cook. Cook was an engineer who came out to East Africa in December 1907 as one of Henry Scott's party to take charge of the new building programme. His most notable work was to construct the mission's own fresh water supply which was opened at the beginning of 1910. For a brief period he was the first apprentice instructor at Thogoto before leaving the mission staff to take up the management of an engineering firm in Nairobi and he was still at the mission when Kenyatta first arrived. Left-handed, a spectacular shot, with a large bushy moustache and somewhat broody eyes, Cook was a popular figure among the mission boys.

Cook's firm went bankrupt and he had to struggle to keep himself in business on his own account. Arthur described him as "too honest for this business world'. In 1916 he was working as the manager of a sisal company at Thika, an area midway between Nairobi and Fort Hall which was one of the first to be opened to white settlers, and the first to receive its own branch railway line in October 1913.[3] Its flame trees provided the setting for Elspeth Huxley's evocative description of pioneer white settlement seen through the eyes of a child before the war.[4] It was flat scrub country below Kikuyuland proper, though many Kikuyu came down to work on the European farms. Sisal, imported from India in 1909, was proving a success. Cook recruited a number of Thogoto boys. Among them was Philip Karanja, Scott's first Kikuyu convert who was emerging as one of the leaders of the new generation of Kiambu Kikuyu.

In 1916 Kenyatta joined Cook at Thika. Cook liked him and entrusted him with the job of fetching the company wages from the bank in Nairobi twenty-five miles away. Kenyatta became a kind of overseer. But he did not remain with the sisal company for long. The trouble with his lungs flared up again and he fell seriously ill. Dr Arthur would have treated him at Thogoto, but Kenyatta chose not to return there; instead he turned to the other Presbyterian mission hospital at Tumutumu more than thirty-five miles away at the bottom of Mount Kenya. Kenyatta's friend Charles Kasaja now worked in the Tumutumu hospital, and Kenyatta made his way to him on foot. He arrived on the point of collapse and in a high fever, clutching a large tin full of rupees and notes. Kasaja begged him to enter the hospital for proper treatment, but Kenyatta refused. Perhaps he dreaded the hot poultices again, or perhaps he knew that between him and the missionaries there was already some kind of barrier. Dangerously ill, he lay in his friend's hut and was nursed by him back to health.

The pressure on recruitment increased as the campaign dragged on. The government had taken compulsory powers, but most chiefs willingly co-operated in supplying young men from their villages. In 1917 von Lettow Vorbeck was retreating towards the Portuguese frontier and a final effort was required to close the noose on his elusive columns. The war council sanctioned raids upon European farms to collect natives who had so far avoided the net. All unemployed males were driven at the point of bayonets into service. Several fights broke out and many Kikuyu made off to the plains to live with the Masai. Throughout the war, this tribe refused to have anything to do with porterage.[5]

Dr Arthur was on furlough in Scotland when the war broke out. In September 1915 he returned to Thogoto to watch with growing dismay the toll in health and morale which the war was taking on the Kikuyu.[6] The area around the mission itself was largely exempt, as the 'mission boys' mostly filled good jobs and could not be spared. But mission outschools in isolated villages were vulnerable. Mission natives were accused of cowardice by their fellows, and beaten.

Early in 1917 Arthur received, as he wrote home, 'an inspiration from God'. The missionaries had been 'saved' a generation before by the Empire, now it was their turn to support the flag. Arthur proposed forming a special contingent of volunteer porters from the missions themselves. The CMS agreed. The government gave every support and within four days the idea went through. The response from the 'mission boys' was 'unanimous and speedy'. On 14 April 1917, 1,800 assembled at Thogoto for training and special discipline in the interests of hygiene. It justified a little 'kibokoing' in Arthur's eyes. The missionaries received temporary commissions in the Army, church elders were promoted to non-commissioned officers, and the Kikuyu Mission Volunteers, as the force was called, became an *élite* corps of porters for the last year of the war. In May 1917 Captain the Reverend Arthur led his men down to Mombasa singing 'Onward Christian Soldiers', 'Hold the Fort' and other militant hymns.

As things turned out the 'Grand Old Duke of York' would have been more appropriate. The train carrying the KMV arrived at the quayside to find the boat was not expected until the following day. Then health regulations further delayed their embarkation. But in July they arrived in Dar and moved into the supply line. For four months they suffered the worst of the weather and the traditional British army mess-ups. In this period the KMV lost only 100 men out of a total force of 1,900, a striking tribute to Arthur's training and to their own powers of self-discipline.

Most of Kenyatta's generation at Thogoto enrolled in the KMV. Philip Karanja and Musa Gitau were among the leaders. Charles Kasaja volunteered but was asked by Dr Arthur to remain at Thogoto as interpreter and assistant to Dr Jones, the new mission doctor now responsible for a special Carrier Corps hospital. All other work at the mission came to a standstill, and the carpentry and masons' shops were closed.

Kenyatta was not involved. Perhaps John Cook sheltered him for a while, but he always risked being picked up in one of the sweeps through the European estates. This appeared to be the fate of his younger brother Kongo who had joined him as a boarder at Thogoto and continued his schooling there after Kenyatta himself had left. At the end of one term, during the war, Kongo went off for his holidays and was never seen again. Perhaps he died somewhere along the line of porters in the fever-ridden swamps of 'German East', an unnamed Kikuyu among thousands who met their end in the Carrier Corps; or perhaps he attached himself to a European and met his fate in an un-recorded drama elsewhere. His family never knew what happened. During the war Kongo just disappeared.

Kenyatta knew how to look after himself. In that fateful year of 1917 the safest place to be was among the Masai. This arrogant tribe would have nothing to do with the Carrier Corps and held normal military discipline to be beneath them. Apart from Delamere's scouting operations they took no active part in the war. After its second move the tribe was now consolidated south of the railway in dry, open country, dotted with sharp-thorned acacia trees which extended for thousands of square miles across the Rift Valley and towards the Serengeti plains in Tanganyika. Their administrative headquarters were at Narok, nearly 100 miles west of Nairobi.

The Masai has a riddle: 'What is it that escapes the veld fire? The bare ground where no grass grows.'[7] It aptly described the Kikuyu exodus to Masaidom to escape the press-gang raids on their villages. Among the Masai a man could lie low. The fire of recruitment would not spread there, for the Masai were too dispersed for close adminis-tration and too fierce for casual interference. Though the Kikuyu and the Masai were traditional enemies, certain clans among both tribes had long maintained contact with each other. Kenyatta's family had these connections. One of his grandfather's wives was a Masai woman and Kenyatta had an aunt married to a Masai chief.[8] He took the opportunity of staying with this family.

The Masai may not have provided soldiers or porters for the war, but they made up for it by supplying large quantities of meat, 'a most important munition of war' as an official noted. It was in Narok that Kenyatta found himself in 1917, possibly with Indians acting as agents for army contractors. He was some kind of administrative clerk or ranching hand, responsible for getting the cattle, sheep and donkeys through to Nairobi.

One letter in Kenyatta's hand survives from those years. From Narok he wrote in August 1917 to congratulate a friend, Paul, on his

marriage. Though a somewhat unformed scrawl, it is the first clear expression of his extrovert personality and he signed it with the flourish
that was to become a characteristic. Kenyatta sent his friend a present:

'I enclosed herewith 15 rupees to help you in your marriage. Hoping
you will excuse me as I have nothing to help you, you know I am a
poor fellow.
Besides this I want to let you know that I don't know what day I
shall be there because I have no idea. Hoping this will find you safely.
Salute for me your sweetheart.
Will you please wait me on 11th at station. I don't know if I will pass
through Nairobi.
I beg to enclosed with best regards.
Your Aye Acquaintance
K. N. Johnstone'[9]

At the beginning of 1918 the Kikuyu Mission Volunteers returned
from Dar. Their work was done; 'German East' was now declared a
British Protectorate.

The pressure on the Kikuyu relaxed; life in the territory began to
pick up more of its peacetime momentum. Kenyatta left his retreat
in Masailand and returned to Nairobi. Here was life; jobs for an
intelligent and hard-working Kikuyu were well paid, and in Nairobi
he could improve his English. He attended evening classes at a CMS
school and for a time worked for a certain Stephen Ellis looking after
a store of farming and engineering equipment. It was near the old
Indian bazaar and at the centre of activity for the polyglot hangers-on
of the European community. Kenyatta shared a corner of the building with the ploughs and saws. Some months later he was back at
Thika again, with another sisal company. John Cook was busy with
further construction work. The Thogoto mission required more
houses for its staff, and Kenyatta was responsible for building them.
One was for his friend Charles Kasaja.

But it was Nairobi that attracted him. Kenyatta was one of an increasing number of Africans who were rapidly adapting themselves
to the new style of life introduced into their world by the Europeans.
They were earning good money, and mastering the new economic
conditions. In the Nairobi bazaar they could buy second-hand clothes
and deck themselves out in the latest fashion—no more eccentric in
their own eyes than the white men they aspired to be. In Nairobi too
there was a new magic: the photograph. Indians were quick to open

studios where the Africans could pose against suitable backdrops. De-mobilized porters were delighted with this visible record of their ad-ventures. Kenyatta and his friends joined in. To be photographed was an essential part of the new style of life.

From the pages of old albums a figure emerges. On one page he wears slouch hat, bush jacket and riding breeches, thick stockings and safari boots. His arms are on his hips and a long kiboko whip is in one hand. A thin moustache grows above thick, slightly parted lips. On the next page he is in a heavy suit with waistcoat, wide brimmed hat, collar and tie. Over the page again: a military man, water bottle slung over one shoulder, glasses over the other, pipe in mouth, feet in cavalry boots, the very image of one of the pioneers who shot their way through bush and jungle—lion, antelope and 'nigger', it was all the same to them.

Here is the new man. Twenty years before he was a child of the centuries, carried in a goatskin on his mother's back in a Kikuyu world outside history; now he was travelling freely beyond the hori-zon, utilizing a new magic, speaking a new language, dressing with a new raciness: 'Your Aye Acquaintance'.

Masai women spent much of their time decorating thin strips of leather with brightly coloured beads. Kenyatta enjoyed wearing their ornaments and he affected some of their customs. The ornaments could be worn round the arm or neck, tied round the waist as a belt, or fastened in a band round a hat. The Kikuyu word for them was *kinyata*. To his friends, K. N. Johnstone, alias Kamau wa Ngengi, baptized Johnstone by the 'Scotchi', was undergoing a transformation.

CHAPTER 7

The Aftermath of War: Harry Thuku

In Europe the Armistice saw a continent in turmoil. The empires of Russia, Austro-Hungary and Turkey had collapsed, flooding Eastern and Central Europe with a tide of revolution which surged up to the Rhine. No longer would the frontiers of the world be drawn to suit the fancies of princes; Tsar, Sultan, Kaiser and Holy Roman Emperor had departed the stage of history, never to reappear. Republican France was bled near to death; republican America soon withdrew back into isolation across the Atlantic. Only for Britain was the outcome one for self-congratulation; the Empire had proved itself, the Empire still stood. God had made her mighty and would make her mightier yet.

The peace treaty confirmed Britain in her imperial role. More areas of the globe were now painted red than ever before: in the Middle East, a new empire which virtually stretched from the Mediterranean to the Himalayas; in Africa, the fulfilment of Rhodes's old dream. When the League of Nations endorsed Britain's mandate over Tanganyika, a broad swathe of red coloured the map of Africa from the Cape of Good Hope to Cairo.

Physically, too, the war transformed the face of Africa and opened up the countryside in a manner undreamed of by the first settlers. In 1914, throughout the whole of the eastern and central parts of the continent, roads capable of taking motor vehicles were negligible. In Nyasaland, there was a single stretch of forty-five miles with two small motor cars and one 15-cwt lorry; in German East Africa, one lorry for a stretch of only twenty miles; in Kenya, perhaps twenty miles of road at the coast and the odd fifty miles between Nairobi and Fort Hall along which Lord Cranworth's two 5-ton trucks plied with difficulty; in Uganda and Northern Rhodesia, nothing at all. Less than a dozen vehicles in all that vast hinterland, and few communications between the territories themselves. At the close of hostilities the scene had changed. In 1922 there were 134 cars in Kenya;

in 1924, 945. Travel throughout Africa by motor vehicle became normal; the territories were linked up along a north-south axis and within their own regions; aeroplanes had appeared. The war brought an end to the world of Livingstone and Stanley and to the string of naked porters following the sun-hatted white man with his gun. The pace of development increased.

The settlers were determined to press home the advances they had secured during the war. At their request the Colonial Office appointed a Major-General as their next governor. He was Sir Edward Northey, who had won renown in the campaign in Nyasaland. He arrived in Nairobi in February 1919.

Northey's period of office inaugurated a new era of controversy in Kenya's affairs. The stage was set as soon as he arrived, when at a special banquet Grogan welcomed him with a two-hour speech of an immoderation unusual even for him. 'We are entitled to know,' Grogan said, 'whether you have been sent out here as another telephone exchange girl, or whether you have been sent out with powers commensurate with the work you have achieved in the world.' Northey and his staff were visibly shaken by this verbal assault. Grogan left him in no doubt about the settlers' point of view: 'We hold that the Secretariat has no function in governing this country . . . men of little more brain than the creatures that crawl about at the bottom of the sea . . . The time has come for them to go.'[1]

The settlers were bidding for self-government, claiming that they knew best how to look after native interests. Delamere had expressed the same view in more measured language in 1918: 'The really important thing to my mind is that the Colonial Office should avoid interference in the local affairs of this Protectorate.'[2]

One of Northey's first acts was to take in hand plans for resettling servicemen on free land made available in newly alienated areas. The offer was widely publicized in the home newspapers. Open to ballot were 250 farms of 160 acres each, all free land, and 800 larger farms available for purchase on generous terms. The response was spectacular. Throughout the summer of 1919 the scheme attracted wide attention, largely, it seemed, because of the high proportion of England's upper classes who entered the lottery. 'Lucky aristocrats' and 'Blue blood in the wilds' ran the headlines.[3]

They were a new type of settler, attracted, no doubt, by the idea of servants at under £1 a month and of escaping the new democracy at home.[4] They had little experience of farming or sense of vocation. Most were hardened by life in the trenches and alarmed by the

spectres of industrial unrest which haunted post-war Europe. They
brought with them the restlessness which disturbed the West in the
years following the war like currents which continue to swirl through
the atmosphere for months after a nuclear explosion. Their occupation of new land roused bitter feelings among Africans who had
served loyally in the Carrier Corps and received no such rewards.
What new meaning would the latter now attach to the words on the
fine war memorials in Nairobi and Mombasa? 'To the carriers who
were the hands and feet of the army: "If you fight for your country
even if you die your sons will remember your name." '

With military despatch Northey set about reconstructing the life of
the territory. In his opening address to the Legislative Council he
endorsed the grant of electoral privilege to the settlers which had
been anticipated by the appointments to the war council. The first
elections to the new council were held in January 1920. In July 1920
the British East Africa Protectorate officially became the Crown
Colony of Kenya. Northey reorganized the finances of the railway
and the country generally to give the new colony a properly balanced
budget. He introduced a new administrative system which separated
native from settled areas and placed the former under provincial and
District Officers responsible to the new post of Chief Native Commissioner. Responding to pressure from the settlers for whom labour
had always been a serious problem, he authorized measures which
implied that compulsion might be used by native chiefs and headmen to supply labour for the European farms. And in keeping with
the strong settler bias of his government, he enforced a system of
registration for all natives leaving the reserves. Here again he built
on the work of the war council.

The *kipande,* as it was called, remained a source of grievance
among Africans for the whole of the colonial period. Every male
African leaving his reserve was required to carry a registration certificate on which were recorded his finger-prints, the name of his
employer and the nature of his work. The certificates were placed
in small tins which most men hung round their necks. To be without one made the African liable to fines and imprisonment. The
system was open to abuse by unscrupulous employers and threatened
to clog the administrative machinery with its detail and necessary
police involvement. The scheme was launched in August 1920 and by
1922 nearly half a million natives had been registered, Kenyatta
among them. He belonged to the category of roving 'detribalized'
Africans whom the government wished to control.

On returning from Masailand Kenyatta had not cut himself off from his stepfather at Ngenda. They were his own family lands for which he, as the eldest surviving son of Muigai, would inherit responsibility. Kenyatta had the right to ask Ngengi for the sheep and goats necessary for each stage in tribal life—when he was initiated, when he entered the grades of eldership, and above all when he got married.

To obtain a wife was an important step for the young Kikuyu men. In pre-colonial days it took seven years' work in the *shambas* to earn the requisite number of goats for each wife—the time it took Jacob to win Rachel. Women were central to the economy of the tribe and a man would only buy himself a wife from a family known to be reliable, one which could be trusted to return the goats if the marriage proved unsatisfactory. Kenyatta's first bid for a wife failed as she turned out to be related to his own clan. But as a wise elder might have told him: 'Is it not one ridge only that has bananas on it; you must cut your bunch from another plantation.'[5] He soon found another girl who was attending the CMS school for girls at Kabete, not far from Dagoretti. Her name was Grace Wahu and her family lived near his own lands at Ngenda. Kenyatta installed her on the family homestead and on 20 November 1920 his first child, a boy, was born. Kenyatta named him after his own father, Muigai.

But Ngengi was no more easy to live with now than he had been when Kenyatta was a small boy. The older man resented the growing sons of his dead brother, and like many of his generation was suspicious of the European ways which Kenyatta was affecting. Whenever his 'stepson' came to visit him, he would slaughter a beast to give him the customary feast, knowing Kenyatta would not stay long in the homestead. But he soon grew irritated at the presence of Grace and the new baby. He resorted to the traditional Kikuyu device for getting rid of people. In this case, the procedure was to cut another door into her hut. It was a form of curse and no one could endure the disgrace of it without moving. Grace took the baby to join Kenyatta at Dagoretti.

Kenyatta had no intention of taking up farming life. He had left home to escape all that. Like all the brighter mission-trained young men he looked for more lucrative jobs with the administration or the Europeans. To do this a man did not need to have a special home of his own; it was enough to buy himself a wife, build her a hut and set her to work on the family land. Men never shared their huts with their women folk, a wife safeguarded a husband's rights of inheritance as well as providing him with a steady income in case of need. Kenyatta's contacts were all in Nairobi or the Dagoretti area, and he was still a member of the church at Thogoto. For a time he was a client, one might say, of the sub-chief of the district, Kioi.

With the descendants of the Waiyaki family Kioi was among the biggest landowners of the district around the Presbyterian mission.[6] After Waiyaki's death Kioi rose like Kinyanjui through the favour of the administration. They represented local tribal authority to whom the Scottish missionaries paid court. Their land straddled the Nyongara River close to the mission estate and they were generous patrons of the mission, present on all important occasions. Photographed by Arthur together they might have struck European eyes as a couple of ruffians. Kinyanjui wore a military cap of sorts with his chief's badge of office, and he always carried a black fly-whisk and stick. Kioi went heavily ornamented and barefooted, in blanket and top hat. For all their comic appearance to Europeans they bore themselves with dignity and impressed the tribe. It is reasonable to suppose that they also impressed the young Kenyatta, and that he borrowed from their style.

Kenyatta lived for a time in Kioi's village, at the home of his circumcision father Musa Gitau. As one who knew his way around the mission and had experienced the white man's ways in Nairobi, Kenyatta was a useful retainer to a chief like Kioi. He called on the young man's services to help him over an important land-case which came up in 1919 before a judge in Nairobi. It was brought by two young men of Kenyatta's generation. Kioi was supported by Kinyanjui. In a previous action the judge had ordered Kioi to remove his huts from a certain piece of land. Kioi had obeyed and placed them on the land now in dispute. It was not, said the judge, a question of ownership, as understood by an English freehold, but of rights to cultivation.

The two young men claimed their father had acquired these occupation rights from the aboriginal hunters of the forest, the Wandorobo. In a raid, the Masai killed their father and 'in the year of the big famine' came to an agreement whereby the Kikuyu deal with the Wandorobo was confirmed. Kioi countered by saying that Kinyanjui was the original party to this settlement and that he, Kioi, had bought the land direct from Kinyanjui 'for 100 goats, four oxen, one daughter, and four fat sheep'. According to him, the young men steadily encroached on his land because the mother of one of them was Kioi's sister.

It was a story of the most complex family relationships, with sisters and 'step-mothers', uncles and 'sons' and a frontier outside any known law where three tribes, Masai, Kikuyu and Wandorobo, met in the forests of Dagoretti in pre-colonial days. Kenyatta's role was to explain to Kioi's European lawyers the precise meaning of these complex kinship ties.

Kioi lost. The trial judge dismissed much of the evidence, some of which Kenyatta had helped prepare.

'The majority of the Akikuyu witnesses,' he said 'have sworn against each other—and at their own request—on their *kithathi* juju stone. I am informed that the oath is a peculiarly binding one and that the penalties for breaking it—temporal and physical rather than spiritual and eternal—are extremely unpleasant. In spite of this there has been an inexcusable amount of barefaced lying on one side or the other, possibly on both—and certainly on the part of the defendant himself.'[7]

The case was significant as it raised the whole question of land 'ownership' and threw into sharp contrast Western legal concepts and immemorial tribal custom. The administration sought definitions in the courts. In 1921 the colony's Chief Justice drew upon the Kioi case in delivering a judgement which took many people by surprise. The only real 'owner' of land reserved for the use of tribes, said the Chief Justice, was the Crown—a legal fiction understandable in Britain, but one which caused consternation to Africans. It made explicit what the imperialists took for granted, that the colonial power was absolute, 'and in consequence all native rights in such reserved land disappear—natives in occupation thereof becoming tenants at will of the Crown.'[8]

It took some time for Kikuyu landowners to become fully aware of the meaning of this judgement, but when they did so it appeared to put their lands more than ever at risk to settler encroachments. It was over-shadowed at the time by a vicious controversy over the status of Indians.

The Indian question arose primarily through settler claims to superior rights over land and electoral privileges. The point was simple. The Indians in Kenya outnumbered Europeans by almost four to one; if they were allowed equal voting rights and to buy land on the same conditions as the European settlers, then Kenya would shortly become an Indian colony.[9] Eliot in 1902 had warned of possible friction if Indians were allowed to take up land, and gave verbal instructions to exclude Indian settlement between Machakos and Fort Ternan on the border of Kavirondo. At the same time the Colonial Office frankly looked to India for the development of East Africa. In the ensuing years government policy was never clearly spelled out but remained a matter of local interpretation. The war heightened the political ambitions of Indians as much as of European settlers, and the Indian subcontinent itself was beginning to stir from the imperial grip. While the Indians of East Africa looked to the Viceroy in Delhi for moral support, the white settlers turned to South Africa and General Smuts. Both Smuts and the India Office carried weight in the imperial cabinet. It was a nice issue of imperial politics which party would carry the day.

The dispute raged throughout Northey's term of office. The settlers used arguments from nature, stock breeding, Darwin and the Bible. They abused the Indians' religious beliefs, accused them of 'moral depravity' and deployed against them the same reasoning as later generations of racists would apply against Jewish and Negro minorities; that they were inherently more prone to crime, disease and vice than the white man. Grogan's hand was much in evidence.

From 1917 the Indian population of East Africa increased spectacularly. Swelled by these newcomers, they contributed enormously to the wealth and versatility of the colony. Included in their number were Ismaili Moslems who were followers of the Aga Khan and possessed a fine record of community development, Sikhs who were excellent mechanics and Hindu clerks who practically ran the administrative system.

Indians permeated all walks of life, in business as in the police, in the professions as in the civil service; they were prominent in Nairobi society and could be found in the smallest townships. Without them the economy of East Africa would have come to a standstill and white settlement been an impossibility short of the creation of a class of poor whites imported from Italy or Eastern Europe. In neighbouring Uganda, where white settlement was insignificant, a government report at this very moment publicly recognized the debt the country owed Indians.[10]

In the autumn of 1920 the Indians of Nairobi produced their own journal, the *East African Chronicle,* to answer the settlers. To the ferment of Kenya politics they brought an awareness of the wider struggle against British imperialism. The *East African Chronicle* featured articles on the Sinn Fein in Ireland, on Gandhi, and on the black racism of Marcus Garvey. It gave a reasonable account of the

Kenyatta wearing a monkey skin presented by Kikuyu tribesmen after his release from prison in 1961

Kenyatta as president

Kikuyu warriors

Kikuyu women carrying firewood

The pioneers. Francis Hall is seated far right

The Iron Snake crossing forest and escarpment

Panorama of Nairobi *c.* 1902

Nairobi *c.* 1954

Nairobi *c.* 1904

Kenyatta at Thogoto

The mission school at Thogoto

Kenyatta and family *c.* 1925. Seated with him is his first wife, Grace Wahu, wearing Kinyata belt, between them their son. Kenyatta's half brother James Muigai is standing right.

Kenyatta with his son Peter Muigai and motor bike *c.* 1929

historical relationship between India and East Africa which 'was long antecedent' to the arrival of European settlers.

In May 1921 the struggle between the Europeans and Indians moved in an unexpected direction. While the settlers formulated what they described as their 'irreducible minimum' position over the Indian claim for equal land opportunities and common roll voting, the Indians turned to another quarter. They attacked the settler bias of the colonial government not from their own point of view, but from that of the Africans. Their chosen instrument was a young Kikuyu telephone operator called Harry Thuku.

Harry Thuku was born in about 1895. He owed his African name to his maternal grandfather who in turn had taken it after exchanging ivory for brass wire with Arab traders.[11] Thuku's father belonged to one of the leading families of southern Kiambu who provided land for the American Gospel Missionary Society's station at Kambui, close to Thuku's home. Thuku spent four years with these American missionaries. They baptized him in 1908. Like Kenyatta a few years later, he chose to be circumcized quietly with a group of mission friends. In 1911 he came to Nairobi to earn £1 a month as an errand boy in a bank. But a foolish attempt to forge a cheque which a friend had stolen from the mission landed him with a two-year prison sentence. He served it in Mombasa building roads and pushing the trolleys on which Europeans travelled about the streets of the town. His prison officers were Indians. When he was released in 1913 he was taken on as a servant on a government tour of Turkana country in the north, returning through Luo country in the west of Kenya.

Thuku was the prototype of 'detribalized' Kikuyu. Few had seen so much of East Africa so young. He had a superior view of tribal tradition and he looked naturally towards Nairobi where, with his intelligence and command of English, he found no difficulty in obtaining jobs. For a time he worked as a compositor on the settler *Leader of British East Africa,* where he fell under the influence of the Goans and Indians who made up the technical staff. He slept in rooms in the Asian quarter off River Road and his African friends were either Nyasas from the old freed slave settlement of Freretown on the coast, or Baganda. These were the two principal sources of native clerks in East Africa at that time. In December 1917 he decided to quit the *Leader of British East Africa* and a few months later he became one of the telephone operators at the Treasury.

By 1921 Thuku was earning over £4 a month. He could afford a bicycle which enabled him to live in Pangani, the native location to the north of the Nairobi River, named after one of the starting points for slaving caravans on the mainland north of Zanzibar from which early IBEA Company caravans were fitted out before Mombasa became properly established. It was the natural habitat of detribalized natives and Thuku's acquaintances were all young men who had broken away from the ridges of Kikuyuland and the kraals of the plains. Here lived African Moslem converts, some Kikuyu-born like Abdulla Tairara, some Kamba like Mohammed Sheikh. Here were the only tea shops which the Africans could frequent, being excluded from the bars, hotels and cafés in the European quarter of the town. Here Giriama from the coast and Masai, Nandi and Kamba and Kikuyu all exchanged gossip in Swahili, the *lingua franca* of East Africa. Chauffeurs, gardeners, compositors and line-setters, Christians and Moslems, half-castes and orphans, all the hangers-on of the white man's world came together in Pangani. By 1921 it was a breeding ground for political agitation.

While he was at the Treasury Thuku came into contact with Indian leaders, and in particular with Desai, the Secretary, and Jeevanjee, the President of the Indian Association. They were the two men nominated by the Governor to represent Indians in his council. They controlled the *East African Chronicle* and, through their community, many employers of African clerks and workers. In June 1921 they began to publicize African grievances. Desai encouraged Thuku to use his office as a headquarters and gave him clerical and financial assistance as well as the use of his printing works. It was enough to turn any young man's head.

The *kipande* registration decree had been received by the Africans, in the words of one of its foremost European critics, 'with remarkable submissiveness'.[12] It was followed by further measures of the Northey administration designed to balance the colony's budget and counter the world trade recession which set in towards the end of 1920, and which ruined many of the newly settled ex-servicemen. These measures included the raising of the hut tax, a change in the currency from the rupee to the shilling, which actually left the Africans better off, and the imposition of import duties. But the most drastic action came from the settlers themselves, when they proposed an all-round cut in native wages from 1 June. It was all that was needed in Pangani.[13]

The missionaries watched the racial dispute with apprehension. They had lived closer to the Africans during the months when the Kikuyu Mission Volunteers were in the line of porters during the war and they had seen them through the dark months of the influenza epidemic which followed. As settler demands for more land and labour increased, so did missionary anxiety over the character of Northey's administration. The relationship between settler and missionary was always uneasy. After the war they drew rapidly apart. The missionaries also took the view that Indians should be prevented from swamping the colony. Both settlers and Indians claimed to be guardians of the true interests of the natives. But the missionaries could show the best reason why they alone should take this role.

Some time towards the end of 1920 reference was first made to a body which called itself the 'Kikuyu Association'. Doubt exists over its precise origins, but its character has been well described as 'a largely informal grouping of leading Christians, government headmen and tribal elders drawn principally from south and central Kiambu'.[14] Whatever its origins the Kikuyu Association received its sense of direction from the missions. The Presbyterians at Thogoto and the Anglicans at Kabete had established strong influences over the leading chiefs of the district who between them virtually controlled southern Kikuyuland. Watchful of the settlers, alarmed at the Indian agitation, and certain in their own minds that anything emanating from Pangani was bad, the missionaries supported these Kikuku chiefs in their representations to the government. On 11 June 1921, a meeting took place in Kioi's village to put the grievances of the tribe into proper form. Barlow acted as interpreter and drew up a petition on behalf of the Association.

Guided by his Indian friends, Thuku moved among the natives of Pangani to rally support for a different organisation. Various names were canvassed, among them the 'African Association' and the 'Young Kikuyu Association'.[15]

On 24 June 1921, the administration held a *baraza* at Dagoretti, the traditional palaver between government officers and tribal representatives. To it came the leading chiefs of southern Kiambu, together with many young men from Nairobi and the surrounding ridges, to present the petition which Barlow had drawn up on their behalf to the Chief Native Commissioner. The Kikuyu complaints in substance remained the basic items of grievance for the rest of the colonial period. They included forced labour, alienation of land, the *kipande*, taxes, lack of educational benefits and other public services. The young men raised the question of the suggested wage cut: would the government bend to settler pressure?

Thuku turned up at the meeting on his bicycle and obtained a copy

of the Barlow memorandum. The meeting broke up with the chiefs
satisfied they had delivered their petition in the proper manner to
the government. Thuku returned to Nairobi with the copy in his
hands.

During the next few days both the Indians and the settlers held
important meetings to define their attitudes towards the racial issue.
Both had delegations canvassing support outside the colony. So
heated were the settlers that the Governor was forced to walk out of
one of their sessions. The Indians passed resolutions which were
clearly intended to gain African support. They took counsel with
Harry Thuku over his next move.

The result was the final choice of the name "East African Association" for Thuku's Pangani group and a decision to break with the
mission-backed Kikuyu Association and the tribal authorities of
Kiambu. On 13 July Thuku sent a summary of the Dagoretti resolutions by cable direct to the Prime Minister in London, thus going over
the heads of both the chiefs and the colonial administration. Furious,
the chiefs repudiated it. From the dawning of their political consciousness the Kikuyu appeared bitterly divided.

Thuku had put his Treasury address on his cable. The administrative officer in charge told him he must give up his political activities or leave government service. Sympathetic Europeans tried to
restrain him. Physically Thuku was a small man but he made up for
it by an aristocratic disdain for others. His own feelings would probably have been enough to make him choose to continue agitation, but
the Indian backing clinched it.

It was easy to accuse the chiefs of being government stooges. Like
Matthew in Roman Palestine they had at first been responsible for
collecting taxes on behalf of the British government, on which they
took a commission. But by the 1920s their position was ambiguous as
the government began to recognize the value of the old council of
elders (*Kiama*) who exercized a greater collective authority. Kinyanjui was forbidden by the administration to sign further protests and
Thuku alleged that he secretly agreed with him. Koinange, a neighbouring chief, and much respected by the administration, once spent
a night in Thuku's rooms in Pangani and told the young man how
his own land had been divided by a road for the convenience of the
settlers, and the section across the road taken for a European coffee
farm. Koinange himself was not permitted to grow coffee on his own
farm, while across the road he could see the settler's coffee prospering

on his ancestral soil. The lost land contained the graves of his father and grandfather.

Clan feeling was strong among the Kikuyu, and Thuku belonged to one of the leading families. Everyone took a certain pride in the success of one of their young men and Thuku derived considerable support, moral as well as material, from his own family land.

He claimed that his Association contained most of the educated Kikuyu, and this was likely to be true as they were concentrated in Nairobi. He also argued, in language which anticipated a later call by Kenyatta, for a wider loyalty than that of the tribe alone: 'I am fully convinced that it is essential for the uplift of my countrymen to be friendly to all races whether Indians, Europeans, Arabs, Somalis or Goans and it is equally essential for the good of Kenya and for its progress and advancement that all races are friendly to one another.'[16] In pursuit of this Thuku aimed to campaign beyond Kikuyuland in Luo and Kamba country.

Within a few months he acquired a hero's reputation in Kikuyuland. Songs about him spread from ridge to ridge; prayers were offered on his behalf by church elders; contributions of a shilling a head poured into his Association; his leaflets, printed on Indian presses, quickly sold out. Whatever role the Indians played at the outset was overtaken by deeper forces of tribal revolt. Thuku was the catalyst for all the feelings of hostility nurtured by the Africans since the arrival of the white man. He gave way to mob oratory in the reserve:

'I, Harry Thuku, am greater than you Europeans. I am even greater than the Chiefs of this country. How is it that I have left Nairobi without being arrested if it is not because I am a great man? . . . I desire if the Europeans tell you to do any sort of work at all, that you tell them Harry Thuku has refused to allow you to make camps, or to make roads, or to work in the station or for the Public Works Department, or to give out food for porters or firewood. Hearken, every day you pay hut tax to the Europeans of Government. Where is it sent? It is their task to steal the property of the Akikuyu.'[17]

Thuku made little headway in Kiambu, the area nearest Nairobi. Tribal representatives from this district toured Kikuyuland after him and held meetings to counter his speeches. Not that they did not share the basic grievances over land, the *kipande,* taxes and

labour, but their approach was more conservative than radical, aiming more to work within the administrative system and alongside the
missionaries than against them. Chiefs in other parts of Kikuyuland
requested the government to deport Thuku. The missionaries assisted by preparing evidence against him. In the evening of 14 March
1922, he was arrested in Pangani by a Sikh Inspector of Police who
brought him back on the rear of his motorcycle to the police lines off
Government Road. At the same time the offices of the *East African
Chronicle* were searched.

Next day a crowd gathered in front of the police lines which were
no more than a range of old tin buildings. The Pangani leaders organized a strike of Nairobi workers, mostly rickshaw-pullers and
sweepers, and collected money for Thuku's defence. Houseboys and
clerks joined in the 'strike'. The tide of angry Africans swelled
throughout the day, ebbed towards the evening of the 15th, and on
the morning of the 16th swelled again, carrying in its front gaudily
dressed town prostitutes. A native delegation came to interview the
Governor's deputy; egged on by the women the crowd moved towards the nervous police, throwing stones and insults. Looking on
derisively was a group of Europeans taking their midday drinks on
the veranda of the Norfolk Hotel.

It was a classic scene from colonial history, ready made for a film
scenario. The reality was tragic. The leaders were unable to control
the mob, which now numbered six or seven thousand, and the police
riflemen—about 150 of them—fired at point blank range. According
to the official report of the 'riot', twenty-one natives were killed, including several women and one 15-year-old boy. Patrols with Lewis
guns kept the natives on the move and Thuku was taken down to the
coast to begin an exile which was to last nine years, though he was
never put on trial. With this sudden outbreak of violence the East
African Association came to an end and Thuku's Pangani group
dispersed.

Unlike Amritsar in 1919 the Thuku shooting made little stir in
Britain. There were the usual questions in Parliament and an official
report on the incident in which the Governor assured the Colonial
Secretary that the crowd had gathered out of curiosity and not because of any genuine sense of grievance. Thuku's agitation was seen
by the Europeans as further evidence of the dangerous influence of
Indians.[18]

The racial issue now moved to a climax. In August 1922 Northey
was summarily recalled by Winston Churchill, Colonial Secretary

from February 1921 to October 1922 when the Duke of Devonshire took over, one of seven peers in Bonar Law's Conservative Cabinet. From Uganda Sir Robert Coryndon moved across to Nairobi as Governor of the fractious Kenya colony.

In September the Indians appeared to have gained their point with the Colonial Office. The Europeans in Kenya were outraged. The settlers counted among their number an unusually high proportion of ex-military men. Led by Delamere, they made plans for armed rebellion under the slogan 'For King and Kenya'. They would abduct the Governor.

Three British cruisers took up station off the East African coast. The Governor was summoned home. 'Gentlemen', he said before leaving, 'you may remember that I am South African born'.[19] He invited the two parties to send delegations as well. Delamere led the settlers. The Indians chose Thuku's old friends and sailed via Bombay where they picked up two members of the Viceroy's Council. Coryndon asked for a missionary to advise him on African opinion. The choice fell on Dr Arthur from Thogoto.

The Protestant missions had been moving towards federation since 1913. The Kikuyu Mission Volunteers gave practical expression to this alliance and in 1918 it was formally endorsed at a conference held at the Presbyterian mission, which set up a representative council. Their long-term hope of a united church was not to be realized and the most enduring aspect of their work was to give Kenya its first secondary school, the Alliance High School, situated on the Thogoto mission estate.

Through their home organizations the Protestant alliance mobilized an impressive weight of opinion which no government could afford to ignore. At the centre, in London, was J. H. Oldham, "a man of outstanding vision, ability and tact', who was reckoned to be 'one of the most deeply thinking and creative personalities who collaborated in the evolution of modern imperial policy in East Africa'.[20]

Before leaving for London, Arthur canvassed all the Kenya missionaries for their views on the subject of Indian immigration and was powerfully armed with their replies.[21] Arguments raged around the question of the franchise, immigration, the number of seats to be allocated on the Legislative Council, the composition of municipal authorities, the allocation of alienated land. Over these matters the settlers retained most of their privileges, and particularly over the preservation of the 'white' highlands. But behind the scenes, through Oldham and the Archbishop of Canterbury, it was the missionaries who made the greatest impression on the Duke of Devonshire. In July 1923 the white paper was issued. Arthur wrote of it as

'the Magna Charta of the rights of the native peoples of Kenya: . . . No finer statement of policy as to the status of the native races in Africa has been produced in the history of our country in its dealings with peoples who have been brought under our trusteeship.'[22]

The Devonshire white paper delivered a crushing rebuff to the settlers. At a time when the settlers of Rhodesia were being offered the choice of incorporation in the Union of South Africa or a limited form of self-government under the Colonial Office, the white paper came down unequivocally on the side of African interests which, it said, in a key phrase, must be 'paramount' in Kenya.[23]

All the settlers had achieved was a firm declaration that self-government was 'out of the question within any period of time which need now be taken into consideration'. In no way did Kenya differ from Uganda or Tanganyika as far as the principle of trusteeship for the natives was concerned. Yet had the decision gone wholly to the Indians, it would have had incalculable consequences for the future of all races in Kenya, and indeed for the whole idea of a multi-racial Commonwealth.

For the Africans it was a milestone. It assured them of a political future, though one they would have to struggle to achieve. But the European and Indian Associations, with their rival newspaper campaigns, their cables and delegations to London and lobbying of interests outside Kenya, had put ideas into the minds of the Africans which they would soon imitate on their own account.

CHAPTER 8

Kenyatta and the Church

Kenyatta took no part in the upheavals which swept through Kikuyu-land after the war. He was acquiring instead a reputation as a lover of the good life of Nairobi. It brought him into conflict with his mission friends which came to a head in October 1920.

The previous month a significant development had taken place in the organization of the Presbyterian mission. Through a representative sent out from Edinburgh, the Church of Scotland set up local church courts, called Kirk Sessions by the Scots, at Thogoto and Tumutumu. United with the existing Kirk Session of the European congregation of St Andrew's, Nairobi, these now formed a new Presbytery of Kenya. In effect power over the missionary church was transferred from Scotland to the Christians, white and black, of the Presbyterian Church of Kenya. Henceforward, the final say in all matters affecting the 'native church'—that is, Kikuyu Presbyterians—rested with the Kenya Presbytery. This was, of course, still controlled by Europeans who reserved for themselves the right of appeal to the General Assembly of the Church of Scotland. But the move gave a larger role to Africans in the running of their own church. It showed that the lead in the development of local institutions in the colony was still being taken by the missionary church when, in contrast, nothing was being done by the colonial administration to encourage African political growth.

The rules of the new Kirk Sessions were based on lines worked out in 1915, which placed a strong emphasis on the *discipline* which is a feature of Presbyterianism. The missionaries often found that when young men broke away from their tribal surroundings, they embraced the new faith with an extreme zealotry. The Scottish tradition encouraged this tendency, though it could be detected all over Africa. Waves of religious enthusiasm periodically swept over Africans with a fervour which apparently owed little to European missionaries. Such a period began during the war. Arthur described it on his return from furlough in August 1915 as 'A Great Awakening', when he held a conference for all baptized members of the Presbyterian Church from every corner of the Protectorate.[1]

Kenyatta was at this conference and took the opportunity to make his first Communion.[2] It is not known what part he took in its discussions, but the 'Young Kirk' party, as Barlow described them, swept delegates up with their reformist zeal. The native church clamped down on drinking, womanizing, and dances—all features of the old tribal life which the young men denounced as evil. The debate over beer drinking was the hardest fought, the old men especially protesting against interference in their personal liberty in this matter. One senior teacher expressed the feelings of most when reluctantly he accepted the decision. 'He wished it to be known that he would never have done so had they come as commands from the white men of the mission staff!'[3]

Domestic brawls, adultery, loose behaviour, questions of tribal custom, drinking—every aspect of life came up for scrutiny. In a society where there was no distinction between private and public morality, nor between religious and secular life, such an approach was natural and wholesome. It gave the Kikuyu Presbyterians qualities of leadership whose real worth was to be proved time and again in the crises which lay ahead. The Presbyterian system built naturally on Kikuyu custom. Good conduct and the esteem of fellow Christians replaced the stages by which a Kikuyu man graduated to the old tribal courts. The terminology—elders, *kiama*—remained the same as did the respect in which they were held by the body of church members. For the Kikuyu Christians to be suspended from the church was analogous to being deprived of communion with the life force of the tribe. Indeed, it may well be asked how real was the distinction made by the missionaries and their converts between the old and the new spiritual concepts.

The new church courts became watchdogs of this puritanism. Membership rose steadily.

No sooner was it instituted than the Thogoto Kirk Session turned its attention to wayward brothers. On 22 October 1920, the name of Johnstone Kamau appeared on its agenda. The elders had been investigating his conduct. Kenyatta was instructed to present himself. Barlow recorded what took place. Among the elders were Musa Gitau and Samson Njoroge, the two men who had attended his tribal initiation and stood towards him in a special relationship.

The charges were grave. Kenyatta had (a) 'committed sin with the girl (connected with the CMS mission) whom he is buying as wife, as the result of which she is with child', and (b) was 'a habitual drinker of intoxicating liquor'. 'He admitted the truth of both charges'. Kenyatta was thereupon suspended from Holy Communion and other church privileges until he had 'made his repentance evident and made amends for his sin to the satisfaction of the Kirk Session. He was strongly recommended in regard to the first offence not to live with the girl but see that she remains at her own home until he marries her legally.' In the eyes of the church this meant Kenyatta would have to obtain a proper civil marriage before the magistrate according to the Christian Marriage and Divorce Ordinance. A marriage according to Kikuyu custom would not do.

Kenyatta agreed to do this. But giving up drinking was a different matter. He told them 'in a manner inclined to be offensive' that he had no intention of obeying the rule. The meeting broke up.

Overnight Kenyatta had second thoughts. His friends reasoned with him. Perhaps he felt oppressed by unknown spiritual dangers and in need of the support of his church. Next morning he wrote to the church elders apologizing for his rude words and saying he would try to mend his ways. The elders, led by Musa Gitau, commended him to God's help.

Next day was Sunday and the sentence was read out in church. Kenyatta was, in effect, cut off from fellowship and spiritual life. A month later his son was born.

It was part of a dialogue with the Church which lasted all his life.

All Africans are aware that invisible forces are at work in the world. For Christian converts it was the starting point of their acceptance of the missionary gospel which transformed their fear of transgressing these forces into reliance upon God's love for all creation. Kenyatta's compelling desire to control this unseen world was what gave him his sense of destiny. The missionaries demanded a response from the individual and this made each African Christian a rebel against his past. From early childhood Kenyatta was a loner and a rebel against authority. He sought to benefit from the power of God, but cared nothing for the commandments of men.

The sentence went into effect. Eight months later Kenyatta was working on a settler farm in the vicinity. He wrote again to the church elders. It was 'urgent'.

'I am very anxious to have your replies to the following questions, because the Kirk Session said that when I have put my affairs in order, I should let them know; and now my questions are as follows:

1. Let me know if I can be married in church "Privacy" because the rule is that, if one of the partners is baptised and the other has reached the stage of second profession* they may be married in church.
2. Let me know whether my child can be baptised.

Remain in peace

Your servant,

K. N. Johnstone'

It was a stilted, barely literate style. Kenyatta seemed neither to understand, nor to accept, the authority of the church courts.

Behind his request was a pressing matter—'URGENT'. According to Kikuyu custom, occasions when the father of a bride could demand goats from the bridegroom's family never ceased and many men bought their wives by instalments. But when Christians were married in church they paid their bride price once and for all. A Christian girl's father knew that he had to obtain from his in-laws-to-be as many goats as possible before the wedding as no further opportunities would arise. Kenyatta wanted to marry in secret—'Privacy' —so that Grace Wahu's father would not hear about it in time to step up his demands.

His friends would recognize the problem. But the leaders stuck to their ruling. As he had not married the girl before a magistrate, according to their instruction, there could be no question of their union being blessed in a church ceremony or of their child being baptized.

In September Kenyatta was at Thogoto and wrote again. There was no change. A year later, on 8 November 1922, he apparently did go through a civil marriage. The following March, 1923, he wrote a third letter, this time to Dr Arthur.

'Sir,

I wish to remind you about my affair about which I wrote last term [the reference is to the preceding school term] because I have heard that there is to be a baptismal service for infants and I am very anxious to remind you about [the baptism of] my child. I wrote you about it on that occasion but I have not received any reply. Now, therefore, I desire greatly to know whether my child may be baptised

---

* That is, in the catechumen's class. This was the rule according to the Christian Marriage and Divorce Ordinance.

now because I have been kept waiting for a very long time without any information on this subject. Further I want to know about my own case; because here also I have sought information and have been told nothing. At one time, I thought there might be malicious intent in this. But, since nearly three years have passed since the case began and all the requirements [laid upon me] I have fulfilled, and since rancour has possibly no suitable sacrifice [or cure], I want to know whether I have been told that I shall never again be eligible for church membership. I have not left it [the church].

I want a reply to this letter by the bearer.

It is your friend,

K. N. Johnstone'

The church elders asked him to appear before them again, and on 6 July 1923 he did so. They were now 'satisfied that he had married the young woman properly', but told him that he could not be restored to full church membership until he had served the requisite six months' suspension in a true spirit of contrition. Hitherto he had challenged the validity of their judgement; on his now accepting it the suspension would run until December that year.

Kenyatta agreed and made formal confession to three standard questions:

'Before God and before these persons do you truly say that you have committed sin?

Before God and before these persons do you truly say that you are sorry for your sin?

Before God and before these persons do you truly say that you will endeavour to forsake your sin?'

The officiating minister spoke of the Bible's message of forgiveness for sincere penitents and of the redemptive love of Jesus. Kenyatta promised he would drink no more *njohi,* the native beer, and Samson and the elders prayed for him.

Here, at last, was Kenyatta, the swashbuckling figure from the Nairobi photographer's studio, standing before the barefooted church elders accepting 'discipline'. These men were not his enemies, but brothers before God and, in the life of his tribe, spiritual fathers. His destiny was linked with theirs; theirs with his. How much, we may wonder, did they wish to share in the freedom he enjoyed in his social life, and secretly envy the escape he had made from the mission stronghold? And he, how much did he yearn for true communion in his church? How much passion was there locked up in his soul for fellowship in the life-force of his tribe? Did he join with them in a new vision of the future?[4]

There is no hint of any political involvement in Kenyatta's dealings with the Kirk Session. The missions had not escaped the unrest which accompanied Harry Thuku's movement throughout Kikuyuland. Apprentices and boarders came out on 'strike' for a time at Thogoto, while at Tumutumu several church members had to be disciplined. It was the first serious testing of the new church courts.

Kenyatta had, on the contrary, landed one of the plum jobs in Nairobi. At the start of 1922 the Nairobi municipal council took over responsibility for the town's water supply from the railway and the Public Works Department. The council appointed John Cook as water superintendent, and Cook at once recruited Kenyatta to be his stores clerk and meter reader. The 'salary' was 250 shillings a month. It was an unusually high wage for an African to earn at this time, higher even than a European girl would receive as a junior clerk. Cook must have enjoyed considerable confidence in Kenyatta to have offered him the job. By now they knew each other well, and it was the kind of work he had been engaged in, on and off, since leaving Thogoto. Kenyatta took up his duties on 1 April 1922, a fortnight after Thuku's arrest. He was not going to risk anything by getting mixed up in political agitation.

In the material sense the job was the making of Kenyatta. It gave him financial independence. He could build his own home, send his brother to the mission, buy better clothes, invest in a bicycle. Above all it gave him a new self-confidence, a self-confidence reflected in the tone of his letter to Arthur and his readiness to bow his head before the Kirk Session.

He became one of the recognized figures of Nairobi, a hail-fellow-well-met who gladly jumped off his bike to greet old friends—it might be Philp, the doctor from Tumutumu on a rare visit to Nairobi[5], or Charles Stokes, now working at the medical laboratory in Nairobi.

While in the photographer's studio the raffish character in safari outfit gave way to a family man in plus-fours and sun helmet, for all the world one of the tweedy sort at the local golf club. No longer the aspiring man about town, Kenyatta, in his own eyes at least, had arrived.

The work itself was not exacting. At this time the water was paid for not by the quantity used but on a fixed charge by way of rental of meters at 10 shillings a month. Kenyatta's task was to cycle round Nairobi checking the meters, making whatever repairs were necessary, installing new ones and reporting to the accounts clerk. His base was at Kilimani, the Swahili word for 'on the hill', where the stores were located. He lived in one of the huts.

Eighteen months after taking up his appointment, John Cook resigned. He had been fifteen years in Kenya and had seen it grow from a pioneer settlement into a Crown Colony, from a missionary idea into a developing imitation of the Western world. He and his kind largely made it what it was, and their work now was done. He had been a good friend to Kenyatta. But it was not the last they were to see of each other.

The post-war years saw the transformation of Nairobi from a raw frontier township to an object of municipal pride. In 1919 it was properly constituted as a corporation, its boundaries were extended to take in some of the outlying residential areas, and the first housing schemes for Africans were laid out at Kariokor and Pumwani. Building in stone replaced the wood and tin structures of the Protectorate era, the pavements and roads were cleaned up, and taxis allotted regular stands. In December 1924 the Mayor took the Duke and Duchess of York down a special processional route to Government House for which the council voted £400 and the labour of 100 convicts.

The work of the water authorities grew accordingly. While Kenyatta was working for them they were tapping fresh sources from springs in the higher land, preparing reservoirs, laying bigger pipes, installing a new one million gallon tank shipped out from an English foundry. They put a street watering cart into service and faced demands from the New Stanley Hotel for more water or a reduced meter rental. Kenyatta moved into better quarters at Kilimani, specially built for African workers, with their own latrines. The supplies in his stores increased as did requests for new meters. In February 1924 he submitted a claim to the council for a cycle allowance and was granted free repairs.

With his regular income, Kenyatta's life style changed. His friends at Dagoretti put land at his disposal at the junction between the road to the mission and a track which dropped down to the river. It was quite near the administrative sub-office. He built himself a simple mud and wattle hut with a corrugated tin roof for Grace Wahu and the baby, Peter Muigai. The hut had two sections, and one of these he stocked with general provisions for the Dagoretti neighbourhood.

He called it the Kinyata Stores. It acquired a dubious reputation in the eyes of the church elders.

Cycling out from Nairobi at the weekend with his friend Charles Stokes he would stop beneath the trees where the road to Ngong forked and where the Sudanese rested their caravans, there buying from them 'Nubian Gin'—fearsome stuff, said to flare up when a match was put to it. Thus provided, he spent convivial evenings at his new home, while Charles Stokes hurried on to his own wife at Thogoto not wishing to compromise his observance of the missionary ideals of abstinence and chastity. The church elders were disturbed at Kenyatta's way of living and sent two of their number, Samson and Barnabus, to investigate. No doubt it was a cause of the delay in welcoming him back to the church.

But Kenyatta's horizons were wider than those of his Kikuyu neighbours. To his stores came a succession of exotic people from all over the colony, some from the government veterinary farm at nearby Kabete, some from distant Nyeri in the north of Kikuyuland; he had Masai visitors and Swahili from the coast and Nairobi acquaintances of all races and creeds.

In this way and in this obscure corner of the British Empire Kenyatta enjoyed the jazz age of the twenties. He divided his life between his hut beside the water tank on Nairobi hill and his Kinyata Stores which was a home, too, for his younger brother Muigai, now a boarder at the mission. In Nairobi there were cinemas and Italian shows, magicians and football matches, and he walked with a swagger and a dare to knock down anyone who insulted his friend Charles Stokes. He could afford to lend money to European clerks in the offices and offer cigarettes all round. And there were plenty of girls.

At weekends at Dagoretti he and his friends danced versions of the latest European steps to a penny whistle and followed the rage for dressing up in clothes bought in the second-hand shops fast springing up in the bazaar and stocked from Birmingham. Though the cast-off silks of Mayfair hung loosely on the African girls, and the men wilted in starched shirts and ill-assorted tails and trousers, the rickety Kinyata Stores became a palace of fun never before seen in Kikuyuland. Why talk of politics when wine, women and song are available?

CHAPTER 9

Kenyatta Enters Politics

The churches of Weithaga and Kahuhia stand on promontories jutting out into the endless sea of Kikuyu ridges. As far as eye can see are steep valleys covered with huts and densely cultivated with plots of bananas, maize and vegetables. Sounds of goats and sheep and small boys playing carry far across the ridges. In the north rises the jagged mass of Mount Kenya; in the west, the long range of the Aberdares. Countless streams flow down from these heights through the Kikuyu valleys to form the Tana River which then arches north and east before draining south into the Indian Ocean at Witu. Its flood waters are heavy with top soil from the red earth of Kikuyuland so that it seems as though the land is bleeding into the sea.

Traditionally this Murang'a district of Kikuyuland was the original entry point of the tribe into the forests and it still claims to be its spiritual heart. It was here that the adventurer John Boyes set up his base in the village of a powerful chief, Karuri, before Francis Hall had built his fort nearby and put a stop to his activities. When the railway arrived at Nairobi and Meinertzhagen was shooting his way towards Nyeri in the north, Karuri invited the newly arrived Anglican missionaries to come to his area. The mission stations of Weithaga and Kahuhia, dating from 1904 and 1906, resulted.[1]

Around Weithaga and Kahuhia lived the most clannish people in the whole world: a man would not tell you which ridge he came from for fear you lived on the next one and were an enemy. Something of that clannishness had been broken by the war, particularly among the Mission Volunteers. But the spirit of comradeship instilled in the Carrier Corps was short-lived; reunions of old porters died out; ancient suspicions returned.

The missionaries lived closer to the Africans than other Europeans, and it was only human for them to condemn everything to do with Nairobi as corrupting. Handley Hooper, who took over at Kahuhia on his father's retirement in 1916, forbade his natives to wear boots

on the grounds that they were alien influence—even though boots
gave protection against jiggers, and became essential when macadam-
ized roads heated up under the equatorial sun and burnt the skin off
a man's foot. The missionaries fought to preserve the integrity of
tribal ways and shunned all political activity. They cherished, rather,
a nostalgia for a rural Arcadia, the Lost Garden of Eden.

'To us it is strange that our Lord was born in a humble shed with
animals standing around: here in Africa it seems the natural, the
proper way to be born which everyone will understand. These might
be His own fields and valleys, and the winding paths of Galilee where
Jesus walked . . .'[2]

But it was the missionaries who saw more clearly than anyone else
the effect on African village life of the settler system, and the abuses
which administrative policies led to in the hands of government-
appointed chiefs and headmen. It was they who first protested over
Northey's encouragement of compulsory labour, knowing that girls
would be forced out to work on roads or other government projects
and be housed at night in the quarters of tribal policemen. The
missionaries saw young government officers who took too keen an
interest in native welfare shifted into career backwaters or else
seduced by Nairobi society. They looked askance at the loose ways
of Northey's set at Government House, and were shocked when the
Duke and Duchess of York, on their honeymoon in East Africa, confined themselves to settler hospitality and made no effort to meet
the thousands of villagers who had waited days to greet them. In
Uganda the bishop had to speak sharply to them of their imperial
duties. Reluctantly the missionaries were drawn into the political
arena themselves.

In the west of Kenya, which then fell within the Anglican diocese
of Uganda, the strongly independent Archdeacon Owen guided the
people of the Nyanza province, mostly Luo and Luhya tribesmen,
into an organization known as the Kavirondo Taxpayers Welfare
Association. They had shown a similar restlessness to the Kikuyu
during Thuku's brief career, but under Owen's tactful hand now
turned themselves into a model institution of self-help. Owen effectively defused any radical political energies which existed in the
second most numerous agricultural tribe in Kenya.

But the missionaries did not always fully understand the impact of their teaching on the African, or appreciate the way Africans saw their own situation literally in terms of the tribes of the Old Testament. Throughout the campaign in German East Africa the African Christians kept up their morale by reminding themselves of Israel in the wilderness; and they preached sermon after sermon in their native churches on these ancient themes.

Typical of this generation was Gideon at Kahuhia. A devout Christian and church elder, he was always suggesting ways of improving his village and of helping his neighbours. Every day he set aside a portion of food for sale in the market, the proceeds of which he gave to his church—'God's portion', he called it. But all the time, a seed of hatred against the Europeans was swelling in his heart, watered, it may have been, by the failure of the government to reward the porters of the Carrier Corps in the same way as they did white soldiers. Gideon formed a cell of similar minded Christians and they prayed together for a Moses to lead them out of bondage. For a time they saw Harry Thuku as their saviour.

'Christians all over Africa . . . we ask you to pray for Harry Thuku our leader and his associates . . . They have been chosen for us now and not in the past, because it is now that we are feeling the slavery which we did not have before the coming of the Europeans to East Africa. Remember too that the Lord God was able to rescue the children of Israel from slavery under Pharaoh.'[3]

Gideon and his small group used to meet secretly in the banana fields or one of the round huts of Kahuhia, often at night. Handley Hooper was aware that something was going on and warned them against secrecy. With Owen's success in mind he promised to assist them in presenting legitimate aspirations to government. He advised against continuing with the name of East African Association because of its Indian connotations. Better something specifically tribal.

Mindful of the existence of the Kikuyu Association of southern Kiambu the Fort Hall members required little originality to decide to call their group the 'Central Kikuyu Association', or Kikuyu Central Association, as it shortly became (KCA for convenience). Possibly they intended it from the start to rival the other, but it was also an indication of the extreme regionalism of Kikuyuland. They belonged to the central district of the tribe, and they also believed they

were the true guardians of tribal orthodoxy. They needed someone
who could properly articulate their feelings. Such a man was James
Beauttah.[4]

James Beauttah was born at the time of full-scale penetration by
the IBEA Company into the Kikuyu highlands. Shortly after, his
mother was killed by a punitive expedition, perhaps one of Hall's or
Meinertzhagen's. As a small boy he was badly treated by an older
brother and ran away to the government compound at Fort Hall
where he worked for a Zanzibari rifleman for one rupee a month.
He then made his way to Nairobi and was taken on as a pantry boy
in one of the first ramshackle hotels. But one day he tripped, smashed
all the china, was thrashed, and ran away again. An officer on the
railway took him in to look after his own small son and asked him to
accompany him to England. At Mombasa Beauttah took fright at his
first sight of the ocean; he remembered a Kikuyu legend about a sea
monster who devoured men, and refused to board ship. Eventually
he came into the hands of missionaries at the coast. His future was
made.

Beauttah's career illustrates the importance of the missionary role
in the development of Africa. At that time missions in Uganda and
at the coast produced most of the African clerks in government service throughout the two protectorates. In 1910 he went to the Post
Office training school at Rabai, the old CMS station of Krapf and
Rebmann; a few years later he married a Christian girl in Mombasa
despite strong opposition from his own people; and after the war
he took charge of the telegraphy school at the CMS headquarters at
Maseno.

Beauttah worked at various times in Uganda, in western Kenya,
at Mombasa, at Kikuyu post office close to Thogoto, in Nairobi itself,
and among the up-country settlers at Eldoret, where he heard over
the telegraph wires of Thuku's arrest. He read American Negro
literature and had European lawyers as his friends. Still in spiritual
communion with his tribe, he yet had a wider vision of the future
than any shared by his contemporaries. It was James Beauttah, more
than any other man, who gave the fledgling politicians of Kahuhia
intellectual leadership, drew them out of their rural confines, and
introduced them to other young men in Nairobi.

Beauttah knew Kenyatta as all 'detribalized' Africans met sooner
or later in Nairobi. But Fort Hall Kikuyu were suspicious of Kiambu
men, particularly those of the Presbyterian mission. In 1924 they ran
into each other at Nairobi railway station. Beauttah was going to a

meeting in Pumwani, then commonly described as a 'tea-party', at which he hoped to bring together the Christian and Moslem Kikuyu. Kenyatta agreed to go along with him, as he had many non-Christian friends.

The meeting led to nothing positive. The Fort Hall members kept to themselves, and Kenyatta was enjoying too good a life to do more than take an amiable interest.

1924 was the year when the first of a long line of Parliamentary commissions descended on East Africa as the consciences of members in London, roused by the extravagant words of men like Delamere and Grogan, wrestled with the problem of how to reconcile the imperial mission with local settler politics. Both the Kavirondo Taxpayers Welfare Association and the Kikuyu Association presented memoranda to the commission, which was led by W. Ormsby-Gore, Under-Secretary at the Colonial Office at the time of the Devonshire white paper. The appearance of this commission stimulated the Fort Hall group into drawing up their own memorandum and may also have decided them to turn themselves into a formal association. Joseph Kangethe was chosen secretary—some said because of his imposing physique. He had risen to be a sergeant in the machine-gun corps during the war and wore his campaign medals with pride. Hooper took a sympathetic interest in their development and gave Beauttah the use of his mission typewriter to produce his memorandum.

In 1925 the government introduced what were called Local Native Councils, LNC for short, throughout the colony, a devolution of Northey's policy for tribal reserves. Membership was open in part to election and in part to the existing system of government-appointed chiefs and headmen. The District Commissioner was ex-officio chairman.[5] They had authority to make recommendations covering a wide range of local matters, and to raise and disburse local revenue. Delamere supported their formation because he argued they implied recognition of separate development for the races; Arthur, too, welcomed them as a safety valve for the feelings that had spilled over into Thuku's movement. At the same time, as prosperity picked up after the slump of 1921–2, greater attention was given to the economic growth of the reserves.

Among the most committee-minded of Africans, the Kikuyu now possessed three formal outlets through which they could openly express themselves. First, they had their traditional grades of eldership —the old *kiama* of the tribe which the administration had come to recognize as a legitimate and valuable institution; second, their native church courts; and third, these new government-sponsored local councils. It was not surprising that these years also saw a sudden crop of associations, secret societies, break-away groups, and a general spirit of restlessness throughout the reserve. Nor was it surprising that considerable confusion should have existed in the minds of most Africans over the purposes of these various bodies. LNC members had to take an oath of loyalty to the Crown.[6] It is said that Kangethe and others were so impressed by the ceremonial of the Fort Hall LNC that they decided to introduce a simple oath into their own organization: 'While a Bible was held up in the left hand, a handful of earth was pressed to the navel, and the member swore to serve his people faithfully and to look after their money should he be entrusted with it.'[7]

The introduction of Local Native Councils stimulated political activity. They were intended to be the means whereby different generations could reconcile their feelings about matters directly affecting tribal development. The idea of an association like the KCA quickly spread throughout Kikuyuland, not as a formal organization so much as a means of expressing opposition to whatever happened to be the local colonial establishment. Kangethe and another KCA man were among the first elected to the Fort Hall LNC. In 1927 old Kinyanjui was beaten to the Kiambu LNC by a member of the Thogoto church.

Equally, as politics entered the ridges some men naturally turned to the administration for help, just as individual chiefs had enlisted the aid of the white man when he first appeared at the forest's edge in their own local power struggles, as Waiyaki had done with Lugard, and Chief Karuri with John Boyes. The government had to support their native officials and they naturally attributed any opposition to 'disaffected Indians' and rootless young men from Nairobi. The chiefs and headmen were also quick to complain of 'agitators' as they had done with Harry Thuku. A senior European officer and an 'elderly headman of many years service' saw eye to eye over 'the young man with a smattering of literacy'. To both government servants he was 'a budding politician of the kind that does nothing but heckle without offering any useful suggestions'. Though the village headman put it in more vivid language: ' "S" is the louse in the blanket. He has been making us itch ever since we started today. I don't know what he wants, nor does he.'

James Beauttah's name never appeared on the documents which marked the emergence of the KCA from its underground cell at Kahuhia into open political activity. But several of Harry Thuku's old associates, like Abdulla Tairara joined it. These Nairobi men still drew on Indian assistance.[8] It was a time of growing unrest in India and opponents of the Raj sought allies wherever they could. By now the Bolsheviks had won out in Russia and were promoting anti-imperialist feelings. Beauttah had contacts among disaffected Europeans, and especially among Irishmen whose own 'troubles' were increased, rather than diminished, by the treaty of 1922 which brought to an end British rule in Dublin, England's oldest colony. Beauttah knew a certain Captain Macdermot who made his living as a journalist and court reporter.[9] The Africans called him *kiri nditi*, 'he who does not care', the 'daredevil', and were enraptured by his stories of the Sinn Fein and IRA. Men like Macdermot gladly thumbed through law archives in Nairobi on behalf of the Africans to check government statements over land and other matters.

In 1925 or early 1926 Beauttah was moved from Nairobi to Uganda. But he kept in touch with the Kahuhia group and also with Kenyatta. In Beauttah's absence the KCA members also approached Kenyatta themselves to assist them in translating and drafting letters. They paid for his services in kind, mostly by providing him, through Goan contacts, with beer and spirits, which he was unable to purchase himself.[10]

But it was not a serious involvement, little more than framing a vaguely abusive letter to the Scottish mission over school fees (not, apparently an Association matter at all), and drafting a series of letters to the authorities asking if the KCA might present a casket as a gift to the Governor. There was as yet no role for an association since most of the points raised by the Kikuyu farmers in the reserve could best be dealt with by District Officers working through Local Native Councils, as the government pointed out. Such were two meetings held in July and August 1927, with KCA representatives present, to discuss topics of exclusively local concern: to do with salt licks, supplies of red earth for painting faces, clay for pot making, and seed plots. Kenyatta was not present.

Even then a wide difference existed between the sophistication of Beauttah's approach and the village politics of the reserves, and there is no indication that Kenyatta shared in the abusive tone of the letter to the mission or even took the matter of the casket seriously. One imagines him, rather, cycling home to Dagoretti well supplied for the weekend and singing the jingle of the Nairobi rickshaw boys, his attitude like theirs that of the undoctrinaire and 'bolshy' taxi-driver class the world over:

'Great and wise and wonderful is the European
He came into our land with his wisdom and his might.
He made wars to cease
He causes our fields to bring forth plenty
And our flocks to increase.
He gives us great riches, and then—
He takes them all away again in taxes.
Great and wise and wonderful is the European.'[11]

The settlers were by no means subdued by the Devonshire white paper. They interpreted it as vindicating their own 'paramountcy' over the Indians. Grogan and Delamere dominated the social scene. Northey's period in Nairobi had seen a decline in moral standards among Europeans, probably no worse than elsewhere in the 'jazz age', but which gave Kenya a reputation for vulgarity and racial arrogance.[12] The settlers' world of polo and champagne, of an aristocratic game preserve and 'I know the nigger better than any damned official in Whitehall', made a mockery of the old civilizing mission. With the arrival of Sir Edward Grigg as Governor in 1925 events took a turn for the worse.

Grigg was a one-time journalist turned liberal politician who owed his appointment to Leo Amery, Colonial Secretary in Baldwin's second Conservative cabinet in which Winston Churchill was Chancellor of the Exchequer. These were the years of the 'pugnacious Imperialists',[13] ushered in by the 1924 Empire Exhibition at Wembley. Grigg professed to be a follower of Smuts and Rhodes in pursuing the ideal of 'equal rights for all civilized men', and like them he saw white settlement as providing the backbone for Britain's civilizing mission.

Grigg was a snob. Before taking up his appointment he had begged permission from the King, whose equerry he had once been, to wear his army uniform, despite Colonial Office regulations to the contrary. He believed in the integrity of the old school tie and was captivated by the upper-class posturing of the settlers. He quickly fell under the influence of Delamere and his cousin, Lord Francis Scott, a fellow Etonian made somewhat peppery by the loss of a leg during the war. Grigg made government by consent his rule—the consent of the settlers.

Riding before breakfast, tennis and golf after tea, and a siesta, of course, in the middle of the day—life for a governor of Kenya was not arduous. There might, perhaps, be time for a few visitors in the

course of the morning and days set aside for the occasional *barazas*
with natives whom Grigg judged, he confessed, more by the looks
on their faces than by their words. It was not surprising that he fell
in with settler pressure for a majority of unofficials in the Legislative
Council thereby lending support to their dream of self-government.
He quoted with approval the aphorism: "Better Nero on the spot
than a committee of archangels in Whitehall.'[14]

Amery confided in Grigg his plan for a federation of Britain's three
East African territories: Uganda, Kenya and Tanganyika. Grigg
hoped to be their first Governor-General and he set about the building of two new and spacious residences at Nairobi and Mombasa in
anticipation of an increased style of entertaining. With federation in
mind he organized regular conferences of governors where matters
of common interest could be discussed (a course of action which
Delamere also adopted in relation to the white settlers of East and
Central Africa). In July 1927 Amery published his ideas in a white
paper and announced the setting up of the Hilton Young Commission to consider federation, or 'closer union' as it was called.

The racial bias of Grigg's administration brought renewed Indian
protests. Federation was at once suspect. Always a hotbed of rumour,
Nairobi found its political temperature rising again. The Africans
felt it too. They saw in the new commission a further opportunity
to present their case direct to London, a game they had watched both
Indians and settlers playing in the past. Sometime towards the end
of 1927 the KCA group wrote to Beauttah in Uganda asking him to
go as their representative to London. Beauttah considered his responsibilities towards his family too great and replied suggesting the
names of several men, of whom Kenyatta was one, who could do the
job just as well. But Kenyatta was his first recommendation because
of his better English.

Kangethe approached Kenyatta. He took his time to consider his
position. Grace Wahu was expecting a second child. He was paying
for his brother Muigai at the Alliance High School and his small son
at the central school at Thogoto. He had a good wage from his job.
To join the KCA as a full-time official meant leaving government
service with little prospect of returning to it. There were, by now,
a growing number of Africans waiting for such jobs, and many of
them had better educational qualifications than Kenyatta.

We can only speculate over what finally decided him to accept.
European detractors later said it was because he was sacked by the
town council.[15] It is more likely that he demanded and obtained high

terms from the Association—at least an equivalent salary and an assurance that his 'expenses' would be generous. One of the objections to Thuku's Association was the way it extracted contributions from villagers which, so the authorities said, went into the pockets of the organizers. Frequent collections of a shilling a head were made on Thuku's behalf when he was in exile, not a cent of which did he receive. Some estimates put the expense allowance of KCA officials as high as £1 a day when away from home.[16]

Kenyatta probably also insisted on being provided with a motor-cycle to enable him to get around Kikuyuland properly. It was how he was remembered by the boys of Dagoretti: a young man, tidily dressed, whose 'piki-piki' bike could be heard a long way off chugging up the hill. They would run out of their huts to greet him and he would stop to chat with their fathers and listen to all that they had been taught in school that day. He gave rides to some of them on the back of his bike. His prestige rose accordingly.

Another factor was the growth of the KCA itself. In 1927 members established an office in Nairobi.[17] They were aiming at something wider than the local councils and bidding for the support of the whole tribe, though there were no political institutions through which the tribe as a unit could express itself. By 1928 the DC of Fort Hall could write: 'It can no longer be said that the KCA is unrepresentative of the Kikuyu people. It includes in its ranks a vast proportion of the more enlightened and progressive youth, and wields an increasing influence on the counsel of the elders.' Kenyatta was stepping into an organization which now stood for something in Kikuyuland. Its increased size was no doubt also reflected in an increased inflow of contributions.

Kenyatta's name was publicly linked with the political movement for the first time at the beginning of 1928. On 14 February he accompanied a KCA party to Government House, Nairobi, to give oral evidence to the Hilton Young Commission, more, it seems, as an interpreter than in an executive capacity. Perhaps he had not finally made up his mind, or else the KCA had not agreed on terms. The KCA delegates made no impression on the commissioners who were pessimistic about the prospects of native representation:

'The present backwardness of the tribes in Kenya makes it easy to think of them as politically negligible. But it is contrary to all experience and reason to suppose that the native peoples will always be satisfied to remain unrepresented in the government of the country . . . It must obviously be a very long time before suitable individuals can be found among the natives themselves. Not only are natives of sufficient education lacking but it would be impossible to find any single man who could represent, or command the confidence of, more than a section of the people.'[18]

Kenyatta's future career was to be the answer to this challenge. However imperfect a tool, the KCA was the only one at hand.

A month later Kenyatta attended a meeting at Kahuhia, at which the Provincial Commissioner and several local chiefs were also present, held to reassure the government officials of the good faith and sound intentions of the KCA. Kenyatta said the KCA was anxious to do things the proper way and would gladly correct any mistakes it might be making. In reply the PC stressed that the Association could not claim to speak for the whole tribe, but, he concluded, 'I wish to express again my pleasure at meeting you and my hopes that the progress and good understanding now in evidence will continue.'[19]

A cordial encounter: nothing radical suggested, no 'bolshy' speeches. Unlike Thuku the new leaders generated little charisma with the tribesmen. Beneath his dirty sun hat and baggy plus-fours Kenyatta struck Europeans as nothing more than an agreeable if somewhat seedy 'Europeanized' native. An increasing number of his kind were to be seen in Nairobi and the smaller townships. To his fellow Africans Kenyatta was a sophisticated man-about-town about whose political earnestness they had certain reservations. They called him John, or Johnstoni, giving an inflexion to the second syllable. But he was also using the name Kenyatta more frequently. It sounded more authentically African.

In May 1928 a Kikuyu vernacular periodical called *Muigwithania* appeared. The KCA slogan 'Pray and Work' was displayed on its title page and the editor's name was given as Johnstone Kenyatta, Secretary of the KCA, the first time it appeared in this form. It was a flimsy, but careful production typical of many similar Indian publications of the same date. A monthly collection of news, articles and homilies in the allusive Kikuyu style made up its contents.[20]

In the summer of 1928 the subject of Kikuyu land rights came to a head. Grigg proposed setting up Land Boards to hold all land in the native reserves in trust for each tribe. The Boards would regulate land exchanges, supervise improvements and generally demarcate the areas within which the tribe might exercise authority over its own land in its own way. The Hilton Young Commission threatened to pre-empt the subject. Questions about native land rights had become frequent in Parliament from the Labour Opposition.

Grigg was anxious to push his legislation through without waiting for the report of the commission for fear of further delays. But the missionaries were again active and on 18 June Amery was forced to suspend the proposed Bill. That very day a select committee of Kenya's Legislative Council heard evidence on the subject from native witnesses, among whom both the Kikuyu Association and the KCA were represented, the former by Koinange and his colleagues from Kiambu, the latter by Kangethe with Kenyatta in attendance. On this, the most emotive subject of all, both Kikuyu groups were in agreement.

Barlow acted as interpreter for Koinange: 'The burden of their complaint was that no recognition is given in the Bill to what is known as Githaka rights.' These were the rights of trusteeship for family estates devolving upon each family head, the nearest the Kikuyu came to individual ownership of land. Witnesses 'could not help feeling anxious as to Government's "bona fides" ' and 'expressed their dissatisfaction at the inclusion of their lands in a definition of Crown Land'.

The following day, 19 June, Kangethe and 'Johnstone Kinyatta' appeared with their interpreter, a Colonel Watkins: 'They had devoted a great deal of time and attention to the Bill but admitted that they had not been able to understand the whole of it.'

Kenyatta and Kangethe raised a number of points concerning native representation on the Board, but their main argument was the same as Koinange's: the Bill

'did not deal with what they had demanded for years—the natives' rights to their own land. They had no wish to dissociate themselves from government, but they did want their rights to be defined by some form of document. They wanted their land to be managed according to their own traditional customs . . . Now they had no security. They wanted Title Deeds now, simply because no individual appeared to have any legal rights to their own land.'

Such was the simple statement, couched in moderate language, of what was the basic and universal feeling of all sections of the Kikuyu tribe. But Grigg was wholly unsympathetic. He was piqued at the disruption of his plans. In reporting to the Colonial Office he complained that the natives 'practically refused to give any information' to the government research officer, which would have surprised no one with experience of the Kikuyu's unwillingness to answer questions *on any subject,* least of all about land. He went on to say:

'I am informed by the Chief Native Commissioner that it was manifest that the two natives who appeared as representatives of the Kikuyu Central Association were incapable of understanding the provisions of the Bill or appreciating its application to any tribe or body of natives other than their own particular section of the Kikuyu. Their attitude appeared to him to be more unintelligent opposition to any arrangement which does not provide for their own unfettered personal control.'[21]

Such views by the Governor of Kenya show how out of touch Grigg was. He and his officials in Nairobi were not prepared to think of the natives as individuals with individual rights and individual contributions to make. Few men at this time bothered to learn the vernacular languages, apart from the missionaries.[22] Grigg's opinion was hardly borne out by his officers in the reserves. But Grigg was not going to allow native opinion to sway him.

Kenyatta had to step cautiously through the minefields of colonial politics. A false move and he knew he would be whisked off into exile like Harry Thuku—and Thuku had still not been released.

Accordingly his contributions to *Muigwithania* were over-correct: he supported the churches, district commissioners and chiefs; he urged on his fellow Africans the importance of agricultural and educational self-advancement; and he praised the role of the British Empire: 'The first thing [about the British Empire] is that all people are governed justly, big or small—equally. The second thing is that nobody is regarded as a slave, everyone is free to do what he or she likes without being hindered.'[23]

Muigwithania means literally 'he who causes the whole group to understand each other'. It might be translated as 'The Reconciler' or 'The Unifier', and its main purpose was to draw the whole Kikuyu people together into a renewal of their tribal consciousness.

In September it featured an article on the word 'association' in which for the first time was used the phrase *kikuyu karing'a*. This meant 'real Kikuyu' or 'pure Kikuyu' and the idea was that all who were true Kikuyu belonged together. It also implied a revival of old Kikuyu customs. Both its progressive articles and its more allusive pieces were an attempt by *Muigwithania* to unite the tribe. A major purpose, of course, was also to raise funds to pay for Kenyatta's passage to England. For this reason, if for none other, he was anxious not to put a foot wrong.

There is no indication of who were the guiding spirits behind the paper. It is unlikely that Kenyatta himself took much hand in it. He had no writing experience and lacked the educational background. His role as editor was probably to advise on suitable material and to translate into Kikuyu articles written by Beauttah's contacts. The Association also wanted to promote its front man; the editor of a vernacular periodical had an added claim to speak for the tribe as a whole.

Grigg was not impressed. He complained of 'baneful influences', by which he meant Indians, and religious hysteria. For *Muigwithania* was being printed on Indian presses and one issue included an extract from the *Book of Lamentations:* 'O God, look and see the insults with which we are insulted. See how our inheritance is given to strangers and our houses made to belong to other tribes [or races] . . .'

Of its editor Grigg said no more than he 'is a Kikuyu native who is Secretary of the Association'. He asked London if he could suppress the paper.[24]

Kenyatta took no risks. He travelled about Kikuyuland on his motorbike, an object of wonder in the remoter areas, and to neighbouring tribes like the Meru and Embu living on the north-east and south-east slopes of Mount Kenya. He set up branches of the KCA and as secretary of the Association he wrote to the Governor pleading for the release of Harry Thuku. He took care to give no offence, but begged 'to remain, Your Excellency, Your Obedient Servant, Johnstone Kinyatta'. The police had nothing on him. But Grigg was not interested, he had a visit from the Prince of Wales to attend to.[25]

Kenyatta was bent on getting to England. In December the KCA decided they had collected sufficient funds and that the time was ripe. At a gathering in Pumwani Kenyatta took a Bible in his hands, with some earth, and swore before them all that he would not betray them, and would return to serve them further. They swore before him to look after his wife and family.

This had received an addition when, on 16 February 1928, two days after his appearance before the Hilton Young Commission, Grace gave birth to their second child, a girl. Kenyatta gave her his mother's name, Wambui. She was later baptized Margaret. Shortly after her delivery Grace was in the native hospital at Pumwani while

Kenyatta was absorbed in political matters in Fort Hall. He sent her two bunches of bananas with his love and greetings from colleagues.

The baby girl scarcely knew her father as a child. But she was to become his closest confidante and the child who seemed most to resemble him. Grace, too, saw little of him. For most of the time he stayed with his associates while she remained at Dagoretti. But, for a short while at least, she was evidently well provided for as KCA support was available and they could afford a servant.

Kenyatta was an affectionate father, but, unlike Beauttah, he was willing to sacrifice family life to his new calling. On Grace fell the responsibility of bringing up their son, Peter Muigai, and providing a home at the Kinyata Stores for Kenyatta's half-brother James Muigai. Using the name James Johnstone he was the first boy to register at the Alliance High School when it was opened on 1 March 1926. Kenyatta paid for his fees, then a nominal 42 shillings a year. James completed only two years at the Alliance High School out of a possible three, but his teachers gave him a good report as a footballer and as a potential teacher himself. He left on 27 January 1928, to join the police.[26] Kenyatta was thus freed from that responsibility, and instead James was now able to contribute to Grace's upkeep himself. In the years ahead he was to become her main support.

In the new year, 1929, the KCA put in its request to the colonial administration to send its secretary to London. Grigg was on his way there too to try to rescue something of Closer Union. On 18 January Nairobi sent a telegram to the Colonial Office about the KCA move. It stuck to Grigg's line about the Association being unrepresentative:

'This Association is an unofficial body claiming to represent the views of the Kikuyu tribes [sic]. This Government does not recognise this claim. There are other and rival Associations for instance the Kikuyu Association, Kavirondo Taxpayers Welfare Association, Arab and African Association and the Native Catholic Union.'

With Canon Leakey of the CMS, Kabete, Grace's old teacher, the administration had tried to dissuade Kenyatta, but the Association was insistent: "and had stated that it will bear all the expenses and that certain West Africans have promised entertainment in England.' Kenyatta, or one of his Nairobi contacts, had evidently been in touch with other negro organizations.

On 4 February the authorities in Nairobi saw Kenyatta and warned him his trip was a waste of time and money. They could not refuse him permission to leave Kenya, but they followed up this meeting with a letter, dated 6 February and addressed to the President of the KCA, which put the official position on the record:

'I am now directed to inform you that in view of the facts that
(a) the views of your President and Secretary as given before the Select Committee of the Legislative Council are before the Secretary of State and
(b) your Association is an unofficial body which cannot be regarded as representative of the whole Kikuyu tribe, the Secetary of State will be unable to grant an interview to Mr. Johnstone Kenyatta should your Association decide to send him to England.'[27]

But Kenyatta's mind was made up. He had already booked his passage on the *Bernadino de St Pierre,* a French liner of the Messageries Maritimes line, due to sail from Mombasa on 17 February. Some months later, while waiting in London for an appointment to see the Colonial Secretary, he claimed that if his Association had known that an interview would not be granted it would never have incurred the expense of sending him to England. But in its paper work, at least, the colonial system was thorough and the correspondence was on the Colonial Office file to refute him.

Mombasa's Fort Jesus was built by the Portuguese in the sixteenth century and loomed over the old harbour. During the years of the Zanzibar Sultanates it had been one of the principal slave markets on the East African coast. Sir Lloyd Mathews, the Wazir of the Sultan, had announced the establishment of the British Protectorate on 1 July 1895 within its walls, now softened to a delicate pastel colour. Since then the main commercial port had moved to Kilindini, on the southern side of Mombasa Island, where Grogan turned in an enormous profit on his original speculation. In August 1926 a new harbour was opened which was now the embarkation point for ocean-going liners. Here, as planned, Kenyatta boarded the *Bernadino de St Pierre* on 17 February 1929.

It was a daunting step for the solitary Kikuyu representative to be taking, a forlorn and wasteful mission in the eyes of the white men, but what a leap forward in the long pilgrimage of the tribe! The *Bernadino de St Pierre* drew away from the quayside, passing Grigg's new Government House, the squat fortress of the Portuguese and, in the distance across the strait, the cross above the graves of Mrs Krapf and her baby, the first missionary sacrifice in East Africa.[28] The shore receded into a line of palm trees and golden sand behind the coral reefs where Africa fell away into the Indian Ocean.

No doubt Kenyatta stood on deck and watched the coast drop beneath the horizon. A fellow passenger was Isher Dass, a young Indian who had only recently arrived in Kenya and was already prominent in Nairobi politics. It can scarcely have been coincidence that they were travelling together. Different races, different cultures, in an uneasy alliance against the British Empire.

What did Kenyatta really hope to achieve? To see the world? To escape from the dead-end of Nairobi? To find a wider political role? Perhaps these were among his thoughts; there would be plenty of time on the voyage to discuss ideas with Isher Dass.

But there was something else. When the KCA first approached him about this trip he had talked it over with Charles Stokes, his half-caste friend whom Mrs Watson had taken to Dundee as a boy. It was one of the few occasions they discussed politics together. Stokes's advice was: if you get to England, get yourself into an institution of some kind for further education. 'Oh yes, I know that,' replied Kenyatta. Before him still was the lure of the white man's magic, the touchstone of knowledge and of all that his race had missed through their centuries of isolation from the rest of the world.

Fluttering on the stern of the *Bernadino de St Pierre* the ship's flag beckoned him forward as, more than twenty years before, the small piece of paper jammed in a forked stick had done in his grandfather's village. He was on the same pilgrimage, and now he carried in his own person the destiny of his people. Confident of that inner power, he set his face towards Europe and the heart of the British Empire.

Part II

CHAPTER 10

London 1929–30

Nothing that an African might see in the silent movie houses of Nairobi or the pages of English magazines could have prepared Kenyatta for the reality of Europe's largest city. London's population itself far exceeded that of the whole of Kenya colony.

Kenyatta arrived in the capital of the British Empire on 8 March 1929, to find there was a mild heat-wave. He had in his pocket the name of the West African organization which had promised the KCA to provide hospitality, and it was to their address in west London that he made his way as soon as he arrived. Their leader was a Nigerian called Ladipo Solanke, then living at 57 Castletown Road, W14. It was a street of tall terraced houses between Baron's Court and Hammersmith.

Ladipo Solanke was a Yoruba law student who came to London soon after the war, one of an increasing number of West Africans seeking higher qualifications in England. He was the founder of the West African Students' Union. He qualified as a barrister in 1926 and the following year published his first literary work, the first of its kind to appear from British colonial Africa in the century. In 1929, when Kenyatta met him, he was about to embark on extensive tours of West Africa to raise funds for, and spread interest in, the organization he had founded. Through the WASU Solanke set out to encourage his fellow Africans to rediscover their history and take pride in their traditional institutions. Solanke had no truck with the colonialist's view that Africans were incapable of running their own affairs but he looked ultimately to the 'joy of independence even in poor surroundings'. His was the first clear expression of African Nationalism: 'West African honour, respect and glory must be pressed and pushed forward and until it has reached its goal it may not stop. Progress! I repeat, Progress!! West Africa, onward to the goal!!!'

For someone coming straight from the settler-dominated territories of East and Central Africa, such views were revelational. Only white men talked about self-government there; it was not a KCA objective.

In Kenya a few of Kenyatta's fellow tribesmen had risen, like James Beauttah, to be junior civil servants or teachers, but none could look for careers beyond this level. For the first time Kenyatta met Africans of higher intellectual attainments than could be dreamed of in his own part of the continent. Among these barristers and writers from Nigeria and the Gold Coast he was at a disadvantage. They had no common experience except their black skins and no common language except English which he spoke slowly, whereas they had picked up the latest idiom of debate.

How was Kenyatta to challenge those grey, unsmiling façades of Whitehall? Africans on official delegations were closely chaperoned by Colonial Office guides who feared they would otherwise get lost or run over in the unaccustomed street traffic—or just, perhaps, spirited away. Before leaving Nairobi Kenyatta was warned of these dangers by missionaries to scare him off coming. The West Africans barely took him seriously, and charged him 'fairly highly' for his board and lodging.[1] To add its cheerlessness the weather turned cold and damp. But Kenyatta had the money raised by the KCA and ample self-confidence in his destiny. He was ready to embark upon a new phase of his life. First he wrote to Grace.

'To my wife, G. W. Johnstone, Kikuyu

Many greetings, and after my greetings I want to tell you that I have arrived in England in the peace of God. Here all is well, except the cold which is very great, for here the sun is not often seen, but there is frequently a heavy mist (or fog), but this season is nearly over for the time has come for warmer weather.

Please let me know what clothes you'd like me to buy for you, but especially I want you to take Peter's measurements and send them to me, so that I can have them made up here—for here clothes are not very expensive.

I want to hear all the news from home, and if anything has gone wrong since I left. Here all goes well with me, though I'm very busy on work for our country. Please don't be sorry for me, for God has helped me much, in all things . . .

                    Peace be with you always,

                            Your husband who loves you much.'

For practical assistance Kenyatta turned to another name on his list: W. McGregor Ross.

Ross had been Kenya's Director of Public Works from 1905 to

1923. He came to Kenya in 1900, and lived through Nairobi's transformation from a pioneering railway township to a colonial capital. He left a permanent mark on the city in the wide avenue which he laid out from Government Road to the Hill. Called first simply 5th Avenue it was subsequently named Delamere Avenue and then Kenyatta Avenue, a sequence which would have appealed to Ross himself.

In 1916 Ross's experience earned him a place on the Governor's Council where his was often the only official voice raised against measures like the *kipande,* the proposed devaluation of the currency, wage cuts and the segregation of Indians in Nairobi. He retired to England in 1923 and wrote a penetrating account of the history of white settlement entitled *Kenya From Within* which Allen & Unwin published in 1927.

With Norman Leys, Ross formed the nucleus of a growing body of influential opinion in the British Labour Party. They were tireless speakers, indefatigable letter-writers and members of countless committees. Both their names were known to the leaders of the KCA in Nairobi.

Kenyatta lost no time in contacting Ross and on 21 March they met at London's Royal Empire Society.[2] Ross was a political animal whose natural habitat was the correspondence column and the newspaper article, blue books and public commissions. Kenyatta was entrusted with a petition to the Secretary of State signed by thirty KCA members and listing the complaints which the KCA had been collating since Beauttah's memorandum to the Ormsby-Gore Commission. It was right up Ross's street and they discussed Kenyatta's tactics. On 28 March Kenyatta sent it to Grigg for forwarding to the Colonial Office:

'I am Mr. Johnstone Kenyatta a Native of Kenya the representative of the above mentioned Association sent to this country for the same purpose. It is the desire of the members of my Association as loyal subjects of His Majesty the King to do all they can to place these petitions before the Secretary of State for the Colonies in a constitutional manner, and I hereby apologise for whatever acts of omission or otherwise I may through ignorance have committed in my effort to conduct things in the proper constitutional way . . .'[3]

Removed from the atmosphere of Government House, Nairobi, Grigg consented to see Kenyatta. Briefed by Ross, Kenyatta came to the offices of the Rhodes Trust on 16 April. The atmosphere was friendly; they kept to the two main issues which Kenyatta was deputed to raise in London. First, Kenyatta asked for the release of Harry Thuku, whom the petition described as 'Chairman' of the Kikuyu Central Association. Grigg had been discussing Thuku's future with the Colonial Office and had agreed a date for his release. With Kenyatta he was non-committal.

They went on to talk about the land problem, and in particular about Grigg's Native Lands Trust Bill, which had been held up the previous year by the Hilton Young Commission. Grigg explained to Kenyatta the purpose of his legislation: that it would enable tribes to make general improvements to their land within their reserves. For example, they could pipe water from streams instead of using those traditional beasts of burden, their women folk. Kenyatta accepted this, but he stressed the Africans' desire for individual security through title-deeds and he queried the good faith of the Crown. Grigg countered with the argument that only the Crown could provide security. He concluded by saying that the Kikuyu must learn patiently to argue their views out through local councils, a democratic process, Grigg added, which was going on at this moment in Britain.

Kenyatta received no reply to his petition and on 23 July he wrote to the Colonial Office asking what had happened to it. Now an anomaly came to light. Not unreasonably Kenyatta believed that the Governor of Kenya was still Governor of Kenya while he was in London. Kenyatta had sent his petition to the Colonial Secretary *through* Grigg, assuming this to be the correct approach. But it transpired that the Governor of Kenya was not the executive head of his government while he was out of the colony. Kenyatta's dealings with Grigg in London, therefore, did not constitute that 'going through the proper channels' on which civil servants always insist. At the end of May they could report that 'Johnstone Kenyatta has not approached, or communicated with, the Colonial Office since his arrival in England'. It was only his letter of July that elicited the information that 'the two petitions which were sent by you to Sir Edward Grigg and handed by him to this department, are being sent to Kenya in order that the views of the Government of that Colony on the various points raised may be reported to the Secretary of State.' It had taken three months for Grigg and the Colonial Office to do anything about them, and he was not to receive a formal reply until January the following year, an interval of nine months.

But Grigg's indifference did not prevent him putting the police Special Branch on to Kenyatta and circulating their report. It told him little that was not to be expected. While Kenyatta kicked his heels waiting for a reply from the Colonial Office he was contacting other names on his list. They included members of the League Against Imperialism, an international organization founded in 1927 and composed mostly of Communists, Fenner Brockway of the Independent Labour Party and Kingsley Martin, a rising columnist on the *Manchester Guardian,* soon to become editor of the *New Statesman and Nation.* Isher Dass, Kenyatta's travelling companion, was an obvious intermediary as India was in the forefront of the anti-imperialist movement.[4]

Kenyatta had arrived in London at a turning point in European history. The jazz age was setting, the world slump just over the horizon. Stalin was now in undisputed control in Russia; Germany had a socialist government. Left-wing analysts spoke of completing Lenin's revolution throughout the world. The days of Western imperialism, they thought, were numbered.

In May 1929 Britain went into a General Election, the first in Britain in which the whole adult nation was allowed to vote, women having gained equality with men the year before. The outcome was a big increase in the Labour Party's representation in Parliament. They now held 288 seats to the Conservatives' 260. The Liberals trailed at 59. For them and for Lloyd-George it was the end. Baldwin resigned, and Ramsay MacDonald returned as Labour Premier for the second time.

Ross was deeply involved in the election and its aftermath and it was not until late summer that he attempted to pick up his contacts with Kenyatta. On 24 August, being in his area, he went round to Kenyatta's new lodgings where he received a shock. Kenyatta was not there. 'He had gone to Moscow, but I saw a girl named Conie Mac-gregor who said she was his friend who had a lot of his papers.' Ross was nonplussed. What had Kenyatta been doing throughout that summer of 1929?

Though Kenyatta was officially on Association business, tapping away at letters to the Colonial Office over a typewriter in west London was not his style, any more than drafting letters at Dagoretti about the KCA casket for Grigg. Kenyatta had come to London with a one-way ticket and a fair amount of money—enough at least to think of buying clothes for Grace and the children. A young, good-looking man, he relished the life of a great metropolis. And when someone appeared who offered to take him round Europe, all expenses paid, he jumped at the offer.

But while he was out of the country, stories about his private life began circulating among those with an interest in Kenya. From Kenyatta's point of view the most damaging was the one which reached Handley Hooper. Since leaving Kahuhia in 1925 Hooper had become Africa Secretary of the Church Missionary Society at their headquarters in Salisbury Square. He was at the heart of the missionary network in London and he maintained a busy correspondence with his old colleagues in Kenya. In September 1929 he wrote to Gideon Mugo about Kenyatta. He told his protégés in the KCA that their delegate had seen the Governor in London and other leaders of the country—'elders', Hooper called them. 'But', he went on,

'Kenyatta was not pleased with their quietness, he forgot how unimportant he is amongst all the many people who go to that office with their needs. He wanted praise (adulation), so he went away to meet a small group of other people who are of no particular account in this country, and they were prepared to flatter him.

And at that time he spent money on clothes for himself and for a young prostitute who lived with him at his lodgings. These things cause trouble and bring shame and bring great discredit on the good name of the Association in the eyes of our Leaders (Elders) .'[5]

To a fellow missionary at Kahuhia, Hooper was more explicit. He had found Kenyatta 'out of his depth' in London and had tried to help him. But 'the boy' was at a disadvantage because of his lack of fluency in English and was 'making a fool of himself'. 'He was spending too much money on his clothes, his morals were doubtful, and he was giving a false impression to those in Africa of the progress he was making.'

Kenyatta's disappearance in Russia, thought Hooper, was likely to be the end of him.

'It's a tragic story: he began fairly well, but his recent behaviour, if known, would discredit him with any British Government, and damn the Association he was supposed to represent. If they can't recall him at once, I advise the Association to drop him and cut their losses. I don't think his case had been prepared with sufficient care, and it's throwing away money to send a man whose character is so unstable. Many of us, who realise better than the Association what an infinitesimal unit in the Empire their numbers are, would do our best to ensure that any reasonable statement should at least receive a hearing: but to send a boy like Kenyatta is worse than not sending anyone, and just makes the friends of Africa in this country sad.'[6]

But Kenyatta survived. On 4 October 1929 he arrived back in England to find an accumulation of trouble. Norman Leys had written advising him to give up politics and return to manual work. Kenyatta's girl-friend, Conie Macgregor, was in distress on Ross's doorstep; another girl, 'Dolly', was asking for more money. There were difficulties with his landlord who had impounded his belongings against unpaid debts. 'Get back to Kenya sharp' was Ross's advice, if necessary by working his own passage. Kenyatta was put out—'very soured' was Ross's impression. But he had made new friends and no longer felt he had to rely on old colonials whose own motives in attacking the system were often mixed enough.

In the communist *Sunday Worker* of 27 October 1929 appeared a long article under the heading: GIVE BACK OUR LAND. It was by a certain Johnstone Kenyatta. The paper reported unrest in Kenya which Grigg, back in his colony, had attributed to 'seditious propaganda'.

Kenyatta's comment was in the form of an 'interview' which ran for two-and-a-half columns. He began: 'The present situation means that once again the natives of the colony are showing their determination not to submit to the outrageous tyranny which has been their lot since the British robbers stole their land.' Strong words! They were far stronger than anything in the KCA memoranda. The article then went on to describe the troubles of 'the natives' who 'have found themselves constantly denuded of their land, and compelled by means of forced labour to work the vast natural wealth of their country for the profit of their interloping imperialist bosses.'

Kenyatta had certainly picked up the language of abuse. But there was more to it. 'Discontent has always been rife among the natives', he continued, 'and will be so until they govern themselves'. This was new. No Kikuyu had made that claim before. 'Sir Edward Grigg talks of "agitation"; there is agitation, an agitation that meets a hearty response from robbed and maltreated Africans, and will not cease until we are our own rulers again.' For the next thirty years this remained substantially the basis of Kenyatta's political message. At his trial at Kapenguria, these very words were thrown back in his face.

In January, Kenyatta followed this article up with two more in the new *Daily Worker,* describing the events which led up to Harry Thuku's arrest in 1922. Its headlines were bold:

AN AFRICAN PEOPLE RISE IN REVOLT

and

A GENERAL STRIKE DROWNED IN BLOOD

Kenyatta did not claim to have taken part in Thuku's organization, but said he was present when the firing took place outside the police lines:

'I was in the crowd myself and saw men, women and children killed, and many others lying in agony. It was a most terrible massacre of people who were quite unarmed and defenceless, and the people of Kenya will not forget it. The official report said that 25 were killed, but this is absurd.'

He quoted a letter from Ross to the *Manchester Guardian* arguing that at least 150 had died.[7]

In the *Daily Worker* 'Comrade Kenyatta' was shown wearing his military outfit with a Boy Scout type of hat, a pipe in his mouth, and hands on his hips. Across one shoulder was slung a water bottle and across the other field glasses. Around his waist was his famous beaded belt. Curiously, the paper at first ascribed the photograph to Thuku. The editors must have failed to recognize in the new London man the old jack-of-all-trades, K. N. Johnstone—'Your Aye Acquaintance' of post-war Nairobi.

There can be no doubt that Kenyatta was strongly influenced by his trip to Russia and his new contacts. Three years later he returned to Moscow for a more prolonged visit, but for the time being he contented himself with the knowledge that he had made a useful reconnaissance. To Ross and others who enquired, he said that an American negro, 'a commercial traveller of sorts', had offered to take him, paying all his expenses, on a 'business trip' which took in Berlin, Hamburg, Leningrad, Moscow, Odessa, Sebastopol, Yalta and Constantinople. They returned via Berlin.[8]

He also persuaded Ross that the tone of the articles was none of his doing. It was fortunate for Kenyatta that Ross was such an open-minded man and did not take offence at his private life. Among Ross's many friends in the Labour Party one, Dr Drummond Shiels, took over as Under-Secretary of State at the Colonial Office at the end of 1929. Shiels placed a minute on the Colonial Office file: 'We must be on our guard against the "Moscow" cry to justify harsh treatment of natives, which would, in fact, provide the raw material which suits Moscow best.'[9]

Before leaving for Moscow Kenyatta had moved from west London to 23 Cambridge Street, where Ross had discovered Conie Macgregor and his letters. On his return he moved further down Cambridge Street to Number 95 and wrote again to the Colonial Office asking for an interview with the Secretary of State. Kenyatta now tried to bluff the civil servants by saying that his Association would never have incurred the expense of sending him to England 'had it known that a personal interview would be refused'. But the record of the correspondence in the Colonial Office files gave him the lie. His story struck the civil servants as a 'deliberate untruth'. 'The more we hear of Kenyatta', they noted, 'the less satisfactory a person he is; the West African Students, Mr Solanke, help him over here and are dissatisfied and disappointed in him.'[10]

The new Under-Secretary of State, however, was not put off. Shiels disliked Grigg and the hardness of the Colonial Office experts. He minuted:

'I would like to have a talk with the young man Kenyatta. The movement for political advancement among the Kikuyus and others cannot be killed by police or missionaries. It is bound to go on. What we have to try is to see that it is directed into constitutional channels. To refuse to see or hear emissaries of the discontented, whether or not they are foolish or wild in expression, tends to make it thought that violent methods are the only ones likely to attract attention.'[11]

On 23 January 1930, McGregor Ross took Kenyatta to see Shiels at the House of Commons. They sat through Question Time in the Strangers' Gallery and then went to Shiels's room where he offered them tea. Kenyatta fenced skilfully with the conventional small talk which Ross afterwards noted down for the record.[12]

' "When did you come to this country?"
"In March" replied Kenyatta.

"It must have been a great change from Kenya weather to March weather in England. Where have you been all this time? In London only?"

"No, I have been travelling about part of the time in England and on the Continent."

"In which parts have you been?"

"In Germany and France and Holland."

"And Russia?" Shiels asked. (Kenyatta's inflammatory articles in the *Daily Worker* had appeared only two days before.)

"Yes, I have been in Russia for a short time."

"How did you like being in Russia?"

"It was very interesting; but the towns were not as good as in France and Germany and England. The people in the streets looked poorer." '

They went on to talk about education. Shiels stressed the need for steady constitutional progress which, he said, can only come through an educated democracy. Kenyatta agreed, saying he had urged his own people to concentrate on education.

'I am very glad', said Shiels, 'to see the stress that you lay on education. Unless you have an educated people to deal with, you may have the misfortune to put into force influences that you cannot control, and grave disaster to all your hopes may result.'

True courage and patriotism, Shiels concluded, lay in holding extremists in check to avoid provoking reactions hurtful to the tribe as a whole. They were prophetic words. How often Kenyatta must have recalled them in later years!

'I added', the Under-Secretary wrote afterwards to the Governor, 'a small homily on the impetuosity of youth and the greater experience of life of the older man.' In short, his advice to Kenyatta was like Ross's: Go back to Kenya, impress on your people the need for ordered constitutional advance and avoid at all costs talk of violence and extremism.

But what did Shiels's advice mean in the colonial context? In the following month Grigg told a meeting of Kikuyu chiefs that he intended banning the collection of money by natives for political associations, thereby cutting off Kenyatta's funds and those of his Nairobi-based colleagues. Grigg asked the Colonial Office whether he had powers to suppress vernacular newspapers; he took powers to curtail the right of native assemblies and the making of public speeches; his government intercepted letters to and from the colony and it operated an elaborate internal intelligence system which depended on nobody knew how many local informers.

In April, Kangethe was arrested for attending a 'tea-party' which the administration declared was a prohibited meeting. Could 'ordered constitutional advance' have any meaning in these circumstances?

On entering office in June 1929 Ramsay MacDonald's cabinet faced the need to take political decisions over the future of East Africa, following Amery's scheme for Closer Union.[13] To Lord Passfield, formerly Sidney Webb, chief propagandist of the Labour Party, fell the task of defining the new government's policy towards its East African colonies.

Passfield, the Fabian theorist, was at a loss. A flurry of white papers issued from the Colonial Office, which reaffirmed the paramountcy of native interests and the long-term goal of full native participation in government. To furious settler objections Passfield replied by referring the whole future of Closer Union to a joint select committee of both Houses of Parliament.

His relations with Grigg became strained. The two men were not on good personal terms, and Grigg came near to open disloyalty in his closing months as Governor, when he was forced to pass legislation against the will of his settlers.[14]

Could democratic theory ever be reconciled with colonial practice? To give British imperial policy a new and radical direction was an exciting aim. It would need time and men on the spot prepared to adjust to these objectives. But the colonial structure was in its very nature authoritarian and its civil servants were by training and background conservative. They viewed their new political masters with suspicion because of their relationship with men like Ross and Leys, who belonged to the policy-forming group within the Labour Party. They knew Leys to be their enemy. Intercepted correspondence told them that he was in touch with the radical Kikuyu leaders. 'Don't send anyone like Mr Kenyatta,' Leys wrote to Kangethe. 'He has done far more harm than good. But make all the noise you can in Kenya. You ought to be able to find Indians to advise you what you can do.' In another letter he added: 'What is needed is that you should do things that would make the papers in this country print sensational telegrams.' Leys suggested a peaceful march on Government House and mass protests.

When forwarding these intercepted letters to the Colonial Office, Grigg's secretary commented: 'it is difficult to believe that he [Leys] is accepting a pension from Government'.[15]

At the Colonial Office, Drummond Shiels echoed Passfield's feelings about Grigg, and their differences came to a head over their conflicting views on the political future of Africans. Kenyatta was a case in point. Shiels felt strongly that the radical tendencies of the KCA should be guided into constitutional channels, and that this was a natural and proper evolution for African politics. He wrote accordingly to Grigg.

'You should know that McGregor Ross, who brought Kenyatta to see me, has been doing his best to keep Kenyatta on right lines. He has seen him about this article and Kenyatta tells him that wild exaggerations have been made in the original draft and lurid headlines inserted without his knowledge. Kenyatta did not know that the article would be published in the *Daily Worker* . . . He stoutly denied that he had the slightest connection with communist circles, and McGregor Ross is convinced that no more writings by Kenyatta will appear in the communist paper.

Kenyatta is now being pressed by McGregor Ross and others to return to Kenya. I understand he goes not later than March, but I feel strongly that the Chief Native Commissioner ought to see Kenyatta as soon as possible after he gets back to Kenya . . . It would, I think, be most unfortunate if he should be allowed to lapse into an attitude of hostility to the Government, and I believe that with careful handling that can be prevented, and his whole Association brought with him. I feel that it is wiser to attempt to guide the Central Association along constitutional lines, by hearing its representations and by showing no open hostility to it as long as it is so guided, rather than to attempt to crush or ignore it. I realise the difficulty with the Native Councils who are your normal avenue of communication with the Kikuyu and whose influence you do not wish to diminish. At the same time, something of the nature of the Central Association is springing up in most colonies, and must be regarded more or less as a permanent feature which Governments have to reckon with.'[16]

Grigg did not take well to this important instruction. He replied that he believed Shiels was wrong to see Kenyatta, as the Nairobi government was doing all it could to bolster the prestige of chiefs like Koinange. Grigg had no time for the KCA: 'It is also the fact that they have collected large sums of money at random and spent them largely on the personal gratification of their own officers.'

He had little good to say for Kenyatta either, and attributed his own difficulties in ruling Kenya to the interference of people in London.

'With regard to Kenyatta, I recognise that he is a harmless individual when left alone. I saw him myself in London, as you know, and I have satisfied myself since I returned to the Colony that he has no real influence or importance with his tribe. How, then, you will ask, has he gained his position? Frankly, as a tool of men who are not friendly to this or any other form of European government . . . It is common knowledge indeed that Kenyatta and other members of his Association have been used by European and Indian malcontents here and elsewhere to further their own ends. Mr McGregor Ross's assertion that Kenyatta has had nothing to do with the Communists takes my breath away . . . We know indeed that he has disappointed his friends out here and is in consequence very short of funds. I got a bill the other day for a typewriter which he had ordered from a London shop and failed to pay for, giving my name as security.

The importance attached to Kenyatta in England is really, therefore, ridiculous. He has done so little even for his Association during his absence that he has ceased to have any serious following here so far as I can judge.'[17]

But Kenyatta was worried that if he returned to Kenya he would be arrested and detained without trial like Harry Thuku in a remote province of the colony. For a young man who enjoyed city life and one where he moved with a sense of his own importance, detention and manual work would have seemed especially abhorrent. He received accounts of Grigg's repressive measures from cables and letters from Kenya. In March 1930 he wrote to Shiels:

'There are rumours in Kenya that the police may try and find some excuse for putting me in prison or deporting me. It is true, as I told you, that I visited Russia without any bad intentions and perhaps the people there may write to me although I have made no arrangements of any kind with them to do so. This might be used as a reason for getting me into trouble, but I am quite willing to let the Kenya Government see anything from Russia if anything is sent. I should be very grateful to you if you will do anything you can to see that I am allowed to reach my home and family and to resume my work among my people without being molested.'[18]

Shiels, too, was worried. To Kenyatta he could resort only to the formula: 'If you conduct yourself in Kenya as a law-abiding citizen, there should be no reason for you to anticipate any trouble with the authorities.'[19] Privately, Shiels minuted, with reference to Grigg, 'I wish I felt more hopeful that our advice would be taken'.[20]

With discussion at its height over East Africa's future, Ross had every reason to keep in close touch with the one Kikuyu representative in London. But he and his wife, Isabel, had another and deeper concern for Kenyatta. Whatever it was that had happened during those first three months in London, Isabel and 'Mac' Ross were not going to allow it to prevent their offering friendship towards the underdog and the spiritually lonely.[21] While doing their best to get him to return to Kenya, they also saw to it, as far as they could, that while he remained in England he would not fall into the wrong hands.

Kenyatta became almost one of the Ross family. He was a regular visitor at their home in Hampstead, and a frequent correspondent. Sometimes Kenyatta would spend most of the day with the Rosses discussing KCA cables and developments in Kenya. Ross helped him draft letters to the Colonial Office and put the correspondence together for printing as a small pamphlet, which Kenyatta was then able to distribute among his contacts in London and carry back to Nairobi to publicize his cause.[22]

Isabel Ross was as concerned for Kenyatta as her husband. One Sunday she took him to a Quaker Meeting—the first he attended—on other occasions it might be to tea parties, or a visit to the sea-side. They introduced him to discussion groups, helped him over appointments and lent him money. Ross sent him with a letter to Transport House to get advice on the running of Unions 'and especially how Union finance is organised, brought to account and audited'. In view of Grigg's threats, Ross added, 'Kenyatta needs all the coaching he can get!'[23]

Through the Rosses Kenyatta became one of the 'Hampstead set', joining in drawing-room discussions and long walks over the Heath. On 26 June 1930, he was their guest at a performance of *Othello* at the Savoy Theatre, in which Paul Robeson played the title role. A strange play, for a visiting African, in which a black man smothers his white wife with a pillow!

Old Kenya hands were of the opinion that the Rosses took a 'town view' of Africans and ignored the realities of colonial politics. It may have been so. But something of Ross's liberalism must have rubbed off on to Kenyatta's shoulders. In East Africa it was still not done for a white man to shake hands with a black man, even if they belonged to the same church; still less were natives welcomed as guests in the home of a white man. A guidebook to Kenya published at this time spelt out the racial difference: 'As children grow up they must be kept from familiarity with Africans; girls must never be left alone with male natives.'[24]

That Kenyatta was ready to listen to Ross may be seen from a letter which appeared in the *Manchester Guardian* on 18 March 1930, under Kenyatta's name. Ross was a regular correspondent to the paper, and knew Scott, the editor, well. The careful phrasing and ordered summary of Kenyatta's petition betray his hand:

'Sir: May I be permitted to throw some light on the so-called "unrest among Kenya natives."

I should mention in passing that I am a Kikuyu, and, with all public-spirited men of my tribe, regard with considerable uneasiness the policy that is being advocated by certain influential people both in Kenya and in this country of further alienating our land from us for the use of non-natives in conjunction with attempts to abolish wholesale our tribal customs. General Smuts has recently condemned most wholeheartedly a similar policy which is being carried out in South Africa.

The Kikuyu Central Association, of which I am the general secretary, is not a subversive organisation. Its object is to help the Kikuyu to improve himself as a better Mu-Kikuyu, not to "ape" the foreigner. Our aims and objects may be summarised briefly under the following five headings:

1. LAND.—To obtain a legal right, recognised by the local government, to the tenure of lands held by our tribe before the advent of the foreigner, and to prevent further encroachment by non-natives on the native reserves.

2. EDUCATION.—To obtain educational facilities of a practical nature to be financed from a portion of the taxes paid by us to the Government.

3. WOMEN'S HUT TAX.—To obtain the abolition of the 'hut tax' on women, which leads to their being forced into work outside the native reserves or into prostituion for the purpose of obtaining money to pay this tax.

4. REPRESENTATION IN THE LEGISLATURE.—To obtain the representation of native interest on the Legislative Council by native representatives elected by the natives themselves.

5. TRIBAL CUSTOMS.—To be permitted to retain our many good tribal customs, and by means of education to elevate the minds of our people to the willing rejection of the bad customs.

Evolving from these five points we hope to remove all lack of understanding between the various people who form the population of East Africa, so that we may all march together as loyal subjects of his Britannic Majesty along the road of Empire prosperity. I would like to ask if any fair minded Briton considers the policy of the Kikuyu Central Association outlined above to savour in any way of sedition? The repression of native views, on subjects of such vital interest to my people, by means of legislative measures, can only be described as a short-sighted tightening up of the safety valve of free speech, which must inevitably result in a dangerous explosion—the one thing all sane men wish to avoid.'[25]

Anyone who knew East Africa would recognize that this letter was not the work of one of the new Kikuyu politicians of Nairobi. It was, however, a masterly summary of the 'constitutionalist' approach to native ambitions, and would have served well as a brief for an editorial in the *Manchester Guardian* itself. Its final sentence might be thought prophetic: a 'dangerous explosion' did indeed break out twenty years later in the Mau Mau Emergency.

But it could be argued that liberalism too helped spark off these explosive situations since its theory never resolved the contradiction of safeguarding democratic rights in the essentially authoritarian society of a colonial Empire. Nor did Ross or his *Manchester Guardian* friends have to grapple with the basic paradox of multi-racial progress towards self-government. History has shown that self-government in Africa implies racial exclusiveness by either white minorities or black majorities. Liberalism and colonialism were incompatible and yet the liberals were, after all, imperialists. They believed that by removing 'all lack of understanding' the different races of East Africa 'may all march together as loyal subjects of His Britannic Majesty along the road of Empire prosperity.'[26] That was a far cry from Kenyatta's bold assertions of the *Sunday* and *Daily Worker*.

Ross and Hooper were both convinced that Kenyatta was a different man since his return from Moscow and they wrote accordingly to their contacts in Kenya. 'The change in the boy during these last months has been remarkable', Hooper wrote to Kenya's Chief Native Commissioner. He felt rather ashamed of his earlier opinion of Kenyatta, especially after he had come to him one morning 'at the end of his tether'. Kenyatta had said that:

'an African when he was short of food looked round to see which goat he could sell, whereupon he produced a typewriter which he bought in his more palmy days, together with the receipt, and asked me whether I could sell it for him. I pawned the typewriter and sent him away with the money, but cast around for some other means of supplying his necessity. We had a young recruit about to sail for East Africa, who was needing language lessons in Kikuyu, and I arranged for Kenyatta to go up to the college twice a week to give those lessons. At the close I sent him a little formal letter of thanks and a cheque for £3. He has insisted on returning the cheque, which I think you will agree speaks well for the boy . . .

Many of us have seen rapid development in his powers of thought and in the depth of his desire to serve his people. His whole personality has grown, and he is now something much bigger than an untutored Kikuyu at the mercy of any sharp who looks to exploit him.'[27]

Barlow was home on leave that year and he made a point of looking up the old apprentice of Thogoto. He came to see Ross and get to the bottom of the rumours current about Kenyatta's activities.

Kenyata joined them for supper and Barlow, too, was immediately struck by the change in him. He was 'quiet and suave' and behaved like any Englishman in his club. Barlow was rather taken aback at such sophistication—'Johnstone offers his cigarettes and lights one's "smoke" in quite the approved fashion!' he wrote to Arthur. Missionaries were never quite at ease with Africans who picked up these 'Western' habits. Kenyatta, continued Barlow, 'more than kept his end up with me: I felt that a cleverer man than I was wanted to argue with him.'

Kenyatta, in fact, was more relaxed than Ross whose contemptuous remarks about Grigg, the settlers and church leaders, spoken openly in front of Kenyatta, embarrassed and annoyed the missionary from Kenya.

But Kenyatta was friendliness itself towards Barlow and told him of all that he had been doing. His work in Britain, he said, was now finished but for a meeting he hoped to arrange with members of the Church of Scotland in Edinburgh. Thanks to Barlow it was soon fixed for the end of May.[28]

To Barlow it was an extraordinary development in a 'mission boy'. Ten years before he had been present at the Kirk Session when Kenyatta had been hauled up for drinking and marital irregularities. Now he saw a man capable of holding his own in political discussion, travelling all over Britain and Europe, making appointments, attending the State Opening of Parliament, taking himself familiarly through crowded London streets, and meeting, almost as an equal, the governing body of the mission church to which they both belonged. Barlow's commitment to Africa was of a different kind from Ross's. He still had personal responsibilities in Kenya and saw his own destiny, and the destiny of Africans, in terms of the old civilizing mission. Kenyatta, Barlow knew, was a portent, but whether for good or ill he was less sure.

Barlow kept in touch with Kenyatta. He wanted his assistance over the final stages of his Kikuyu dictionary, on which he had been working for many years, and, in any case, he felt it was his duty to prepare his people in Kenya for the time when Kenyatta would return. He came to see him in his rooms in Victoria and met his landlady—'a friendly wee body'. 'It was quite a nice bed-sitting room, though decidedly shabby in some respects.' There were books on Africa and souvenirs of his travels.

Barlow was interested in the photographs with which Kenyatta surrounded himself. They seemed to be mostly of his Russian tour and of his lady acquaintances—'interpreters and guides', explained Kenyatta. Barlow could believe it, as 'they appeared to be middle-aged, serious looking, plain and intellectual'. Kenyatta was evidently quite at home in the world of London bed-sitting rooms.[29]

Barlow now discovered that by a strange chance Kenyatta's old employer, John Cook, had reappeared in his life. How or when this occurred is not clear, though it would have been natural for Kenyatta to have kept a note of his address. Cook turned up from time to time in lodgings near to Kenyatta's digs in Cambridge Street. The old engineer had fallen on bad times. His attempts to patent a sisal machine had failed and left him hard up. But Kenyatta was glad to give what help he could to his old friend in the changed circumstances in which they both found themselves. From Cook Barlow learnt new and disconcerting stories about Kenyatta's life, the details of which appeared to mystify Cook also. Kenyatta kept strange company—one was a Somali, another a virulently anti-British young Indian, others again to whom his landlady forbade entry. He was liable to disappear suddenly for days on end without saying a word to anyone. An Irish Mohammedan called Ryan was a frequent visitor, and tried to convert Kenyatta to the Moslem faith. He had a rich acquaintance who stayed at the nearby Grosvenor Hotel and took Kenyatta on a flight to some European capital.

Kenyatta, according to John Cook, 'was not in the habit of attending any place of worship, but he often went to hear the Atheist speakers in Hyde Park'. Not that he accepted their teaching: he was keeping his mind independent and forming his own opinion. 'John Cook thinks he still retains the faith taught him in the Mission.' A strange pair they must have made, the old, down-and-out Kenya pioneer and the young Kikuyu, who for a time wore a fez and posed as an Egyptian. Of his private morals, Barlow was not disposed to be censorious. He repeated Ross's view about police reports that Kenyatta had been photographed with nude white girls: 'Dirty minded liars!' . . . 'What leprous reptiles the police can be!' and 'Noisome tripe.' A humble and intensely spiritual man, Barlow looked for the best in everyone's character, but he was absolutely loyal to his church and to Dr Arthur, his comrade in mission work for more than twenty years. No one knew better the crisis through which the Kikuyu Church was passing nor felt a greater sense of responsibility to report fairly on this Kikuyu spokesman who, in such a short space of time and in so convincing a manner, had broken through the attitudes of centuries. 'He may have been playing a double, if not treble or quadruple game . . . I would not yet condemn him without further evidence, but . . . he has grown to be more and more of an enigma . . .'[30]

On 4 August 1930, he wrote at length to Arthur. No greater insight into Kenyatta's character and situation was subsequently to be vouchsafed by any other white man.

'I greatly admired J.K.'s enterprise and courage in undertaking this mission of his, and his apparent diligence and perseverance in carrying it out. Looking at it from the point of view of those who are enthusiasts for African progress and political liberty, he has probably accomplished a great deal of good, and if he were not under the shadow of his connection with the KCA we should all concede him the honour due to a courageous man and a patriot. It is most un-fortunate that, from the beginning, we have been out of touch with the KCA and have no influence with it, and that it fell under the spell of extremists. On the other hand, as M'G. Ross would say, in all movements of reform and of progress it is generally the extremists who manage to get a move on. I do not think that J.K.'s experiences have 'spoiled' him. I think, on the contrary, that he may have benefited from them. He seems to have a sincere desire to foster peace and harmony, as well as to work for the security and progress of his own people and country . . . I do not go the length of trusting him beyond what I can see, and he may have succeeded in throwing dust in the eyes of his friends and supporters at home, or he may be just a clever diplomat. He may be a Communist agent by now, for all I know. After our late experiences in Kikuyu I have often wondered whether one can ever fully trust a Kikuyu again, except in very special cases.* But . . . I have been impressed by his apparent level-headedness and quiet bearing. The Kikuyu have gained an able champion, and he has opened doors through which many may pass in the future. He has demonstrated the ability of a Kikuyu to mix on equal terms with the Europeans and to hold his end up in spite of all his handicaps, educationally and socially. He has shown, too, that there is no great gulf between the African and the Legislative Council. If the uneducated Johnstone Kenyatta can do these things, are there not potential Aggreys amongst our High School and other pupils?'

Everyone connected with Kenyatta's eighteen months in London now shared a concern to get him back to Kenya. Though reluctant to feel he was being pushed around, he could not put the moment off for ever. He was, in any case, without funds of any kind. Supplies from the KCA, never amounting to more than driblets, were long since exhausted. Once again the Rosses came to his rescue. They arranged for their friends in the Anti-Slavery Society to advance Kenyatta the money for the passage home and enough ready cash to pay off his debts in London.

---

* A reference to the female circumcision controversy. See next chapter.

But the committee took the precaution of asking Isabel Ross to handle the actual cash disbursements for Kenyatta on the grounds, as they explained, 'that it might be unwise for you to have so large a sum of money about you as £32. 10. 0.'[31]

Kenyatta swallowed the insult. He continued firing off letters to the Colonial Office, and he left a quantity of unfinished business for Ross to send on to him in Kenya. On 2 September 1930, the Rosses were on the platform at Victoria Station to see him at last board the train for the East Africa steamer. Subsequently a card from Suez reassured them that he had indeed caught the boat.

But there was a surprise in store for them all. A week after Kenyatta had departed, Barlow received a letter from John Cook. On the day Kenyatta was due to catch his train, Cook, who knew nothing of this, went round to see him. He found a taxi waiting stacked with luggage. Kenyatta emerged from the house—

'dressed in the latest fashion. He for a moment looked much taken aback but soon recovered and in an offhand manner explained that he was going off on a visit for about 3 weeks. On my previous visit his room was cumbered with at least 4 new tweed suits and a large collection of good underclothing, enough to keep him going for years. I asked him why he was laying in such a stock and he explained that, although he had no idea when he was returning to Kenya, he was quietly preparing so as to be ready when the call came. Upon my insisting upon his telling me when he thought he would be going he stated that he did not expect to go for some time yet.'

His suspicions roused, Cook returned to Kenyatta's digs and spoke to the family that was looking after him. He discovered that no one else knew he was leaving either,

'judging from the number of phone calls they have had. When he did leave he treated the landlady very shabbily by deducting from the bill all the meals which were prepared for him but which he wouldn't take the trouble to eat, and on several occasions lately came down to the kitchen and ordered dinner after 9 p.m. and grumbled if he didn't get served within a few minutes. I warned his landlady months ago that she was spoiling Johnstone, now she knows. One thing is certain; if Johnstone returns as he has told them he will, he has lost a good home because they now consider him to be the most selfish of men. A sister told me they were wondering where Johnstone got all the money he spent so freely from, because his outfit must have cost many £s, yet at the last this sister, to oblige Johnstone, let him have a handbag for 15/- and received only 10/-, the bag having cost £2/2/-.

"I fear", concluded John Cook, "Johnstone has been deceiving the English Church Mission as well as the Rosses." '[32]

Kenyatta had lived for eighteen months in London in an atmosphere of deepening mystery. He had kept his thoughts and his impressions to himself and his different activities separate from each other. He left no clues to the development of his ideas, but only feelings of mistrust in others. The secrecy with which he surrounded himself, with his enigmatic acquaintances, was fostered for reasons deeply embedded in his nature. That he intended returning to England was clear. In London he was a free man, in Nairobi the subject of a totalitarian state.

To have succeeded in making his mark in the capital of the British Empire was itself a notable achievement. The settlers in Kenya would never give him credit for this. They believed Nairobi corrupted natives; how much worse, they imagined, was the effect of London, not to mention Moscow. Bolshevik, licentious, dishonest—such judgments came easily to their minds and Kenyatta's future career only confirmed them in their view.

And what of Barlow's sane and humane assessment of him? That would now be put to the test in the ferment in Kikuyuland towards which Kenyatta was heading.

CHAPTER 11

Female Circumcision

At his interview with Shiels in January 1930, Kenyatta was shocked to learn details of the murder in Kenya of an elderly American missionary, Hilda Stumpf, of the Africa Inland Mission. She was stone deaf and at first it looked as though her murder was the work of a thief. The real facts had been hushed up since the post-mortem showed that she had been sexually mutilated in a brutal fashion. Her attackers had smothered her face with a pillow to stifle her cries and she had died from suffocation. Behind this outrage lay the drama of the female circumcision controversy.

Among the Kikuyu, as with certain other African tribes, the circumcision of girls as well as boys formed an important part of the initiatory rites associated with age-sets and entry into full membership of the tribal community. It was the outward symbol of a girl's reaching the end of her education and marked her readiness to indulge in sexual activities. It entitled her to a marriage settlement and consequent negotiations over goats and land for the benefit of her parents. Beer in the short term, and in the long term rights of inheritance, all depended on circumcision.

For girls the operation itself entailed a cutting away of the soft tissues surrounding the entrance to the vagina, in medical terms the removal of the clitoris, labia minora and half the labia majora. After elaborate preparations during which she was carefully briefed on her role, the initiate girl took her place on a special skin laid out on the ground and leaned back against her sponsor who supported her body with her own, twined her legs around the girl's and held them wide apart for the circumciser's knife—a piece of sharpened iron. The important thing was for the girl to show no sign of fear or pain, and there was no question, of course, of anaesthetics. Older women attended the ceremony and watched intently as each girl in turn was operated on, and they praised the bravery of those who took the knife

[155]

without flinching. Immediately after, leaf dressings were applied and the wound was left to heal of its own accord.

Though wholesale abandonment by tribes of such customs was not unknown, particularly under strong outside pressures, some anthropologists took the view that circumcision among the Kikuyu held a much deeper meaning in the spiritual life of the community than the physical operation alone suggested. But the precise significance of the outward symbol was not clear.

In this, as with most tribal practices, the habits of centuries had blurred whatever was the original sociological or religious purpose behind the custom. The word used by the Kikuyu for initiation also carried an association with the idea of pain. Circumcision of men and women was part initiatory, part sacrificial, part sanctification, and probably derived from some earlier rites connected with fertility and reproduction. To these had been added a whole course of preliminary and post-initiatory ceremonies which lasted several weeks, induced a high degree of emotional excitement among adolescents approaching puberty, and were thought by some western observers to be as important, if not more so, than the physical operation itself. Some sections of the tribe practised a less drastic form than others, and it was assumed that this was because they had come into contact with the Masai as the less severe operations were normally found among the southern Kikuyu.

The educational content of the ceremonies included explicit instruction in sexual matters and often took the form of dances and other displays of a more or less obscene nature. In so far as sexuality lies close to the centre of the human persona, it can no doubt be said that everything connected with female circumcision had 'enormous implications' in the life of the community. But no adequate explanation was offered as to why girls should suffer such a traumatic end to their childhood.

The most plausible anthropological explanation of the significance of both male and female circumcision is that it inculcated a strong sense of corporate identity, and so was more deeply felt than mere initiation, but exercized, rather, a mystical hold over the people of a religious nature. Through mutilation and blood-letting were invoked the blessings of the ancestral spirits; they gave the seal of blood-brotherhood to fellow initiates in their earthly life, and, as in the Jewish idea of a covenant with God, confirmed the tribe's sense of a divinely appointed destiny in the world. Thus circumcision bound the community together, both the living and the dead, in a solemn and irreversible act which mingled blood with earth and so united them in the source of all life, the soil of Kikuyuland. Socially, circumcision determined the age-grades of boys and so the whole structure of eldership within the tribe; for girls it meant sisterhood with their fellow initiates and a sharing with the boys of the same age-grade, though this did not have the same importance in a woman's life as it did for men.

European medical opinion condemned female circumcision outright. Apart from the agony suffered by the girl, and the risk of infection from the crude instruments employed and the lack of adequate aftercare, when the wound healed it formed a hard scar tissue at the opening of the birth canal which often made subsequent childbirth difficult and dangerous, and in some cases led to the death of the child in first births. There was always a danger of other complications affecting the urinary system. Anthropologists who were otherwise sympathetic towards African customs admitted the harmful aspects of female circumcision, but there were some who defended it with an interest unrelated to personal observations, and assumed that missionary objections were based on a prudish attitude towards anything to do with sex. The real ground for conflict lay much deeper.

In some respects the most revolutionary aspect of European contact with Africa lay in the Christian attitude towards women. The missionaries taught that wives and daughters were equal with men in the eyes of God and deserved love and respect as individuals. Only in this light could sense be made of the Bible's teaching about family life and the consequent insistence in Christian communities on monogamy, chastity, and the emancipation of women from their servile role in the tribal economy.

The impact of these ideas was profound. Christianity threatened to turn African society upside down, as it had done the world of first-century Rome. The missionaries found their hardest task was to convert girls, but once they succeeded the possibility existed of Christian marriages between Africans. Only in this way, in effect, could a new, native church be born.

The question of female circumcision was one consequence of this struggle over the status of women.

At the Scottish mission it was, significantly, the two outstanding women, Mrs Watson and Marion Stevenson, who first taught against female circumcision, and because they were the first to base doctors at their stations it was the Scottish missionaries who became most actively involved in its medical implications.[1]

The missionaries, it must be remembered, were concerned primarily with their own church members. Understanding the social importance of the custom they tried to give a positive lead, as they did with the initiation of boys, by providing proper medical supervision and ensuring that the girls' sponsors were Christians. In this way, at least, they could prevent much of the dancing and sexual 'instruction', to which they objected almost as much as to the physical operation. In 1914 and '15, at Thogoto and Tumutumu respectively, experiments were tried of bringing girls into the mission hospital for the operation to be performed by the village circumciser under the eye of a European doctor. But it was too much for the doctors, who then actively campaigned against it on medical grounds. In this they were supported both by the other Protestant missionary societies, who welcomed their professional guidance, and by leading native Christians on whom their medical exposition made a devastating impression.

The result was a steady growth of feeling within all the Protestant churches in Kikuyuland against female circumcision. The Presbyterian churches and some others introduced rules forbidding its practise or encouragement by church members upon pain of church discipline—which might mean suspension from fellowship or denial of Communion or a setting back in instruction.[2] Roman Catholics were not concerned about it.

Administrative officers and settlers with direct experience of female circumcision likewise opposed it. Government reports described it as 'horrible mutilation' and a 'horrible practice', one of a number of 'barbarous ordeals'. But government action in the form of legislation was deemed inappropriate on the grounds, apparently, of unenforceability.

Officially the administration took the view that only 'education' and time would see it wholly eradicated, though district officers, called out to investigate ceremonies, were often as horrified by what they saw as were the doctors. One officer reported his experiences. Hearing screams from a banana plantation, he found the village women engaged in the traditional method of treating young girls after their operation. They were holding down each one in turn and forcing her legs apart so that one old woman could spit into the wound and swab it out roughly with chewed banana leaves. 'The girl suffered intensely and the cries she emitted as her wound was treated in this way denoted an agony which shattered her self control.' The other girls lay 'moaning and whispering covered by the usual oily cloths'. All their wounds 'were bleeding profusely'. There was no doubt in the mind of this observer about the 'obvious sufferings' of the girls and the futility of a passive approach towards 'education'. He concluded his report with the challenge: 'I now feel very strongly . . . that Government should prevent it if possible.'[3]

But government—by now it was Grigg's government—refused to take the 'strong action' urged by its officers in the field. The conference of East African governors in 1926 decided that as the custom 'was of very ancient origin' it 'should not be interfered with' and an attempt should be made instead to persuade tribes to abandon 'the more brutal forms of it and return to the more ancient and less brutal form'. It was believed that this 'less brutal form' consisted in the removal of the clitoris only, which, according to the governors, 'would appear to be harmless'. To this end, from 1926 most Local Native Councils were persuaded to pass resolutions 'whereby the operation may only be performed by skilled women authorised by the Council, and no operator may remove more than the clitoris'. Such regulations satisfied neither the old tribalists nor the reformers, and they were widely disregarded in the reserves.[4]

In March 1929 a conference of all churches working in Kikuyuland was held at Tumutumu. Among other matters the subject of female circumcision was reviewed. Three resolutions were passed:

'1. Resolved, with one dissentient, that this custom is evil and should be abandoned by all Christians.
2. Resolved, by 30 to 9, that all Christians submitting to it should be suspended by Churches everywhere.
3. The Conference makes no recommendation as to the period of suspension. It refers the question back to the Churches, asking that it be carefully considered with a view to getting a definite decision at a future Conference.'[5]

It must be stressed that these resolutions were put forward, debated and passed by the Africans themselves, and on their own initiative. Kikuyu Christians themselves, in other words, were taking their rejection of female circumcision one stage further by seeking for a uniform approach in all their churches.

Kenyatta by now had left Kenya for London. He was therefore absent from the country for the ensuing eighteen months during which time the issue of female circumcision suddenly blazed into a controversy of unprecedented heat. The KCA made it a political matter by including it among several tribal customs for which they canvassed support in the reserves. Their argument was that the culture of the tribe was threatened and its traditional structure in danger of being broken up. It was a highly emotive subject and their campaign was immediately effective, even though it was being pressed hardest by elements in the tribe who had departed furthest from their old way of life.

Dr Arthur at Thogoto was at the heart of the crisis. He felt that at stake was the whole question of church discipline—that important Presbyterian concept. For him it was a simple matter of principle. His African church had passed certain laws and all members vowed to obey them in accepting Christian fellowship. To oppose those laws *from within* the church was not just a matter of rebellion against the way the church was being run—the sort of trouble which all missions encountered from time to time—it was a question of spiritual deception. Those guilty of it were sinning against their own promises, against their own souls.

As a result the African elders at Thogoto decided they must purge their membership. In an atmosphere of rising tension, in which Arthur invoked the spirit of the Scottish covenanters and his loyal elders were fired with similar zeal against 'Apollyon', the Kikuyu mission was put to the test.[6]

First, all teachers on the mission payroll were asked to state their acceptance of the church ruling on female circumcision and to repudiate membership of the KCA 'until that body should cease from its anti-Christian propaganda'. Of fifty-three teachers, twelve refused and were dismissed.

Next it was the turn of the elders. How many would now accept the church law *they themselves had helped draw up?* For them non-membership of the KCA was not made a requirement, 'this being considered a matter for the individual conscience'. Of fifty elders, thirty-two agreed at once, followed later by another two. Sixteen— a third—refused and were suspended.

Finally the mission turned to its rank and file membership. As with the elders 'a simple declaration' of their acceptance of the church ruling was required. In the first month of testing, nine-tenths of the body of the church were lost.

In the middle of October 1929, almost overnight it seemed, a scurrilous dance song swept through the villages to add to the dismay of the missionaries. It was supposed to be derived from a Swahili tune, but the Kikuyu added ingredients of their own in imitation of the European fox-trot, and with an exotic accompaniment of bells and pieces of metal struck to the rhythm of the dance. Masters of improvisation, they invented any number of verses, most of which Europeans regarded as 'quite unprintable'. Less offensive stanzas were quoted as examples of the hostility being directed against the Church:

'*Little knives in their sheaths,*
that they may fight with the church, the time has come.'

'*I used to think Jesus was the Son of God;*
I have now found out that he was an Indian' (or '*Picture*' or '*Mohammedan*'.)

'*When you hear the baboons in the wood barking it is Musa*
They are waiting that he may go and baptise them.'

Musa Gitau, to whom this last verse referred, Kenyatta's circumcision father, was now the ordained minister of the mission church. He was one of Arthur's staunchest allies throughout the crisis. In its most vituperative respect the campaign had turned against 'loyal' Christians, rather than against Europeans.

By October 1929, when the trouble was at its height, it was known in Nairobi that Kenyatta was visiting Moscow and was 'in close touch with Communists and Communist Organisations'.[7] The verses of the *Muthirigu* song glorified Kenyatta and abused the chiefs and government.

'*Elders Koinange and Waruhiu when John Kenyatta comes you will be given women's loin cloths and have to cook him his food.*'

'*The Governor is called a big man but when John (Kenyatta) comes he [i.e. the Governor] will have his teeth extracted like a Kavirondo because of all the lies he told in Europe.*'

'*We Kikuyu are delighted that John Kenyatta has been made Governor of all Kikuyu by the Secretary of State. Praise Elders of Kikuyu Central Association for sending John Kenyatta to Europe who is stronger than the Governor of Kenya for he defeats the Governor of Kenya.*'

It was not surprising that Grigg felt at odds with the Colonial Office and their boosting of Kenyatta's standing. In January 1930 he outlawed the song as seditious.[8]

Arthur took a serious view of the crisis. In Africa religious hysteria often ended in bloodshed.[9] Intimidation was rife. Young girls were being circumcised under conditions which were quite unusual according to tribal custom. Organizers were often thugs who had served prison sentences for crimes of violence. The new song rang out at night across the ridges like the 'evil' dances which greeted the missionaries when they first arrived in the forest a generation ago. Loyal Christians were threatened, services were disrupted and rival services held alongside. Schools were boycotted, school buildings raided, equipment removed, and parents abused. These incidents, which culminated in the murder of Hilda Stumpf in January 1930, all went to show how raw conditions were beneath the surface of Grigg's settler colony.[10]

The government was disinclined to take the sudden disturbance seriously, though officials were puzzled by it. The KCA, they opined, were no more than 'sillies' behaving like schoolboys 'who make bombs to blow up their form master'. In view of the stand the missionaries had taken in proclaiming the paramountcy of native interests against Grigg's plans, his government took a sly pleasure in their discomfiture. Arthur, of course, was an obvious scapegoat and Grigg asked for his resignation as representative of native interests on his council.[11]

In London, female circumcision, or clitoridectomy as the fastidious called it, became the talk in advanced circles and Kenyatta was sought after by hostesses at tea-time discussions. A powerful group, headed by the Duchess of Atholl, a Unionist Member of Parliament and protagonist of women's rights, was well briefed by the Scottish Church. They called female circumcision barbarous mutilation and pressed for its outlawing by government action in the same way as governments had not hesitated to put a stop to cannibalism and human sacrifices and the burning alive of widows in India—and, they might have added, to other African customs like trial by ordeal and abandoning babies and sick people in the bush for the hyenas. Was not this one of the objects of the civilizing mission?[12]

Shiels raised the issue with Kenyatta at their meeting at the House of Commons. Kenyatta then accepted Shiel's suggestion that it would be helpful if the government were to send medical teams into the reserves to explain why the operation was a danger to health. And he helped Ross and Hooper in the drafting of a letter written in Kikuyu to the KCA which Ross, Norman Leys and Josiah Wedgwood MP all signed. They asked the KCA leaders not to mix up circumcision with land and taxation matters. For medical reasons, if for none other, they wished that 'the Kikuyu people themselves would follow the lead of all the civilised nations throughout the world and discontinue the circumcision of their girls'.[13]

In associating himself with this letter, Kenyatta appeared to identify himself with moderate Western attitudes. It was a posture which contrasted with the tone of his articles in the *Sunday* and *Daily Worker*.

Helped by Ross, Kenyatta also wrote to the Colonial Office on the subject.

'I would respectfully draw your attention to the fact that any attempt to coerce my people by "force majeure" will have the very opposite of the desired effect as it causes my people to attach accentuated importance to the maintenance of this custom.'

Ross, Leys, Isabel Ross, Mrs Hooper and Hooper himself took much the same line, though the Anglican missionaries were divided on the issue and fearful of running into the same kind of show-down as Arthur encountered.[14]

We must now consider Kenyatta's appearance before the twelve members of the Church of Scotland in Edinburgh on 30 May 1929.[15] Among them were Barlow and Dr Philp, both with personal experience of the trouble. Philp was in charge at Tumutumu throughout an agitation which culminated in an agreement between KCA agents and local chiefs to make a return to old tribal customs the basis of their electoral campaign for the Local Native Councils in March 1928. He was an unfriendly witness. Barlow had left Kenya only seven weeks before the meeting.

Kenyatta was in a predicament. He knew little of the details of the row and his personal feelings were not strong. If anything, he was against the practice and he evidently gave this impression to his relatives. A few weeks before he had received a letter from his 'uncle', Lawi Iguku, an elder of the Thogoto church, appealing for his support:

'I exhort you to remember that where you are—it is God who helps us, and you have been brought up by the Scottish Church, so if you

see the matter is lies, you are on our side always as we hoped. I remember that from the beginning you led me that this matter of circumcision is *not important,* thus I hope that you are the spokesman
of the Kikuyu, and especially the magnifier of the Church and of God
[who] helps us.'

On the other hand, Kenyatta learnt that Grace Wahu had followed
the anti-church party.[16]

Kenyatta adopted the position that the KCA was not against the
church. How could they be, he asked, when so many Christians were
members of the Association? It was the church, he said, not the
KCA which had provoked the row and he, like the KCA, felt that it
was wrong for the church to press for the abolition of the custom by
legislative action. Its abolition could only be achieved through education, perhaps by sending doctors like Dr Philp, he added, around
the reserves. It was the point he had agreed with Shiels.

But Kenyatta stoutly denied that KCA members were involved in
intimidation and rowdiness, or that the Association, as a matter of
policy, was in favour of female circumcision. In what was an uncanny
foretaste of a later argument, Kenyatta said that it was easy for the
opponents of the KCA—a legitimate political organization—to give
it a bad name by attributing to it the irresponsible views and actions
of non-members.[17] This was the crux of the matter as far as Kenyatta's
own attitude was concerned. The Scotsmen pressed him:

'I gather that, speaking generally, you say that this mutilation is a bad
thing. Then if it is a bad thing, why should not the Church do its best
to get it abolished by every means in their power?—that is why the
Church exists.'

To this Kenyatta relapsed into Kikuyu:

'I put it in this way, to sum it up in a nutshell, their way of looking at
it is that the way of gradual conviction is to be preferred to that of
a direct attack by means of spear and shield.'

This was as far as Kenyatta would go. He claimed that he had written to the KCA telling them 'they had no right to take action of any
kind in the matter of circumcision' as 'it was not the business of a po-

litical body'. He was referring to the letter jointly signed by Ross, Leys and Josiah Wedgwood; but he had not signed it himself.

Both Kenyatta and the church leaders appeared well satisfied with the encounter. The chairman concluded:

'We are really in agreement when we come to think of it, that the Church is really the educative factor that leads people, whether in your country or in ours, to see what is right and what is wrong . . . You do agree with us that every step should be taken to rid your people of what is a very cruel custom. Now we look to you as a representative of the KCA to bring all your influence to bear that your people may be continuously under the Christian educating influence.'

Kenyatta replied that he would do his best and to Ross he reported 'loud in his praise' of his reception in Edinburgh.

By the autumn of 1930 Arthur felt he had the situation in his own church under control. Naturally he was apprehensive about Kenyatta's return. Letters intercepted by the police to Kenyatta's colleagues revealed little. They were too allegorical to be meaningful. From CID sources Arthur knew about his debts;[18] he had Barlow's frank assessment of his ways in London and a detailed report of the Edinburgh meeting. Whatever may have been his earlier feelings for 'the lad', as he called him, which dated back to Kenyatta's refusal to finish his apprenticeship and his brush with the Kirk Session over his way of life at Dagoretti, Arthur did not allow them to come between his Christian duty as a pastor towards 'an erring member of our Church'.[19] Members of Kenyatta's family were loyal supporters of that church; Musa Gitau, Kenyatta's circumcision father, was the African minister at Thogoto. Kenyatta was often in their prayers and Arthur was ready to welcome him back, as he wrote to Barlow:

'I can assure you that I shall not be in opposition to him, if he comes back determined to tell his KCA people they have made a mistake in attacking the Church. *Their political propaganda I have nothing to do with and would not keep him out of church for, if he will stop his beer etc.* [author's italics] I may not like his politics, though even there if he has learned anything at Home, and if it is true he is out for 'uiguano' [reconciliation], I shall be prepared to listen to. There lies a great future before him, if he will become first of all a good man and be reconciled to his Church (I can see no hope for him otherwise); and second if he will then lead his Association into right ways, that all Europeans can sympathise with and stop this communism and up-against-Governmentism as rebellious subjects . . .'[20]

Such was the situation facing Kenyatta on his return to his homeland. He landed at Mombasa on 24 September 1930. James Beauttah, now working at the coast, was there to meet him. For a few days Kenyatta lay low in order to bring himself up to date on all that had been going on in Kikuyuland in his absence. Ironically, Grigg was on his way out as Kenyatta came in. The Governor made his farewell speech to the settler community in Nairobi on 23 September and departed, according to his own words, 'a sad and disappointed man. My mission had failed so far as Closer Union was concerned.' He had found it 'not a happy thing to be Governor of Kenya in 1929 and 30'.[21] At the end of the month Kenyatta made his way to Nairobi where Grace was waiting with leaders of the KCA.

One of his first actions was to send a brief note to Arthur saying he was back. It crossed with one from Arthur to him.

'Dear Johnstone Kenyatta,
I am writing to you not as Secretary of the Kikuyu Central Association but privately as a friend of ours who was one of our earliest scholars in this school and as the minister of the Church to which you belong . . .
You have had a wonderful sojourn in England, and God has given to you the unique opportunity of seeing many new things and learning many new lessons . . .
And now you have come back to your family and to your people and to your work again. There is a great future before you in your life, if you will let God dominate your life and allow Jesus Christ to be Lord and Master of your soul and therefore of all your ways. We want you to return into Church fellowship again, and that as soon as possible. You will remember that talk Rev. Musa and I had with you about two years ago, and how we urged you to come back. We are still waiting and praying for that return.
I know that you have come back to a very difficult life, how difficult God alone knows. If you will let God help and guide and strengthen you, as He wishes to do, in these difficult early days, there is nothing that is not possible for you to do or to become.
I have been praying often for you, while you were away in England, that God would help you and keep you. I am praying every day just

now that He will strengthen your heart and will to do just now only what is right and in accordance with His will.'[22]

Kenyatta did not respond immediately to Arthur's olive branch, but a Sunday or two later he came to church and after the service Arthur invited him in for tea at the manse. Kenyatta had Grace Wahu with him and a group of his Association people, one of whom he introduced as his 'secretary'. 'Conversation was rather slow and difficult.' Arthur asked Kenyatta to come to see him alone, but Kenyatta said his people insisted on always being with him. 'Evidently they don't trust him', thought Arthur.[23]

Arthur never did get to see him alone. But on 5 November Kenyatta came out again to the mission to meet the church elders. They were chosen with care to bring the greatest spiritual, and tribal, influence on him. Dr Arthur was the only European; with him were the Revd Benjamin, a son of the old Dagoretti chief Waiyaki, and the Revd Musa Gitau. Among the others was Charles Stokes, brought in specially because of his old friendship with Kenyatta.

As before, Kenyatta had with him four men from his Association, all mission educated. The encounter was more like a *shauri*, a meeting between rival parties, than the simple 'interview' for which Arthur had hoped. A generation ago disputes like this would have been handled by the tribal elders of the district cloaked in skins and squatting on the earth with sticks in their hands to represent the points each side wanted to make. Now everyone carried a veneer of sophistication. Kenyatta was in one of the many suits he had bought in London, his colleagues wore the latest styles from the Nairobi bazaar. Opposite them was Arthur, trim, ageing, an elder statesman of the colony and no longer the boyish sportsman with the handlebar moustache who taught them all to play football in those days before the war when Kenyatta was a 'mission boy'. With him were the barefooted church elders who were looking not for anathema but restoration. But the language was still the same—that elusive Kikuyu phraseology with which they once used to invoke the shades of their forefathers and, perhaps, still did.

For the benefit of the KCA people present, Arthur described how Kenyatta had met with the church leaders in Edinburgh, and

'We have seen how you, Johnstone, told those elders [i.e. the Overseas Committee of the Church of Scotland] that you did not agree with Joseph Kangethe or the KCA in regard to this matter of Female

Circumcision and that you had written to your people to tell them so. We are glad to hear that.'

Kenyatta, continued Arthur, should tell his people to obey government officers, Kikuyu chiefs, and missions in control of schools,

'because we do not see how things can improve unless people do obey their rulers. It is good for you to tell your people that the abolishing of the Female Circumcision is a matter for one to decide himself with his own conscience and it is not a thing to be ordered by the KCA.'

The church, no doubt under Arthur's guidance, had prepared a long document setting out its case. The detail and argument were impressive. But Kenyatta refused to be drawn.[24] He repeated 'that for himself he was opposed to the practice but that the thing could only be done away with by education'. It was an inconclusive meeting, as inconclusive as the one in Edinburgh. But Arthur now felt he knew his man. He had hoped that Kenyatta would influence the KCA, but he realized that his tribal situation made it impossible for him. 'What was important for him was to retain his position, which was not very secure, as Secretary of the KCA. He has remained so but probably at the cost of having to oppose us.'[25]

The likelihood of Kenyatta's reconciling himself with his church on Dr Arthur's terms was never great. His visit to Europe had opened his mind to too many new ideas, too many new influences, for the old missionary appeal to call him back. He had always been a rebel at heart and Arthur's paternalism was what he most rejected in the European attitude towards Africans. Added to which the austerity of the Scottish mind and character was particularly frustrating to a man like Kenyatta who enjoyed earthy pleasures in life.

Kenyatta's own people now looked increasingly to him for a lead. His prestige stood high as the one who had been to London and interviewed the greatest in the land—and Kenyatta was not shy in stating what he had done. The dialogue with the church at Thogoto was fast drawing to a close.

But there was one approach still open to him. The boycott which followed the dismissal of teachers who refused to take the oath demanded by the church was followed by an uneasy period during which both parties waited to see what attitude the government would adopt. Eventually it was agreed between the missions and government that no teaching against female circumcision would be given during school hours. Intimidation against teachers and parents was then at its height, and school attendances were poor. The mission, however, kept them open, staffed by teachers agreeing to the ruling on circumcision and the repudiation of the KCA.[26]

While Kenyatta was still in England, KCA representatives appealed to the government to intervene and open government schools in these areas on their behalf. For a moment the Director of Education hesitated. By now the CMS had fallen into line with the Scottish Church, and a head-on collision between all the Protestant missions and government loomed. The Director refused the KCA request, and in the six months before Kenyatta returned attendance at the church schools was steadily building up again.

Shortly after arriving back in Kenya, Kenyatta approached the administration with the KCA request for the government to provide teachers. He received the same reply: they were mission schools and the missions made the appointments. So, on 22 December 1930, Kenyatta came out again to Thogoto for a final attempt to get round Arthur.[27]

He was accompanied this time by Jesse Kariuki, a small dapper man who intermittently acted for the KCA when Kenyetta was abroad. He was now stated to be their President.

Kenyatta spoke words of honey to sweeten the way to peace. It was only a question of schools he was concerned with now, he said, and had nothing to do with the church. His heart was sad at the way his people were going backwards for lack of schooling, and all because of a misunderstanding. He wanted to help the mission and his people. 'He wished to seek for a way of reconciliation by way of a compromise.' Let us have two teachers, Kenyatta suggested, one who has not taken the vow against female circumcision and one who has. The children will surely then come back.

But Arthur was not deceived. 'First of all I could not agree that school and church could be separated . . . it would be worse for them to receive education without Christianity than no education at all.' And, of course, it would be impossible to run a school with teachers looking to two, conflicting, sources of authority.

They discussed matters for nearly two hours, and when he left Kenyatta said he felt very sad. Well he might, for Arthur had now made up his mind about Kenyatta and his Association. They were not truly seeking reconciliation, but their own advantage at whatever cost to their people. There was no room here for compromise. Arthur's duty lay in protecting the African church which had remained loyal throughout the crisis and on which, he believed, hung the future destinies of the people. In Arthur's eyes Kenyatta chose to place himself outside this destiny. He was soil in which the seed of progress was smothered with the thorns of this world's ambitions. Arthur had nothing further to say to him. He drew up a detailed report for Scott, the Director of Education.

One by one he went through the points Kenyatta had earlier raised with Scott and demonstrated their falsity:

Kenyatta had said that the eight schools on his list were all practically closed. It was 'untrue', three only were closed, the remaining five had two resident teachers and over twenty scholars attending at each.

Kenyatta had said that these schools were paid for entirely by natives, with no mission funds. It was 'again not true', and the natives who helped with the building included Christians loyal to the mission. 'In every case the building was built as a *Church* and allowed to be used as a school during the week.'

Kenyatta had repeated the charge he made in front of the DC that Arthur was demanding that no child should be allowed to attend school who had not signed the oath. 'Every one knows this is a lie . . . at the central school here, there are scholars in the day school morning, afternoon, and night, who have signed and others who have not signed, the latter more than the former.'

Kenyatta had said that none of the money paid by way of government grant to the missions actually went to the teachers—it was another 'misrepresentation, so typical, of the KCA people'. Scott could have disproved it himself by simply asking his departmental accountant to produce the monthly receipts signed by all the teachers for their wages. Arthur commented acidly: 'Perhaps, however, you did not know that such receipts have been demanded for years by Government.' Kenyatta was trying to have it both ways, concluded Arthur.

'He is a man of guile, and thought he could gain credit with the Mission and at the same time keep up his end with his people . . . Since Johnstone's return, the opposition all over has stiffened and the numbers attending school have gone down. He has therefore failed, even if he has tried . . .'

Arthur's final words on the subject bear repeating. They were framed in the terms of the old civilizing mission. That remained his ideal and the basis on which he judged men and their motives.

'I believe, as I have always done, that if we as a Mission come down on this thing, and these people and the KCA win the day, then it is only a matter of time, till the Chiefs and headmen are forced to fall into line, and that means Government . . . Again I would express the opinion, and I feel I cannot too often reiterate it, that this fight is a fight for good government, and for all that is good. If these forces of evil are allowed to have their way, they will ruin the country, and the peace of the Kikuyu people, to say nothing of the Europeans.'[28]

The female circumcision controversy was a portent. Its true significance was not to be realized until twenty years later. As it turned out, school membership and church attendances in the affected areas suffered only a brief recession in the overall steady growth of the African church. But that it provided a dress rehearsal, as it were, for a later emergency will strike many a reader.

It is often said that the Kikuyu independent schools movement arose directly out of the female circumcision controversy. There is no evidence to support this. Scott, writing some years later of his personal experiences as Director of Education, could not sustain it. The controversy, he thought, was the occasion, not the cause, of interest in private education.[29] A problem exists in trying to distinguish in these early days between church and school. The missions, as Arthur pointed out to Kenyatta, made no distinction. Independent schools appeared as early as 1922 in the Fort Hall area in the form of an independent church. Then, too, the occasion, but not the cause, seems to have been the restlessness which accompanied Harry Thuku's movement. Other schools sprang up during the twenties depending, rather, on the whim of the administrative officers in charge. A few which were begun as an experiment in 1928 were closed by government a year later because of their unsatisfactory condition. Among these was a school at Githunguri, later to become Kenyatta's headquarters in the period before the Mau Mau Emergency. Towards the end of 1930 this school reopened. The chiefs at once complained that it was a centre of political disaffection. No one could control it. 'They could have any kind of secret meeting they wanted under the guise that it was a school.' It was another foretaste of later troubles.

During the thirties two types of independent school came into prominence. One, called the Kikuyu Independent Schools Association, borrowed heavily from the missions. It was as much an independent church following African pentecostal lines as an independent educational system. The second incorporated the expression *karinga* in its title and had less clear objectives. *Karinga* denoted tribal purity and seemed connected with the female circumcision controversy, the pure Kikuyu being those who stood out for the old tribal customs. Initially this organization banned all religious content for seven years. Afterwards it too succumbed to African independent church influences from elsewhere.[30] Its supporters came mostly from the region nearest to the Thogoto mission, and it was always closely connected with the KCA.

Kenyatta went along with the independent schools though he played no part in them. At the beginning of 1931 he removed his son Peter Muigai, now aged nearly 10, from the central school at Thogoto and placed him in a private school which had been in existence for six years and was backed by the KCA. Arthur spoke well of it.[31] The following year Kenyatta's brother, James Muigai, became headmaster of another independent school.

For a young man like Kenyatta, who was still in his early thirties and had experienced the freedoms of Europe, life in Kenya was frustrating. Grigg's measures were taking effect. It was impossible to hold meetings without permission—a few friends who gathered after church might be arrested for holding an unauthorized meeting.[32] The collection of funds was impeded by the laws promulgated in March 1930.[33] The CID, the settlers and the missionaries were all on the look-out for 'sedition'. Reports came to the administration that in the more distant parts of the reserve secret meetings were being held at night, with dances and sing-songs to attract the crowds, at which collections were made. At these meetings hot-heads bandied about Kenyatta's name 'as our new king'. Missionaries in the reserves said he was sounding people out for a campaign of civil disobedience.[34] Would all this get out of hand in the same manner as Harry Thuku's movement?

Yet among those nearest him Kenyatta found himself surrounded by an uneasy atmosphere. Gone were the carefree days when the Nairobi Water Board clerk bicycled out to Dagoretti for a weekend of fun. In their place he faced Kikuyu sullenness and lack of commitment. Accompanied by Jesse Kariuki, Kenyatta spent some days driving round the schools in a large car. He would stop, ask questions, take a photograph or two and move on. But everywhere he met an air of suspicion.[35]

Then came the news he was half expecting and half fearing. On 6 January 1931, when most of the Kiambu tribesmen were enjoying a large agricultural show on the sports-ground at Kabete, word got around that Harry Thuku was back.

Harry Thuku! He was the real 'King of the Kikuyu' whom the young men glorified in their forbidden *Muthirigu* song. Thuku had been in exile for almost nine years without trial or sentence. Three years he had spent at Kismayu, and then when Britain ceded Jubaland to Italy in 1925, as a reward for her joining the allies in the war, Thuku had trekked up with his gaolers through the desert to the beautiful, remote oasis of Marsabit. Here he had spent his time learning to farm and engaging in profitable trading with the local Boran tribesmen. When told he was to be released, he had taken several days to pack up all his belongings.

Kenyatta waited twenty-four hours after getting the news that Thuku was home and then he too paid his respects. During the following days he and Jesse Kariuki took him out in a taxi in the evenings to see how Nairobi and the surrounding area had changed in his absence. Their prestige was nothing beside his. Though he had to keep quiet for a while, Thuku was universally recognized as the returning hero. He belonged to one of the most influential families of Kikuyuland. Christian chiefs and the Kambui church leaders were glad to be seen in his company. Thuku's return brought back to the KCA their real leader. Kenyatta's own position was less certain.

Before leaving London, Kenyatta had discussed with Ross the setting up of the joint select committee of Parliament announced in Passfield's white paper of 1930. Kenyatta had written to the Colonial Office urging that native evidence should be heard. The committee began work in December 1930 and the following March it was announced that in addition to members of other races, official delegations of three natives would go to London from each of the East African territories under Colonial Office rule: Uganda, Kenya and Tanganyika. The names of the Kenya native delegation were announced: one was the President of the Kavirondo Taxpayers Welfare Association, another was a Kamba headman from Machakos, and for the Kikuyu, Chief Koinange. Koinange was the most widely respected Kikuyu leader and was often described as Kinyanjui's successor as Paramount Chief (though the Kikuyu had no such traditional title) .

But the KCA objected. The Kikuyu Association, now renamed the

Kikuyu Loyal Patriots to avoid confusion with the KCA, did not have the latter's widely-based appeal. The days were past when at a *baraza* the chiefs could dominate the proceedings and threaten to throw a little man like Harry Thuku over the Chania Falls. Though the KCA lacked coordination, and was little more than a loose confederation of young men with some education working in Nairobi and tribal elements disturbed by contact with civilization, it was a new and growing force. They wanted one of their own men attached to the official Kenya delegation.

A new burst of telegrams sped between Nairobi and London, and the usual circle of KCA sympathizers was alerted, including Ross. Kenyatta cabled the Anti-Slavery and Aborigine Protection Society to try and get funds for a ticket. Jesse Kariuki for the KCA requested permission for Harry Thuku to give evidence. Shiels at the Colonial Office would have welcomed this and regretted that he was not nominated. But that would have been, he minuted, "too much to expect from the Kenya Government'. 'Docile "Chiefs" ', he went on, 'will tend to emphasise the lack of capacity of the African.'[36] The colonial government, however, refused to allow Thuku to leave Kenya so soon after his release and deprecated the idea that Koinange was an inadequate spokesman for the Kikuyu. They took the line that if the KCA felt called on to give evidence they should submit it first in writing. If they sent a delegate uninvited to London he must pay for himself.

But the KCA were not content with one delegate only. Perhaps some members were suspicious of Kenyatta and remembered how he had previously disappeared for several months from London.

Their second choice fell on a man called Parmenas Githendu Mockerie, a school teacher from Kahuhia who belonged to Gideon Mugo's group. At the beginning of 1931 he was in Uganda attending a teachers' refresher course at Makerere College when he received a cable from KCA headquarters asking him to represent them in London. Of course the missionaries tried to dissuade Mockerie from quitting his career, just as they had tried to dissuade Kenyatta two years before. But the offer of a free trip to England, even though it might be on a political goose errand, was a tempting prospect for any young African. Mockerie told the missionaries that the KCA were willing to finance him for a year's studies in London, which illustrated the lack of confidence which this generation of Kikuyu felt in the opportunities open to them in their own country.[37]

Meanwhile Kenyatta was busy collecting material for his own return to London. He was in touch with Ross and sent him a draft memorandum for presenting to the select committee. On 18 April Ross cabled back his approval. By now the KCA had collected £300 ('by very doubtful means' according to the missionaries) and their intention of sending two delegates to London was known to the Colonial Office. Predictably it was regarded by the permanent officials as 'a scandalous waste of money . . . but they cannot be stopped from coming to England as individuals if they wish and can pay their way.' Nairobi pressed that they should not be invited to appear before the select committee as this would damage the prestige of the Kenya government. 'If they are admitted they will not of course say anything that is the slightest importance to anyone.'[38]

On 28 April a large crowd of Kikuyu well-wishers came to see Kenyatta and Mockerie off at Nairobi station. In London the very same day Koinange and his fellow Kenya Africans appeared before the Parliamentary committee. It made the journey of the two KCA men 'a fiasco' in the eyes of European observers.[39] But Kenyatta and Mockerie each had his own motives for wanting to leave Kenya at this time and there was always the possibility that the committee would still call them. On 2 May 1931, Kenyatta boarded the *Mazzini*, an Italian liner bound for Genoa.

Behind him an era was coming to an end. Delamere was ailing and unable to go to London himself to put the settler point of view to the select committee. His death in November the same year removed one of the most colourful figures of the pioneering period, the man who had made the settler life possible. The circumcision controversy brought to an abrupt close the paternalistic phase of missionary activity; henceforward the emphasis would be on the growth of native churches. The high noon of imperialism, when Churchill and Amery dominated the cabinet, and Grigg sought to extend white dominion over all of East Africa, was over.

Behind him, also, Kenyatta was leaving his youth, the companions of his twenties, and his Kikuyu family. But he did not abandon them in the European sense, for African society made provision for these separations which in the past arose frequently through deaths in intertribal fighting or natural mishaps. A wife had her place in the tribal economy and Grace Wahu and his two children "belonged" to the wider family of his clan who could be expected to see to their material needs. Though hardship might occur, and the separation be long, neither his wife nor his children could feel he had utterly deserted them. Nor would they do so later when he took other wives and had other children. They remained in spiritual contact with him and this, too, belonged to the psychology of Africa. In serving the destiny of his people Kenyatta was also keeping faith with that extended family of his own which embraced his dead ancestors, their living representatives, and members as yet unborn. This was the mission to which he dedicated himself.

On board the *Mazzini* the voices of Italian-speaking Africans were new to the Kenya natives, but at the calls the boat made on its voyage Kenyatta felt at home again with the Arabs and Somalis and Adenis, the Egyptians and Maltese and the freemasonry of the sea. The shadows of colonial Africa lifted, and ahead the prospects, though indistinct, brightened: England, Europe and Moscow, perhaps even America. Ahead were his negro contacts and the freedoms of the West. Ahead lay new experiences, new ideas, new faces and the possibility of another life altogether. He was not to see Kenya again for over fifteen years.

CHAPTER 12

Return to London

The *Mazzini* docked at Genoa on 20 May and Kenyatta and Mockerie took the boat train to Paris where they stopped a day to watch a French colonial exhibition. To their astonishment they learned that African representatives had seats in the French National Assembly. There was nothing like that at Westminster. From Paris Kenyatta sent Ross a telegram telling him the time of the train's arrival in London and on the cold, wet afternoon of 22 May they pulled into Victoria Station. Ross was on the platform to welcome them. Handley Hooper was also there to greet his old Kahuhia protégé.

Kenyatta arrived in London just a week after the official native witnesses to the joint select committee had left to return to East Africa. Koinange and his colleagues had spent a little over a fortnight in London at the government's expense. There had been some problem over accommodation as it was felt that normal guest-houses would be unsuitable. White women might not like to eat in the same rooms or sleep under the same roofs as a Kikuyu chief and his fellows! But an international hostel was found in Sydenham which was run by a Mrs Mellor, 'a very genteel and sensible Manageress'.[1]

The attention paid to the official delegation contrasted starkly with that accorded to Kenyatta and his rival mission. The official witnesses were given a guinea a day expenses and the Colonial Office chaperoned them throughout their time in England. They were taken to see the Changing of the Guard, the Mint and the Tower of London; they visited hospitals, museums and factories; they had excursions to Portsmouth and Aldershot and were treated to a bombing display at Farnborough; one day was spent at Oxford and they attended the Cup Final at Wembley. But the high spot came at Windsor when they caught sight of the King in his car. The driver came right over to their side of the road so that they could all bow to the ground before that august ruler, King George, whose name meant everything in Kenya. 'They will count it', they wrote in appreciation, 'as the culminating moment of their lives that they should have been allowed to see him as he left Windsor. They are overwhelmed with his condescension in noticing their presence.'[2]

Kenyatta might have hesitated to join in such an effusion of loyalty had he been a member of the official party, but no one was left in doubt as to Koinange's loyalty also towards his own people. The chief was a model of courtesy and firmness. He 'charmed everyone' on the committee and detailed the grievances from which he knew, as well as anyone, the Kikuyu suffered.

Kenyatta hoped he might also be invited to give evidence and the committee had a long discussion among themselves over whether they should hear him. They decided against it, but two members pressed that at least his memorandum should be included in the published Appendix to their report. One of these was C. R. Buxton, the Labour Party's expert on colonial affairs. He was a friend of the Rosses and belonged to the Hampstead set. Like Ross he took an interest in every African who came to London and was keen to promote understanding of native problems among the rank and file of the Labour Party, who generally showed little concern in such matters. Buxton used to meet Kenyatta at Belsize Park underground station for a walk over Hampstead Heath before tea. In pressing strongly for the inclusion of Kenyatta's memorandum, Buxton argued that:

'He represents a large body of Africans who are troublesome, because they are *vocal;* but his views are in reality most moderate. It will cause much *more* trouble in the long run if they are not only refused a hearing, but refused publicly for their rather pathetic observations!'[3]

The committee decided otherwise and Kenyatta's memorandum was left out.

Kenyatta lost no time in picking up his old contacts. The weeks were crowded with ILP summer schools, Fabian gatherings and special meetings of those with African interests. Within a month of his arrival he was on his travels again. Towards the end of June the Save the Children Fund held an international conference on African children at Geneva. Handley Hooper's wife, Cicely, and Isabel Ross were members of the British delegation. The Duchess of Atholl was there and spoke about female circumcision. Suddenly, Kenyatta turned up and intervened in one of the sessions to refute what the

Duchess had said about Kikuyu customs. He offered the ladies no explanation as to why, or how, he had come to Geneva.[4]

Perhaps Roden Buxton brought him, but Kenyatta evidently had other business as well. In October the Foreign Office received a mysterious enquiry from the Belgian Embassy in London: 'The Belgian Government have received information that a negro named Johnstone Kenyatta who is a native of East Africa . . . and is known to be a dangerous communist, is at present in London.' Who was this Kenyatta, asked the Belgians, and what was this 'negro society' known as the Kikuyu Central Association? 'It is understood that in no case will the Belgian Government allow Kenyatta to enter Belgium,' the Foreign Office note concluded.

There was a good deal by now on the Colonial Office file about Kenyatta, but nothing to arouse suspicions. Accordingly, the Foreign Office was told that:

'He seems to be a harmless individual if left alone, but is apparently susceptible to outside influences, some of which I am afraid have not been good. The view taken here hitherto has been that the wisest course is for him to be handled sympathetically by the Government of Kenya with the object of guiding him and his Association on the right lines.'[5]

The autumn of 1931 was a turning point in the destiny of the British people—as indeed of Europe—in the twentieth century. Throughout the year an air of unreality hung over the political scene as Philip Snowden, Labour's Chancellor of the Exchequer, guided the economy on to the reefs of orthodox budgetary policy. Unemployment was over the two million mark.

On 30 July Parliament rose and ministers dispersed for the holidays. On 11 August the crisis broke. Ramsay MacDonald was hurriedly recalled to London to be told by the bankers that there was a run on the pound. Though agreed on the orthodox remedy of balancing the budget, which meant cuts in unemployment benefits, the Labour cabinet were divided on who should carry out this policy. On 24 August MacDonald drove to Buckingham Palace to hand in his resignation as Labour Prime Minister and drove away again as Prime Minister of a National Government, to be repudiated by the Labour Party who charged him with premeditated treachery to the Labour movement.

On 7 October Parliament was dissolved. Kenyatta was back in England for a second General Election, marked this time by a vicious split in Labour's ranks. The result was a personal triumph for Mac-Donald and the annihilation of his party. On 27 October the Conservatives headed the poll with a massive hold of 473 seats; Labour retained only 52. Meanwhile, on 21 September Britain came off the Gold Standard. A whole epoch was at an end.

Drummond Shiels lost his seat in the election and the possibility of the Labour intellectuals being able to give British colonial policy a radically new direction disappeared. In MacDonald's National Government a Conservative, Cunliffe-Lister, took over as Colonial Secretary, and in Whitehall the civil servants breathed more easily.

With illness, holidays, and a trip to the United States which kept him away for all of September and October, Ross was out of things throughout that fateful autumn. He saw Kenyatta and Mockerie only briefly for tea on a day late in August and left them in the hands of his Hampstead friends. Kenyatta and Mockerie had little in common, except a shortage of funds. Kenyatta knew how to look after himself but Mockerie's future gave Handley Hooper much anxiety. He warned his CMS colleagues in Kenya of the danger that the African's situation in London would 'throw him to the arms of a very advanced socialist group which is contemptuous of Christian Missions.'

After a good deal of correspondence with Kenya, Hooper was able to arrange for Mockerie to take a year's course at the Fircroft Working Men's College in Birmingham, one of the Selly Oak group of colleges. There were good Christians there, and Hooper trusted that Mockerie would be out of range of the 'pernicious influences' he feared would get at him if he stayed in London, and which, in his view, had already got at Kenyatta.[6]

The problem of further education was one which gnawed at the heart of the East Africans. They found themselves at a disadvantage in the company of their black brothers from the west coast of Africa and constantly at the mercy of white prejudice, which derided their efforts at self-advancement. Kenyatta also desperately wanted to increase his intellectual standing. Education! That was the bait which first tempted him into Thogoto. 'Get yourself into a college' Charles Stokes had advised him. But where? And how?

As Christmas 1931 approached, Ross felt Kenyatta should return to Kenya. The select committee published its report on 3 November. It recommended that a further commission should investigate fully the whole question of native land rights in Kenya. This was just what the Kikuyu had been agitating for for years. Ross considered Kenyatta's duty was to return at once to Nairobi to prepare his tribe's case.

But Buxton had now taken Kenyatta under his wing and offered to finance him for a few months at the Quaker College of Woodbrooke, also at Selly Oak, Birmingham. In London Ross found that Kenyatta's contributions to drawing-room discussions were ineffective; at least at Woodbrooke he could improve his English.

So Kenyatta travelled up to Birmingham at the end of November and remained there until Easter the following year, 1932. He found himself living in a large country mansion set in spacious grounds to which came men and women from all over the world. Quakers living nearby took him into their house for Christmas, and the ladies at the college made a fuss of him. For the first time in Britain Kenyatta felt relaxed and at peace with himself. He was free to come and go as he pleased, to read the papers and spend what time he liked in the library. He was not obliged to follow the regular courses but could work in his own way on another memorandum to the new commission. Members of the staff helped him with daily English lessons.[7]

The fellowship of Woodbrooke made a great impression on Kenyatta. It was a life of pullovers and slacks, of wide-ranging discussions on topical affairs and long walks in the country. Everyone was treated as an equal. The five years at Thogoto, the vows made before the Scottish missionaries and his Kikuyu church elders, the prayers offered in the past on his behalf, all these began to have meaning. Woodbrooke brought spiritual rewards he had not found in Kenya. Before leaving, he wrote an unusual testimonial in the College Record Book:

'It is the spirit [of Woodbrooke] which forces men and women to realise their mutual responsibility in life—it teaches them to think of others and not to take thought alone for their own comfort, pleasure and salvation. This spirit I hold must grow and pervade all classes of the community irrespective of rank and station, colour or race. It is a spirit which will raise men by its unselfishness; will redeem them by its personal appeal, will broaden their views so that where now they are but creed and dogma, they will see Truth. It will indeed teach that we, the children of humanity, being brothers and sisters must serve one another in the love of all mankind, and the benefit of all life and to the advancement and ultimate perfection of those who are yet to come. Surely the spirit of Woodbrooke teaches us patience in trial, resignation in affliction, humility in success and virtue in whatever position in life it has pleased God to place us. Above all it is the spirit of true Fellowship.'

On 23 March, 1932, the Woodbrooke College broke up for Easter and Kenyatta returned to London to spend the next week as guest of the Rosses. They were typical days in the life of a member of the Hampstead set, with visitors from Africa home for tea and visits out to left-wing intellectuals, long walks over the Heath and drafting Kenyatta's letters to the papers.

Isabel Ross was an independent-minded woman and staunch feminist with many activities of her own. Kenyatta enjoyed the company of such white women, perhaps more than he did that of their husbands, and he had a great attraction towards them. Where Ross was concerned with Kenyatta's political development, Isabel took more of an interest in his personal life and his views about his tribe. Above all it was Isabel's Quaker beliefs which predominated in the Ross household.

Both the Rosses were pacifists, and their convictions made a strong impression on a man who was otherwise fond of boasting of his entry into the warrior grade of Kikuyu society. Another influence in the same direction came from Gandhi, whom Winston Churchill had recently dismissed as 'a seditious Middle Temple lawyer, now posing as a half-naked fakir'. Kenyatta met the Indian leader in November 1931, and Gandhi then inscribed Kenyatta's diary with the words: 'Truth and non-violence can deliver any nation from bondage.' Kenyatta was to give much thought to reconciling that idea with African tradition.[8]

Quaker pacifism, Quaker concern for freedom and for the weaker members of the human race, Quaker emphasis on practical service as 'mission'—no doubt these were subjects of many a discussion over tea at Ross's house and during the long walks over Hampstead Heath. That Easter Sunday, Kenyatta accompanied the Rosses to a Quaker Meeting. It was a wet and blustery day and in the afternoon they went over for tea with Roden Buxton's wife to find her near to tears over the news of floods in China resulting in the deaths of thousands of families. It was a reminder of the violence and distress which seemed in those years to be gathering from all quarters of the world—in Manchuria, in India, and, looming over all, in Germany.

When Kenyatta left at the end of the week to stay with other friends of the Rosses in Bloomsbury, anxiety grew in Ross's mind about Kenyatta's intentions. He had no permanent accommodation and no regular means of support. He added little to the numerous discussions organized by groups like the Union for Democratic Control, except a certain curiosity value. His letters to the papers contributed nothing that was new, brought in no revenue and even, Ross might have thought, tended to encroach on Ross's own special province. Where, Ross asked himself, was all this taking Kenyatta?

Kenyatta had already submitted to the Colonial Office the long memorandum about land and other matters which he had drawn up while he was at Woodbrooke. The day Kenyatta returned to London from Birmingham, 23 March, Ross had taken him to hear an important debate in the House of Lords. Lord Olivier, spokesman for the old Ross/Leys lobby, mentioned Kenyatta's memorandum in the course of a speech criticizing the government's land policy in Kenya. In reply, the government announced the setting up of the land commission recommended by the joint select committee. Its chairman was to be Sir Morris Carter, a man with Rhodesian experience, and he was due to leave for Kenya at the beginning of June.

By the end of May, Ross concluded that Kenyatta was loitering in England when he ought to be back in Nairobi helping his people prepare for the land commission's arrival. Furthermore, he began to have serious doubts about the authenticity of information Kenyatta purported to receive from his Association. In particular he questioned Kenyatta's charges that in the Maragwa area of Fort Hall district land had recently been taken from its African owners, and their huts burned down in order to evict them. Kenyatta forwarded these charges to the Colonial Office and repeated them in a letter to the *Manchester Guardian* which appeared on 19 April. Ross asked Kenyatta to confirm his sources and when this was not forthcoming he checked on them himself through three of his own contacts in Kenya. Their replies satisfied him that Kenyatta had made 'a sensational mis-statement of fact'. It worried Ross that the credibility of the KCA was being destroyed (and, no doubt, that he was being taken for a ride himself) by Kenyatta's blunders.[9] He wrote to him accordingly in his forthright manner:

'It is possible that some trouble with Kikuyu and even some hut burnings may have occurred *years ago* . . . and your Committee lump all these episodes together, believing that they are thus making

a really grave charge against the Government. This is rubbish. If you
can't teach them to be truthful and extremely and entirely accurate
you had better close down and disband the K.C.A. Otherwise you will
all end up in jail as certain as your name is Kenyatta.'

Whatever the KCA were doing sounded 'very fishy' to Ross. Secret
meetings and collections of money were unnecessary if their evidence
to the new commission was well and truthfully prepared:

'So why are they bleeding the peasants of money for their own personal pleasure? If so, shut down the K.C.A. sharp, or else you'll be in
court on a charge of "receiver of stolen goods" or something of that
sort. You are a salaried servant of the K.C.A. and if they as good as
steal money from ignorant Kikuyu and you receive part of it, they
(the Police or Govt.) will get you into jail certain; and you must not
complain, because you ought to be back in your office insisting on
honest behaviour by your colleagues . . .

'You are positively doing nothing now in London to help the cause
of the Africans for this land business. You are just having a pleasant
holiday, and you surely must know that the proper place for you at
present is in your office at Nairobi working hard on preparing evidence for Sir Wm. Morris Carter to receive. Not only are you not
helping but you are hindering, and, as has been explained to you,
your last letter to the "Manchester Guardian" was most unwise and in
all probability spoilt a very promising move that other people were
making and which you should not have interfered with, without asking permission first.'[10]

Largely due to Ross's prompting, Carter delayed his departure by a
month in order to hear the evidence of interested parties in London
first. It meant that Kenyatta could now also give evidence in London.
Ross spent the evening before his appearance going over the ground
with him.[11]

Sir Morris Carter was a man whose experience in Rhodesia led him
to believe in the value of separation between the white and black
races, and not the inter-penetration for which Eliot aimed when opening up Kenya for white settlement. The other members of his commission were a retired Kenya administrator and a landowner from the
Machakos district, both of whom were in Kenya. They insisted that a

verbatim record should be taken of any evidence given to Carter in London.

Carter had not read Kenyatta's memorandum nor studied his map. Had he done so he might have challenged Kenyatta on his claim that before the settlers arrived Kikuyu territory stretched well out along the Athi River, beyond the forest boundary, beyond even the far environs of Nairobi. They were now prosperous European farms and no Kikuyu could have settled there in pre-colonial days when Masai warriors ruled the plains. Had Kenyatta persuaded himself that his claim was true, or was this another case of an obvious 'brick' which Ross had not spotted?

They met on 16 June. Kenyatta spoke about his own background and of his childhood days when the Kikuyu reached the forest boundary and there encountered the first white man.

Chairman Where were you born?

Kenyatta I was born in Ng'enda, near Thiririka, just north of the Theta River. Then later we moved to where my grandfather lived, about a mile and a half north of Dagoretti. I was just a small boy, and we used to take our sheep and goats to the Gitiba. I did not know about the land question or anything of the kind then, but I do remember going with other bigger boys and men with our goats to these Gitiba salt-licks.

Chairman Do you say there was no station at Dagoretti then?

Kenyatta No. I did not see a station.

Chairman There must have been, because Lord Lugard bought it about 1890.

Kenyatta I was a young boy, and I do not know whether there was a *boma* there, but I did not see it myself.

Chairman Did you see no European when you were a boy?

Kenyatta No. The first European I saw was one who nearly killed my father. My father was appointed a chief or sub-chief—I do not quite know which—and he returned from this place near Dagoretti to Ng'enda, and became a chief, and the first European I saw was a European who quarreled with my father. The European became very angry, and he tried to shoot my father.

Chairman Was he a settler?

Kenyatta He was a settler.

Chairman That was before you went to school?

Kenyatta   Yes.
Chairman   At that time were you old enough to marry?
Kenyatta   No.
Chairman   Would you be 10 or 12?
Kenyatta   I should say I was about 10 or 12.
Chairman   You would be 10 or 12 when you left this place near Dagoretti?
Kenyatta   Yes.
Chairman   Is there anything else you can speak of from your own personal knowledge on the point as to whether the place belonged to the Agikuyu and has been taken away?
Kenyatta   I can give you the case of my own people's land. It is near No. 5070, which is marked on the Nairobi map, Sheet South A–37/G.H. This land at Magomano (which means 'where the rivers meet') used to belong to my own family, and in the early days, before I had seen any European, our cattle used to be there. My people used to cultivate sugar-cane and *nduma*. They used to have their garden there for *nduma* and sugar-cane. It is now a European coffee farm.
Chairman   To whom does it belong now?
Kenyatta   I do not know.
Chairman   That was where you lived?
Kenyatta   Yes.
Chairman   You saw the sugar-cane and the *nduma* growing there which had been planted by your family?
Kenyatta   Yes. Afterwards, when I went to school, I went home again to visit my family. I passed that place, and I noticed that it was all a European farm. A few years ago, the White Sisters claimed the ownership of that land at Mangu, and people were told to go away and that the land had been bought many years ago by the White Sisters. That was at Mangu. You will find it explained in my memorandum. There is the Razario Mundia. That was not taken long ago. The people were living there until recently, and they were then told to go away. They had been there for many generations, and the White Sisters said the land belonged to them. You will see the people coming before you in Kenya, and explaining about it.[12]

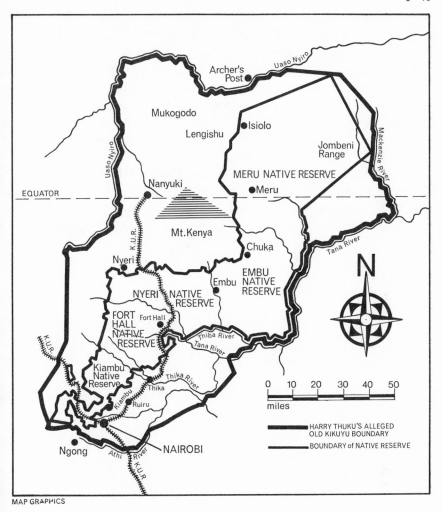

III Extent of KCA land claim submitted to Carter Land Commission
Based on map lent by courtesy of Her Majesty's Stationery Office

The following day Mockerie was called, and on 20 June Ross gave his evidence. In a written memorandum he corrected one point in what Kenyatta had said. The Dagoretti *boma* referred to was the new government building put up by Indian contractors in 1902–3. Ross was followed two days later by Arthur who was home this year on furlough. In Kenya Ross had been a good friend of the Thogoto mission and usually worshipped there; now Arthur came to tea at Hampstead and upbraided Ross for his support of the KCA in the female circumcision controversy. 'Bitterly resentful', Ross described him in his diary. But there was no indication that Arthur met Kenyatta or even tried to get in touch with him. Kenyatta's name had been struck off the Communion roll at Thogoto in October 1931 for lack of attendance. Arthur had nothing further to say to him.[13]

Morris Carter then sailed for Kenya and Ross continued to press Kenyatta to return also. On 11 August, while he was on holiday with the family, Ross 'got a letter from K with no address, posted at Dover, saying that he had left 95 Cambridge Street and would write to us later when he had "settled down again" '. A further communication arrived giving his address as the Westfalia Hotel in Berlin, to which Ross immediately sent a registered letter. On 22 August he received a final letter from Hamburg. Then there was silence.

CHAPTER 13

Moscow

On his first visit to London in March 1929 Kenyatta had made any number of contacts with the different left-wing organizations which proliferated in Europe by the end of the twenties—Fabians, Trotskyists, Marxists, members of the ILP, of the League Against Imperialism, of the British Labour Party, Trade Unionists of all descriptions, Socialists of the Second, or Amsterdam, International and Communists of the Third. In those first few months in England he must have been bewildered by the ideological subtleties which distinguished the groups from each other, as, one suspects, were their own propagandists.

To someone coming fresh to the European scene only one thing seemed really important. In the Russian Revolution of 1917 the mighty had been put down from their seat and the humble and meek apparently exalted. For Kenyatta as for all oppressed people in the world the Red Star now shone beckoning in the east.

By 1928 Moscow began to see in the races under colonial rule the possibility of fresh territory for ideological conquest, and at a meeting in March 1928 of the Red International of Labour Unions, RILU, held in Moscow, the call went out to mobilize negro workers behind the Soviet banner. This was the cue for the entry on to the international stage of a certain George Padmore.

Padmore was a West Indian, born in 1903 in Trinidad, the son of a local schoolmaster, James Nurse, whose own father had been born a slave on the nearby island of Barbados. Padmore was christened Malcolm Ivan Meredith Nurse and it was as Malcolm Nurse that he spent his schooldays in Trinidad, graduating without distinction from a Roman Catholic college to become a reporter on a local Trinidad newspaper. He married a local girl in 1924, his best man being a certain Errol Padmore, and at the end of that year left for America for further studies at Fisk University in Nashville, Tennessee. Here he switched from medicine to law and began to interest himself in politics. He soon made a name for himself as a speaker on the campus and came into contact with other radical negro intellectuals, among them the Nigerian Benjamin Azikiwe. From Fisk he moved to New York and enrolled at the Law School of Howard University, an institution which contained an unusually large contingent of students from British dependencies. Here he joined the Communist Party and adopted the cover name of George Padmore. His intelligence and fluency, both as speaker and writer, brought him rapid advancement in negro communist circles, just at the time when Moscow was reaching out for such men.

In 1929, using false passports and his new cover name, Padmore came to Europe with an American negro communist, J. W. Ford, to attend the second congress of the League Against Imperialism. But the League Against Imperialism turned out to be an unsatisfactory instrument for the Comintern's probing of colonial discontents. It contained many non-communists, like Fenner Brockway of the British Independent Labour Party, and it lacked representatives of the oppressed colonial peoples.

Padmore and Ford were instructed to find them and the Comintern set up another front for this purpose in the form of an International Trade Union Committee of Negro Workers, a black arm, as it were, of the Red International of Labour Unions. Padmore searched for likely candidates among the African and West Indian students in London, and the coloured dockers at British ports. Kenyatta was just the sort of person he was looking for.[1]

Of Kenyatta's first trip to Moscow in the autumn of 1929 nothing further is known apart from what he himself told Ross and Barlow. It may have been Padmore himself who took him to Russia—his 'American negro friend' who was 'a commercial traveller of sorts'—or one of Padmore's fellow communists making a report to Comintern headquarters. America did not recognize Soviet Russia at this time and any non-American citizen visiting Moscow automatically risked losing his re-entry permit into the United States. Clearly there was more to Kenyatta's trip than a straightforward sightseeing tour.

In July 1930 the International Trade Union Committee of Negro Workers held its first conference in Hamburg.[2] They originally planned to foregather in Berlin, but Hamburg appealed more to Ford and Padmore. It was the stronghold of Ernst Thaelmann, the leader of the German Communist Party, and, being a great international port, it was a useful centre for disseminating propaganda and for clandestine movement in and out of Europe. Padmore set up his headquarters at 8 Rothesoodstrasse, in the seamy waterfront district, under cover of a seamen's club.[3]

The report of the conference showed Johnstone Kenyatta's name on the list of the Provisional Executive Committee, representing the 'Central Association of Kenya, East Africa.'[4] Ford opened the conference with a long speech which gave a résumé of the negro workers' movement and in the course of which he attacked the bourgeois connections of other racial organizations, such as Garveyism in America and the West African Students' Union in England. They were 'negro reformist fakers' and represented 'the most dangerous obstacle to the development of the struggle of the negro workers'. Missionaries were dismissed as 'dope peddlars', and no reliance was to be placed on legislative reform. The ILP was condemned in equally strong terms.

No doubt it was his interest in the conference that led Kenyatta to prevaricate so over his movements with Cook and Ross. The mysterious stranger who arranged his flight to European capitals was probably a communist agent.

On his return to Britain in May 1931, Kenyatta was 'interviewed' for *East Africa,* the fortnightly organ of the Kenya settlers. This was almost certainly Ross's doing. Ross was incensed by the slanders, as he believed them to be, which were propagated by Joelson, the *East Africa*'s editor, concerning Kenyatta's private life, and he now saw to it that the journal made amends. Kenyatta too was anxious to appear moderate, and though he repeated the KCA charges against the Church of Scotland, to which Arthur had already given the lie, he was conciliatory towards the settlers. No doubt prompted by Ross, Kenyatta was at pains to remove the 'bolshevik' label attached to him during his previous time in England.

'His visit to Moscow last year had been purely for sight seeing purposes, and neither then nor at any time subsequently had he had any communication, direct or indirect, with any Bolshevik or Communist organisation. He admitted that communication had been addressed and continued to be addressed to his Nairobi box office by correspondents in Moscow, who, however, could only have taken his name and address from letters he had contributed to the Press; he did not know them, and had never had any communication with them.'[5]

Kenyatta had already repudiated the violent overtones given to his articles in the *Daily Worker* in January 1930. Now he again denied having any involvement with communists. That he succeeded in convincing Ross, Shiels and others of his detachment is proof of his consummate ability to keep his true purposes and opinions to himself. The very same month as the article appeared in *East Africa,* Kenyatta was in Geneva, apparently for the *Save the Children Fund* conference. It could hardly have been coincidence that with him that week in Geneva were Ford and several other footloose negroes. Ford intervened in one of the *Save the Children Fund* sessions, and Kenyatta was observed by Mrs Hooper to be consorting with a negro whom she did not know and who made a point of being rude to her.

Padmore had by now entered fully into the work of a professional Comintern agent. From his base in Hamburg he moved about Europe, attending to business in Moscow, Vienna, Berlin and Paris, and even, it is said, making secret visits to the west coast of Africa. In Hamburg he edited the *Negro Worker,* the periodical of the International Trade Union Committee of Negro Workers.[6] He ranked high in the confidence of the Comintern, and was entrusted with funds to enroll agents from the colonial races for Moscow's long-term plans. By the summer of 1932 Kenyatta was again being urged by Ross to return to Kenya and was running out of sympathy and money. His answer was to join Padmore in Germany where the shadows of Weimar decadence were lengthening. A staggering total of six million workers were unemployed, and the struggle between Nazi and communist thugs had moved to the streets.

The atmosphere of dissolution well suited George Padmore with his false passports and underground contacts. Throughout Europe negroes enjoyed an exotic appeal. London witnessed a craze for New Orleans jazz, for the music of Louis Armstrong, for Al Jolson and the new sound movies, for the magnificent voice and physique of Paul Robeson. In Paris Nancy Cunard, daughter of the shipping millionaire, held court with her negro lover, the American pianist Henry Crowder, to a strange mixture of professional revolutionaries and dabblers in surrealism. She was a passionate advocate of all black causes and a useful source of funds. Padmore became her close associate. But it was Berlin which most attracted the intellectual dilettantes of the West and where negro entertainers, like Josephine Baker, were most in demand. Nightly her ebony limbs girated across the footlights to saxophone, trumpet and trombone. While elsewhere

Kenyatta the water meter reader (with bicycle) and friends

Kenyatta seated, right, with Kangethe, centre, and Jesse Kariuki, left

Kenyatta with Kessie in Russell Square

Kenyatta photographed by Mc-Gregor Ross

C. F. Andrews (with beard), Isabel Ross and McGregor Ross in their garden in Hampstead

Kenyatta at Manchester, October 1945

Scene from *Sanders of the River* with Leslie Banks as Commissioner Sanders

Edna Kenyatta with their baby Peter Magana

Kenyatta holding Peter Magana

Kenyatta speaking at mass rally, Kiambu, August 1952. Beside him on
platform is Waruhiu

Sir Evelyn Baring

Kenyatta with his third wife (left) and their daughter. Centre and right, members of the Kenya Women's League at Githunguri

The settlers march on Government House, Nairobi, January 1963

The shadow of the Emergency: Camp for Mau Mau detainees

Kenyatta at Lokitaung shortly before his move to Lodwar

Kenyatta at Kapenguria

in brothels, strip clubs and cabarets, black bodies reflected the exotic glare of Weimar decadence.

Kenyatta followed Padmore into this cosmopolitan jungle. Only a few months remained in which he could enjoy it.

On 21 February 1933, a telegram reached the Foreign Office in London from the British Consul-General in Hamburg. It reported that the German police were deporting one 'Malcolm Ivan Nurse, native of Trinidad . . . Steps are being taken to safeguard his trunk which contains communistic correspondence.' A letter followed which gave a few more details, including names and addresses copied from the deportee's notebook, and a copy of the *Negro Worker* for January 1933.[7]

Padmore, alias Malcolm Nurse, was fortunate in being in possession of his British passport. In the past sympathizers among the Hamburg police had tipped him off when a raid was being planned on his premises along the waterfront. But Hitler's arrival in power at the end of January 1933 brought an end to this accommodation with the authorities. Padmore was lucky not to find himself in a concentration camp. Other refugees found their way to Paris, Vienna and Copenhagen. From Britain Padmore had no difficulty picking up his contacts. The *Negro Worker* resumed publication in the Danish capital.

Kenyatta escaped the Nazi purge. Some time before the blow fell in Germany, Padmore had taken him to Moscow and installed him in a special institute for members of the colonial races. Whether he actually joined the Communist Party is in dispute. CID reports assumed that he had.[8] Fenner Brockway and ILP friends later denied it. But one thing is certain, in Moscow Kenyatta was being trained as a professional revolutionary.

Moscow in the winter of 1932–3 was a different city from the one Kenyatta had visited briefly three years before. In 1929 an air of expectancy still hung over Russia and Kenyatta may well have looked around with the eyes of a tourist. No doubt he paid his respects to Lenin's corpse lying embalmed in its glass case in the heavy stone mausoleum by the Kremlin's walls. It was guarded by soldiers with fixed bayonets and the face always looked in need of attention—an unwelcome sight to a Kikuyu. Kenyatta's guide would have taken him to the Pushkin memorial to look up at the flared nostrils of the Russian poet whose great-grandfather was a negro slave at the court of Peter the Great. They would have done the rounds of the Opera and the Circus, proletarian culture one evening. Chekhov or the ballet the next. Kenyatta would have stood in Red Square and seen for the first time the huge red flag hanging over the Kremlin, a lazy flame of revolution curling over the onion domes of former palaces and cathedrals. In 1929 Kenyatta might have seen in Soviet Russia an alternative world system to the British Empire.

But when he returned in the winter of 1932 the icy winds of Stalin's policy of collectivization of the farms were blowing in across the Moscow River. By Christmas 1932, when the policy was in full operation, famine and terror stalked through the Russian countryside cutting down in their thousands the old and the young, the weak and the sick, all who stood in the way of the dictatorship of the proletariat, that grim myth in whose name Stalin ruled. According to recent estimates, up to six million peasants are believed to have died of starvation, and a further ten million small farmers, kulaks, to have been liquidated.

The full horror of those winter months can never be fully known to outsiders. Mothers would sooner kill their own children than watch over their sufferings; fathers disappeared and were never seen again. Throughout the Russian countryside whole villages were emptied, mile upon mile left deserted. Weeping survivors might occasionally be seen pleading on their knees in the snow for bread. Along the railway small groups would gather in the hope of catching scraps thrown out from carriage windows by Western travellers. Men and women fought over garbage like wild cats. It was an abyss of misery which destroyed the little that had been gained by the revolution of October 1917. Yet few of the journalists sent from the West saw through the propaganda put about by the Comintern agencies and repeated by their Intourist guides. Even fewer wanted to see for themselves what was actually going on. Those who did were marked for life, and for them the Russian experience was a turning point, the end of one kind of search and the beginning of self-discovery.

Malcolm Muggeridge was there at exactly the same time as Kenyatta. He captured the scene brilliantly in his book *Winter in Moscow*.

'. . . the streets of Moscow were illuminated. Everywhere red streamers decorated with revolutionary slogans; soaring graphs; figures that mounted to dizzier and dizzier heights; cardboard battleships and motor-cars; printed placards marking where new hotels and skyscrapers were to be built; busts of Lenin and Stalin; silhouettes of Marx and Engels and Lenin and Stalin shading into one another like

Jesus sitting in the lap of Mary and Mary in the lap of Anne. It made the city more than usually fanciful and unreal. The dreams and aspirations of the Dictatorship of the Proletariat took tangible shape in terms of limelight and pasteboard . . .

Dark masses of people strolled amongst these slogans and graphs and figures and cardboard motor-cars and busts, staring at them; quite silent; their faces expressionless; like a river flowing through an empty lighted town. They were the proletariat. For them it had all happened.'[9]

Kenyatta responded to the warmth of the Russian people; to the way children clung to the legs of negro visitors and laughed from the sheer joy of seeing black men; and to the simplicity of the peasants who used to rub his skin to see if it were really black and not dyed as a propaganda trick.

He apparently travelled as far as Siberia, ostensibly to see how the Russians were dealing with their own backward areas.[10] It must have been an official tour, like those Westerners were treated to, to see Magnitogorsk, the city of steel behind the Urals, or Dnieprostroi, the giant new hydro-electric works in the Ukraine. Perhaps, too, he met other nationalist leaders from China and India, maybe even a rising Mao Tse Tung or a Nehru.

But most of the time he spent at the special revolutionary institute in Moscow. Here he received some kind of para-military training, together with a full grounding in the Marxist classics and the inevitable political indoctrination. Some idea of this institute may be gathered from an account which appeared in the *Manchester Guardian*. It came from a West Indian sailor who found himself stranded in Odessa. He was taken to Moscow where he 'attended lectures at a kind of college for "Communist Workers of the East".' It was:

'a large building with white washed rooms and many small cubicles. The desks were rough and ill made. There was a blackboard and a few exercise books, and of course the usual communist literature and photographs of Bolshevik leaders. The dining-room was sprinkled with saw-dust. We used to line up, plate in hand, for our food . . . As for the lessons, we first learnt to sing the "Internationale", and then we read histories of the different revolutions.'[11]

It was not an inspiring education. The will-o'-the-wisp which drew Kenyatta to Thogoto in 1909 still eluded him, and the streets of Moscow offered bleak comfort compared with those of London and Paris. Did he not see the grey, expressionless faces of the men and women shuffling in queues; did he never visit the markets where the bread was sour and pulpy from much handling and where a piece of sausage would pass from hand to hand until it found a purchaser who would suddenly swallow it and as suddenly retch it up again from a stomach too long emptied of the means of life?

No doubt Kenyatta enjoyed certain privileges and was provided with special funds which enabled him to buy food and clothes in the stores reserved for foreigners.[12] In their lighted windows little pyramids of fruit attracted the gaze of starving passers-by: inside an illuminated lie, outside the dark truth. But perhaps the poverty did not strike him so harshly, for he would have known it himself from Africa. Perhaps the idea of revolution was an inspiration in itself.

Padmore was high in the negro section of the Comintern. He reputedly lectured at Kenyatta's training school for African revolutionaries; he knew well the leaders of Indian and Chinese communist parties, and was even briefly elected a member of the Moscow City Soviet which entitled him to stand alongside the highest Soviet dignitaries at a May Day parade. Moving in such circles he was far removed from the realities of Russian life under Stalin. But it was a dangerously exposed position, and in the course of 1933 a crisis arose.

Hitler's arrival in power in Germany forced the Russian leaders to rethink their foreign policy. Officially Russia was hostile to the League of Nations—that 'robbers' den' in the words of Lenin. In communist jargon the Versailles treaty was regarded as a capitalist yoke to enforce colonial oppression on other races. On this reasoning Germany was welcomed as a fellow sufferer from the imperialist forces which dictated the peace, and in the twenties Russian policy had been to hold out towards Germany the hand of friendship. The policy was enshrined in the Treaty of Rapallo, signed originally in 1926, and prolonged in 1931. In May 1933, only a few months after Hitler's installation as Chancellor, Stalin confirmed the Rapallo treaty.

But the reality of Hitler's intentions towards communists left the Comintern bewildered by Stalin's policy, and Russia herself was now dangerously isolated. Simultaneously, therefore, Stalin ordered a revision of Comintern propaganda. From being identified in communist jargon as the 'twin' of fascism, social democracy in all its Western forms was courted as Russia's ally. From being bitterly hostile towards the imperial powers, France and Britain, Russia moved towards accommodation. The result was that in September 1934 Russia joined the League of Nations, and in 1935 signed alliances with France and Czechoslovakia. Meanwhile, in November 1933, the United States officially recognized the Soviet government. Revisionism could scarcely go further.

Kremlinologists became aware of these impending changes months before they were translated into official utterances; to none were they more fraught with meaning than to the negro and African members of the Comintern. To them the anti-imperialist phraseology of communist propaganda was the main point. The switch in Comintern policy now demanded of them an abrupt about-turn in their whole thinking, which in turn raised the basic question of national liberation movements throughout the colonial world.

Communist orthodoxy declared that the underdeveloped peoples lacked the wherewithal to produce their own revolution. Only in the West had capitalism reached the point where the workers could make a revolution; the effort of the world-wide communist movement should therefore be directed to safeguarding the USSR and extending the Russian revolution into the bastions of Western capitalism. In other words, it would have to be a white revolution first, in order to destroy the imperial powers, and the white workers could then bring the revolution to the colonial peoples.

To Padmore, Kenyatta, and others, this made little sense. They recognized that Africa lacked a proletariat in the Western sense, but they placed their future in the revolutionary potential of their own people. This was Kenyatta's strength. Unlike Padmore and the other negroes from America, he had been born and brought up under the colonial system. His was the practical experience of Africa which they lacked.

Kenyatta in Moscow had to face one of the central contradictions of Marxism. The 'unhistorical races' were proclaiming themselves. 'It is class, not race, which counts', the Stalinists propounded, and any coloured intellectual who objected was denounced as a petty bourgeois nationalist. To Kenyatta this was just the language of the white man again—similar in intent, though not in origin, to the settlers' talk of law and order. The intent was to impose a white man's pattern on the world, an appeal to the white man's history. It would take another generation before the coloured intellectual, in the writing of Fanon, reached the bleak analysis of violence for its own sake. By then the white man had his back to the wall and was ready to come to terms with the 'petty bourgeois nationalist' in Kenya as well as in Algeria. But for Padmore and Kenyatta the goal of self-rule was distant enough. For them, the American-sponsored Liberia must be defended because it was at least a black state; even Ethiopia, the most reactionary state in all Africa, must be defended against white aggression. For them it *was* race, not class, which was the first priority.

In August 1933 the Comintern decided to disband the International Trade Union Committee of Negro Workers, ITUC-NW, which was the front under which Padmore and Kenyatta were both operating. Padmore learned of the decision on 13 August and immediately resigned his official posts. Vilification soon followed. 'He is branded as a filthy scoundrel, as a betrayer of the struggles of the Negro masses', the communist press charged. Ford, among others, turned against him. In February 1934 he was expelled from the Comintern and in June from the Communist Party.[13]

Kenyatta was Padmore's protégé and his position was equally at risk. Would-be African revolutionaries were in a dangerously weak situation in Russia. They had burnt their boats and the Russians knew it. In consequence anyone who fell out with the communist authorities was liable to be treated with callous brutality. He could be turned out into the streets without food, shelter or medical attention, with no means of supporting himself and no hope of assistance from his former colonial government. And just at this moment when the Comintern was ordered to change front, a more sinister shadow darkened the Russian sky. Behind the scenes in the Kremlin the grim apparatus of Stalin's great purges was being prepared.

There is no record of how Kenyatta—or Padmore, for that matter—succeeded in leaving Russia. Years later the CID reported that after Padmore's fall from favour 'Kenyatta was mentioned as Padmore's successor but no actual proof that he succeeded him was ever obtained.'[14] It would have been, in the circumstances, unlikely; though Kenyatta could not afford to defy the Comintern while he was in Moscow himself. Padmore later wrote dispassionately enough of the break: 'I have never permitted my political objectivity in regard to the Soviet Union to be influenced by my experiences with the Comintern.' Kenyatta adopted much the same attitude. In later years he claimed that he was doing no more than completing his education in Russia. In a sense it was true—he had acquired new tools and new experiences. Whatever it was that had taken him to Moscow, he remained the master of his destiny.[15]

Kenyatta never spoke of his time in Russia in any detail, nor did he ever give a hint in public of his real feelings towards the communists. Back in England a news item might prompt the aside that he had been at Yalta, or had known such and such a Russian mentioned in the bulletin, but he kept his experiences and his ideas about Russia to himself. For their part the Russians evidently had no dossier on his activities in the Soviet Union which they thought worth using at the time, or indeed subsequently. References to his time in Russia by men who claimed to have known him were rare and guarded and only began to appear on Moscow Radio or in articles when Russia began courting potential leaders of future independent African states some quarter of a century later.[16] Other visitors to Russia who must have known him from the same period have been even more reticent. Yet on a personal level Kenyatta apparently found individual Russians warm-hearted and he made some close friends there.[17]

The fact of his being in Moscow was always held against him by the militant settlers of Kenya, but no evidence was ever forthcoming that he received any material assistance from them after he returned to Kenya. Not being of a doctrinaire way of thinking himself, he was unimpressed by Soviet propaganda and detached in all his subsequent dealings with the Russians. Perhaps the one thing he took to heart in Russia was the importance of not being trapped into commitments which would restrict his own freedom of action.

CHAPTER 14

The Long Wait

Despite his furtive departure from London in August 1932, Kenyatta's movements became known in Kenya. His visit to Moscow had not been authorized by the KCA; his presence there added to the confusion which reigned over Kikuyu tribal politics in the aftermath of the female circumcision controversy.

In June 1932 Harry Thuku, the 'King of the Kikuyu', was elected President of the KCA, heavily defeating Kangethe. For reasons that are obscure, this produced a split in the Association. On behalf of the defeated party Jesse Kariuki promptly requested permission from the authorities to reopen their old office at Kahuhia. Nairobi, he said, was now too expensive. George Ndegwa, styled as Assistant General Secretary, repudiated the Kahuhia move. By the end of August 1932 the Kenya CID reported that the split was so wide 'Jesse Kariuki is forming an opposition party'.

The following year the row broke out in public. Kariuki circulated members with a document accusing Thuku of misuse of Association funds. Thuku sued him for criminal libel. The case came to court in Nairobi in May 1933. Kariuki's case was that he had collected 1,200 shillings 'for the people in England', but Thuku 'did not send it because he did not want them to come back'. Thuku's lawyers appeared to ignore this point, but the judge upheld it. Kariuki's circular was certainly defamatory, the judge said, but was made in good faith as he had the interests of the two Association members in England uppermost in his mind. He therefore dismissed the case without commenting on the rights and wrongs of the issues raised.[1]

Thuku's subsequent defence was that the KCA 'offices' were in reality no more than a poky room in a broken-down mud and wattle shack in the Pumwani slums. When he took over he saw to it that the Association put on a better front. With his standing he was able to obtain permission to build new offices in the latest development quarter close to Eastleigh airport. They were opened at the same time as the court case. But the rivalry continued, and in April 1935 Thuku officially took his supporters into a new party called the Kikuyu Provincial Association. His reputation in Kikuyuland assured him of a wide following.

Over the following years Thuku became increasingly 'loyalist' in his approach to the colonial authorities. By contrast the KCA reverted to small cells of disgruntled people without a leader. Outside these local rivalries, Kenyatta was playing a lone hand. He appeared to have cut himself off from tribal politics.

This first became apparent during the hearing of native evidence before the Carter Commission, whose arrival in Kenya stirred the Kikuyu into new activity. Their anxiety over land had been the refrain to everything they had said or written since the earliest days of political activity. Here, now, was their chance to voice their claims. They did so by the score with bewildering detail and optimism.

On 16 February 1933, Harry Thuku appeared before them, and now a curious thing came to light. Thuku had heard nothing from Kenyatta. He did not know that Kenyatta had already given evidence in London, nor that he had promised the Commission a special paper on Kikuyu land-holding customs.[2] It was a strange lapse in a delegate in such an important matter. Thuku was evidently uncertain where Kenyatta stood in relation to the split in the ranks of the KCA. But his suspicions were further roused when he learnt of Kenyatta's sojourn in Russia. In March 1933 Thuku wrote to Roden Buxton:

'We are very disturbed by Mr Kenyatta, because we heard that he have gone to Germany and Russia where we do not want him to go. He do not represent us in those countries as he went there against our wishes, so he is alone responsible for all he do there.'[3]

Buxton forwarded Thuku's letter to Ross who kept its contents to himself. At CMS headquarters in London Hooper was under the impression that Kenyatta was in America and he was more concerned with the future of his own protégé, Parmenas Mockerie. Mockerie's year at Fircroft, Birmingham, had been followed by further study at Ruskin College, Oxford. His development pleased Hooper. He had managed to keep Mockerie away from the 'dangerous influences' which he believed had corrupted Kenyatta as he wrote to Kenya:

'. . . there is no danger at the moment of his becoming a sinister revolutionary . . . I used to think that, compared with Kinyatta Parmenas need not be rated very seriously. My opinion has changed, and I know that he carries heavier metal than I ever suspected. We want to save him from becoming an embittered and discontented critic of things as they are.'[4]

The problem was how to fit a man like Mockerie after his European education into the employment pattern of Kenya colony. The mission could only offer jobs at low salaries—lower than his qualifications might lead Mockerie to expect. Political activity was likely to be frustrating, as Kenyatta had found, with an unsympathetic administration on the one hand, and ignorant and suspicious colleagues among the tribesmen on the other. In England Mockerie had written a short book entitled *An African Speaks For His People*. It was published by Leonard Woolf at the Hogarth Press with a foreword by Professor Julian Huxley and was the first account to appear in England by an intelligent Kikuyu of his tribe's background and attitudes. But what could he look forward to in Kenya?

On 17 May 1933, Hooper received a cable from Jesse Kariuki asking for the cost of the return fare for Kenyatta and Mockerie from London to Nairobi. £100 would cover both, replied Hooper, and in the course of the summer this sum was deposited by someone in the KCA with the Union Castle Line. But there was no sign of Kenyatta. Whereupon, at the end of August, Mockerie bought himself a first-class ticket and pocketed the balance. Hooper explained that Mockerie must have thought the money was safer in his own hands than left on the books of a shipping company in London 'when for all he knew Kenyatta might be dead'. There had been no word of him for a year.[5]

Kenyatta, however, chose this moment to reappear in London. On 30 August 1933 he telephoned the Rosses out of the blue and two days later was out at Hampstead again for supper 'just back from a year on the Continent'. Evidently he kept his past movements very much to himself. There was no word about Russia and Ross ignored, or forgot about, Thuku's letter to Roden Buxton. Hooper was equally in the dark, writing to Kenya on 12 September:

'. . . now I have heard from friends that Johnston Kinyatta has arrived back in England after a year in Germany. He has not troubled to keep any of his friends informed as to his activities; but the fact that the Nazis did not intern him in a concentration camp suggests that he was not consorting with any known communists in Germany itself.

I have always thought him too cautious ever to become a fanatic. The problem which is troubling me at the moment is that he is not very well.'[6]

Kenyatta naturally asked Hooper for his return passage money and had to be told that Mockerie had just left with it. According to the Kenya CID, Kenyatta at once wrote to the KCA 'imploring them to send him £150 immediately in order that he might settle his debts and return to Kenya.'[7] But no money was immediately forthcoming. He was stranded.

Kenyatta now took stock of himself. As far as the Colonial Office was concerned he no longer had any standing. Apart from desultory requests for interviews with senior officials, Kenyatta's memorandum from Woodbrooke was his last serious attempt at dialogue with the civil servants in Whitehall. Thereafter, it was the brush-off. Alive now to 'the unwisdom of encouraging Mr J. Kenyatta by too punctilious a treatment of his effusions', the officials instructed the Kenya Government to deal directly with the KCA in Nairobi and so 'short circuit' their man in London. At the end of 1932 they closed their file on Johnstone Kenyatta.[8]

By now the intense interest in East Africa, which had given Kenyatta his opportunities in 1929–30, had shifted to the work of the Carter Commission, whose report was anxiously awaited. When it was finally published in May 1934 it fell to the Kikuyu leaders in Kenya to make further representations on behalf of their tribe. The activity which went into the framing of their evidence to the Carter Commission seemed to take the bitterness out of Kikuyu politics. The different groupings in Kikuyuland tended to come together to present a united view. The administration also developed a technique by which they hoped to 'short circuit' local agitators as effectively as the Colonial Office bypassed Kenyatta in London. The Provincial Commissioner described it candidly to one of his district officers:

'. . . the policy which experience has shown to be the best is to obtain privately as much information as possible of the aims of the political agitation and in so far as they are in accord with general

policy, to put them into effect without recourse to the agitation themselves. Such reform will effectively cut the ground from under the
feet of political agitation.'⁹

Kenyatta, of course, still had his communist contacts. According
to later CID reports they provided him with some funds and further
introductions—a printing establishment was mentioned, and other
"communistic and revolutionary organisations'.¹⁰ There is no evidence that Kenyatta thought of these contacts as more than temporary expedients to see him through a difficult period in his life.

But they left a mark on his thinking. In the January 1933 issue of
the *Negro Worker,* which was on George Padmore when he was deported from Hamburg, there was a long article by Kenyatta entitled
'An African Looks at British Imperialism'.¹¹ It was as extreme as
anything he had written for the communist press three years previously.

Kenyatta began with a résumé of Kenya's development under
colonialism. 'The history of British rule is one of the blackest spots
in the black history of British imperialism.' He dismissed the Carter
Commission out of hand. The land was stolen by the white men,
and the natives chosen to speak for the people were no more than
stooges.

Missionaries 'are the agents of the imperialists, who teach Africans that they must tolerate all oppression and exploitation in order
that they shall have a good home and better conditions in heaven
when they die!' Nothing, concluded Comrade Kenyatta, would do
but 'the unconditional return of the land to the Native Africans and
the evacuation of the imperialist robber from the land, which is the
natural property of the Africans by all canons.' It was, in fact, an
explicit call for 'complete self-rule'.

The phraseology and thinking behind this article betray Padmore's influence. It may be supposed that the idea of self-government
for the natives of colonial Africa was also borrowed from the tradition
among West Indian intellectuals of revolt against slave owners. As
we have noted, this idea led Padmore into a passionate defence of
Liberia, despite its bourgeois, American-backed regime, simply on the
grounds that Liberia at least was a black state.

Kenyatta's association with Padmore also showed itself in a contribution included by Nancy Cunard in her anthology *Negro*. This
massive tome, which ran to over 800 pages, was published in 1934 and
consisted of essays, poems and articles written by men and women

from many different backgrounds covering all aspects of the racial conflict between the black man and the West. Padmore worked closely with Nancy Cunard in Paris over its compilation.

Kenyatta's article was entitled simply 'Kenya'.

'Kenya' he began 'is the most important British Colony in East Africa . . . During the past 35 years these people have been robbed of their best land and are today reduced to the status of serfs forced to work on their own lands for the benefit of the white "owners", and even in some circumstances to work without pay or food.'

He lampooned the European way of life in East Africa, with its golf and polo, food, drink and disinfectants, and contrasted it with the bare subsistence earnings of African families and the exploitation they were subjected to in taxation and working conditions. But the African was awakening, he cried:

'The soul of the African is stricken nigh to death by confiscation of its ancestral lands, the obstruction of its free development in social and economic matters, and its subjugation to an imperialist system of slavery, taxpaying, pass carrying and forced labour. This policy of British imperialist robbery and oppression aroused the greatest alarm and anxiety amongst the Kenya Africans, the outcome of which was the revolt of 1922, when defenceless Africans, men, women and children, were shot down by these filibusters.'

There was nothing original in these statements, but Kenyatta also attacked the British Government's attitude towards the detribalized native and here he touched a more significant point. 'British imperialism supports the backward form of social relationships in Kenya.' The authorities, he said, felt no need to listen to the opinions of those natives who had succeeded in breaking out of their tribal background. 'By operating on tribal differences, British imperialism's age-long policy of "divide and rule" is enhanced, while the Kenya African national liberation movement is arrested.' Tribal society, Kenyatta implied in a penetrating insight, could never break loose from the colonial grip. Only the detribalized native could effectively lead that new, twentieth-century, phenomenon 'the Kenya African national liberation movement'.

Kenyatta's article was accompanied by a photograph. It was Kenyatta the dandy, in shirt, collar and tie, in elegant suit and waistcoat with his handkerchief in his breast pocket; Kenyatta the young and earnest writer, politician and man of the world. This was the model negro type, the one Nancy Cunard and her Parisian circle idealized, the noble savage of the romantic past brought up to date with Savile Row suits and Parisian wit.

In the circle of George Padmore and Nancy Cunard, Kenyatta aspired to something higher than the Nairobi version of the detribalized native. He identified the person of the black revolutionary —himself—with the soul of Africa. The links with the American negro struggle and the Africans from other European colonies whom he met in Paris enabled him, perhaps for the first time, to see his own situation in its full racial context. His role was not to 'ape' the white man, as he put it, but to create an autonomous African alternative to the white man's view of history. Behind the jargon was a search for blood brotherhood—the elevation of the African into the full dignity of man as a race, not as a class.

Kenyatta needed time to develop this theme. On returning to Britain from Russia in the autumn of 1933 he found it easier to work up the clichés of his Marxist instructors. An outlet was provided him in the *Labour Monthly*, then edited by the British communist leader, Palme Dutt. In the November 1933 issue Kenyatta contributed an article on 'The Gold Rush in Kenya'.[12] Repeating whole paragraphs from his Nancy Cunard piece, he condemned the way in which the Kenya Government had handled the discovery of gold in March 1931 at Kakagema in northern Nyanza. No sooner had the absolute inviolability of tribal reserves been proclaimed in the Kenya Native Lands Trust Ordinance of 1930 than pressures were exerted to release land for European prospectors. The government yielded and hurriedly passed an amendment to the 1930 ordinance, to the outrage of watchful critics like McGregor Ross.

In his article Kenyatta showed that he could utilize all the art of vilification picked up from his communist experience. The gold hunters, he said, were seducing African girls 'to satisfy their bestial lust, they are dragging their "honour" in the mud and slush, their civilisation is all in the interest of capitalist greed and imperialist exploitation.'

It was no worse a scandal than the successive moves of the Masai, and was certainly less emotive than the subject of Kikuyu land. But it brought from Kenyatta words as strong as any he was to utter:

'Perhaps many will ask: "what can we do against an imperialist government which is armed with machine guns, aeroplanes and guns etc?" My answer to that is, we have learnt examples from other countries. And the only way out is the mass organisation of workers and peasants of various tribes, and by having this unity we shall be in a position to put up a strong protest against this robbery and exploitation.

There, all Kenya Africans must fight for their liberation. We cannot forget how we have been exploited and oppressed through these "solemn pledges". Let none of our countrymen have any faith in these imperialist hypocritical "promises" which mean nothing but the oppression and exploitation of the masses. In this fight we shall have the support of all who are oppressed by the British Slave Empire —the Indians, the Irish, the South Africans—all these people are revolting against this damnable Empire whose days are numbered.

With the support of all revolutionary workers and peasants we must redouble our efforts to break the bonds that bind us. We must refuse to give any support to the British imperialists either by paying taxes or obeying any of their slave laws! We can fight in unity with the workers and toilers of the whole world, and for a Free Africa.'

No one advancing such views would be allowed free expression in Kenya. Indeed at this point of time none of his contemporaries even thought in these terms. In a letter to Ramsay MacDonald written in June 1933 from his American university, the young Peter Koinange said: 'It is an undeniable fact that the natives of Africa have benefited by British Administration, for, regardless of its failures in some respects, the British Government has shown a desire for fair play in its dealings with the natves.'[13]

Harry Thuku took much the same line in his evidence to the Carter Commission. Asked 'Would you rather have the old days?', Thuku replied 'I prefer modern times.' Jesse Kariuki's comment was similar: 'I think that the Government and the white people will do their best to help us to raise up our country and our fear should vanish because we are children of His Majesty the King and we should obey him.'

Every Kikuyu, of course, could raise particular objections to colonial rule. Koinange and the chiefs, Kangethe and the rump of the KCA, and the spokesman for the PKP of Nyeri, all came together in February 1934 to present a joint list of grievances.[14] The familiar items were there: inferior educational facilities, the hut tax and the *kipande,* restrictions on coffee growing, land rights—always land—and fears of European domination. This last item was the clue to their thinking; the Kikuyu leaders in Kenya at this time all looked to the British Government for their welfare and saw their future only in colonial terms. Kenyatta alone looked for African self-government. In the context of the colonial Africa of the 1930s, it seemed a mythical prospect.

So, taking stock of himself as the winter of 1933 approached, Kenyatta concluded that there was no place for him yet in his own country. There was nothing for it but to struggle along in Europe. But one thing was missing: compared with the other negroes he had met his own education still lacked credentials. He had no diplomas or degrees to his name, no university pass-out except the somewhat dubious claim of Moscow, nothing which gave him intellectual respectability. To make up the deficiency he decided to become a student again.

CHAPTER 15

Kenyatta the Student

As early as the winter of 1929 Kenyatta had been introduced to language specialists at London University, when Hooper asked him to give Kikuyu lessons to young missionaries about to set off for Kenya.[1]

The Phonetics Department of University College always welcomed the opportunity of studying any new language or obscure dialect. They paid for foreign or native visitors to attend regular sessions where a proper phonetic record of their own vernacular speech could be made. In this way the structure of all languages, however obscure or complex, could be analyzed and translations compiled. The pay was not much—at first 5 shillings an hour, later raised to 10 shillings, perhaps for two two-hour sessions a week during the university term—but it helped needy students. Kenyatta was a rare find for these language experts. Few natives of East Africa were available in London in those days, and none from Kikuyuland.[2]

For several years Kenyatta was able to make a small income from these sources. Between 1935 and 1937 he contributed towards a book called *The Phonetic and Tonal Structure of Kikuyu* by Lilias Armstrong, who died just before it was published. Kenyatta provided the material for a number of texts, simple stories and conversations which were annotated to show how the principles of translation and pronunciation applied.[3]

He showed, too, an acute sensitivity to the tonal nuances which are especially subtle in Kikuyu, and he was meticulous in spotting inaccuracies in translations. He quickly picked up the method of recording the sounds of the human voice and, perhaps over-valuing his early help to Barlow's Kikuyu dictionary, prided himself on his own expertise in this new field. So much so that when the book was eventually published he was not satisfied with the warm appreciation paid him in the preface but claimed co-authorship with Lilias Armstrong.

At the same time Kenyatta began to study anthropology under the world-famous Professor Malinowski, then teaching at the London School of Economics. How he succeeded in joining Malinowski's classes is something of a mystery. He was the most sought-after anthropologist in Europe, perhaps in the Western world, and in theory he only accepted students who already possessed a degree or equal academic rating. His diploma course was supposed to last three years, of which one was field work. At the end there was a thesis to be written before the diploma could finally be given. Presumably Kenyatta persuaded Malinowski that he possessed sufficient qualifications. Malinowski also was keen to encourage native participation in anthropological research, and he would have found in Kenyatta, as the phoneticians did, a unique chance to include in his group someone with personal experience of tribal life.

The formal records reveal little. Kenyatta was on the books of University College, London, from January to July 1935 for a course in English, and again from October 1935 to June 1936 for a three hours a week course of phonetics. These were intended mostly for overseas teachers of English, and it may have been that Kenyatta toyed with the idea of returning to Kenya in this capacity. The fees were only six guineas, and they gave him an entrée to the University life.

In the end it was the International African Institute which came to his rescue. Kenyatta applied for a grant in 1934, but the award was not 'finalised' until December 1936. It covered his fees at the London School of Economics for the academic year 1936–7 and may have included back payments for the previous year.

Ross, as it happened, also counted Malinowski among his numerous contacts and he may well have effected the original introduction. On Kenyatta's return from Moscow, Ross came to his aid once more and obtained for him a Reader's Ticket for the British Museum Reading Room. But their relationship grew strained. Kenyatta was apt not to keep appointments made for him by Ross, and Ross had doubts as to Kenyatta's political usefulness. A coolness developed between them which lasted a further eighteen months until Ross finally broke with him.

The problem was Kenyatta's debts. On his arival back in London from Russia, Kenyatta returned to his old digs at 95 Cambridge Street and because of his sick appearance prevailed upon his landlady, Mrs Hocken, to take him in again. The Rosses felt a certain responsibility and Isabel Ross took it upon herself to help Mrs

Hocken out. Between the Rosses and other well-wishers like Roden Buxton and CMS headquarters in Salisbury Square there was a steady correspondence over Africans 'on the borrow' in London. Kenyatta soon learnt how to play on their feelings. After Mockerie had gone off with the KCA deposit, Hooper also found himself lending Kenyatta money and involving himself with Isabel Ross over his other debts. Kenyatta wrote disarmingly to Hooper about them himself:

'I just receive a letter from Mrs Ross saying that she sent the £7–10 to you. I shall be glad if you will kindly send it to me. I know I owe you £7, and it is my wish to pay you, but as I have no money at present, and the landlady is terribly worried for her rent, I want to pay her whatever little I can. You know she is a poor woman, and besides this, she have helped me a great deal And I consider her a great friend of Africans, & therefore it my bound duty not to let her down. I trust that you will understand my point of view in this case.'[4]

Hooper left it to Isabel Ross to sort out. Kenyatta apparently satisfied her and they continued to see each other in London for the occasional lecture or meeting. But in August 1934 the Rosses were shocked to find that Kenyatta had paid Mrs Hocken nothing for the past twelve months. His landlady was 'critically embarrassed' and the Rosses cabled Jesse Kariuki at once to send funds to London. But no money was forthcoming. A fortnight later the Rosses received 'an SOS letter' from Mrs Hocken. 'She was out of pocket more than £100 for Kenyatta's board and lodging.'

The Rosses sent airmail appeals to their Nairobi contacts to see what had happened to the KCA and Ross went personally to enquire at a steamship company about the possibility of Kenyatta's working his passage back to Nairobi 'as a pantry boy'. By October Isabel Ross felt Mrs Hocken should turn Kenyatta out as his debts had mounted to £120.

McGregor Ross was a Scot who had schooled himself in government service to be meticulous over financial matters. He lent money himself generously out of his own small pension, often on poor credit, but Kenyatta's behaviour towards Mrs Hocken scandalized him. Christmas 1934 came and Kenyatta received no invitation to spend it with the Ross family. And then one day early in the new year Ross decided to have it out with Kenyatta. On 22 January 1935, 'I had a heated talk with Johnstone Kenyatta and rated him soundly for continuing to sponge on his landlady instead of returning to Kenya.' It was the last Ross saw of the man he had done so much to defend against the prejudices of the Colonial Office.

To an African, accustomed only to tribal hospitality, such indebtedness would have meant little. But Kenyatta had lived in Europe long enough to know what life was like for families like the Hockens in the lean years after the depression. He must have exercized an unusual hold over them. They continued to serve him meals and welcome him to their billiards table in the basement of their house. Ross wrote several times to Kenyatta, and once Isabel called at Cambridge Street to see what was going on. Mrs Hocken and Kenyatta were both out, but she learnt that Kenyatta had recently made one of his mysterious trips to Paris, 'pitching a yarn to Mrs Hocken that it was necessary he should see a Greek princess there on business!'

Some money from Kenya did trickle through. In March 1935 a meagre £20 came for Mrs Hocken and £15 for Kenyatta, which was hardly enough to support him and finance his trips abroad. The Rosses felt they could no longer rely on him. In November Ross wrote to his old friend, C. F. Andrews,

'Isabel and I have ceased taking steps through, or with, Kenyatta. He is ruining his pathetic landlady. When she tries to give him "notice" he bursts into floods of (crocodile?) tears—and sits tight as before! He must surely owe her £150 or £180 by now. Too bad.'[5]

It was against this background of constant, nagging poverty that Kenyatta spent the five years that followed his return from Russia. There were occasions when he had to lie up in his room for days, shivering from cold and waiting for the mail from Kenya. By selling the stamps he could then buy himself a penny bun. He had to walk to save bus fares, allow girl-friends to pay for an evening's outing, and stay in his room while his one shirt dried on the radiator. Sometimes his down-at-heel appearance shamed his friends and they were forced to replace his more tatty garments. No one who has not experienced them himself can tell what such hunger and deprivation cost in personal indignities. But Kenyatta had been toughened by his boyhood trials. He never allowed his sufferings to destroy him.

In the spring of 1934 he joined the Student Movement House, an international hostel inaugurated in 1917 as a memorial to British students killed in the war. Known simply as 'the House', it was then located in Russell Square, in one of the last grand Georgian houses whose Adam fireplaces, painted ceilings and huge mirrors were all that was left of its former elegance.

The hostel was founded by the Student Christian Movement and though many of its inmates were Moslems and Hindus, they all found in its spirit of Christian fellowship a respite from the bitter hatreds which were dividing the world outside. It was a non-residential club where all nationalities mixed freely, Italians and Abyssinians, Jews and Germans, White Russians and aspiring communists, Egyptians and Zionists, Indians, Africans and representatives from Britain's white dominions.

Kenyatta was no exception in being hard up; most of the young men and women who came to Russell Square were in a similar situation. Many were lonely and carried locked up inside them a secret fear of being slighted in some unforeseen manner. There were misunderstandings, fights and troubles with the police; homesickness and thwarted passion drove some to suicide; several died from undernourishment, tuberculosis or pneumonia.

A less resilient man than Kenyatta might easily have given up. Away from his own family, with whom he seemed to have lost all contact, and facing an existence empty of prospects, he needed all his sense of destiny to save himself from despair. Instead, Kenyatta recovered something of the style of the old Dagoretti days. He took to wearing a fez and cloak. Rings still flashed on his fingers and he carried a thin, silver-topped black cane. Conveniently situated near the University, the club was a useful base for him. He could drop in for tea in the late afternoon, read the papers and pick up a friend for the evening. He had no difficulty in attracting girls; nor, remembering some of his Nairobi experiences, was he above the occasional skirmish with Indians, who formed the largest single group of students in London. On one occasion he turned up dishevelled at the warden's door late at night and asked for her protection from some Indians with whom he had been out drinking.[6]

And there were occasions when he, too, looked on the club as a haven from the raw, foggy London streets. In its warmth and activity he felt again something of the spirit of Woodbrooke. Thus it was that he was among the party from twenty different countries who gathered on Christmas Day 1935 for food and company and to listen to the voice of the ailing King George V around the fire in the big room over the square.

Kenyatta was an extrovert and he liked being at the centre of life.

At the students' hostel he met a young English girl, Margaret Bryan, working on post-graduate studies at the University. She too had visited Berlin and since she also spoke Swahili Kenyatta struck up a casual friendship with her. Margaret was lively and intelligent, the kind of 'modern' girl who was ready to argue on any interesting topic; Kenyatta was good company and pleased to have a friend who treated him naturally and not in the patronizing manner of the ex-colonials. On and off, during these years, they saw quite a lot of each other.

With people like Margaret Bryan, Kenyatta could relax and speak his mind, not in that artificial language of the political world of Padmore and the newspapers, but as an individual airing his personal feelings. 'If I were a dictator of Africa', he would say, and then launch into a tirade about the differences between Europeans and Africans. Margaret Bryan was a good listener; she felt he needed to let off steam. They would go off together for coffee at a Lyons Corner House or a meal at the Chinese restaurant in the Strand and continue talking for hours. He struck her as a man whose attitudes were firm and always relevant to whatever was going in Kenya.

At Russell Square there were always other Africans who might join in: law students, doctors, teachers, writers. Kenyatta had one particular friend called Kessie who described himself as the nephew of an Ashanti king. A lady's man himself, Kessie's high-sounding title and good looks impressed society women, and Margaret Bryan photographed the two of them in the gardens. They wore blazers and white trousers, Kenyatta with a cane, Kessie sporting colours on his white pullover, two 'Burlington Berties'. With his fellow Africans Kenyatta compared witchcraft and magic and their different tribal customs; often he sang Kikuyu songs and waxed eloquent about his people. Though he never mentioned Grace Wahu or the two children he had left in Kenya, his homesickness was apparent. 'I do love to see his devotion to his beloved Kikuyu,' his friend noted in her diary after one such evening.

Soon after joining the students' hostel, Kenyatta had an opportunity to earn a little money in a novel manner. Alexander Korda required some 250 coloured extras for his new film *Sanders of the River* which was to star Paul Robeson. Anyone with a black skin would do, and among the 250 enrolled were students from London, dockers from Bristol and Liverpool, buskers from Hyde Park Corner and professional out-of-work actors and actresses—and Kenyatta. In all, they spoke more than twenty different languages.

In the autumn of 1934 the film went into production at Shepperton Studios on the River Thames just outside London. It was an exhilarating experience for Kenyatta. He enjoyed the world of grease-paint and the company of his fellow extras, and it brought him a guinea a day expenses. Kenyatta's was a small role, one of a number of minor chiefs drawn up to be lectured by Sanders, before he leaves for a year's furlough in England, to 'keep the King's Peace, lest the great shame come upon me before my King!' Bosambo, played by Robeson, comes from another tribe and has been promoted by Sanders to be a spokesman for the chiefs—a Kinyanjui figure, who stands by the white man when the 'bad' chiefs stir up trouble. In the scene in which Kenyatta appeared, they all bow to 'Lord Sandy':

Minor Chief (not Kenyatta)	'Lord we all love one another now, because if we did not your Lordship would punish us very cruelly.'
All bow	'Yes Lord Sandy.'
Sanders	'I have called you here today because I go on a long journey over the great sea, and there I shall stay for twelve moons.'
Bosambo	'Lord Sandy, it fills our hearts with sorrow to see you go away from us.'
Sanders	'Thank you Bosambo. And in my place the Lord Ferguson will stay here and give the law to all the peoples of the River. I want you to obey him as if you were his own children.'

Sanders was the creation of Edgar Wallace who, as a young reporter, had followed the Empire-builders in the opening up of Africa. Sanders distributes rough justice to the natives and is loved by them for it. His methods would never stand up to a Parliamentary Question in the 1930s, but they suited the temperament of the tribes in the previous century—a summary whipping or a quick hanging from the nearest tree.

'By Sanders' code you trusted all natives up to the same point, as you trust children, with a few notable exceptions. The Zulu were men, the Basuto were men, yet childlike in their grave faith. The black men who wore the fez were subtle but trustworthy; but the browny men of the Gold Coast, who talked English, wore European clothing, and called one another "Mr", were Sanders' pet abomination.'[7]

This was the British colonial approach at its frankest. Sanders was the archetype British DC who dislikes the detribalized native and wants to keep the tribes uncontaminated by politics and religion. As interpreted by Robeson, Bosambo becomes a loyal British servant whose courage and magnificent songs evoke the world of the noble savage as he enters battle. He represents the best qualities of tribal Africa in popular imagination. As *The Times* put it, the film 'will bring no discredit on Imperial authority'.[8]

Subsequently *Sanders of the River* aroused controversy. Young African nationalists thought it degraded the black man. Robeson was attacked for being a 'white man's nigger' and Kenyatta's participation came in for criticism. Margaret Bryan was having tea with him one day when a West African joined them and 'argued frantically' about the film. 'I quite see the other man's point,' she wrote afterwards, 'that Kenyatta shouldn't have acted in it, that he was letting down his principles for the sake of his pocket.'

Yet Korda had gone to great trouble to make the scenes as authentic as possible. He spent many weeks in Africa shooting location material and recording songs and dances. Perhaps because of his own Jewish sense of persecution, heightened by what was happening in Germany at that time, Korda was intensely sympathetic towards the negro situation, and years later he did it full justice in his production of Alan Paton's great novel *Cry The Beloved Country*.

Robeson was himself looking for a new sense of direction to his life, and shortly after Christmas 1934, when the greater part of *Sanders of the River* had been shot, he paid his first visit to Moscow.[9] Both the visit and the film made a deep impression on him. Russia changed his life, but it was on the set at Shepperton that he discovered his racial identity with his African past. One day he was astonished to find he could understand what two Ibo extras were saying to each other in their own dialect. The meaning of their words came to him from the depths of his childhood subconscious, from words incorporated into negro spirituals sung by generations of slaves and from his own father who had been the son of a slave and born on a plantation in North Carolina. The experience decided him finally on continuing his career as a singer and against returning to the law studies which his family were pressing him to do. He defended his decision in this way:

'All Negroes are exhibitionists, and this I say with no intent to slight myself or my race. Rather I mean that we have a natural ebullience.

And this, too, stems from Africa and not from Harlem. Thus I have no call to the law, challenging the white man. I have a definite call to delineate the Negro and to dispense, so far as my talent may permit, his art.'[10]

It was a strange accident that brought Kenyatta and Robeson together in this way, and both were affected by their encounter. While Robeson was thrilled to discover his African soul in *Sanders of the River*, Kenyatta, too, delighted in the music and the spirit of the African scenes. The film's splendid songs and dances, its powerful rhythms and pattern of spears and shields, its sense of a living tradition, all belonged to the same cultural sensation that Nancy Cunard portrayed in her book. Here was the myth of the noble savage in celluloid form. Both Robeson and Kenyatta were struck with the potential of the new medium.[11] Kenyatta later confided that he would have liked to have made music his real career.[12] They became better acquainted with each other. Robeson gave Kenyatta his records and a gramophone, and no doubt Kenyatta told Robeson about his experiences in Russia and colonial Africa. They visited each other's flats—Robeson's a bookish, unpretentious set of rooms off the Strand, Kenyatta's the modest bed-sitting room near Victoria Station which Mrs Hocken kept tidy for him.

Kenyatta never spoke later about his appearance in *Sanders of the River*. But at the time he was glad to join in the presentation of a gold cigarette case to Korda and add his name to the inscription inside, 'with deep admiration and gratitude'.[13]

Living in his hand-to-mouth way, Kenyatta struggled through the nineteen-thirties. He was catholic in his friendships and accepted hospitality whenever it was offered. One friend was an insurance clerk, Geoffrey Husbands, whom Kenyatta met at an LCC evening class soon after his return from Russia. Husbands was a member of the Communist Party and then lived in a flat in Bloomsbury where he brought his friends back for soup after their classes. He detected no ideological bias in Kenyatta's views, but, on the contrary, found him remarkably open-minded, especially about the backwardness of his own race. With Geoffrey Husbands and his wife Lucy, Kenyatta could enjoy the company of young children again. He spent Christmas 1936 with them after they had moved to a house in Hertfordshire.

In complete contrast to Geoffrey Husbands was Prince Peter of Greece, with whom Kenyatta struck up an acquaintance at the University. Prince Peter had written a thesis in Denmark on co-operative

societies which brought him to the LSE as a pupil of Professor Malinowski's. He was the grandson of George I of Greece, son of Prince
George of Greece and Denmark, and married to a striking White
Russian *émigré*. They introduced Kenyatta to an aristocratic, cosmopolitan world far removed from the privations of Cambridge Street.
Prince Peter brought him over to Paris to stay with his mother, Princess Marie Bonaparte, at St Cloud. A pupil of Freud, and a highly
intelligent woman, she took a great interest in Kenyatta. He spent a
month with her in the spring of 1936 and then went on to Denmark
where Prince Peter arranged for him to live at the International
School and visit Danish co-operative farms. His stories to Mrs Hocken
were not all the moonshine Ross assumed them to be.

All these years Kenyatta showed he was adept at keeping his life
in compartments which were well sealed off from each other. While
his debts mounted at Mrs Hocken's he was also earning his fees as
an extra at Shepperton. All the time he was seeing Geoffrey Husbands
he never mentioned *Sanders of the River*. With Margaret Bryan he
spoke little about his university life, though they had much in common there, while to his university colleagues and tutors he said
nothing about his life in Cambridge Street. Prince Peter knew he had
been to Russia, but nothing of the details. Fenner Brockway once
found him stranded in Paris and gave him his return fare to London,
but he never understood what he was really doing in the French
capital. Thus Kenyatta maintained an air of detachment which made
him seem older than he was and more experienced than his contemporaries. He did not volunteer explanations about himself, nor could
he be pressed to give any. As Arthur and Barlow, Ross and Hooper,
dropped out of his life, he presented himself in a different light to
the new generation of white intellectuals.

Kenyatta attended Malinowski's classes for something like two
years. The two men apparently became close friends. They shared
certain prejudices, among them a dislike of Indians. 'My lectures are
not for Indians' Malinowski was known to open a session, and Kenyatta would follow up by describing how Indians exploited Africans
in Kenya.[14] Malinowski's classes included names subsequently famous
in the field of anthropology like Audrey Richards and Lucy Mair, as
well as African specialists like Elspeth Huxley, who wrote later that
Kenyatta 'was one of Dr Malinowski's brightest pupils . . . A showman to his finger tips; jovial, a good companion, shrewd, fluent,
quick, devious, subtle, flesh pot loving . . .'[15] Not everyone saw this
at the time; on other students Kenyatta made little impression. David

Abercrombie, the son of the poet, was a fellow member and found Kenyatta dressed soberly, even poorly. They collaborated together to raise funds for the defence of negro causes.

Each student was expected to give a paper in rotation and this was followed by discussions and lectures. On 14 November 1935, it was Kenyatta's turn. Prince Peter of Greece was there and took down notes of his friend's paper. Its subject was female circumcision. Kenyatta gave a factual account of the ceremony as it was performed by the Kikuyu. 'Europeans and missionaries consider this rite disgusting and barbarous', noted Prince Peter, 'the Kikuyu consider it very important for the solidity of the social structure.' In anthropology Kenyatta had found the weapon he needed to answer the philosophy of colonialism. The outcome was his book, published in 1938, *Facing Mount Kenya.*

CHAPTER 16

Facing Mount Kenya

Facing Mount Kenya is a collection of studies in Kikuyu life and customs based on the papers which Kenyatta wrote for Malinowski's seminars. Its pages contain scattered autobiographical references and a wealth of ethnological detail which have provided material for writers ever since.[1]

'It is one of the first really competent and instructive contributions to African ethnography by a scholar of pure African parentage. . . . As a first-hand account of a representative African culture, as an invaluable document in the principles underlying culture-contact and change; last, not least, as a personal statement of the new outlook of a progressive African, this book will rank as a pioneering achievement of outstanding merit.'

The value of Kenyatta's contribution to anthropology must be left to experts to judge. It is a science which claims an objectivity outsiders cannot always recognize. The historian especially must remain sceptical of a discipline which places such emphasis on description and offers no criteria for critical appraisal. But the accolade Kenyatta earned from Malinowski showed that he had mastered the technique.

What appeared to impress the seminar most was his paper on magic. Kenyatta wrote this from first-hand experience of his grandfather's trade, and he was at pains to make his hearers understand the real efficacy of these magical arts in African society. His descriptions of the different potions and invocations once in use in his part of the country were an original and valuable record, and he clearly was deeply convinced by them himself. At the phonetics laboratory he refused to speak into the instrument used for recording vowel sounds for fear of the possible evil consequences.

Kenyatta's purpose in writing *Facing Mount Kenya* was to challenge the white man's view of history. He was incensed by the European assumptions of superiority he had met throughout his life in Kenya, and he used the language of anthropology to propound a different philosophy—that of the golden African past. He described the principles of order, self-sufficiency and virtue underlying the Kikuyu way of life before the arrival of the white man. He tried to show in scientific terms, as George Padmore and Nancy Cunard had tried to do in literary and artistic terms, that the negro was not a benighted savage groping towards European enlightenment, but a man who inherited his social and cultural ideals from a different, and equally worthy, past. Taken by themselves, the factual and descriptive parts of his book were a contribution towards his chosen science, but *Facing Mount Kenya* as a whole was a masterly propaganda document.

Malinowski welcomed the slant of the book. In Kenyatta he saw a spokesman for the 'educated, intellectual minority of Africans, usually dismissed as "agitators"', who were 'catalysing an African public opinion even among raw tribesmen'. The process of disintegration through the West's false idea of progress, argued Malinowski, must not be repeated in Africa.

As in his texts for Lilias Armstrong's book, Kenyatta returned to his childhood world, remembered perhaps through the lullabies of his mother, where a Kikuyu infant grew up to learn the moral and practical meaning of life in terms of the tribe's communal loyalties. Each institution and activity was upheld by tribal law and custom— sex, love, marriage, war, work, friendship, justice and prayer. The division of tasks in the fields and homestead, the choosing of additional wives by the husband, and his offering of them to visitors and members of his own age-set, were all essential to this collective harmony: 'To live with others is to share and to have mercy for one another'.

Everything found strength and unity from the land. The dead, the living and the unborn lived through the soil and 'through incarnation' were fused into 'one organic whole'. God's blessing and prosperity rested with the tribe provided the ancient sacrifices were made beside the sacred trees, for the sacred tree

'is one of the key institutions of their culture. It marks at once their unity as a people, their family integrity (for their fathers sacrificed around it), their close contact with the soil, the rain and the rest of

Nature, and, to crown all, their most vital communion with the High God of the tribe.'

Kenyatta's thesis was that in its economic, social, religious and political aspects, Kikuyu tribal custom had a cohesion and integrity better than anything that the colonial system could offer. Chapters on land, education, religion and ancestor worship, political institutions—each in turn challenged the assumptions of the West.

'In the old order of the African society, with all the evils that are supposed to be connected with it, a man was a man, and as such he had the rights of a man and liberty to exercise his will and thought in a direction which suited his purposes as well as those of his fellow-men; but today an African, no matter what his station in life, is like a horse which moves only in the direction that the rider pulls the rein.'

Kenyatta's moral was unequivocal. The colonial theory of tutelage was oppressive and alien:

'In our opinion, the African can only advance to a "higher level" if he is free to express himself, to organise economically, politically, and socially, and to take part in the government of his own country. In this way he will be able to develop his creative mind, initiative, and personality, which hitherto have been hindered by the multiplicity of incomprehensible laws and ordinances.'

Facing Mount Kenya was a propaganda *tour de force*. No other African had made such an uncompromising stand for tribal integrity. Men who knew Kenyatta's background were astonished at his achievement and readers could not fail to be impressed by his skilful blend of fact and polemic, his confident references to Aristotle and Blue Books, and his clear, though not compelling, language. Even Arthur paid tribute to his powers of description.

There was one critic present at that seminar in November 1935 when Kenyatta had read his paper on female circumcision. L. S. B. Leakey, son of Canon Harry Leakey of the CMS 'Mother Church' at Kabete, had made a point of attending it. Like his father, L. S. B. Leakey regarded Kenyatta's potential influence on the tribe as mischievous. He had been initiated into the Kikuyu age-grade of *Kihiomwere,* the same as Kenyatta's, and had also written on the

subject of female circumcision in an anthropological journal in
1931. He and Kenyatta had a disagreement about the subject in front
of Malinowski's class. Both men shouted in Kikuyu at each other
and the reason for the quarrel was lost on the others. But Leakey
understood Kenyatta to argue that Kikuyu politics needed the type
of exaggeration that he had given.[2]

By the time *Facing Mount Kenya* came to be published, Kenyatta
had arrived at the appropriate scientific defence of female circumcision which he had lacked at his interview with Shiels in January
1931. This feeling of being at a disadvantage with European intellectuals was one of the reasons which had led him into the study of
anthropology. Some of the arguments in his book he borrowed from
Leakey's article.

Naturally he played down the physical ordeal. According to him
the circumciser operated 'with the dexterity of a Harley Street sur-
geon . . . with a stroke she cuts off the tip of the clitoris . . . the
girl hardly feels any pain'. The physical side was no more than a
'trimming' which, elsewhere, he suggested may have been designed
originally to help girls control their sexual feelings and keep them
chaste.

Kenyatta's advocacy of female circumcision was now unconditional.
It lay at the very heart of Kikuyu culture. The missionary 'attack' was
'misinformed' and he ridiculed their medical objections:

'The Gikuyu look upon these religious fanatics with great suspicion.
The overwhelming majority of them believe that it is the secret aim
of those who attack this centuries-old custom to disintegrate their
social order and thereby hasten their Europeanisation.'

Scoring points off the missionaries, however, was not his chief
aim and there was much else in *Facing Mount Kenya* that was controversial. But attention must be drawn to one aspect of the book,
namely the place Kenyatta accorded to the individual in Kikuyu society. Throughout *Facing Mount Kenya* the individual was down-
graded in the interests of group loyalties: 'The selfish or self-regarding
man has no name or reputation . . . An individualist is looked upon
with suspicion . . . and is likely to end up as a wizard.' While
'everything good comes from the collective life of the community.'
Where did this leave Kenyatta himself? He was the loner, the outsider, and such men were to be thrust out of the tribe. In Biblical

terms they would be cut off in their generation, a fate worse than death itself. In old times they were thought to be poisoners who did their work in the dark and were burned alive.

The distinction Kenyatta drew between the practitioners of beneficent magic and the evil wizards was among the most fascinating passages in *Facing Mount Kenya*. The latter met in secret and at night, usually in disguise. They dealt, according to Kenyatta, in 'genital organs of both male and female, breasts, tongues, ears, hands and feet, blood, eyes, and noses' extracted from both human and animal bodies and mixed with various burnt ashes and powders. They were 'a few nefarious men and women'. But the former were the real tribal leaders and they consisted of

'the majority of chiefs . . . especially if they command the respect and leadership of the tribal organisation. The qualifications for this position require, from the African's point of view, that the chief must be brave, a philosopher, and a seer; that is to say, to be practically a magician.'

Europeans were later to examine *Facing Mount Kenya* for clues to Kenyatta's own position in his tribe. Many of them failed to see that an individual could find self-expression by contributing leadership that was acceptable to the community. In Kenyatta's terms that meant associating himself with the destiny of the tribe. On those occasions when the pressures of the community placed a strain on his personality he could not, in the end, deny his Kikuyu heritage.

He originally called his book 'Voice of the Gikuyu: Echoes from Mount Kenya'. Its eventual title came from the final words of his preface, where he wrote that land 'is the key to the people's life; it secures for them that peaceful tillage of the soil which supplies their material needs and enables them to perform their magic and traditional ceremonies in undisturbed serenity, facing Mount Kenya.' The frontispiece showed a photograph of a new Kenyatta altogether. He wore a beard and carried a skin cloak slung over one shoulder, leaving the other bare. In his hands was a spear and he fingered its point reflectively. He had a new signature too; here, for the first time, the world saw the name *Jomo* Kenyatta.

Kenyatta was creating a new myth to rival the white man's view of history. This was what, finally, was striking and original about *Facing Mount Kenya*. Western intellectuals believed that myths could be among the most revolutionary forces in history. Consciously or un-

consciously Kenyatta was inventing one for Africa. The most significant part of *Facing Mount Kenya* was its dedication:

'To Moigoi and Wamboi and all the dispossessed youth of Africa: for
perpetuation of communion with ancestral spirits through the fight
for African Freedom, and in the firm faith that the dead, the living,
and the unborn will unite to rebuild the destroyed shrines.'

Muigai and Wambui were both his son and daughter and his father
and mother. But there were echoes here of all the influences that had
come Kenyatta's way, of Isaiah and the promise to the remnant of
Israel, or Padraic Pearse's call to Irish men and women to honour the
dead generations at Easter 1916, of Mazzini and the *Risorgimento*
and of all the revolutionary nationalisms of the West. *Facing Mount
Kenya* was in this historic tradition.

CHAPTER 17

Kenyatta the Pan-African

Facing Mount Kenya sold only 517 copies. As a publishing gamble it was 'a dismal flop' and Kenyatta's advance on royalties of £30 was 'barely earned'. But Frederic Warburg, to whom Kenyatta had been introduced by Fenner Brockway, saw in its pages a work for the future and Malinowski's introduction—he was a friend of Warburg's also—gave it intellectual respectability. On the whole it was well received. Barlow called it 'an excellent book in good English'. Arthur was less enthusiastic, being unable to accept Kenyatta's evaluation of the good life in terms of African culture.[1]

Though the book reflected many of the influences which had come into Kenyatta's life at the university, his new name and the photograph of him as an African tribalist were the result of another encounter which was destined to have more far-reaching consequences.

In the autumn of 1936 a fellow Kikuyu, Peter Mbiyu Koinange, the son of senior chief Koinange, arrived in England from America where he had completed his studies, begun in 1927, with a degree at New York's Columbia University. The Koinanges were childhood friends of the Leakey family, and L. S. B. Leakey arranged for Peter Mbiyu to spend a year at his own college, St John's College, Cambridge, on a Rhodes Trust grant while he attended classes in anthropology and African religions under a Professor Driberg, a former African administrator.[2]

Leakey discouraged Koinange from seeing Kenyatta, but in November 1936 Kenyatta came up to Cambridge to visit him. Koinange knew him only from a brief acquaintance in 1926 when Kenyatta was wearing his beaded cowboy-style hat and beaded belt, his khaki safari outfit and riding breeches. He was then still the Kenyatta of the Nairobi Water Board and Dagoretti, while Koinange was starting at the Alliance High School with Kenyatta's brother Muigai. In America all Koinange had heard was that Kenyatta had opposed his father's appointment as Kikuyu representative to the joint select committee.

In England the two men sized each other up. Kenyatta explained his own position. He acknowledged that Koinange's father had made an effective stand before the parliamentary committee. 'We misunderstood the old man,' he said. According to Kenyatta's interpretation all the tribal organizations in Kenya, including even the Local Native Councils, were really pursuing the same goal. To Peter Koinange, Kenyatta appeared now as mellow and friendly. He arranged to attend Malinowski's seminars in London once a week and so was enabled both to check on Kenyatta's tribal researches and meet his circle of left-wing intellectuals.

Whatever Koinange might have thought about the contents of *Facing Mount Kenya,* he was anxious to help in its presentation. He lent Kenyatta his hyrax and blue monkey cloak for the photograph, and they sharpened a piece of wood into the shape of a spear. Their object, according to Koinange, was to make the author of the book seem more like a tribal elder than a Western student. That way it would carry greater conviction.[3]

But then arose the question of coining a suitable name. 'Johnstone' clearly would no longer do; it smacked too much of the European tradition. What's wrong with Kamau wa Ngengi?' asked Koinange. 'You see, I am known by the name Kenyatta, I want to retain it,' his companion replied. Together they went through the alphabet trying out different combinations of vowels and consonants. From these efforts emerged the word Jomo. It sounded good, and it was close to a Kikuyu word describing the pulling of a sword from its scabbard. So Jomo Kenyatta he now became.

With his intelligence and American experience, Koinange was stimulating company for Kenyatta. In the deteriorating international scene of the thirties, London drew many African and negro leaders to witness, they hoped, the final act of the capitalist drama. Instead and to their fury they were treated to yet another adventure in European imperialism. The stage, this time, was Abyssinia.

The background to the Abyssinian tragedy lay in the diplomacy of nineteenth-century imperialism in which Britain, France and Italy competed for strategic advantage in the Horn of Africa. The Italians were not content with their sizeable colonies in Somalia and Eritrea which they had picked up in the 1880s. Despite repeated affirmations of friendship towards Ethiopia and her young and vigorous monarch

Ras Tafari, who was proclaimed Emperor Haile Selassie in 1930, they dreamed of revenge for their defeat at Adowa in 1896.

On 2 October 1935, the fascist armies, with huge supplies of the most up-to-date equipment, crossed into Ethiopian territory claiming they were acting on behalf of civilization.

The nineteenth century had left Abyssinia with a precarious independence based on some of the gains of Menelik's bloodthirsty rule. But she was still slave-ridden and 'backward'. Intervention by a European power at any time before 1914 would have passed with little comment. But in the nineteen-thirties, when the Western powers were already searching for a new philosophy to contain the totalitarian nationalism of Japan, Italy and Germany, the old call of the civilizing mission had a hollow ring. Grigg, however, could be relied on to make it in defending Italy's action, as did his former master, Leo Amery. Churchill wisely kept out of Britain and refused to comment.

The left, fearful of another war, was even more split between the pacifists and those driven to outbid the hated National Government in calling for sanctions, which left them open to the charge of war-mongering. Britain and France between them controlled Mussolini's lines of communication, but they preferred to see Ethiopia dismembered than risk a war on her behalf. They sought Mussolini's friendship as a counter to Hitler. With the aid of mustard gas and heavy aerial bombardments, the Italians overwhelmed the Ethiopian forces.

The Emperor's appeals to the League of Nations went unheeded. In March 1936 Hitler saw his chance and marched into the Rhineland in defiance of his generals who were prepared to remove him if things went wrong. No one stirred against him. The League was finished; another world war was now inevitable. Abyssinia was the nemesis of imperialism.

In 1935 Padmore came to live permanently in London where he joined up with C. L. R. James, an old friend from his Trinidad schooldays.[4] James formed a body which called themselves the International African Friends of Abyssinia. Kenyatta was strongly influenced by Padmore and ready to join with him in anything. He became an honorary secretary of James's body. It was an 'all Negro organisation . . . to assist by all means in their power in the maintenance of the territorial integrity and the political independence of Abyssinia.' Their 'office' was a restaurant in London's Oxford Street, run by Mrs Marcus Garvey. In September Kenyatta signed an article for the *Labour Monthly* called 'Hands off Abyssinia' in which he traced Italy's move to the European scramble for Africa and de-nounced the hypocrisy of the West. He described Abyssinia as 'the last remaining relic of the greatness of an Africa that once was.'

Kenyatta was out walking in Hertfordshire with Geoffrey Hus-bands when they saw newspaper headlines announcing the bombing of Harrar. Kenyatta was deeply affected by it—as deeply as others were later by the bombing of Guernica. In Abyssinia spears and ar-rows were being pitted against aeroplanes and mustard gas. Kenyatta knew what an unequal contest that was.[5] He had been in Kenya when the colonial police shot down the crowd protesting at Harry Thuku's arrest. Better than any of his colleagues in the Afro-Negro group in London he had learnt the true weakness of African tribes in face of modern weapons. On 2 May 1936, the Emperor was forced to leave his country. A British warship awaited him at Djibuti to carry him to a five-year exile. A month later, he arrived at Waterloo Station, a small, lonely, but immensely dignified figure, to begin his bitter campaign to secure international justice for his people.[6]

Kenyatta and the Friends of Ethiopia were waiting to demonstrate their solidarity with the Emperor. According to one eyewitness ac-count, an African in the watching crowd broke through the polite cordon of officials. It was Kenyatta. Contemptuous of protocol, he went up to the Emperor and embraced him man to man, African to fellow African. It was a moving scene between two exiles.[7]

But the Emperor's cause was submerged in the larger threat which now loomed over the world. In the West there was talk of appeasing Hitler by returning former German colonies like Tanganyika to the Nazis, while in Ethiopia resistance to the invader cast a shadow over the spectacular programme of public works on which the Italians embarked. In the course of three days in February 1937, 30,000 Ethiopians were massacred in Addis Ababa as a reprisal for a bomb attack on Italian soldiers. In May a further 5,000 were cut down while attending a religious feast.[8] The Emperor could do nothing but wait in the country house provided for him near Bath.

But his plight and that of his country were the catalyst for the Afro-negro movement. The atrocities reported from Addis Ababa en-sured an emotional response from the expatriate journalists, lawyers, students and politicians who gathered in London, Kenyatta and Peter Koinange among them. Doctrinal differences were forgotten; the Em-peror was held up as a model 'progressive' monarch. Kenyatta grew a beard as a gesture of support, which is how he came to be photo-graphed for *Facing Mount Kenya*.

The International Friends of Ethiopia were an *ad hoc* group responding like many such ephemeral organizations to a specific situation. In March 1937 it gave way to the more purposeful International African Service Bureau, which was launched chiefly by Padmore and James as a central powerhouse of ideas and information to propagate the pan-African idea. Its message was simple: to win 'domestic rights, civil liberties and self-determination' for the African. It aimed to co-ordinate the varied activities of London's coloured intellectuals, like Solanke's old West African Students' Union, to which Kenyatta's friend Kessie belonged, and the League of Coloured Peoples, which was founded in 1931 by a Jamaican doctor working in London, Harold Moody, as a Christian reform body.[9]

But the hard core of the IASB was made up of activists who believed in revolution—men like Padmore and James, and Padmore's old contacts in the International Trade Union Committee of Negro Workers like I. T. A. Wallace-Johnson, a West African born in Sierra Leone who was about the same age as Kenyatta. Wallace-Johnson had served in the Carrier Corps in the war and had been enrolled by Padmore into his Moscow university course, where he probably met Kenyatta. Having founded the Nigerian Workers Union in 1931, he was actively engaged in political developments in West Africa.

The business side of the IASB was managed by a British Guianan named Griffiths who graduated from Cornell University in America in 1933 and went to Denmark, ostensibly to study agriculture. Like Padmore, Wallace-Johnson and Kenyatta, he then adopted a footloose clandestine style of living and flirted with communism. On publicizing his discovery that Denmark was manufacturing mustard gas, he was deported to Britain where he changed his name to T. Ras Makonnen in sympathy with the Ethiopian cause. His business flair kept the IASB going throughout the thirties.

Kenyatta took an active part in the Pan-African movement, as he did in anything which might suit his purpose, but with a down-to-earth approach which sometimes worried his more doctrinaire colleagues. His single-minded attention to the future of Kenya seemed to exclude their flightier ideas. But he alone supplied authentic experience of Africa and his pragmatism was justified. The British public were quite unmoved by the IASB publicity. No section of British society proved itself more racially conscious than the working class in whose vocabulary the word 'blackleg' denoted someone more hateful than an imperialist or even a capitalist. While members of the liberal intelligentsia like Ross were advocating non-resistance to fascist aggression, whether in Abyssinia or Europe, Fenner Brockway and others on the left were preoccupied with India.

One day when he was attending a rally in Trafalgar Square, Kenyatta met a woman who was to play an important part in his life. She was Dinah Stock, the secretary of the British Centre Against Imperialism, a group drawn from the non-communist elements of the League Against Imperialism. At Oxford she had been the first woman to be chairman of the Labour Club and she had graduated in 1926 into the thick of left-wing politics moving steadily away from the official Labour Party.

By profession Dinah Stock was a WEA lecturer and in 1937 she had just returned from a journey which took her through Nazi Germany, Soviet Russia, China and India, when she was introduced to Kenyatta as a man who needed help with a book. She was then thirty-five, a handsome, intelligent and progressive woman, and she made an immediate impression on Kenyatta. He took a room in her flat in Camden Town and they began a period of collaboration which lifted Kenyatta out of his student world of petty debts and intrigue into a new political maturity.[10]

Dinah Stock first helped him put the scattered essays from his seminars into the order in which they appeared in *Facing Mount Kenya,* correcting where necessary his English and his spelling. As she read his typescript, she recognized at once that he was a man with a mission. She had lived through the Easter Rising in Dublin in 1916 and its sequel, and from those experiences she could add to his faith that the Africans of Kenya would one day be free. Unhesitatingly she supported him in his own sense of destiny.

Kenyatta had no regular income. He and Dinah Stock were hard put to it between them to find the rent for the flat in Camden Town. The KCA periodically tried to raise funds, ostensibly to bring Kenyatta home, and in 1935 their paper *Muigwithania* made a brief reappearance with this as its declared objective, but it is unlikely that much reached him in London and even less likely that he intended returning. He was enjoying life. Hardship was shared: 'When we had nothing to eat we shared it.' They shared too an interest in the cause of the oppressed. Kenyatta's first action in their new home was to paint the furniture with the Abyssinian colours. Dinah Stock made no emotional demands on him but was a loyal and diligent collaborator. She accepted absolutely his position and made no attempt, as McGregor Ross had done, to see that he conformed to the white liberal's concept of ordered, constitutional development. That way, the way of Ross and Leys, would have neutered Kenyatta. Better, in fact, were the out-and-out white settlers, the Delameres and Grogans, for at least their position was unequivocal. Dinah Stock represented the opposite pole. If Africa for the Africans meant anything, it meant acceptance of African traditions wholeheartedly and in their own right, even if that were to involve violence and an appeal to the dead generations. Had not Padraic Pearse declared that 'The tree of liberty must be watered with blood'? Ireland, India, Africa—for all true anti-imperialists it was the same struggle.

While *Facing Mount Kenya* was a theoretical rejection of everything to do with colonial rule, Kenyatta maintained a continuing interest in the development of Kenya. His main concern was over the implementation of the Carter Commission's recommendations which affected most directly the Kikuyu tribe. The Commission found that some land had been removed from the tribe's ancestral territories and proposed that compensation for the individual clans affected should be paid in the form of new land excised from the forest reserve. This left the way clear for the Kenya Government to define the European farming areas as an exclusive 'white' reserve—what was popularly known as the White Highlands.

The Kikuyu were slow to react. At first the local leaders appeared to accept the proposals, and Koinange and the chiefs limited themselves to a request that their sacred Mount Kenya should not be included in the White Highlands. But then more general opposition grew to the whole idea of an exclusive white reserve.

Moving the families from the designated area, Tigoni, gave rise to renewed bitterness. It turned out that nearly 4,000 individuals were involved. Carter had spoken of only 200 families and allowed them £2,000 financial compensation, and at least one official breezily foresaw that there would be trouble: 'there is likely to be quite a spot of bother with the Kiambu Kukes if the Morris Carter proposals are carried out . . . they're naturally not happy at getting only 10/- a head, and a problematical patch of inferior land miles away!'

Naturally the hard core of the old KCA were active and the delays in getting the legislation through gave them an opportunity for stiffening resistance; but Koinange, Harry Thuku and the tribal elders were now united in their concern at the way things were going.[11]

The Tigoni move did not affect the bulk of the Kikuyu tribe; but it added to the general sense of grievance and of something lost, thus strengthening Kenyatta's idea of a past golden age which the white man had destroyed and which might yet be regained if the land could be recovered. Nor was Kenyatta alone in holding this view. By May 1939 Koinange wrote the Governor a courteous but warning letter, which gave a striking illustration of how his own restraint was beginning to give way:

'A large bulk of African people still retain their ancient religious rites and beliefs that to be removed from their trees, ceremonies and graves of their ancestors is to be suddenly torn in their spiritual body . . . If Government do not change their policy people might become disobedient. We do not like this but it is our duty to say it without fear.'[12]

Political activity had hitherto been largely confined to the Kikuyu and the Nyanza tribes around Lake Victoria, who were stimulated into renewed interest by the Kakamega gold rush. But in 1938 trouble arose with the Kamba people over their stocks of cattle, which the tribe regarded as the index of prestige and wealth in a mystical sense akin to the Kikuyu's feelings over land. The Kamba were the tribe living around the hills of Machakos to the east of the Kikuyu, and they supplied most of the recruits for the Kenya police and the King's African Rifles. Since the removal of the Masai and the introduction of Western veterinary science their herds of cattle had grown rapidly. Simultaneously their capacity to expand out of their traditional lands was restricted by their early confinement within a reserve, and the granting of the ranching land along the railway line across the Athi plain to Europeans.[13]

The result was soil erosion, a decline in agricultural output and growing poverty. For ten years the government tried remedial action. The Carter Commission recommended de-stocking, and by 1938 the situation had become so grave the government accepted that a drastic reduction in cattle was necessary if disaster was to be avoided. A special meat factory was set up on the edge of the reserve and inducements were offered to the tribesmen to reduce their stocks willingly; but most refused and stock culling, as it was called, was undertaken by force. The Kamba reacted by marching in a body on Nairobi to see the Governor, and some 3,000 men, women and children camped for days near the race course. But the Governor declined to see them, being otherwise engaged in polo and the races.

Again the KCA were active. The Kamba also received strong sup-

port from Isher Dass, now a member of Legco. A certain Samuel
Muindi emerged as spokesman for the tribe. Using the KCA address
in Nairobi he resorted to their tactic of sending cables and protests
to sympathizers in London, Kenyatta among them. The Kenya Government wrote him off as no more than a KCA-type agitator, an
'ex-policeman who holds no responsible position in the tribe.' Muindi
was accused of holding an illegal 'cursing' *baraza,* and in October
1938 the government deported him to Lamu. Compulsory de-stocking
was suspended while other approaches were considered, and the war
solved the problem, at least for the time being, by creating a large
demand for meat.[14]

Kenyatta saw the Kamba affair as another example of the one-
sided effects of colonial rule and he refused to eat any meat that came
out of a tin. Though tenuous, the KCA link with the Kamba and
the Nyanza tribes enabled him to claim to speak for all Africans in
Kenya. He found a way of turning the flank of the Colonial Office in
London by using Arthur Creech Jones as an intermediary. Creech
Jones entered Parliament in 1935 and soon became official opposition
spokesman on colonial affairs. The KCA and Koinange sent him
copies of their cables and petitions and from 1937 Kenyatta kept
him regularly supplied with information. Creech Jones sent copies
of the replies he received from the Colonial Office straight on to
Kenyatta, asking him to keep his friends in Kenya informed.[15]

As the tempo of international politics increased and the dictators of
Europe got the measure of the appeasers in Britain and France, so
the IASB stepped up its own propaganda. The year 1938 was Kenyatta's busiest in his new political role. With Dinah Stock's assistance
he wrote a number of articles for the *Manchester Guardian* about
the Kamba troubles and he threw himself into a speaking campaign
which took him all over the country, to meetings organized by the
Fabians and the ILP, by the Workers Educational Association, Ro-
tary Clubs and anyone else interested in colonial problems.

His line was to translate into political terms the message of *Facing
Mount Kenya.* At a one-day WEA school in Horsham, for example,
he described how as a boy he had watched 'hundreds of natives,
chained together by the necks, being marched to work on the white
men's estates.' 'In 1895, when I was in my own country I was a man;
now I am no longer a man. I am a slave.' He returned time and again
to the problem of land: the Europeans had stolen it; they had bribed
the chiefs with gin, beads and blankets; the government 'took away
with one stroke of the pen practically all the land held by Africans.'

And in the *New Statesman and Nation,* writing about the Kamba troubles: 'The people's land is filched, and now their cattle are cut down by force to match the reduced grazing area.'

In May that year the IASB put on an anti-colonial display to rival London's Empire Day exhibition, and when the latter moved to Glasgow in September the IASB followed with its counter-demonstration. Posters of Kenyatta in his *Facing Mount Kenya* outfit formed part of the display and he took his turn on the platform to relate to Kenya the general attack on the Western democracies mounted by the Pan-African propaganda machine. The IASB took the line that in war the colonial peoples had the right to rise against their governments, and at the time of the Munich crisis they brought out a manifesto with the title *Europe's Difficulty is Africa's Opportunity.* Kenyatta was too cautious to call for rebellion, but he implied as much by questioning whether the British could expect the support of its subject races in another war against fascism unless they convinced them 'that British methods are different and that British claims to stand for democracy and freedom are true.'

It was a theme he repeated throughout those months. In October 1938 he was at the Manchester Fabian Society:

'I not only say there is British Fascism in the colonies but can give you examples and facts for you to judge whether the Jews in Germany are treated worse than we are in the colonies. The natives have no freedom of speech, freedom of association, or freedom of movement.'

In November he was at another one-day WEA school in Eastbourne:

'I think the time when the Englishman's word was his bond is gone. In 1914 thousands of Africans helped in the war, over 30,000 from Kenya alone, but I very much doubt how many will turn out next time to fight for democracy. We say "No thank you".'

(He did not of course mention that he had opted out of the first war himself.)

At the end of the year he was in Salisbury:

'We are not asking too much by asking for human rights. A democratic country must extend its democratic principles to the people for whom it is trustee. It is only by doing so that we can find the difference between British rule and rules such as we see in Germany and other countries.'

Kenyatta's activities led the Colonial Office to reopen their files on him. 'Jomo Kenyatta: Libellous statements made to the WEA' was the heading the civil servants gave to his new dossier, as cuttings from local newspapers reached them with headlines like: BRITISH RULE MORE FEARED THAN ITALIAN OR GERMAN, and 'I AM A SLAVE' SAYS WEA SPEAKER.' 'Mr Kenyatta is becoming increasingly mischievous' noted the officials. 'The difficulty is, however, that he is spreading his poison by word of mouth at relatively obscure meetings organised by a perfectly reputable organisation.'[16]

As war approached, the Colonial Office came alive to the danger that the IASB group might form a fifth column. Requests went out to the different colonial governments for CID information on the ringleaders. In April 1939 the Governor of Kenya forwarded his police chief's report on Kenyatta. It contained little that was new, and many of its details are now unverifiable. Kenyatta's early days in London were recalled in the terms to which Ross took such exception, in that 'he was associating with white women of doubtful moral character'. The police assumed he was still receiving communist financial aid, but they admitted that no one could be sure whether the money raised on his behalf in Nairobi ever reached him in London. Kenyatta, concluded the report, was not to be rated seriously.

'The articles written by him . . . and his speeches . . . are notable for their inaccuracy, exaggeration and false portrayal of conditions in the colony and he certainly cannot claim with any authority to speak on behalf of the people in Kenya whom he purports to represent.'[17]

The government found nothing in Kenyatta's past or in his present activities which could be construed as seditious enough to warrant prosecution, though they were able to do this successfully with Wallace-Johnson.

But the Colonial Office knew also that Kenyatta had some grounds for his attacks. Despite the presence of Malcolm MacDonald at the Dominions and Colonial Office, which partially restored Labour's political influence lost in the débâcle of 1931, the gulf between Whitehall and Nairobi which had shown itself in Grigg's day was as wide as ever.[18]

Thus the Kenya Government's opposition to Peter Koinange's

proposed course of study in England received this comment in London: 'A dreadful despatch. It seems to have been conceived in a thoroughly narrow-minded, illiberal and suspicious spirit.'[19] The handling of the removal of Kikuyu farmers from the area newly demarcated for white settlers drew the rebuke: 'The Government of Kenya seems to have behaved with almost criminal ineptitude in its arrangements for the removal of this tribe.' And again, on the same subject: 'it seems clear that, whether as regards the quality of the new land with which they are to be provided or as regards the amenities of life, many of these natives will suffer very considerably by the exchange.' While the Kenya Government's attitude was that 'the Kikuyu is an ungrateful and omnivorous creature when it comes to land.'[20]

With hindsight it can be seen that Kenya on the eve of the war showed every sign of a growing political awareness spreading among all sections of African society. Trade unions had come into existence, thanks largely to Indians, and proved their effectiveness in a strike in Mombasa. The Nairobi-based 'agitators' had succeeded in forming links between the Kikuyu and other tribes. Detribalization had spread. The Kenya Government could not long continue to treat opposition to its policies, as did the Governor of Kenya, then an Air Marshal, with harangues in the language of *Sanders of the River;* nor complain if the young African politician lobbied for support in London instead of looking to his DC 'as his father and mother and his chief source of help'.

Furthermore the thirties had seen a dramatic change in the nature of communications with the introduction in 1931 of the Empire News Service of the BBC and the growth of Imperial Airways. The effect was double edged. Though it gave the white settlers of Africa a feeling that they now shared more closely in their European heritage, it also brought to the natives a growing consciousness of the outside world. A broadcast, for instance, which announced the ending of the Kamba protest also contained news of a terrorist outbreak in Palestine, which must have given many food for thought.[21] Small wonder the film censors were particularly strong on anything which reflected unfavourably on colonial officers and the white man generally in a colonial context; or that men like Paul Robeson looked to the film as a potent means of expressing their support of the Pan-African idea.[22]

In 1938 the KCA hard core reconstituted themselves as the 'Kikuyu Central Association (1938) ', with Jesse Kariuki and George Ndegwa taking the lead. Though the Governor reported that they did not represent the opinions of the Kikuyu tribe, he allowed that the KCA was now supported by 10,000 of them. That was a sizeable number by any standards. Furthermore, he was forced to acknowledge that:

'There are perhaps two subjects upon which the Association might be said to have the bulk of Kikuyu opinion behind it, namely, land claims, upon which the tribe feels strongly, and the desire for increased educational facilities.'[23]

Here, before the war swept these things from sight, were all the makings of a mass movement: a wider political awareness, better communications, fertile ground for emotional propaganda—the only thing lacking was a leader. Kenyatta had no doubt that his destiny was to be that leader. He had watched the success of the leaders of Europe and studied their techniques. But could he be sure that his moment had come?

In 1938 Peter Koinange prepared to return to his country after an absence of nine years, and having put in an extra year in London for a teaching diploma. For Kenyatta it was a testing situation. He had no illusions about Koinange's better standing in the colonial world. He was the son of the senior and most respected Kikuyu chief and he could now boast a university degree and an English diploma. Koinange's future seemed bright, while he, Kenyatta, was losing touch with his Association and with his own family. No word from Dagoretti had reached him for a long time. Koinange's departure was a reminder to Kenyatta of his own lengthening separation and isolation. He watched him go with mixed feelings.

The Colonial Office, too, looked forward to Koinange's return with misgivings. His Cambridge tutor spoke highly of his loyalty and desire to serve his people. But the civil servants knew only too well how these feelings might be rebuffed in the colony:

'His own view of his mission in life is clearly very different from that of the Government of Kenya . . . He will find that these aspirations will be viewed with a considerable measure of frigidity in Kenya . . . There is not in Kenya, as there is in West Africa a local educated African "society" in which he could find a place. He will be an "odd man out" with no social background.'[24]

These forebodings were justified. Koinange's homecoming proved a bitter disappointment to him. The administration offered him only a minor post in the educational department, and at a salary less than Europeans with poorer qualifications were receiving for the same job. Koinange refused the offer.

Looking back, one is stunned by the folly of the colonial government in thus snubbing one of the ablest of the new Kikuyu generation and one who, moreover, belonged to the most influential family in Kikuyuland. It showed how far the racial attitudes depicted in E. M. Forster's *A Passage To India* had permeated the British Empire.

The closer the coloured man approached the white man in education and standard of living, the more the latter insisted on social exclusiveness. In Kenya Peter Mbiyu found the racial barriers had grown while he was away. His father, too, was hurt and now turned slowly, and with reluctance, from loyalty to opposition.[25] White society in Nairobi helped the cause of African Nationalism far more than white socialists in London. The Koinange family began to see that Kenyatta might be their man after all.

Helped by his father, Peter Mbiyu now took the problem of the independent schools in hand. On 7 January 1939 he founded a Teachers' Training College at Githunguri, near to his estates, to provide the shock troops for the independent schools movement. It was to play an important role in nationalist politics after the war.

It is likely that Kenyatta and Koinange talked about the political value of the independent schools while they were in London. Certainly, Kenyatta asked Koinange to help with the education of his own family. At Christmas 1938 he heard from his son at last. On 28 March Kenyatta replied, in what perhaps was *his* first letter to his son:

'To my son Muigai,
First receive my greetings—which come from your father's heart whom you have not forgotten these many days past, and who always remembers you in his heart . . . please understand it is not that I have forgotten you, but that I have much other business. My greetings to your sister and your mother, tell them that I'm all right.
Now what I want to tell you is in the matter of which you asked, i.e. your schooling . . . I shall be glad to hear that you have started worthwhile education, and that you are keen to learn. If there's anything worrying you in your desire to study, please let me know at

once. And tell me honestly what you want and what you need for
study, for perhaps you have been drifting, but if you really try you
will go ahead without difficulty . . . Please let me know also how
far your sister Wambui has reached in her studies. And please also
send me photos of you both, so that I can see what you are like . . .
I am all right. I have work for the country. Here there is now much
cold weather, but warmer weather is just around the corner.
Greet all those at home and all your friends

Your loving father,

Jomo Kenyatta

P.S. Perhaps you have seen the book I wrote? It is called "Facing
Mount Kenya". If you want a copy, let me know and I'll bring you
one.'

While visiting Paris in May, Kenyatta heard that Peter's schooling
had been fixed up with Mbiyu, and in August he wrote his last letter
before communications were lost, asking for details of the fees and
further news. 'I've received the photos and see that you have become
a big lad; if you hadn't told me it was your photo, I would have
guessed you were like your uncle.'[26]

Within a month the British Empire was at war. For the second time
in his life Kenyatta found himself in the middle of a struggle in which
he had no wish to take part.

CHAPTER 18

World War II

The leaders of the IASB were not unprepared for war. For the past eighteen months they had been looking forward to a European conflagration as the means whereby the colonies would be shaken free of the imperial grip. In the crisis which preceded Munich they believed the moment had come, and T. R. Makonnen made arrangements for four of them, including Kenyatta, to move to Norway. There, they thought, they could watch in safety the collapse of Europe's empires. Munich deceived them. In September 1939 they found themselves trapped in Britain, except for James who had gone to America in 1938 on a lecture tour and was able to remain there, and Wallace-Johnson who was under arrest in Sierra Leone. During the months of the phoney war the others looked to their own future. Makonnen eventually made his way to Manchester to start a restaurant business. Padmore remained in London in his flat in Cranleigh Houses, nearly next door to Dinah Stock's. But Dinah Stock decided London in war-time was no place for Kenyatta and herself. They left to stay with friends at Storrington in West Sussex.

The war brought a clamp-down on Kenyatta's communications. The last thing he heard from Kenya was a letter from a certain Makhan Singh, calling himself General Secretary of the Labour Trade Union of East Africa, who told him that he had been given his name by George Ndegwa of the KCA. He invited Kenyatta, together with Krishna Menon, to represent his organization at an international conference planned for the end of September in Brussels. Kenyatta did not know who Makhan Singh was, and he must have read one sentence with a wry smile: 'Please note that it is impossible for us at the moment to bear the expenses of the journey [to Brussels], and we think that you will be able to manage for that.' Kenyatta accepted, but the further information he asked for never arrived; nor did the conference take place.[1] Though Kenyatta did not know it, the Colonial Office suspected Makhan Singh of communist sympathies and in May 1940 he was arrested in India.

Kenyatta heard nothing further from the KCA either. Nor had the Colonial Office apparently replied to the various petitions which accumulated in the months before the war. Kenyatta reopened his correspondence with the Colonial Office in July 1939 about these matters, and in April 1940 he wrote again from his war-time address, asking for an interview with the Colonial Secretary. None was granted. Instead, and again unknown to him, a cable from Nairobi warned the Colonial Office of police reports that the KCA leaders were in touch with the Italian Consul in Nairobi. They also reported a new development: secret oathing was taking place at night, something which was illegal and contrary to tribal custom.[2] Three days later, on 30 May, the KCA was banned, and Jesse Kariuki, George Ndegwa and other ringleaders were arrested and exiled in the north of Kenya. Their arrest and the government's security measures sealed off Kenyatta from his country.

Creech Jones also wondered what was going on. In 1940 he formed a Fabian Colonial Research Bureau under Rita Hinden to help formulate Labour Party thinking on colonial matters. It coincided with the government's Colonial Welfare and Development Act which adopted a new principle of 'aid' to overseas territories. But the Fabians were suspicious of Kenyatta and his communist past, and Kenyatta for his part treated Creech Jones as little more than a posting box. In August 1941 he replied somewhat casually to an enquiry from Creech Jones: 'I have had no news from Kenya for over a year, and am therefore quite out of touch with recent developments. I don't know what has happened to your African correspondents, and have unfortunately no way of finding out.'[3]

Storrington is a peaceful west Sussex village lying a few miles inland from Worthing. It is a countryside of bracken, silver birches and adders, of rich farmland and copses and views across the Arun Valley to the South Downs. Though reluctant at first to leave London, Kenyatta found it in 1939 the perfect retreat from bombs and busybodies and he made it his home for the duration of the war.

Dinah Stock's friend was an extra-mural lecturer from Southhampton University called Roy Armstrong. He was building his house himself in stages with large rooms below and wings off at each side which gave it a colonial appearance, like one of the houses Nairobi folk built for themselves on the estates outside town at Karen or Muthaiga. It lay down a secluded lane in rough heathland which reminded Kenyatta of parts of his own country. Dinah Stock and he rented the flat, and Armstrong gave him his own plot of scrub to clear which Kenyatta soon brought under control. He planted mixed vegetables in the manner of Kikuyu agriculturalists, brought in some chickens, and soon had a miniature *shamba* going in the west Sussex heath.

In August 1940 Kenyatta took a job on a neighbouring farm. As an agricultural worker he could avoid conscription, and experience at first hand English farming methods. Later he moved to the tomato houses at Lindfield. In both places he earned the standard labourer's wage.

Through the WEA and his trade union contacts, Kenyatta was also in demand as a speaker. In the long, dark months of the war his exotic appearance was a distraction from other news. His line was the familiar one: land, settler oppression and native sufferings.

'In the last war 300,000 of my people fought in the British Army to drive the Germans from East Africa and 60,000 of them lost their lives. In this war large numbers of my people have been fighting to smash fascist power in Africa and have borne some of the hardest fights against the Italians. Surely if we are considered fit enough to take our rifles and fight side by side with white men we have a right to a direct say in the running of our country and to education.'[4]

Often he would raise a laugh with a reference to African customs which he knew how to make sound outrageous, or to some aspect of European behaviour which he could ridicule:

'You may say the world wants gold. I am not so sure. It seems to me gold is taken from the ground, taken to America, and then put underground again. Anyhow, our point is that the land belongs to us and we want some of the gold to decorate our women and ourselves.'[5]

Kenyatta's diploma also came in useful. It made him eligible to join the panel of lecturers to army educational classes in the southern counties. On these afternoons a jeep called after lunch to take him out to training camps or gun emplacements in the Downs. He spoke to the troops of his own country, choosing his words carefully. It was an ironic role for a Moscow-trained revolutionary. He also tried to join the Home Guard but here, as he said in his letter to Creech Jones, 'there seems to be some red tape somewhere'. No doubt officials drew the line at issuing him with a gun.

The war forced on Kenyatta a period of reflection. There was not much point in writing to the papers, and he had to be careful of the powers of arbitrary detention vested in the government under wartime regulations. For a time Dinah Stock provided an important stimulus to his thinking. She encouraged him to continue writing. Kenyatta had an ambition to compose a large work on Kenya which would incorporate and supersede *Facing Mount Kenya*. He began a novel about the upbringing of an African (himself) in a British colony which he intended submitting for a competition. A chapter was to describe how Kenjimoo, the hero, came to London; but he never completed it.[6]

One result, however, was a pamphlet which eventually appeared under the title *My People of Kikuyu* and, as a subtitle, *The Life of Chief Wangombe*. It was a further essay in legendary history. The first half described the traditional political organization of the Kikuyu and stressed its democratic structure through age-grades. Kenyatta ended it with a strong plea for Kikuyu independence:

'The spirit of independence, love of freedom in thought and action, and hatred of autocratic rule, are ingrained in the minds of the Kikuyu people . . . In their highlands and mountain homes, the people cherished the system of democratic government, the principles of which have been passed down from generation to generation. Their love of freedom and manhood has made them defend their country fearlessly. Warriors armed with spears and shields, bows and arrows, have shed blood to defend their freedom, for they said: *"Kindo kiega gitiumaga hega"* (meaning "The tree of liberty is watered with blood," or "A good thing is not easy to get.") That was when they depended on their strength in the settling of frontier disputes.

In recent times physical force has given place to diplomacy as a means of defence. It is a difficult and disheartening weapon to use, but the Kikuyu still show their devotion to their land by the way in which they handle it.'

A passage which should have given English readers occasion to pause. Kenyatta had equated the Irish freedom fighter's slogan 'The tree of liberty is watered with blood' to a Kikuyu proverb. The phrase suggested a call to violence. Did Kenyatta mean this? As the passage continued, he appeared to say that the fight must now be conducted not with the spear but with diplomacy. 'Spear and Diplomacy' was a theme he planned to write about with Dinah Stock. Kenya, he would say later, had been conquered by Blue Books and Royal Commissions and the Africans must fight back with similar weapons.

The second part of the pamphlet continued with the idea of a Kikuyu paradise which Kenyatta said existed before the white man's arrival. It was created by the integrated system of leadership upwards from clan elders through district chiefs to the 'national chiefs', Wangombe and Waiyaki. They were the great heroes. Peace reigned between them and the Masai and 'in this way the country and the people were kept united, and feelings of contentment prevailed everywhere.'

Ostensibly this section was an account of the life of Chief Wangombe, a man prominent in the northern district of Kikuyuland at the time when John Boyes entered the country. It was an account which Kenyatta, coming from the southern district of the tribe, was unlikely to have received first hand. But tradition and invention ran in close parallel to the men of Kenyatta's generation who grew up under the impact of European penetration, and the booklet was an illustration of the strong feelings of pride in his tribe which Kenyatta held. The most important part of his story was the words he put into the mouth of the dying Wangombe:

' "Remember how many battles we have fought to protect our country from invaders," he said in a slow sinking voice. "Don't forget that you have a great task in front of you; you may not have to fight with spears, shields or bows and arrows, in the way with which you are familiar. But in the short time in which I have been in contact with the Athongo (Europeans), I have seen how hard it is to deal with them. They know how to dazzle your mind with praise, when they know that by doing it they will achieve their own ends. Learn their clever way of talking for it is by using your wisdom that you may safeguard your country . . ." '

In other words, diplomacy must replace the spear.[7]

In all Kenyatta's writings it was never really clear where fact ended and invention began. Was the life of Wangombe real history or legend, and were the two distinguishable in a society which lived on oral traditions? Was the autobiographical chapter of his novel a true impression of Kenyatta's earliest memories or merely propa-

ganda? Were his descriptions of Kikuyuland his own, or did he come
by them, as others thought, from hearing how Europeans talked about
the highlands of Kenya? Was the myth he was creating a reality in
his own mind, or was he seeing his future only through the idealism
of Dinah Stock?

Soon after moving down to Storrington, Dinah Stock was offered
a teaching job in Yorkshire. Her salary enabled her to send remit-
tances for Kenyatta to keep the flat on. Early in 1940 while seeing
a girl-friend off on the bus to London, Kenyatta met a family looking
for a house in the country. He offered them the use of his half-empty
flat while they searched. Within a few weeks they found what they
wanted in the neighbouring village of Ashington, which was close
to the greenhouses where Kenyatta was working. He fell into the
habit of eating his lunch with them every day, and so became a regular visitor at their household.

With his new friends lived a companion and governess called Edna
Grace Clarke, the daughter of a marine engineer in Yarmouth. One
morning in May 1941 she heard that both her parents had been killed
in an air raid ruring the night. With that instinctive sympathy which
Kenyatta always extended to people in distress, he at once offered to
help, and accompanied her on the train as far as London, seeing her
across the city to the train to Yarmouth to attend to the sad business
of clearing up. Returning alone to Sussex, Edna welcomed the protection of Kenyatta's warm and powerful personality. A year later,
on 11 May 1942, they were married at Chanctonbury Registry Office.

Edna was a bright, straightforward girl of thirty-two. On the marriage certificate Kenyatta put his own age down as thirty-seven and
gave his profession as 'author and lecturer', describing himself as a
bachelor. Though he hardly ever spoke of Grace Wahu and the two
children in Kenya, he emphasized that one day he would have to
return to his own people. On 11 August 1943, in Worthing Hospital,
Edna gave birth to their son. They named him Peter Magana, after
Kenyatta's grandfather.

Kenyatta soon fitted himself into Sussex life. His *Facing Mount
Kenya* outfit was always good for a couple of drinks in the local pub.
Never one for worrying about status, he mixed on equal terms with
the villagers. They reacted to him as any group will to a stranger.
Some took to his gregarious nature, others were repelled by his flashi-
ness.

For his friends, life was always exciting when Kenyatta was around and in form. One day he would be singing one of Paul Robeson's songs and swinging children over his head to the music, on another he would mimic with great accuracy the sounds of Africans taking off a British DC at a *baraza:* 'Phut phut phut yers, phut phut phut . . .' One Christmas there was a party round the fire at Storrington and one of the group described a bullfight he had seen in Latin America. Eyes turned to Kenyatta as he took up the poker and mimed a Masai stalking and killing a lion with a vividness that took their breath away. He was indeed 'a showman to his fingertips'.[8] From his childhood he had learnt the value of being out of the ordinary. First there had been the bright beads around his hat and his belt which gave him his name; then there had been the large garnet rings and swagger sticks, the fez and the cloak and the beard; recently he had taken to using green ink for all his writing. From Russia he had come away with an astrakhan fur hat which he wore with aplomb; but he was equally at home in Dinah Stock's straw boater tied up with a red ribbon, and he could stand at a bus stop and inform the staring queue that he was an Eskimo with a seriousness which stupefied his questioners. Not even his closest friends could ever really be sure when he was inventing a story himself.

These powers of imagination saved him from sinking into mental apathy. His was never a doctrinaire mind, and he never became as obsessed with politics as did George Padmore and most of the Pan-African group to the exclusion of other interests. Kenyatta's belief in the supernatural was another source of his strength. His colleagues at the phonetics laboratory might think him merely superstitious, but in the Sussex countryside he drew close to the forces which controlled his destiny. He soon located a sacred tree in the garden at Storrington and maintained communion with the spirits of his people through libations and prayers. Words, too, had an almost magical appeal to him, words like rhododendron and hallelujah. The latter became a kind of password among his inner circle and he was overjoyed when Handel's *Messiah* was performed in Storrington and he could listen to its great 'Hallelujah Chorus'.

His imagination helped him overcome the routine of life in wartime. In the greenhouses at Lindfield he was able to address the tomato plants as though they were a Soviet meeting; he could stalk a fox in the heathland as though it were a leopard in the bush; and there was an occasion when he was invited to preach in a nearby Congregationalist chapel and he recreated the atmosphere he had first known at the Scottish mission. As a cook, as a horticulturist, as a handyman about the house, Kenyatta drew on his experiences with a cheerfulness which was infectious.

But for all his apparent extrovert nature Kenyatta kept his inner thoughts to himself. There was always something devious about him. Often he gave the impression of one who was afraid he was being watched, and that strangers might be police agents. Somewhere into his character had entered a fear of the unknown and a corresponding desire to master his environment. It was this mixture of fear and ambition which had driven him to Thogoto, to Europe and to Russia, and into staying in England when everyone was urging him to return to Kenya. And the deviousness showed itself in his use of other people, about which Kenyatta could be quite unscrupulous, even brutal. Mrs Hocken, his old landlady at Cambridge Street, was one of the main sufferers, but he was using Dinah Stock and Edna too, and anyone else who might serve his purpose for the moment. There was one afternoon at Storrington when Kenyatta invited to tea Lady Cynthia Asquith and her children, who were neighbours of the Armstrongs, and he insisted on Mrs Armstrong's acting as though she were some kind of housemaid or secretary.

Not that he was obsequious to those in authority—quite the reverse. His showmanship was intended to impress. He knew he was on his own and if he did not assert himself others might take advantage of him. At a party it was Kenyatta who had to hold the centre of the stage or he was liable to sulk and turn stubborn or argumentative. At Storrington his strong personality dominated the household: even the chickens appeared to obey his shouts alone. But if crossed, he would lose his temper; if asked to wait when he thought he should be shown straight in to see someone, he would storm out in a rage. It was the same arrogance that had upset his relations with the publishers of Lilias Armstrong's book when they refused to credit him as co-author. And the same swagger which had once led him in Nairobi to offer to knock down anyone who insulted his friend Charles Stokes could as well lead to a pub brawl or a fight with Indians. Hostesses, especially, found he took them for granted and he often left them resentful of his pushing manner.

Men found it hard to feel real affection for such a person. There was mutual respect, a sense of comradeship, between, say, Geoffrey Husbands, the insurance clerk, and Kenyatta, but not brotherly love. While to women, Kenyatta's sensual mouth and yellow, leopard-like eyes had a special appeal. They felt he needed looking after, and the assortment of pullovers, dressing-gowns and socks which accumulated in his wardrobe testified to his amorous success in the different capitals of Europe. Kenyatta had a disarming openness about these relationships. He was an African; the monogamy of the West was an interesting anthropological phenomenon, no more.

It was a personality made up of contradictions. He was at once gregarious and secretive, at once assertive and cautious, at once sympathetic and distant. Such men who keep their inner thoughts to themselves like company if they can control it, and if they find they cannot, then often they show the less pleasing side of their natures. This was Kenyatta, and those who did not recognize and accept the African quality in his make-up felt let down and betrayed by him. But it is also worth reflecting that his readiness to marry a white woman showed he was troubled by no racist impulses, but inspired rather by that spirit of 'anything you can do I can do better' which marked so many of his actions. What perhaps was his most consistent and remarkable characteristic was his love of children and his sympathy for the underdog and outsider. He shared with them a feeling that life was for all men and for all God's created world. For all his personal idiosyncracies, for all those accusations which the missionaries made against him, and for all his deviousness which some might call dishonesty, never once did Kenyatta show any sign of physical cruelty or nihilism.

Life at Storrington was restricted. Kenyatta could not feel that lecturing to British troops and insurance clerks was his true mission. The WEA audiences were not inspiring: 'Ach, they're just a lot of incompoops', he remarked to Dinah Stock after one session. What good would they ever do his own people? 'I feel like a general separated by 5,000 miles from his troops', he exclaimed in exasperation to Edna. He took every opportunity to slip up to London, perhaps to spend an afternoon at the School of Oriental and African Studies, perhaps to call on the Fabian Colonial Bureau or the Lutterworth Press about a new book.

As the war dragged on, he tired of his retreat. Friends noticed he was drinking more heavily and turning more assertive in his conversation. He sat in the garden at Storrington and brooded. The landscape reminded him of Kenya and he was troubled by nostalgia and fear that his destiny might be slipping away. From sound recordings sent to him by contacts in the overseas section of the BBC for review, he learnt that Kikuyu mothers were teaching his name to their children and that he was not forgotten. But how could he reach them?

Padmore was still at the heart of things in London and the Pan-African group kept abreast as best they could with the handling of racial problems in Britain's armed forces. Complaints reached them of African troops suffering from unequal pay and living conditions, and there were incidents of mutiny at sea involving coloured seamen and discrimination at home against coloured workers.

The arrival of American servicemen in Britain brought renewed outbursts of racism, to the surprise and shock of many Englishmen. Thanks largely to Padmore the BBC were persuaded to drop the use of the word 'nigger' in broadcasts and to take a more balanced view of racial problems.[9] The IASB maintained contacts with racial communities like the Somalis in the ports around Britain. They attended court hearings, briefed lawyers and worked out the most effective defence techniques for coloured defendants in English courts.

The activities of a handful of coloured intellectuals scattered through Britain did not rate seriously in the titanic struggle being waged between the western democracies and the totalitarian powers. But the underlying importance of the Second World War in the history of imperialism can now be discerned. Two events may be singled out for their historic consequences.

The first was the signing of what came to be known as the Atlantic Charter between Churchill and Roosevelt in August 1941. The declaration of certain basic human rights which the Charter enumerated was directed primarily at restoring to liberty those people whom the Nazis had struck down. Churchill did not intend them to apply to Britain's subject races. America had not then entered the war, Britain appeared to have survived the worst that the German war machine could inflict; Hitler in June 1941 had turned against Russia. With Italy's challenge in Africa eliminated, the Middle East saved, and Germany's big ships either sunk or contained, it looked momentarily as though it was business as usual as far as the British Empire was concerned. By judicious use of allies like the Free French and Norwegian resistance forces, and by support for the Russians despite their brand of totalitarianism, Hitler it might seem could be brought down as Napoleon was brought down by the Grand Alliance in 1814. The principles of the Atlantic Charter in Churchill's view embodied the old philosophy of Empire.

It was a false reading of history, and it was soon shattered by a second event whose historic significance was more momentous even than the Atlantic Charter. On 7 December 1941, the Japanese destroyed the American Pacific Fleet at Pearl Harbour and four days later sank the *Repulse* and the *Prince of Wales,* the strongest ship in the Royal Navy, off the coast of Malaya, both attacks being made from the air. On 15 February 1942 the Japanese captured Singapore, Britain's great base in the Far East and the lynch pin of her imperial defence system east of Suez. For the British it was the darkest moment of the war.

It marked also the end of the old British Empire. Not only had Britain lost command of the sea in the Far East, but Burma and Malaya were gone and India herself threatened with invasion. Had Ceylon fallen, East Africa too would have been vulnerable. The speed and savagery of the Japanese entry into the war turned it overnight into a truly global struggle, in which Britain found herself locked in alliance with Soviet Russia and Republican America, both of whom were ideologically opposed to imperialism. The fall of Singapore presaged the transference of world power from the old imperial order to the new era of super powers, nuclear weapons and intercontinental missiles.

The relationship between Britain's imperial armies and her subject races also changed overnight. From being primarily a force held in reserve to quell local disorders within the Empire, the imperial army now welcomed all colonial troops as comrades in arms in the wider struggle in which all free people were engaged. The principles of the Atlantic Charter could no longer be withheld from them. Sir Stafford Cripps was at once despatched to Delhi to offer self-government to the Indian Congress leaders. In England the members of the West African Students' Union in April 1942 demanded immediate internal self-government for Britain's West African colonies and complete independence in five years. Padmore looked hopefully for 'a new Commonwealth of Nations, bound together in equal partnership.'[10]

BBC radio discussions also raised the future of Britain's colonies after the war and reminded Kenyatta of the challenge he still had to face. In 1944 the first African was nominated to represent Kenya's natives in Legco, a sign of the changing times. He was Eliud Mathu, a Kikuyu teacher who was a contemporary of Peter Koinange, one of the new Alliance High School generation. Mathu had paid Kenyatta a visit in 1940 while he was completing a course at Exeter College, Oxford. Some intimation that Mathu was being singled out for preferment must have reached Kenyatta, perhaps by instinct, a few months before his appointment was announced. In August 1943 he heard a wireless talk between Leonard Woolf, an old supporter of the Africans in the Labour Party, and Elspeth Huxley. Kenyatta wrote to the *Listener* challenging the view that Africans were unable to speak for themselves. His words anticipated Mathu's appointment and implied a challenge to the legitimacy of that too:

'education is not the sole quality needed in a representative: it is essential that he should also . . . express their needs. If any African does this, the Europeans brand him an "agitator". On the other hand, if he conforms to the standard of complacency expected of him by the Europeans, he will hardly be doing his duty by his country-men . . .

Africans who want self-government are always put off with: "Not yet. Not till you are fit for it." Certainly we aspire to be fit for self-government. But we should like to know who is to be the judge of our fitness, and by what standards will his verdict be pronounced?'[11]

Throughout the war Kenyatta kept in touch with Padmore and the Pan-African group, and as the allied victory approached he found himself spending more and more time in Manchester where Makonnen's restaurant business had expanded through the appeal of his exotic menus in those days of rationing. He now ran a series of eating houses in the smart quarter of Manchester. Makonnen once paid Kenyatta a visit to Storrington and commandeered all his chickens. Kenyatta followed him north and helped with the running of one of the restaurants. Manchester became the headquarters of the IASB.

The group considered their next move. They had been joined in 1943 by Peter Abrahams, the coloured South African writer, whose literary talents added to their publicity outlets; and in early 1945 there arrived from America a young Gold Coast student called Kwame Nkrumah. In America Nkrumah had joined the negro rights movement and met C. L. R. James who had given him an introduction to Padmore. He had a youthful revolutionary spirit and he fell quickly under Padmore's influence, while Padmore too came to see that the Africans themselves, men like Kenyatta, Wallace-Johnson and Nkrumah, must take a more active role in the freedom struggle. Peace was to bring them their opportunity.

In February 1945 a World Trade Union Conference opened in London, to which the British Government admitted seven coloured representatives from the colonies. They at once launched into an indictment of imperialism because of the racial discrimination suffered by coloured workers. The IASB executive invited the coloured delegates up to Manchester where, with Dr Milliard, a West Indian physician, they decided to call a fifth Pan-African Congress. The arrangements went with unexpected smoothness and in October the same year, 1945, around 100 delegates assembled in Manchester.

Kenyatta was up to his neck in the preparations. Throughout the summer excitement mounted as victory in Europe was followed by a General Election in July. There was talk of the IASB putting up its own candidates to publicize the African's point of view, and Kenyatta's name was among those suggested.[12] He had witnessed every general election in Britain since 1929. When Churchill, the arch-imperialist, was swept from office and Attlee became the first Labour Prime Minister to have an absolute majority in Parliament, the future for the Pan-Africans suddenly looked bright beyond imagining five years before. The pre-war IASB circus was on display again in Manchester and enjoyed its finest hour. Peter Abrahams handled its publicity with Nkrumah as his secretary. Kenyatta appeared on the platform as chairman of the credentials committee. The widow of Marcus Garvey, in whose restaurant in London's Oxford Street they had met ten years before, was there and the veteran Pan-African, DuBois, flew over from America to be acclaimed as the founder of the movement.

DuBois was an American negro scholar who had first brought the Pan-African idea to the attention of the world by intervening at the Paris Peace Conference which followed the First War and urging the acceptance of the principle of self-determination for all coloured people. Further conferences were held in Brussels and London, Paris and Lisbon, but after the fourth, which met in New York in 1927, the movement lapsed due to lack of African support. No doubt Padmore was at that New York conference, and it was largely his idea to hold the fifth congress following the Second War.

The philosophy of the Pan-African movement was expressed in the phrase 'Africa for the Africans'. It was the burden of all that Padmore, freed from his Comintern loyalties, had been saying and writing about in the intervening fifteen years, with Kenyatta in close support. What gave it a new edge at the Manchester congress was the question of the legitimacy of violence. Nkrumah and the younger delegates were impatient at the gradualist approach of the pre-war period. Padmore seemed to agree with them. Moderate bodies like the WASU and the League of Coloured People held aloof, fearing that the conference would turn out to be a racist front, or communist controlled, or both.

Kenyatta made no special impact on the congress. On 17 October he spoke about East Africa and ran through the familiar list of grievances. 'One thing we must do,' he ended,

'and that is to get political independence. If we achieve that we shall be free to achieve other things we want. We feel that racial discrimination must go, and then people can perhaps enjoy the right of citizenship, which is the desire of every East African. Self-independence must be our aim.'

The conference closed on a note of vague militancy:

'The delegates to the Fifth Pan-African Congress believe in peace. How could it be otherwise when for centuries the African peoples have been victims of violence and slavery. Yet if the Western world is still determined to rule mankind by force, then Africans, as a last resort, may have to appeal to force in the effort to achieve Freedom, even if force destroys them and the world . . .'[13]

For Kenyatta this renewed activity was a relief after Storrington. He worked on a pamphlet which was issued as an IASB publication called *Kenya: The Land of Conflict*. The cover design was of a map on which light radiated from East Africa. Beside it there was an African with a fur cloak round one shoulder, fingering his spear. It was Kenyatta of *Facing Mount Kenya* now stylized into a propaganda motif. Padmore wrote the introduction and took a major part in assembling the material.[14]

Kenya: The Land of Conflict was a frankly polemical pamphlet with little pretence at scientific analysis. It was an odd mixture of straightforward IASB political argument with Kenyatta's theme of an African Eden before the appearance of the European serpent, when there was plenty of land for all. 'Thus they lived in freedom, roaming their own territories and enjoying the gifts that nature had bestowed upon them.'

From a brief historical sketch and a list of grievances, Kenyatta moved easily into Kikuyu legend and then back again into political history. He made no real distinction between legend and politics. The prophecy of Mugo wa Kabero and the fate of Waiyaki led naturally into the beginnings of political activity among the Kikuyu which resulted in Harry Thuku and the driving underground of his Association (though Kenyatta, by now, did not mention Thuku by name) :

'Forbidden to hold meetings, the members divided into groups of three and four, kept in touch with each other secretly, and continued their work of protest and agitation. The Africans of Kenya had their Maquis long before Hitler appeared on the European scene.'

Though he shared in the resolutions of the Manchester congress, Kenyatta's deep-seated caution held him back from an open commitment to violence or even to a more active political style. As he stressed in his pamphlet, the British were just too strong to be dislodged by rebellion:

'Whatever we may think of their methods, their foothold is secure, and it would be impossible to turn them out without a bloody insurrection. Africans do not want this insurrection. What we do demand is a fundamental change in the present political, economic and social relationship between Europeans and Africans.'

For fully a year after the congress, he continued to move between Manchester, London and Storrington, as elusive as ever in his intentions. One moment he would drop into Dinah Stock's new flat in Hampstead, where she was acting as Secretary of the Pan-African Federation, another he would suddenly turn up for his son's birthday at Storrington. He was at Clacton for a Socialist conference, where he joined in attacking Creech Jones over the Labour Government's colonial policy. Several Kenyan Africans were in England for victory celebrations and they brought him news of home. Finally, in September 1946, the call arrived for him to return.[15]

The months of activity which accompanied the Pan-African Congress and the year that followed it provided Peter Abrahams with the material for his novel *A Wreath For Udomo*. Kenyatta was Abrahams's model for his hero, Udomo, and it is an interesting portrait of him from the point of view of a fellow African at this crisis in his career. In the thirties his IASB colleagues had not been over-impressed with Kenyatta's style; but they all recognized in him someone who was authentically African. Where Europeans were struck by his earthy approach to drink and sex, these negro intellectuals were impressed by his detachment from the European scene. They themselves had been brought up in the West Indies and America to be black Europeans; they took European thought-patterns for granted. Successful negroes like Paul Robeson, Joe Louis, Jessie Owens and Louis Armstrong were subject to white capitalist pressures and as a result were always in danger of being labelled a white man's nigger. They had no role outside Western civilization.[16]

As Udomo, the hero of Abrahams's book, Kenyatta is seen first as the hero in exile and then as the African statesman whose wisdom appears too conservative for the forces released by independence. The book ends with Udomo being struck down by his own people whom freedom has intoxicated. The first part of the book was entitled, significantly, 'The Dream'. In London Udomo is a noble figure waiting for the call from his people. He is calm, with a hidden strength, sure of his mission. Passion contorts his face when he speaks.

Abrahams was impressed both with Kenyatta's sense of history and his humanity, and in his novel Udomo is involved in an emotional dilemma in England. He is befriended and falls in love with Lois, an English left-wing supporter of African causes in her mid-thirties. Udomo is tempted to settle permanently in Europe, but in a moment of weakness he seduces Lois's pretty flat-mate. She becomes pregnant, Udomo arranges an abortion, Lois finds out and ends their association. Noble even in his frailties, Udomo breaks free of the European hold on his life and gives himself up wholly to his mission.

Did such a tension exist in Kenyatta's mind too? It was not uncommon for Africans to feel it. The only clues he left to his emotional states were elusive Kikuyu references and the signs of weakness in his character which were such an essential part of his humanity. But when the time came for him to break with his life in Europe, with his wife and child at Storrington and his friends in London, it was with a decision and finality which struck many of them as brutal. By September 1946 Edna Kenyatta was again pregnant and unable to accompany her husband to Southampton where he was booked aboard the *Alcantara*. She did not expect to see him again.[17]

On 5 September 1946, the *Alcantara* at last took Kenyatta away from England and back to his own people. As the ship made her way past the great fortresses of Gibraltar and Malta, through the Canal, Port Said and Aden, Kenyatta saw what appeared to be a mighty empire still as powerful as ever. Did the brave words spoken at Manchester have any meaning outside England? Had nothing changed in the fifteen years since he had left the soil of Africa?

Quietly he helped with daily Swahili classes held on the ship for newcomers to East Africa and he spent hours with one young woman pacing the deck and discussing the future of the world. He never mentioned the family he had just left in England. Wife, child, friends, they all belonged to a phase in his life which was over. Instead, as the *Alcantara* put in to the familiar harbours along the Red Sea and African coast, he picked up a different set of contacts among the Egyptians, Arabs, Somalis, Goans and Adenis who bridged the gulf between Europe and Africa. Somehow he had forewarned them of his arrival, and in several ports there were cars waiting at the dockside to take him off while the boat was in harbour. No one could tell what passed between them.

In his conversations with his fellow passengers Kenyatta was reserved to the old colonialists, but open to the new and the impressionable. Europe had transformed him. If he had held himself slightly apart from his Pan-African brothers it may partly have been because of their implied racism; and he had been cautious towards other Africans ever since the days of Ladipo Solanke when he first arrived in England. His vision embraced all humanity; in practical terms he knew well enough that his people could not do without Europeans whatever he might have said about the integrity of the tribe in *Facing Mount Kenya*. He welcomed white backing if it was given as generously and unconditionally as Dinah Stock's, and had he not, after all, married a white woman? On board the *Alcantara* Kenyatta spoke about a single Kenya in which all races, white and black, Arabs and Indians, could live and work in peace alongside each other. They should all think of themselves, he said, as Kenyans, not as Africans or Europeans or Asians.

But he did not doubt his own mission to be their leader. In him was incarnate the spirit of Wangombe and Waiyaki and of the father of the tribe, Gikuyu himself. Knowing his name had been kept alive in Kikuyuland, he was a living legend entering upon his inheritance, the Kikuyu Messiah whose message would set free all the people of Kenya. In his real ancestry there mingled both the arrogance of the Masai and the cunning and resourcefulness of the Kikuyu. And to these were added the experience of fifteen years in Europe. It was a formidable combination and several fellow passengers recognized that in him were forces that must affect, for good or ill, the destiny of East Africa.

Part III

CHAPTER 19

Kenya 1946–52

For the second time in half a century, Africa had felt the impact of a European war. Its effects this time were revolutionary and nowhere were they more unsettling than in Kenya, which proved itself to be a vital strategic base, first for Britain's successful campaign against the Italians in East Africa, and then as a stepping-off point in the long-drawn-out struggle against Japan. To Kenya came West African, South African and Commonwealth troops, prisoners-of-war and refugees from Europe; while from Kenya East Africans went to join allied forces in Ethiopia, the Middle East, Palestine, Burma and India. In all the railway carried a total of 1,820,000 troops and prisoners-of-war; some 75,000 men enlisted from Kenya alone.[1]

Overseas these East African servicemen mixed with American negroes, Africans from other European colonies, Indians and members of different cultures, creeds and races. Their eyes were opened to the racial discrimination under which they suffered in their own country. They returned to Kenya determined to achieve something more positive than the old political associations like the KCA had done. Many of the Kikuyu among them belonged to the same age-grade, initiated in 1940, and were known as the Forty Group. They shared an aggressive, let's-get-on-with-it attitude to politics, which was to show itself first in organized resistance to government policies in the tribal reserves, then through Kenya's trade unions, and finally in armed rebellion.

This time war had brought prosperity to Kenya's European farmers. Deprived of her usual markets and sources of supply, Britain turned to her colonies. In Kenya agricultural production was stimulated to unprecedented heights by subsidies and incentives. As a result the value of Kenya's domestic exports during the war years nearly doubled; the acreage put to agricultural production expanded to the full, and the White Highlands seemed to justify all the claims

made in the past for the policy of European settlement in Africa.*[2]
Following the war, the European population of Kenya again sharply
increased.

As after the 1914–18 war, the settlers were determined to consolidate their position politically. In 1944 they formed themselves into
an Electors' Union which replaced the defunct Convention of Associations. They pledged themselves to the old ideal of 'the common
good' which, as in the past, meant continued European superiority.
Their aim was to secure unofficial control of the government, or at
least to acquire executive influence in the running of the country.

In this their leader was F. W. Cavendish-Bentinck, heir presump-
tive to the dukedom of Portland. The Electors' Union faced up to
the constitutional battles of the post-war era confident that the tide
of history was bearing them forward to new positions of power and
responsibility. A £11½ million scheme to settle British soldiers and
officers in the Highlands gave substance to their dreams.

By September 1946 many of the faces known to Kenyatta from the
old days were gone. Dr Arthur had retired at last in 1937, leaving as
his permanent memorial the beautiful and spacious Church of the
Torch in the centre of the grassy square at Thogoto.[3] Canon Harry
Leakey, the pioneer CMS missionary, had died in 1940, and Barlow
had retired in 1941. In March 1943 the death of James McQueen
removed Kenya's oldest settler, the Scottish blacksmith who had
trekked on foot from the coast in 1896 and settled at Mbagathi, a
few miles from Nairobi. His first child was born in Uganda, perhaps
the first European child to be born in the highlands of East Africa.

Superficially the Africans might congratulate themselves on having
made political progress, with the appointment of Eliud Mathu to
represent African interests in Legco in October 1944. To support him
a composite body drawn from different tribes formed themselves on
1 October 1944 into the Kenya African Union. Though the government obliged the leadership to change the name to Kenya African
Study Union, this proved a formality only, and in February 1946
it reverted to Kenya African Union, or KAU as everyone called it
(pronounced 'cow'). With the KCA suppressed, KAU provided Africans with their only political outlet.

In other respects African advances were also notable. In 1937 the
Kenya Missionary Council included for the first time three African

---

* See map on p. 13 for Kikuyu land area in relation to the White Highlands.

church leaders among its number. Likewise the Board of the Alliance High School took on African representation. Stemming from the formation in 1933 of a Christian Council of Race Relations, a positive drive was being made by the churches towards a multi-racial approach to Kenya's future. These churches were themselves moving towards greater African control. European missionaries, having recovered from the setbacks of the female circumcision controversy, were among the foremost champions of African rights. The appointment to Legco in 1943 of Leonard Beecher of the CMS, who was identified as a missionary 'of the militant type' through his persistent criticism of administrative abuses, ensured that African interests had powerful advocacy.

Kenya had a new Governor in Sir Philip Mitchell who was appointed in 1944, one of the Colonial Office's most trusted experts on East African affairs. Mitchell had been with Cameron in Tanganyika where he inherited much of Cameron's opposition to the ideas of Amery and Grigg over Closer Union. He had spent five years as Governor of Uganda, between 1935 and 1940, and he came to Kenya from a brief spell in the Fiji Islands.

There was nothing of the racial snob about Mitchell. He was an enlightened man, but he belonged to the old school which saw Africa as a *tabula rasa* on which Britain could write the word 'civilization'. He believed that Africa's past offered nothing on which Britain's civilizing mission might be built; progress, therefore, towards African self-rule must take generations and could only be realized through multi-racial institutions based on European experience. Mitchell reorganized the administration into what amounted to an embryonic cabinet system in which portfolios were made available to unofficials. As yet, only Europeans were judged capable of taking up these posts. Cavendish-Bentinck became Member for Agriculture.

Mitchell's fundamental assumption about Africa's tribal past was provocative, to say the least, to those Africans who were struggling to find an identity for themselves in the modern world. 'Great empty hunting grounds is just about all this land was, 50 years ago', Mitchell once said. The British found

'no more than the raw materials of a country . . . and African man today stands at long last, by our doing, many centuries after most other man, at the edge of the Bush, looking out at the highway, in the bright light of the civilised modern world, with all opportunity be-

fore him. It is not surprising that he is blinking a little in the sun-
shine.'[4]

The reader must make the effort to realize that Mitchell's views
about Britain's role as trustee for the future represented the liberal
wing of colonial thinking at the time and that throughout his period
of office Mitchell faced problems from settler extremists. But to Kenyatta his words sounded like all that he had grown up to hate about
the racial pride of the English. 'You have been ruling the world so
long, you've all grown arrogant', he once said to Geoffrey Husbands.

Early in the morning of 24 September 1946, the *Alcantara* arrived
off the coast of East Africa. Kenyatta was up at dawn to watch the
coastline take shape along the horizon. On the quayside at Mombasa
an excited deputation of his people awaited him. He was the first to
leave the boat and all the African porters at once crowded round him,
leaving the European passengers to struggle through the customs as
best they could. Among the first to greet him were Grace Wahu and
his two children. Peter Muigai was now twenty-five, and Margaret
Wambui eighteen. He had sent word of his homecoming from Port
Said, but had not expected the letter to reach Kenya much before
the boat.[5]

Kenyatta was deeply moved by his reception. His friends had
arranged a special lunch party and he made a short speech of thanks:

'I am very grateful to God who has made it possible for me to see you
again, and also for enabling me to return to my own country where I
was born. I can tell you that this morning at dawn I came out of my
cabin and looked outside and I watched enthralled by this country
where I was born, and as soon as I set my eyes over it I felt tears
streaming out of my eyes.'

He took up the theme, about which he had been speaking on the
boat, of the need for unity. It was time, he said, for Africans to stop
speaking of themselves as members of separate tribes and to acknowledge their common destiny. 'Let us pray God so that he may give us
strength to serve our beloved country given to us by God.'

But the reception at Mombasa was nothing compared with what
awaited Kenyatta at Nairobi. As news of his return spread through
the bush, groups of tribesmen gathered at each stop along the railway
line to catch a glimpse of him. Hours before the train arrived at

Nairobi hundreds of men and women thronged the station until it looked from a distance as though one dark-brown mass had been poured over the platform. Kenyatta's beard made him easily recognizable. It was a new thing among the Kikuyu and added to the excitement of seeing a living legend. As the train drew in, the crowd cheered and the women set up their peculiar, trilling cry. Kenyatta could not properly step down from his carriage, so dense were the bodies, and he was carried shoulder high from the station.

He was given little time to notice how Nairobi had grown in his absence, with double the population and many new industries resulting from war-time demands. There was the *joie-de-vivre* of Victory Parades and medal-giving still about the streets which added to the enthusiasm of the crowd's welcome.

Yet Kenya's old racist restrictions were as bad as ever and despite half a century of British administration deep poverty was still the harsh reality of life for the majority of the people. The African population was rising towards five million, the Europeans numbered less than 30,000. The Africans were soon to realize that they were in an economic trap in which the development of their own resources was frustrated by the European hold over the country and their only earning power lay as wage-labour in Nairobi and the bigger towns. The restlessness this gave rise to made fertile soil for the new radical politicians.[6]

The welcome at the station moved out to Dagoretti. Old KCA colleagues and neighbours streamed in for the celebrations organized by Peter Mbiyu Koinange and for photographs.[7] But around midnight Kenyatta excused himself and made his way over to Peter Mbiyu's home at Banana Hill, some ten miles distant. It was an action which provided the key to much that was to follow.

Kenyatta still had to reconcile his claim to leadership with the traditional forces within the tribe. One powerful focus of these tribal feelings lay in the person of Peter Mbiyu's father, Senior Chief Koinange, who, though government appointed, had earned for himself something of the respect tradition accorded to the chiefs of the past, men like Waiyaki and Wangombe. Kenyatta set out to make his peace with Koinange and his family.

His path was eased by the blunders of the administration. Following the snub that was given him on his return from America and Europe in 1938, the younger Koinange was further embittered when the Governor nominated Eliud Mathu to Legco, despite a preference for Koinange expressed by the Kikuyu themselves. Peter Mbiyu there-

after abandoned all attempt at co-operation with the colonial regime
and retired into nationalist opposition.

He brought his father with him. But the old man had already been
humiliated by the administration. In 1937, as a result of the Carter
Commission's findings, Koinange received back some of his lost
land—about one-tenth of what he claimed. It now contained coffee
bushes planted by the previous European owner. Because Africans in
his district were at that time forbidden to grow coffee, Koinange was
ordered by his local District Commissioner to dig up his bushes.
Koinange took the case to court, but lost. By the outbreak of war
his name had been added to the list of those to whom the KCA sent
copies of their protests and cables.[8]

Kenyatta's relations with the Koinange family were all important
to him. In the past he had joined in the general KCA abuse of government-appointed chiefs, and old Koinange had been singled out for
vilification. In London Kenyatta appeared to change his attitude, at
least as far as Koinange's son was concerned. Back in Kenya, Kenyatta
sought alliance. Koinange gave him one of his daughters as a wife.
Politically and socially Kenyatta was established among the traditional leadership of the tribe—or, at least, of the Kiambu section of it.

Among the many subjects Kenyatta discussed with Peter Mbiyu
during that midnight talk was the future of Koinange's Independent
Teachers' College at Githunguri. Peter Mbiyu offered Kenyatta the
post of Vice-Principal; in May the following year, Koinange left for
England and Kenyatta took sole charge. Koinange did not return until February 1949 and he left again in November 1951, this time to
remain away for ten years because of government prohibition orders
on his re-entering Kenya.[9]

With one son away so much, old Koinange increasingly looked on
Kenyatta as more than a son-in-law. They formed a deep affection for
each other, cemented by mutual respect and confidence under stress.
Koinange's home, Banana Hill, turned into one of the storm centres
of nationalist politics.[10]

Kenyatta had first to find somewhere to live himself. Dagoretti no
longer appealed to him. Before the war, Grace Wahu had moved
some hundreds of yards from the site of his old Kinyata Stores. She
had found life difficult without him. The family had had trouble
with Ngengi too, and Kenyatta's brother, James Muigai, had brought
a law-suit against his father to restrain him from disposing of parts
of the family estate at Ngenda. In England Kenyatta had often
thought of that strip of land between the two streams which he

called *Ichaweri*. It was where he planned to retire as a farmer. Now it was time he asserted his rights.

'You see,' he said to Peter Mbiyu, 'eldership in Kikuyu is meaningless unless one has a home, a real home. Men in my age-group received me in their homes. I have got to reciprocate it, not in a house built on another man's land but on my legitimate land. At Dagoretti I always feel myself a foreigner and a beggar. I must get myself established at Ichaweri.' So, on the ridge between the two streams near to Gatundu, and close to where he was born, he built himself a small bungalow and began farming his thirty-two acre estate.[11]

Meanwhile through the new vernacular press which had sprung up after the war, Kenyatta issued a manifesto to raise money for the college at Githunguri.[12] It consisted of little more than its stone foundations. Further building had been abandoned at the outbreak of war and their intention was to get every age-group in Kikuyuland to contribute towards the completion of the buildings and the running costs of the college (which included, of course, the substantial expenses of its new Vice-Principal). Kenyatta's manifesto was directed at the Kikuyu traditionalists.

'To all the members of the House of Mumbi wherever they may be. I greet you with all my heart which is full of gratitude and overjoyed for the way Almighty God has helped by giving us the opportunity of seeing and greeting one another with our hands.
I would like to inform you that African people throughout the continent are awakening and beginning to trust with mutual confidence in each other determined to work hard for the benefit of their countries. Therefore arise all of you and let us be united as we set about working hard to do some creative work of lasting value for the whole children of Mumbi.
One of the first object which I want with all my heart is to see how we could build one beautiful school where Mumbi's children could be educated. What I have in mind is that, before we start doing anything else, we ought to complete the school building which you started at Githunguri so that it may be like a great gift or a memorial to our father Gikuyu and our mother Mumbi.
May the Peace of Almighty God keep us united and give us the strength and ability to accomplish that work with love.
I am your servant.
Jomo Kenyatta'

Out of the funds produced by this campaign, Kenyatta was able to build himself a large stone house at Githunguri. It commanded one of the most spectacular views in Kikuyuland and Kenyatta made it his headquarters. The number of boys had increased by the time he took up residence from the 250 enrolled by Peter Mbiyu before the war to around 900. Their ages ranged from eight to eighteen, and there was a small contingent of about thirty girls. But the school itself had little further to show for the substantial contributions paid in. Its main block never rose higher than one floor and progress gradually slowed to a standstill. Kenyatta had to call in Indians to supervise the work. The school organization was under constant scrutiny by the administration, and periodic demands were made for Kenyatta to publish accounts, which he and his subordinates consistently refused to do. There were strikes by teachers for long-over-due wages; standards were never very high and soon declined still further, and numbers fell away.

Kenyatta sought to make Githunguri the focus for the whole independent schools movement which he regarded as a convenient tribal network for political propaganda. Estimates vary of the number of independent schools then in existence in Kenya. In general it may be said that in 1946 there were some 150, with a total number of pupils of around 20,000, and these increased to about 300 schools with pupils numbering around 30,000 by the end of 1952. But their significance has often been overstated. By no means all accepted Kenyatta's leadership nor the ideology of Githunguri. Many of the independent schools strongly upheld Christian standards; their leaders were individualists who rejected much of what they took to be implied in Kenyatta's approach to tribal custom.[13]

It was at Githunguri that many a visitor sought out Kenyatta. They found him, as likely as not, sprawled asleep in the grass, African style, and enjoying 'so far as material things go . . . a very comfortable life'. Books, photographs and souvenirs of his European days filled his rooms. He had servants, women to entertain guests, and a large Hudson car. He disliked Nairobi now because of the racial discrimination to which he, in common with all Africans, was subjected. But he was as flamboyant as ever. Late in 1947, the journalist Negley Farson summed up his impression of him:

'A big, paunchy man, bearded, with slightly bloodshot eyes, a theatrically monstrous ebony elephant-headed walking stick, a gold-rimmed carnelian signet ring about the size of a napkin-ring, an outsize gold wrist-watch fastened to his hefty arm with a gold strap, dressed in European tweed jacket and flannel slacks—with as pleasant, ingratiating and wary a manner as you have ever met. He has a series of grunts—"UNH-HUNH!"—whose rapidly switching inflections might mean anything. He struck me as being a born actor, an evident leader, and, perhaps just because of this, a man born for trouble.'[14]

There was a vaguely pentecostal atmosphere about Githunguri which disconcerted some newcomers to Africa.

In theory Eliud Mathu was the official spokesman for African political interests. He was the one who appeared at all important functions in the colony, a short, natty figure with briefcase and dark suit. Kenyatta had no official position. Soon after his return he went to see the Governor about his own future.[15]

Mitchell advised him to get himself back into the swim of things by joining his Local District Council (the old LNC renamed). There is no reason to think Mitchell intended this as a snub, though he regarded Githunguri as 'a pretentious institution', and in his memoirs wrote that he thought Kenyatta's 'own ideas ran to immediate nomination to Legco'. But Kenyatta was never at ease in English debating circles and he would have been at a disadvantage among the hostile settlers in that chamber. His ambitions could not be limited to this role. But in March 1947 he accepted a post on the African Land Settlement Board which he held for two years.

Kenyatta did not take up the suggestion of joining his local council. Other nationalist leaders like James Beauttah had done this before the war and used the councils as a platform for KCA views. But the scope was too restricted and Kenyatta preferred to remain uncommitted. He had always kept to the outside of every situation, and he was careful to do as much now with the old KCA group as with the government. He was able to appear all things to all men, a man of mystery and of hidden power.

Thus he soon built up for himself an unofficial status as an alternative source of tribal authority to the government. When there was trouble in the Fort Hall district the District Commissioner called on Kenyatta to tour the area with him and help quieten the people. When Kenyatta spoke out over African feeling against the *kipande* the Chief Native Commissioner at once intervened and told him of the government's new proposals for an identity card for all races. And when Kenyatta came to see the Governor a second time about lifting the ban on the KCA, Mitchell handed the matter over to his officials to discuss directly with Kenyatta and Mathu.[16]

On 1 June 1947, at its annual meeting, Kenyatta was elected President of KAU, James Gichuru stepping down to make way for him. No one among the younger men disputed his right to national leadership.

It was a meeting which brought together various different strands in the Kikuyu political struggle. James Beauttah was there, recently back from representing KAU on a delegation to India. Kenyatta had given him a letter to take to Nehru, and Beauttah returned with a message from Nehru reminding Indians in Kenya that they were there only as guests of the Africans. It was an important response. After India's independence in 1947, Nehru's support grew more telling. With the appointment of A. B. Pant as High Commissioner in Nairobi in 1948, it was given in practical as well as moral terms. Through Pant the Indian community were led to subscribe money and scholarships for Africans in India, while other unofficial contacts supplied legal advice and, in some cases, weapons and ammunition.

At this meeting Eliud Mathu also committed himself to independence as the ultimate goal. It was something they could not expect for themselves, he warned, but for which they must work for the benefit of their children. For Mathu, the sole African representative in Legco, this was an important declaration of principle. It placed him alongside Kenyatta in, and placed the Kikuyu in the van of, the political attack on colonialism. But it was still a muted call, and it was not taken up by the conference in that form. Kenyatta himself made a cautious speech.[17]

The power of Kenyatta's name to draw the crowds was soon demonstrated. Within a fortnight of the June conference he was in Nyeri and nearly mobbed. For some minutes he was unable to start his speech because of the crowd. The *East African Standard* wrote of 'scenes of enthusiasm, probably without parallel in Kenya'. Everywhere Kenyatta went in Kikuyuland it was the same. For some Sundays after his return he made a practice of turning up at important religious centres in Kiambu, Fort Hall and Nyeri. Normally overcrowded, the churches on these occasions were deserted. It was obvious that a new force had entered Kikuyu politics.

His physical appearance was enough to draw attention. He joked about his beard, and explained how his cloak was a present from the

Emperor of Ethiopia and his black stick a present from a West African leader. Its elephant's head, he said, reminded him of the Kikuyu proverb 'the elephant is not overpowered by its own tusks' (if a burden is your own you can carry it) . The Kikuyu broadsheets wrote him up as the 'Hero of our Race', a 'Saviour' and 'Great Elder'. If Kenyatta first took his style from old Kinyanjui and his black fly whisk, he certainly exploited his showmanship to the full.

Kenyatta threw himself into the task of building KAU into a united and ordered party. In the years immediately following his return, he grappled with the problem of control, which all mass movements present when they are denied legitimate outlets. From the start he campaigned vigorously for unity, hard work and ordered progress. He did not hesitate to attack the wave of petty crime which appeared to afflict the country; he tried to channel Kikuyu energies into their taking pride in themselves as a community. 'We cannot achieve freedom if it is demanded by one tribe only' he would begin a speech, and then continue by condemning thieving and thuggery which, he said, were getting the Africans a bad name. Dishonesty by Africans entrusted with money, and needless litigation, were destroying 'our reputation and our trustworthiness'.

At the annual meeting of KAU in 1948 he made this his main theme:

'If we want freedom we must eschew idleness, for freedom won't come falling from heaven. We must work, and work hard, particularly on our shambas and on soil conservation. We must build clean houses; whether of wood, corrugated iron or stone they must comply with the laws of health. We must eat only clean food which has been properly cooked, whatever sort of food it is . . . After getting rid of idleness we must get rid of our reputation for robbery and theft. If any man knows that another is a "spiv" or a drone let him have nothing to do with him.'

Prostitution, he added, must stop and everyone must seek to educate himself, and not by getting hold of books and a pen, but by 'a knowledge of how to work. If we use our hands we shall be men; if we don't use them we shall be worthless.'

He kept to this theme throughout the year. In October 1948, at a meeting to open a branch of KAU at Ndya, Kenyatta and old Koinange spoke more directly to their African audience than any European would have dared to do. The hostile settler press for once

gave them full coverage, under the headline KIKUYU LEADERS
TELL SOME HOME TRUTHS.[18]

Kenyatta was quoted at length:

' "People say that the European is doing the African down—but the
man who is keeping the African down is the African himself." Warm-
ing to his theme, he said that Africans kept asking for more land, and
when they were given it, they let it go to rack and ruin—"If you want
more land you must start by looking after what you have got properly." They were too fond of shouting for something and then doing
nothing about it when they got it, he went on. They had demanded
permission to grow tea and coffee. Permission had been given—but
not a single person had done anything about it at all. Too many
people were loafing about doing no work and leaving their land to
spoil. "If you want to be respected, you must tell the truth, work
hard at everything, and stop all this stealing and robbing." Mr.
Kenyatta then had something to say about the African in trade. The
particular line of business in which the African was specialising was
cheating. He cheated because everyone wanted to be wealthier than
his neighbour and would do everything in his power to damage his
neighbour's trade. "Trade isn't for dishonest people or for those
who don't believe in fair dealing," he said. He also appealed to
the Kikuyu to give up bribery and corruption. Justice was impossible
among people who depended on graft.'

These were strong words. At the same time Kenyatta knew that he
must win the backing of other tribes and other communities if he
was to carry any weight on a national scale. From the moment he
landed at Mombasa in September 1946 a consistent theme of his
speeches was that all men in Kenya shared a common destiny. If it
was to an audience of Indians he would point out that beneath men's
skins the colour of their blood was the same; if Somalis, he would
remind them that their future lay in Africa and they must make common cause with Africans; and if Europeans were present, he would
appeal to the white man's pride in justice and fair play.

Kenyatta faced two problems. The first was to establish himself
as the accepted leader of the whole Kikuyu tribe, and the second, to
bring all the tribes of Kenya to follow his call for self-government.
Neither offered easy solutions, nor could the one be approached apart
from the other.

Among the Kikuyu, bitter divisions still existed as a result of the female circumcision controversy and the antagonisms of the twenties between Harry Thuku's followers and government-appointed chiefs. Harry Thuku now aligned himself with the latter group. Mitchell's doctrine of multi-racial progress made a strong appeal to those who had raised themselves above tribal society. The new *élite* in Kikuyu-land, men like Eliud Mathu and James Gichuru, would require persuading that their personal future lay in opposition to the colonial power. It required faith to pursue an objective which seemed to most people unrealizable in the foreseeable future. Not even Kenyatta expected to see Africans ruling themselves in his own lifetime. While among the younger men of the Forty Group who had not arrived among the *élite*, the Kaggias and Kubais, the Mathenges and Kimathis, there were feelings which no amount of reform could mellow. As early as 1947 it seemed to outsiders that these men from the Forty Group had Kenyatta 'on the spot'.[19]

For Kenyatta to unite the other tribes behind his call for self-government presented even deeper problems. To the Luo or Masai, traditional enemies of the Kikuyu, he risked appearing as a spokesman of Kikuyu domination. As it was, the Kikuyu enjoyed many advantages in Kenya because of their proximity to Nairobi and their natural versatility. To less fortunate tribes the continued presence of the British administration was a surer guarantee of their sharing fairly in the benefits of progress than joining a struggle against the colonial power the consequences of which seemed too distant and hypothetical, if not downright unwelcome.

Kenyatta's appeal did not extend outside Kikuyuland, and for this he may have been partly responsible himself. Odinga has recounted how on Kenyatta's first visit to Luo territory he did not even get out of his car to talk to the Luo members of KAU in their new office in Kisumu.[20] Links between KAU and other tribes were under constant strain because of the Kikuyu dominance of the political scene. Kenyatta always insisted on maintaining a show of inter-tribal representation on the KAU executive, and of conducting party business in Swahili, but whether through expediency or on principle was never clear.

Tribal feeling still represented the most basic force in Africa. European officers in the field at this time annually recorded incidents of stock thieving and murder between the Masai and the Kikuyu whom no amount of tinkering with the Constitution could reconcile. Kenyatta faced within KAU the same dilemma as did Britain in all her colonies: how to create new institutions without building upon tribalism. For KAU effectively to override tribal feelings posed a threat to those very forces within the tribes which Kenyatta wished to preserve according to the theory of *Facing Mount Kenya*.

But however successful Kenyatta might have been in his objectives, he was bound to encounter opposition from the settlers—the one group which were organized, articulate and privileged. In the end it was European attitudes which decided politics in Kenya.

It must again be emphasized that the idea of multi-racial progress towards self-rule represented the extreme liberal wing of European opinion at this time. Mitchell had problems with his settlers as every Governor had done since the days of Charles Eliot. For Mitchell they were increased by settler prejudice against Britain's Labour Government which had ousted their hero, Winston Churchill, and was proceeding on the most wide-ranging programme of social reform ever seen in Britain in so short a space of time. To the group-captains and major-generals who came to settle in Kenya in the late 1940s, it was tantamount to communism. And just as after the first war there had been talk of rebellion over the British Government's proposals for a common roll with Indians, so this new generation of white settlers spoke of ending Colonial Office rule and the creation of a new East African Dominion facing south towards Salisbury and Pretoria.

In September 1949 the Electors' Union published these ideas in what they called the *Kenya Plan*. It was an outspoken affirmation by white men of their determination to retain power in Kenya. They called for greater British investment of men and capital, further white settlement, and they looked for economic and moral support from the Rhodesias and South Africa. Among other matters the Electors' Union were concerned about the future of Tanganyika whose status as a mandated territory gave openings for United Nations interest. The settlers wanted Tanganyika brought within the Empire and incorporated within their new British East African Dominion. It was Grigg's Closer Union scheme brought up to date. 'Any attempt to hand over power to an immature race must be resisted', a spokesman said in June 1950. 'To the Africans we offer sympathetic tutelage which will lead them to full participation in the government of the country. But we have made our position clear. We are here to stay and the other races must accept that premiss with all it implies.'[21]

From the moment of his return, Kenyatta was regarded by these men as their principal enemy. The scandals propagated by Europeans in the early 1930s, Kenyatta's visits to Russia and his communist contacts, his marriage to an English woman, these all damned him in their eyes, whatever he might have said or done. Government officers, too, had their own dossier on him and it seems that early on the government circulated some kind of warning notice about him which poisoned relations from the start. They attributed to Kenyatta responsibility for apparently thoughtless opposition to administrative policies aimed at improving local conditions, such as terracing and cattle dipping, which led to strikes, rioting at the Uplands Bacon Factory, and the closing down of a dried vegetable factory in Nyeri.

In his official report for 1947, the District Commissioner for Kiambu already branded Kenyatta as an agitator:

'Jomo is . . . the most accomplished agitator of them all. He has been very clever in his organisation for collecting money from Age Grades for the Githunguri College. He has collected various political elements round him and is probably financing much of the quasi-political activities that are focussed on Githunguri. Results may not be commensurate with funds collected (possibly over £40,000) and they may well fall out financially. If Jomo wishes to appear a moderating influence for his own ends I believe he is even more destructive in his subtle way.'

It was much the same language as government officials had used about Kenyatta ever since he joined the KCA in 1928. In 1949 they were referring to KAU leaders as 'specious and mealy mouthed opportunists', and the European press wrote of them as 'loud mouthed hypocrites'.[22]

Kenyatta was reported to say one thing openly and then to take his tribesmen off by themselves where he spoke in that allusive Kikuyu idiom which defies translation into language comprehensible to Western political tradition. A favourite metaphor he used compared religious sects with weevils. 'The many Kikuyu religions (or sects), are weevils which spoil the food in the granaries. We are the food, and the religions (or sects) are weevils.' The missionaries understood him to refer to Christianity, and one of their informants at these meetings may have reported his words in this sense, which the written record conceals.[23]

There was often no real telling what he meant, as his words *were* ambiguous, perhaps intentionally so. 'A panga is meant to be used. If you put it on a table and leave it there it is useless. Similarly, if we don't help ourselves, God isn't going to come down from above and help us. But if we exert ourselves, he will be on our side.' 'Kenya would be a Paradise if the Europeans went back where they came from . . .'[24]

The tendency of Africans towards secret cults, often of an aberrant Christian form, seemed a sinister development to those who believed Kenyatta was some kind of witch-doctor. To others who had lived through the female circumcision trouble the appearance of Kenyatta's name in pseudo-religious 'hymns', replacing that of Christ and sung to Christian tunes, pointed to the same powers of darkness, and was reminiscent of the hated *Muthirigu* song of October 1929.

The settlers did not scruple to pass on to the government any information which they thought might discredit Kenyatta. From as early as October 1947 they were in touch with police officials over him and in December that year they met the Attorney-General of the colony, who was the official responsible for law and order, with a view to getting Kenyatta deported. The government apparently then took the line that such action would only 'confer upon him an aura of martyrdom'.

For security reasons the Electors' Union were asked to keep no records of these discussions, the implication being that important witnesses might be involved. But the settlers maintained the pressure, reinforced by information supplied by a missionary claiming to have good contacts in the Kikuyu reserve. At the unanimous request of the unofficials in Legco, the Governor in 1948 agreed to appoint a standing committee on security. The settlers were in effect setting themselves up as vigilantes and prompting leading Kikuyu figures to feed them with information against Kenyatta.[25] It gave an unhealthy air of double-dealing to all political activity.

In 1950, following a speech from Mitchell, the Europeans became aware of the communist bogey. These were the years of the great spy scandals in America and Britain, of Russia's explosion of an atomic weapon and of the Korean war. Against this background of aggressive international communism, Kenyatta's role appeared even more sinister.

Kenya's economic situation favoured a rapid advance in trade union activity which had been held up by the war. In January 1947 some 15,000 Africans went on strike in Mombasa for higher wages, in which they were partially successful, thanks to the intervention of Mathu and a government-appointed tribunal. The leader of the strike, Chege Kibachia, at once became a hero throughout Kikuyuland. His name appeared in the quasi-religious Kikuyu songs along with other heroes from the Kikuyu pantheon. In August he was arrested by the government and held under a detention order near Lake Baringo, where he was to spend the next ten years.

The same month Makhan Singh returned to Kenya from India and took up his trade union activity. He succeeded in fighting off a government expulsion order and played a major part in the organization of a body which united six of Kenya's largest unions, among them Kubai's transport workers and Kaggia's salaried officials. On 1 May 1949, the new East African Trade Union Congress, EATUC, was formed with Makhan Singh as General Secretary and Fred Kubai as President. With their headquarters in Nairobi and their own network of informers and activists, they spearheaded a drive for greater militancy in the political arena.

Kenyatta was not involved in the Mombasa strike in January 1947, though the Europeans did not hesitate to attribute its outbreak to his return the previous September. On the contrary Kenyatta was at pains to oppose all illegal activities. Knowing both the power and the limitations of trade union action from his European experiences, he remained cautious in his relations with the new body.[26] Makhan Singh was a self-confessed communist. Kubai and Kaggia were both members of the Forty Group. Though Kenyatta shared in their long-term objective of liberating Africa from colonial rule, he was concerned to give unified and disciplined leadership to the freedom struggle. The idea of unity raised the question of oaths.

To a European or American, accustomed only to his own model of civilized life, the rituals and ingredients of African oathing ceremonies may at first seem repulsive. Eyeballs skewered with thorns, blood and milk and earth and bile, raw meat and entrails, armlets of skin cut from freshly killed animals, bones extracted from warm carcases—these and many other features of oathing ceremonies were so much a part of the East African scene that Europeans experienced in Kenya scarcely found it necessary to comment upon them. The Kikuyu had practised them for centuries. Different oaths suited different needs. There was one kind for cleansing an individual from a broken taboo, another to test his innocence in a court of elders, others again to impart power over an enemy or as occasion demanded. Missionaries discouraged them absolutely, not primarily because of the alleged barbarism in the customs, but rather because of the Biblical teaching against the need for a God-fearing man to resort to magical sanctions of any sort. The Kenya administration, however, allowed recourse to them to be made in difficult legal cases, such as the Kioi land dispute at which Kenyatta had assisted.

Supposedly the first KCA members, many of them church elders, introduced a form of oath in 1925 consisting of a Bible held in one hand and earth pressed to the navel with the other. They were impressed, apparently, by the oath of loyalty to the Crown which everyone was obliged to take on becoming a member of the Local Native Councils. It is said that the KCA leaders who were restricted during the war decided to drop the Bible and substitute goat's meat as being more in keeping with Kikuyu tradition. They then repeated phrases such as: 'If I become an enemy of my land or my people and if I become lazy in working for my country, let this meat and blood kill me straight away. If I am ever bribed to abandon my people, if we have changed our minds since we went to detention, may this oath kill us.'[27] The terminology is reminiscent of the Old Testament, as when Job says: 'Let mine arm fall from my shoulder blade, and mine arm be broken from the bone'. In other words: 'Let me be damned'.

A more important development came from a dispute between the administration and a section of the Kikuyu living in an area known as Olenguruone, which lay in Masailand at a height of 8,000 feet, on the southern edge of the Mau plateau. Behind the dispute, and stretching back long before Kenyatta's return to Kenya, lay a bitter history of squatters' rights and the status of families with lost land resettled from Kikuyuland proper. Some 11,800 men, women and children were involved.

This large Olenguruone group of Kikuyu steadily resisted every move by the government to enforce its resettlement terms. Their solidarity as a tribal unit was cemented by an oath which all of them took, including the women and children. This was a radical departure from Kikuyu custom as traditionally only men took part in oathing ceremonies. In February 1947 Kenyatta and Peter Mbiyu Koinange visited Olenguruone. No one could fail to be impressed by the unity shown by the people of Olenguruone throughout the dispute, which reached its climax late in 1949. On 20 February 1950, at a meeting at Koinange's headquarters at Banana Hill, the Kiambu leaders decided to resort to this new oathing as a means of unifying the whole tribe behind themselves. No doubt they also intended to use it to bring pressure upon their fellow tribesmen who were in government service, a counter-oath, as it were, to their oath of allegiance to the Crown.

It was a fateful decision. Once the leadership had committed itself to a policy of deliberately breaking Western and Christian conventions of behaviour it found it increasingly hard to resist a tendency for the oaths to degenerate in form and content. This in turn led to an increasing isolation of the Kikuyu from the other tribes of Kenya to whom such oaths were repugnant, and it gave rise among Europeans to long suppressed fears about the supposed primitive forces of 'darkest Africa'.

But this is the judgement of hindsight. At the time oathing was not seen as especially sinister or significant in itself. Stress was rather placed on the continued existence of the KCA as an underground society. Because the KCA was still proscribed, prosecutions could, and were, brought against oath administrators on these grounds alone, and accordingly reports in the *East African Standard* drew attention to the political objectives of the nationalist movement rather than to any supposed signs of barbarism. But of course it also suited the supporters of the *Kenya Plan* to argue that Kikuyu methods showed how unfitted the African really was for normal political life.

Oathing added secrecy to a political situation which was already fluid. In 1948 a new word, Mau Mau, came into usage which purported to belong to an underground terrorist movement pledged to kill every white person in Kenya. Thugs saw their opportunity and stepped up their criminal activities under cover of oathing ceremonies. Cases of intimidation were reported. There were murders which Europeans assumed were the work of the new secret society. Dedan Mugo Kimani, the first man in Kiambu convicted of administering an oath in July 1950, belonged to the Forty Group and was prominent in the running of Githunguri.[28] In August 1950 the government outlawed what it called the 'Mau Mau Association'.[29]

Its decision to do so was again primarily political. The oaths of this period were, in the words of a later government report, 'comparatively innocuous'. 'Relatively harmless' was how L. S. B. Leakey described them.[30] Though the rituals in use were more often connected with evil magic, it was not the fact of the oath-taking itself that was objectionable so much as the seditious purpose for which they were taken:

'If you see your enemy, a servant of the Government, whether European or chief or headman, and you refuse to kill him, may this oath kill you. If you divulge any of the secrets of this society, may this oath kill you. If you refuse to subscribe to the funds of the society, if you give any European, Indian, Chinese or Seychellois any land . . . may this oath kill you.'

A certain amount of force would be shown, there would be some mingling of symbols such as the sign of the cross made on the initiate's forehead with the blood used in the ceremony, and perhaps those taking it would be obliged to undress and hand over any money on them. Clauses might be added to cover a local contingency, such as non-cooperation with administrative policy: 'If we refuse to dig terraces and anyone agrees to dig, may this oath kill him'.

These were the forms of oaths which Kenyatta was later charged with having 'managed'. In reporting the case from which the words quoted above are taken, the *East African Standard* (29 September 1950) referred without comment to the ceremonial paraphernalia of earth mixed with blood on a banana leaf, which was passed seven times round the head and licked, and ropes of grass and banana leaves placed around the wrists and neck. There was nothing remarkable about these aspects, and accordingly the paper emphasised instead the political motivation of the ringleaders. On this occasion fifteen Kikuyu were involved, charged with membership of an unlawful society (the KCA) and unlawful administration of an oath. They included local KAU officials and the headmaster of a Roman Catholic school at which some six hundred people were said to have gathered for a meeting. It was a typical case of resurgent Kikuyu nationalism. The word Mau Mau was not mentioned in the report. Oathing as such was not the issue, but the direction in which African politics seemed to be moving.

On 23 April 1950, a joint meeting was held between KAU and the East African Indian National Congress to oppose the *Kenya Plan,* and particularly that part of it which implied holding up Tanganyika's progress towards self-rule. Eliud Mathu was in the chair and the delegates passed a resolution calling for 'the complete independence of the East African territories'. Kenyatta spoke in support of the resolution:

'We have today passed a resolution demanding complete independence. There is nobody who wants to remain a slave . . . Europeans would never say that we are fit to govern ourselves . . . I always like co-operation, but I do not want the co-operation of the cat and the mouse. We must support our friends in Tanganyika, and unitedly continue our struggle for independence.'[31]

It was another fateful decision, which effectively ended any hope of compromise between African political leaders and the government. No member of KAU could remain in doubt that the party was moving towards greater militancy. No African in government service could any longer give whole-hearted support to KAU and also hope for an assured future within the colonial system. Complete independence invited a trial of strength with the European colonists.

In response to the move towards greater militancy, the East African Trade Union Congress called for a boycott of the Nairobi City Charter celebrations in March 1950. A rumour spread that a large area of Kiambu would be incorporated within the new city boundaries. KAU officially dissociated itself from the EATUC boycott. Kenyatta was not present when this decision was taken, and he disowned the KAU disclaimer.

Two assassination attempts followed, one on the moderate, non-Kikuyu, Tom Mbotela who was a senior KAU executive official and a strong opponent of oathing, and the other on Muchohi Gikonyo, a leading Kikuyu city councillor. Fred Kubai and Makhan Singh were arrested for being officers of an unregistered—and therefore illegal—trade union; their followers came out in a general strike which led to scuffles with police and increased rowdyism. This time Kenyatta, with the KAU leadership, opposed the strike. Makhan Singh was exiled to the Northern District of Kenya; Kubai was fined and then rearrested on the further charge of the attempted murder of Gikonyo. In February 1951 he was acquitted. But the judge came within a hair's breadth of finding him guilty.

The militants now moved against the moderates within KAU. On 10 June 1951, at a meeting in Kaloleni Hall of the Nairobi branch of KAU, with Kenyatta presiding, they swept the old officers from their positions. Kubai was elected Chairman, Kaggia General-Secretary and Paul Ngei, a Kamba, ex-British army, ex-part-time actor with an abusive tongue, became Assistant Secretary. They immediately repeated their call for independence within three years.

Kenyatta moved with the times. Though he insisted on a semblance of inter-tribal representation among KAU's office holders, he accepted the legitimacy of the corporate will as expressed through these events. In August 1951 he was reported as saying in a speech at Thika that 'the tree of liberty must be watered with blood'. But the exact context in which he supposedly used the words remains obscure. In October, Kenyatta produced a KAU flag, green, black and red—green for the land, black for the African skin, and red for the blood of liberty. It implied racially exclusive objectives for the African independence movement and confirmed the settlers in their worst fears.

At the end of the year at its annual meeting, KAU endorsed the call for independence within three years. The militants secured strong representation on the national executive of the party. Peter Mbiyu Koinange and Achieng Oneko, a young Luo, were deputed to carry a final plea to Britain for constitutional changes and to appeal also to the United Nations in Paris. Failing any response, the militants were decided on direct action.

The pressures on Kenyatta mounted. KAU was now virtually in the hands of the younger men in Nairobi. In January 1952 they formed their own secret Central Committee and began building up a network of subordinate secret cells throughout Kikuyuland. They used Kenyatta's name freely in their propaganda, which included a stepped-up programme of oathing. Ceremonies now involved up to several hundred initiates at a time. Those responsible were less discriminating in their methods of selection and enforcement, and the oaths were general in their terms. In some respects they corresponded, in Kikuyu nationalist terms, to meetings of Revival Christians which were sweeping through the territory at this time. The same mass emotionalism was present, the same sublimation of the individual in a larger cause and submission to forces greater than the individual will. It was in this context that the hymn books, creeds and prayers of the nationalists came to be seen as especially significant. In place of Christian features they glorified the 'House of Mumbi' and Kenyatta as 'the foundation stone of the Kingdom', the 'Judge of the Kikuyu' and 'King'.

It was thought later that the oaths now included 'positive killing' clauses, though many who took them also said they had no idea what was actually involved. At the same time the men of the Central Committee in Nairobi made secret plans for armed rebellion, and the oathing ceremonies gave them an opportunity to enroll recruits. They began collecting arms and ammunition, either by theft or by murdering African policemen in possession of weapons. A tariff was placed on anyone bringing guns in, which quoted as little as 25 cents for a single round of ammunition and ran up to 500 shillings for an automatic Bren gun. 100 shillings was the average value placed on a pistol. Nairobi prostitutes were said to take rounds of ammunition for services rendered. Some Indians also played important roles as suppliers, and prominent among them was Pio Pinto, a Goan born in Nairobi in 1927, who was thought to have communist contacts. Koinange's home at Banana Hill was believed to be a regular hiding spot for arms.

Anyone suspected of betraying information to the administration was murdered. Bildad Kaggia has recounted how he personally supervised the 'trial' of such a man, who was found guilty, and then executed, in the back of a taxi.[32] African police disappeared, sometimes without trace, sometimes with a limb inadvertently left behind after dismembering. Bodies turned up in rivers, some tied with wire. Women were stripped and beaten if they did not co-operate by taking the oath or otherwise helping the movement. The atmosphere grew heavy with fear, suspicion and hatred. Despite Kenyatta's attempt to make KAU inter-tribal, the Kikuyu were cutting themselves off from the rest of the Africans in Kenya, and the moderates among them were isolated. Tribal morale was disintegrating.

Kenyatta's ability to control events was limited, even supposing he had the will to attempt it. He had to ask permission for every meeting he held. His own movements were under constant watch by police.[33] If he stayed for a night in the house of a local party member, women would be listening behind doors to his conversation; he could not stop for a drink at a tea-shop in the villages without someone pricking up his ears and passing on tales to the authorities; neighbours at Gatundu were bribed to report anything suspicious at his home.

Friends as much as enemies now found Kenyatta's posture equivocal. He had been born with the cautious nature of all his people, and in the deteriorating atmosphere of Kenya's politics he found it difficult to trust anyone, not even his own family. He suffered a personal tragedy when his third wife, Peter Mbiyu's sister, who had already given him one daughter, died in childbirth. The strain told. He missed appointments. His friends began to doubt his reliability. There were signs that drink might be getting the better of him, and on one occasion the Luo treasurer of KAU, Otiende, threw the cash box at him and accused him of spending funds on his own comforts.[34]

Yet Kenyatta retained an unrivalled hold over the mass of the Kikuyu people. His presence drew thousands to meetings. Self-government was now the avowed aim of KAU, and so long as it remained a lawful and law-abiding party, its appeal to the masses was irresistible.

But if KAU stood for 'freedom', what did Mau Mau stand for? No one really knew, except that it was confined to the Kikuyu tribe and had to do with land. Female circumcision was also involved. In April 1952 Kenyatta went on a speaking campaign throughout Kiambu to dissociate KAU from Mau Mau. In June he spoke at Naivasha, in the Rift Valley, and was reported as saying that freedom must be achieved by peaceful means, and that once they had gained their independence, Africans would safeguard other races living in Kenya. In speech after speech Kenyatta declared that KAU stood for all-round improvements in the Africans' living and working conditions, and the party expected its followers to work hard and abandon laziness, theft and crime. Let everyone, therefore, become members of KAU, he would conclude. It was almost a set speech, the same one he had been making ever since his return to Kenya.

The climax to these meetings came at Nyeri on 26 July 1952. The crowd was estimated at around 50,000—an unprecedented size for those days. The government had allowed it as an experiment. Over forty buses brought out KAU shock troops from Nairobi to provide what was now the customary paraphernalia of banana-leaf arches and other Kikuyu symbols, as well as the KAU flag. They were mostly 'thugs and prostitutes' in the official view, and the symbols were similar to those used in oathing ceremonies.

The meeting had all the emotionalism of a revivalist gathering, and Kenyatta himself had difficulty controlling it. 'I am the leader of Mumbi and I ask you again to be quiet', he appealed to them. An African clergyman then opened the meeting with the prayer: 'May God lead us on to our goal. Jomo is the disciple of God who will lead you along the righteous path. In the name of Jesus Christ and the people of Mumbi, I give you my blessing.' Whereupon the crowd hummed three times the traditional Kikuyu answer to such invocations.

Then Kenyatta stood up and let out his characteristic cry of 'eeee!' to which the crowd responded warmly. He spoke of their democratic rights:

'God said this is our land, land in which we are to flourish as a people. We are not worried that other races are here with us in our country, but we insist that we are the leaders here, and what we want we insist we get. We want our cattle to get fat on our land so that our children grow up in prosperity; we do not want the fat removed to feed others. He who has ears should now hear that KAU claims this land as its own gift from God and I wish those who are black, white or brown at this meeting to know this. KAU speaks in daylight. He who calls us the MAU MAU is not truthful. We do not know this thing MAU MAU.'

The Kikuyu idiom Kenyatta employed here apparently had greater force to it than its English translation as 'know' implies. Kenyatta was saying, rather, that 'we do not want' or 'recognize' or 'approve of' Mau Mau. At this point in his speech there were jeers as well as applause. The crowd appeared restless, and an African District Officer, one of the few in government service, asked Kenyatta what he was going to do about Mau Mau. Kenyatta continued:

'I think Mau Mau is a new word. Elders do not know it. [see above for 'know']. KAU is not a fighting union that uses fists and weapons. If any of you here thinks that force is good, I do not agree with you. Remember the old saying that he who is hit with the club returns, but he who is hit with justice never comes back. I do not want people to accuse us falsely—that we steal and that we are Mau Mau. I pray that we join hands for freedom, and freedom means abolishing criminality. Beer harms us and those who drink it do us harm and they may be the so-called Mau Mau.'

The crowd cheered Kenyatta. But when Chief Nderi, son of old Wangombe, tried to speak of the need to co-operate with government, he was barracked into silence. To the European police inspector who was watching, a man born in Kenya and who spoke perfect Kikuyu, it seemed that 'the mood of the meeting was bad. I personally feel that all that remains is for the cooking pot to be brought on.'[35] Kaggia and Oneko (back from Europe) made inflammatory speeches. Kenyatta himself was uneasy. The size of the crowd alarmed him and he said afterwards that he must keep the numbers smaller in future. He left as quickly as he could.

The settlers thought Kenyatta's words were ambiguous, to say the least. What, they asked themselves, could his call for self-government mean but a direct challenge to the colonial power? Unity, whether achieved through his political party, or through Mau Mau oathings, had as its ultimate objective the destruction of their privileged position as the dominant race in Kenya. In their eyes Kenyatta was adopting a 'heads I win, tails you lose' position, and they pressed government to issue a statement that the call for self-government along African Nationalist lines was in itself seditious. The government declined. A sane view of the oathing campaign had been drawn up in February 1952 by the colony's Director of Intelligence. It was, he said, 'to rouse political consciousness, unite the African people in their political objectives, in particular the acquisition by the Kikuyu of more and better land, and to raise money.'[36] Only the last item might be said to be open to true criminality, the remainder were legitimate political aims.

Throughout July 1952 the settlers pressed the government to declare a state of emergency. Information about their intentions reached Kenyatta and the Nairobi leaders. The secert Central Committee ordered selected units to set up guerrilla bases in the forests. On 16 August Waruhiu Itote, the 'General China' of the Emergency, was one of a party of eight young men who came to see Kenyatta at Gatundu after receiving these instructions.[37]

They found him in his garden, dressed in open shirt and baggy trousers, the garb he habitually wore at this time which identified him as a man of the people. It was a warm, sunny day and he led them out of earshot of the house down to the stream at the bottom of the ridge. They told him of their instructions and asked for his advice. Kenyatta knew it could not be long before he was arrested himself, and he spoke of leadership and sacrifice: 'Some of you, too, will be imprisoned, and some of you will be killed. But when these things happen, my sons, do not be afraid. Everything in this world has to be paid for and we must buy our freedom with our blood.'

He told them of the wider cause of freedom for which men throughout the ages had given their lives; he told them of the negro slave, Toussaint L'Ouverture, who rose against the French on the island of Haiti in 1791. Kenyatta had heard about him from C. L. R. James in London.

'We too, after suffering, will get what we want', he continued.

'But we must be courageous and determined, and have faith in our ultimate victory. When I first went to England in 1929 I vowed to myself that Kenya would be free, and I have never lost sight of this goal. I shall go to prison, and perhaps I shall die. But if I die, remember that I shall never change; even then, my blood and my heart will remain with my people.'

Kenyatta referred to Itote's war service:

'You learnt many things in the army, my son, and now you can lead our people. If you had died in Burma no one would have remembered you, for you were fighting for the British. But should you die tomorrow in our struggle, you will die for your own people and your name will live in our hearts.'

He made a strong impression on the young men. As they left he stressed again the need for secrecy. He gave them some pineapples from his garden and wished them good luck. No one could tell on that sunny hillside how things would turn out. By a strange twist, fate brought Kenyatta and Itote together again in very different circumstances. Itote was then to save his life.

The young men departed for the forest where Itote adopted the cover name of China and began to organize his forces and train them in the kind of jungle warfare he had himself experienced in the British army in Burma. The few weapons which had already been collected were distributed and they set about ambushing any Africans they knew who carried guns. Food and other necessities were supplied by local sympathisers; camps and special listening posts were set up; plans were worked out for raids into the reserve against hostile chiefs and headmen. By moving carefully through the banana groves and sugar cane which covered the ridges of Kikuyuland, and keeping away from the main roads where they might run into police checks, China and his men, and others like them, were able to penetrate far into the reserve and retreat to their secret bases without encountering any serious obstacle.

At the same time a new kind of oath was introduced to emphasise the military nature of the undertaking. Known as the *batuni* oath, from the British army word 'platoon', it seems to have evolved naturally from the need to bind forest fighters closely to each other and to their leaders. For this reason it was also called the forest oath and since most of those taking it had already taken the common nationalist type oath, there was a tendency for the new oath to become stiffer in its requirements and more violent in its appeal. In some bands the new oath allegedly contained puritanical terms forbidding improper sexual behaviour and the drinking of English beer; various leadership tests were also introduced as the need for secrecy became greater; sometimes the opportunity was taken of adding practical instruction in guerrilla activities. As these men became cut off in the forests from their more sophisticated leaders they took to inventing their own variants to the oathing procedures to strengthen their hold over their followers and eliminate spies or waverers. In both form and content the oaths gave way to a reliance on violence for its own sake. But it was some time before details of these came to light. The situation by then had passed beyond anybody's control.[38]

Kenyatta knew the crisis could not long be delayed. The Electors' Union prepared for the 'neutralization or liquidation' of what they called 'subversive leaders'.[39] Kenyatta's agents warned him that his life was in danger. At the same time a group of Europeans approached him. They realized that his constitutional approach had failed and they offered to get him out of the country. A Moral Rearmament conference was due to open at Caux at the end of August. Eliud Mathu was booked to go. The Europeans urged Kenyatta to follow suit. They would provide asylum for him in Switzerland until the storm blew over.[40]

Kenyatta once told James Beauttah that he did not want to know too much about the plans others in the freedom movement were making. Throughout his life he had shown a remarkable ability to keep his activities in separate compartments, while he remained detached from the passions of the different groups around him. But though he may have avoided direct implication in what others were planning, he did not necessarily disapprove of them. Nor could he escape his share of responsibility for the consequences. If the paths in the labyrinth of African politics led anywhere at this time, they led to him—to Gatundu, where he talked privately with young men about to take to the forests; to Githunguri, where the KCA diehards and the independent schools and churches looked to him as their spiritual head; to Banana Hill, where secret councils were held by moonlight at the home of old Koinange who, through marriage, was Kenyatta's 'father'; to Nairobi, where KAU had its headquarters and the younger activists gathered and thought out new oaths in Kenyatta's name. Kenyatta was the only link between them all.

But it is an oversimplification to see the tensions of these years as existing only between the moderates and the militants, between the constitutionalists and the advocates of violence; nor was it simply a stress between old tribal loyalties and Kenyatta's attempt to build bridges between the Kikuyu and other tribes in Kenya. These tensions certainly existed; but they describe the complex African scene in terms only of European political thinking and do not fully explain

Lokitaung prison: Kenyatta's kitchen

Lokitaung prison

Kenyatta at the Maralal press conference after his release

Kenyatta at Kitale, March 1959, at Rawson Macharia's trial for perjury

Kenyatta with his daughter Margaret Wambui at the Maralal press conference

Kenyatta with Field Marshal Mwariama, a former Mau Mau leader, in December 1963

Kenyatta greeted by his first wife, Grace Wahu, at Gatundu

Kenyatta with Tom Mboya at Gatundu

Kenyatta wearing leopard skin robe, 1965

Kenyatta speaking at KANU rally

Kenyatta with his youngest son, Uhuru, and daughter Myokabi

Kenyatta greeting his wife, Ngina, now first lady of Kenya

Kenyatta, wearing KANU shirt, cutting tape

the real aspirations of the few men like Kenyatta who had succeeded in rising above their tribal past.

Kenyatta was a solitary figure. In political awareness he stood head and shoulders above all other Africans. His experiences in Moscow and London, his marriage to Edna and his life at Storrington, his association with the Pan-African movements, all gave him a maturity and knowledge of the world unattained by most Europeans. He did not seek personal advancement under the colonial system, but he longed simply for cultural acceptance. It was denied him by the racial prejudices of the settlers and the backwardness of his own people. Socially and spiritually he was on his own.

He was now in his fifties. Until the upsurge of militancy he enjoyed a comfortable life between his farm at Gatundu and his house at Githunguri. He had taken as his fourth wife, Ngina, one of the young girls attending his college. She was the daughter of a chief from his home area of Ngenda, and she presented him with another daughter. The prospect of farming and watching his children and grandchildren grow was not in itself displeasing.

In England he had never been as single-minded over politics as other Pan-Africans like George Padmore; but in Kenya there was no opportunity for social life of the kind he enjoyed with Dinah Stock in London. The settlers kept him at arm's length and they insulted his few European friends. In their eyes Fenner Brockway was dangerous and ignorant; when he came out to visit Kenyatta with Leslie Hale the settlers threatened to beat them up. One went to the length of dropping a pair of socks from an aeroplane over Leslie Hale's head because he went round in open sandals.

Some Indians might serve Kenyatta in Nairobi restaurants, but not if he was accompanied by other Africans. When his friend Peter Abrahams visited Kenya, in the summer of 1952, they had to be careful to hide the drink Kenyatta brought for their picnic as Africans were still not allowed to buy spirits. It was a frustrating existence from which Kenyatta saw little chance of escaping. Patronized, humiliated, isolated, he might well have wondered if the invisible forces that controlled his destiny had deserted him. For their picnic that summer of 1952 Kenyatta took Abrahams up the Ngong Hills with old Koinange and a few friends. It was an Old Testament scene, as the old men, like prophets of ancient Israel, looked out over their promised land now lying in the hands of strangers. Both Koinange and Kenyatta were inspired by Biblical imagery and they spoke in timeless fashion. To Abrahams the visitor, as to many others within Kenya, catastrophe seemed imminent and Kenyatta resigned to it.[41]

He declined the offer to go to Caux. His attitude was to let the colonial administration take responsibility for any breakdown in the colony, perhaps in the belief that he could then pick up the bits. He preferred to let events decide his future for him.

On 24 August 1952, another large meeting was held, this time at Kiambu in the heart of Kenyatta's own district of Kikuyuland. It was called expressly to allow Kenyatta to 'denounce' Mau Mau. The government gave it top billing. For twenty-four hours Kikuyu villagers had been assembling on the sports ground at Kiambu township. Many hundreds came out by taxi or bus from Nairobi. Special police stood by. Microphones and recorders and film cameras were laid on to capture, on celluloid and tape at least, Kenyatta's words. The government intended broadcasting these throughout Kikuyuland.[42]

All the leading figures of Kiambu were present: old Koinange, Harry Thuku, Eliud Mathu and the chiefs. But the main force behind the meeting came from Waruhiu, now a senior chief, a church elder and the pillar of the local 'establishment'. Tall, well dressed, and with considerable presence, Waruhiu personified respect for British colonial authority and for the ideology of the civilizing mission. His was the law and order approach.

After prayers had been said—it was a Sunday morning—Waruhiu climbed on to the table with a bunch of tough elephant grass in his hand. He waved it backwards and forwards in the air. 'Kikuyuland', he said, 'is like this grass, blowing one way and another in the breeze of Mau Mau. We have come here to denounce this movement; it has spoiled our country and we do not want it.'

Then Kenyatta came to the microphone. He had taken off his coat and his shirt sleeves were rolled up on his fleshy arms. Around a sagging waist he wore his *kinyata,* his broad, gaily beaded belt. In one hand he carried his black carved stick, and his large ring was prominent on his finger.

Kenyatta was out of the ordinary in any situation. That morning there was concentrated on him the attention not just of the 30,000 pairs of eyes present, but of all the unseen forces which were preparing for the final struggle. He could not be sure what use the government might make of his words, nor how they would be taken by his own people. He stood alone, with a hold over the crowd which no one in Kenya could rival.

'This meeting,' he began, 'is of the Kikuyu elders and leaders who have decided to address a public meeting and see what the disease in Kikuyuland is, and how this disease can be cured. We are being harmed by a thing called Mau Mau. Who wants to curse Mau Mau?' Every hand in the crowd immediately went up. It was a technique which Kenyatta had perfected. He would ask a rhetorical question and then wait for the crowd to supply the rhetorical answer. He went on to use Kikuyu proverbs with which he was so skilled, and solemnly cursed Mau Mau: 'Mau Mau has spoiled the country. Let Mau Mau perish for ever. All people should search for Mau Mau and kill it.'

Kenyatta then outlined the objectives of KAU. After all, he was there as the President of KAU. The first objective was self-government:

'We want the government to give us freedom to rule our own country, so we may live in happiness in this country which we were given by God. We do not want to oust the Europeans from this country. But what we demand is to be treated like the white races. If we are to live here in peace and happiness, racial discrimination must be abolished.'

That is, in education, farming policies, trade union organizations and political rights, there must be equality between the races.

When Kenyatta had finished, Harry Thuku, Eliud Mathu, James Gichuru (now a chief and vice-president of the Kiambu African District Council) —one by one the leaders followed and 'denounced' Mau Mau. Kikuyu people must work hard, was the repeated theme, Mau Mau was bad: 'It will put us back fifty years,' Chief Njonjo said.

Then old Koinange spoke. He was now eighty-four. He faced the Europeans present and singled out one of them. 'I can remember when the first European came to Kenya. I worked alongside your father and you are my son.' Here he pointed to the European.

'In the First World War you asked our young men to go to fight with the British against the Germans and many were killed. In the Second World War you came again and asked us to fight against the Germans and the Italians and our young people were again ready to go. Now there are Italians and Germans in Kenya and they can live and own land in the highlands from which we are banned, because they are white and we are black. What are we to think? I have known this country for eighty-four years. I have worked on it. I have never been able to find a piece of white land.'

It was a bitter little speech which was later held against him by the authorities. But it went to the heart of that love-hate relationship which existed between subjects and rulers throughout the British Empire. Deep within themselves, most of his fellow Kikuyu on the platform felt as Koinange. But the crowd had ears only for Kenyatta. When Chief Josiah Njonjo urged co-operation with the government and mentioned land terracing he was shouted down, as Chief Nderi had been at Nyeri a month before. Kenyatta had to seize the microphone to restore order. Put away drink, put away crime, we must work hard together, was his eternal message. He wound up the meeting finally with the words: 'Go home peacefully. There are askaris waiting for those who try to cause trouble.' It was late in the afternoon and it had been Kenyatta's day.

Both the European and the African Press gave wide publicity to the meeting, 30,000 KIKUYUS DECRY MAU MAU, ran the headline in the *East African Standard*. The government felt it had the upper hand. Kenyatta's speech, officials believed, had done the trick and the Member for Law and Order wrote accordingly to the Colonial Office on 2 September:

'For the time being it looks as if the thugs, who are the militant element in Mau Mau, have got their heads down. Last Sunday Jomo Kenyatta himself publicly condemned Mau Mau at a meeting of 30,000 Kikuyu, all of whom held up their hands at his request to signify that they approved his denunciation of Mau Mau. If this resistance movement gathers strength, then I think we shall succeed in rolling back the Mau Mau movement before too long.'[43]

Further meetings were planned. But some officials and most settlers still doubted Kenyatta's sincerity. Kenyatta complained to his local District Commissioner: 'How can I bring these young "forty" types to heel if I am not allowed to hold meetings?'[44] At the same time the African militants in Nairobi felt he had said too much already. At a secret, emergency meeting they warned him that his denunciation had been too strongly worded. And to deter others they embarked on a campaign of selected assassination. Their targets were those chiefs and headmen who were most fully committed to the colonial system.

Everyone in Kenya now waited for the crisis to break. The key to the situation lay with the Africans in government service. Law and order in the reserves depended on them. European officers were thinly spread and they relied for the execution of government policies on locally appointed chiefs and headmen, who controlled their own native police. This was what was meant by indirect rule. These African government servants owed their positions and their future to the colonial system; but they also genuinely believed that the best interests of their people lay in co-operation with the colonial government. They accepted the fundamental assumption of the colonial philosophy, that Africans must first advance through their local institutions before they could expect to share in the political control of the whole country.

African Nationalism directly challenged this philosophy, for the nationalists reversed the order of priorities: we must have political control first, they said, then we can remodel our local institutions as we like. When Kenyatta first put this idea to Oginga Odinga, the Luo leader, it came as a revelation to him, and he was at once converted to nationalism. In the west of Kenya the Luo had hitherto looked for self-expression only in independent churches and their own business enterprises. Odinga himself had been notably successful in establishing himself as an independent business entrepreneur.[45]

The Kikuyu too had gone in for a host of local associations and business ventures. These led to many rivalries and personal disputes in which Kenyatta was sometimes involved as mediator. Oathing represented one attempt in tribal terms to give coherence to their activities while KAU articulated the philosophy on a nationwide scale.

Anyone who was forced to take an illegal oath had five days in which to report it, otherwise he was liable to be charged with being an accomplice. If the oathing parties were not reported, the chief's authority was undermined; while if the chief did not respond vigorously when oathing ceremonies were reported, his credibility was destroyed. Thus as the nationalists, based in Nairobi, stepped up the pace of oathing, the greatest pressures built up on the local chiefs and headmen. Most of them cared little about the nature of the oaths themselves; sooner or later the weaker among them probably took some kind of oath. The tribal element would have appealed to them. But the linking of oaths with the nationalist movement threatened their personal stake in Kenya's future. Kenyatta was the leader of the nationalist movement. Though they did not dare openly to accuse him of being the driving force behind the oathing and the intimidation which accompanied it, it suited them to convey as much secretly to their European officers. Only if Kenyatta was out of the way, they sincerely believed, could they maintain their own, and the government's, authority.

The settlers had always taken this view. They had little contact with the reserves. In their White Highlands they had their own local councils and were sufficiently organized to look after themselves. Indeed, the colonial officials were fearful that the settlers might take the law into their own hands. Though there were signs of arson and cattle-maiming on European farms, oathing did not seem to pose the same threat as nationalism. Rather, oathing enabled white men to point to the 'backwardness' of the Kikuyu and helped support their argument that they represented the best interests of the country as a whole. Arrest Kenyatta, they said, and all will be well.

The final decisions lay with the government, which maintained an optimistic front throughout those last fateful months of 1952. In London, in March and on the eve of his retirement, Mitchell spoke of Kenya as being as peaceful as he had ever known it. His fishing holidays were undisturbed and he saw only happy, smiling faces wherever he went in the colony. Right up to September there were officials who believed the corner had been turned.

They may have been right. The moderate African leaders could also point to steady, if unspectacular, advances: an increase in Legco representation to four in 1948, and from four to six in 1952 with the promise of a fullscale constitutional conference in the near future. A seat was open to them on the Governor's Executive Council, which Mathu was invited to fill.

But the facts looked grim, as Baring, the new Governor, discovered on arriving in the colony at the end of September. He had to be driven from the airport to Government House by a circuitous route for fear of attack. He went immediately on a week's tour of Kikuyuland and everywhere was told the same story, by Africans, missionaries, officials and settlers. During the previous three months twenty-four headmen and thirty-six potential witnesses in Mau Mau cases—all Africans—had been murdered. Law and order was collapsing.

The African militants were bent on provoking a showdown, and the question everyone asked himself was why did not Kenyatta put a stop to it?

Waruhiu knew he was a marked man. In Kiambu he rivalled the Koinange family in prestige. Who knows what clan jealousies were involved? Waruhiu was a strong Christian and he never faltered in his opposition to secret oathing. On 7 October 1952 he attended a court hearing to answer to a trivial land charge. It was a tactic often employed against government servants by the nationalists. Before leaving the court, Waruhiu made a short speech:

'There are men who are going to be murdered, they eat with their friends, they laugh with them and they sleep at night. They die in a short moment and they have known no fear before. Their relatives will weep one day but then they will be happy again because his life was good. But there are the others, they are the murderers, they cannot sit and laugh with their friends and drink tea with them. They think about what they are going to do and at night they do not sleep, they have no rest. They do their evil things and in the end they will be caught and killed themselves. And their relatives will never forget it and their children will still know about it that their father was an evil man.'

On his way home the driver of Waruhiu's car noticed they were being followed. 'Have you got your revolver with you?' he asked the chief, as he cut off the main road down a dirt track. But the other car was blocking their exit. A man came over, asked who was Chief Waruhiu and shot him dead. The police found him, as he had been sitting, on the rear seat with his feet still up on the back of the seat in front. The killers escaped. They had clearly been hired for the job and were never caught. The Koinange family were implicated in a vague way, and on the strength of it the old chief was arrested. But no conviction against him was made.[46]

The crime had taken place in broad daylight on an open road. More than anything else that had happened, it crystallized government opinion. Waruhiu's funeral next day was attended by an impressive procession of church leaders, senior members of the government, leading Europeans and Africans. The last were shaken and subdued. Eliud Mathu made a speech, as did Sir Evelyn Baring, the new Governor.

Kenyatta stood among the mourners in a solemn frame of mind. As he and Baring looked into each other's eyes across the open grave, each knew well enough what would follow. It was their only meeting. On 9 October 1952, Baring cabled London for emergency powers to arrest Kenyatta and other African leaders, and to restore 'law and order'. The necessary preparations were made. The armed services were alerted and ships and troops disposed. A list of wanted men was drawn up, with Kenyatta's name at its head.[47]

In the evening of 20 October Baring signed the Emergency proclamation and 'Operation Jock Scott', as it was code-named, went into action. During the night police and army units swooped on their targets. Mysteriously Kenyatta's bodyguard of Kikuyu spearmen vanished in the dark. Relatives urged him to go into hiding. Around midnight the specially strong unit detailed to pick him up arrived at his house at Githunguri. He was allowed to take one suitcase with him. Then he was driven straight to the military airfield outside Nairobi where a light aircraft was waiting for take-off.

Kenyatta had no idea where he was being taken. All he could see from the window of the aircraft was the jagged silhouette of the Aberdares against the bright African night, and he had a momentary fear that his captors intended ejecting him from the plane somewhere in the forests of Mount Kenya where his body would never be found. It seemed like the end of everything.[48]

CHAPTER 20

Kapenguria

The Kikuyu were temporarily stunned by the Emergency measures. Of the KAU executive, apart from Kenyatta himself, Kaggia, Kubai, Ngei and Oneko were removed, leaving the party in the hands of the next echelon of men who included Joseph Murumbi, a highly intelligent young man of mixed Masai/Goan ancestry whom Kenyatta had personally enrolled a few weeks before his arrest.[1] Indians like Pio Pinto were still active, and KAU itself continued in existence, protesting against the Emergency measures, until it was banned in June 1953. Most of the independent schools were also closed down, including Kenyatta's college at Githunguri.

But the secret Central Committee in Nairobi had received warning that something was about to happen. On 19 October, twenty-four hours before Baring signed the Emergency decree, they issued their own order to their guerrilla forces in the forests to take independent action. Instead of killing the 'hydra', of which the government spoke, the Emergency gave it new life in this fragmented leadership which of necessity was at a lower level of political sophistication. The situation after 20 October rapidly deteriorated.

A few days later a frightening indication of what was soon to overtake Kikuyuland occurred in Nyeri district when Chief Nderi, a strong supporter of the government, surprised a group of 500 Kikuyu taking part in a mass oathing ceremony on the banks of a river.[2] They turned on him with their pangas and hacked him to death. Their leader was a certain Dedan Kimathi, a branch secretary of KAU, and a man about whom subsequent enquiries revealed a history of violence and childhood rebellion. In police eyes he was a psychopathic 'odd man out' who found in Mau Mau an appropriate outlet for his repressions. Kimathi was briefly apprehended by security forces. But he escaped to the Aberdare forests and was to defy capture for fully four years, in the course of which his name became a byword for acts of terror and for an elusiveness which astonished his pursuers.[3]

Then, early in the morning of 27 November, a European on his way to work came upon the body of Tom Mbotela lying in a muddy pool beside the ramshackle Burma Market in the Kaloleni location of Nairobi. Mbotela was one of two Africans nominated to the City Council. He had been a vice-president of KAU until the purge of May 1951 and an outspoken opponent of oathing. A non-Kikuyu, Mbotela had pressed for a multi-racial future for Kenya, which implied co-operation with the government albeit while stressing the need for African advances. Mbotela had been to a mayoral party in Nairobi Town Hall on the evening of 26 November and was evidently struck down on his way home. His body had been left all night in the mud beside the road.

These murders shocked the African leaders who had escaped the Emergency round-up into a mixture of fear and rage. Eliud Mathu in Legco backed the government in taking stern counter-action. Though his own life was constantly at risk, he remained one of the few bridges between the government and the Kikuyu nationalists. In the reserves, communities formed their own 'Home Guard' units; one chief nailed the Union Jack to the side of his stockade and rallied his villagers to his side. The government was quick to seize on the possibility that the Kikuyu could be divided into two classes: loyalists and Mau Mau. It was not too particular about the activities of the loyalists. To defeat Mau Mau became an overriding objective.

European opinion quickly hardened. The settlers welcomed Baring's decision and as in past emergencies they looked to achieve greater control over the colony's affairs. But they, too, were shaken by the violence of the Kikuyu reaction.

On 27 October an old settler, Eric Bowyer, was found murdered and disembowelled in his home on the North Kinangop, the farming plateau above Naivasha. A month later, on 22 November, an elderly couple whose farm lay on the edge of the Aberdare forests near Thompson's Falls were attacked by a gang with pangas in the evening as they were sitting down to coffee after dinner. The husband, Commander Meiklejohn, collapsed as he was assembling his shotgun and died two days later in Nakuru hospital. His wife, cut to the bone and covered with blood, managed to drive for help. But their assailants were never caught. On 1 January 1953, two partners on a farm at Ol Kalou, another centre of the White Highlands, were

killed by their own servants, and on 24 January, again on the North
Kinangop, occurred one of the worst tragedies to date. A popular
young family called Ruck were hacked to death in a running battle
across the lawns of their house. Bloody strands of Mrs Ruck's long
golden hair were found scattered across the grass where she had
tried to run from her murderers. Having completed their work on
the adults, the gang then entered the house and cut down their child
of six whom they found cowering in his room.

These savage deeds revived in the minds of Europeans deep-laid
fears about the supposed primitiveness of Africa. The settlers were
suddenly made terrifyingly aware of their isolation and small numbers. Most of them lived alone with their families at considerable
distances from each other and from police assistance, and generally
without telephones. As they sat in their armchairs after their last
evening meal and watched the sudden descent of the African night,
loaded pistols in their hands or under their pillows, so their imaginations began to relive the experiences of those who had first penetrated the 'dark' continent little more than half a century before.[4]
They adopted again the attitude of men like Francis Hall and
Meinertzhagen. You could trust a 'nigger' no further than your gun-
sight.

The morning after his arrest, Kenyatta found himself more than
400 miles to the north of Nairobi at a small station called Lokitaung
near to Lake Rudolph and the Abyssinian border. It was a watering
place for the Turkana people and as remote a place as could be found
in Kenya. He was alone, closely guarded, and without any news of
what was going on. After two days he was allowed to send a letter to
his family. All correspondence, he was told, had to be in Swahili.
Kenyatta wrote to his daughter, Margaret. She was the closest to him
in spirit and she still enjoyed a measure of freedom to contact others
on his behalf. It was the first word his people received of what had become of their leader.

'This is to tell you that I am well, there is nothing wrong, don't be
afraid or grieved in your heart. As you may have heard I was arrested
on 20th October night, and immediately sent to Nairobi, and put in
a plane and brought here to Turkanaland. The journey went well,
there was no trouble on the way, and here too I am in no trouble.
I have a house to myself to sleep in and there are four soldiers to
guard me. I can not go anywhere except just around the place here. I

spend my time reading books, I have nothing else to do. The purpose of this letter is to let you know where I am so that you may not be worried, for these days there are many rumours.'[5]

In the past the Kenya Government had not hesitated to exile men it considered 'seditious'. Harry Thuku had spent almost nine years under restriction without so much as a trial. More recently, Chege Kibachia and Makhan Singh were both arrested for their political or trade union activities and held in indefinite detention.

As we have seen, the settlers had long pressed the government to do the same with Kenyatta, and the government had refused on the grounds that it would turn Kenyatta into a martyr. On taking up his appointment as Governor, Baring took the view that it would be a mistake for him to meet Kenyatta formally since if he then had to arrest him he would appear to have double-crossed the Africans. The first assumption of the Emergency operation was that once the nationalist leaders were out of the way, peace would return among the normally law-abiding natives of the colony.

The government was as shaken as everyone else by the Kikuyu reaction to the loss of their leaders, once the initial numbness wore off. It left them with the problem of having to decide what to do with Kenyatta. In London questions were raised in Parliament where Kenyatta had powerful friends in Fenner Brockway and Leslie Hale. Peter Mbiyu Koinange was also at large and able to denounce the Emergency measures. The confusion of thinking that led to Kenyatta's arrest compelled the government to find some pretext for his detention. Perhaps the most obvious solution was to bring him to trial and to try to make him out to be a common criminal. But of what offence should it accuse him? And how could they make the charge stick?

They made vigorous efforts to find something. A ton and a half of documents, books and papers had been removed from Kenyatta's house at Gatundu, the night of his arrest, and a senior police officer was immediately detailed to go through these and prepare a case against him. He was given three weeks to complete his enquiries. It is fair to say he found nothing.

It is probable that a prosecution was not in contemplation at the time of Kenyatta's arrest and that the government's legal advisers were caught unprepared. To conform with the colony's legal procedure an accused person had to be tried by the court of the area in which the crime allegedly was committed, or by that of the one in which he was 'apprehended'. As Kenyatta's alleged crimes and the place of his arrest both lay in the Kiambu district of Kikuyuland, the natural and proper course would have been to try him in Nairobi. But the government feared the attention and demonstrations which this would attract and wanted to carry the case through as quietly as possible, at some remote spot.

Kapenguria was ideal for this purpose. It lay in a restricted area, to which no one could go without a permit; the scanty local population was backward and uninterested; it had never had a resident magistrate, so that the government could pick someone on whom it could rely.[6] Had the prosecution been decided on from the start, the accused could have been sent straight to one of the prisons at Kapenguria where it would be simple to 'apprehend' them and give some plausibility to the holding of the trial there. But, as it was, the government had to go through a legal farce. On 18 November Kenyatta and his colleagues Kaggia, Kubai, Ngei and Oneko, all of whom were also executive members of KAU, and Kunga Karumba, who was chairman of an important regional branch of the party, were brought down to Kapenguria, technically released from custody and immediately re-arrested, thus creating jurisdiction for trial in Kapenguria. They were now charged with the management of Mau Mau, which was a proscribed society. The offence carried a maximum penalty of seven years' imprisonment. Their trial was set for 24 November.

This was apparently the first Kenyatta heard of the government's intentions toward him. He managed to get a message out requesting that defence lawyers be briefed on his behalf.[7] Within Kenya, feeling among the European community was running so high that no white man in the colony dared join in the defence, which was now being handled from Nairobi by the Indian supporters of the nationalist movement, led by a young barrister, A. R. Kapila. But immediate offers of help came from elsewhere, and soon an impressive international team of counsel was assembled, including Chaman Lall, a member of the Upper House of the Indian Parliament and friend of Nehru, H. O. Davies from Lagos, and Dudley Thompson, a West Indian practicing in Tanganyika. Two Kenya residents also took part, a Goan, Fitzwell de Souza and a Sikh, Jaswant Singh.

To lead this team, Koinange, Brockway and Hale invited the services of D. N. Pritt QC, one of the ablest advocates at the English Bar. On 24 November the six accused were again brought down to Kapenguria where a judge recently retired from the Supreme Court of Kenya, R. S. Thacker, had been specially appointed to hear the case. He adjourned proceedings until 3 December to allow the defence team time to come together.

D. N. Pritt QC had as great an experience of political trials as anyone in the British Commonwealth. A Member of Parliament for fifteen years and known for pro-Soviet views, he had long been an opponent of imperialism. In the Parliament of 1945–50 he had sat as an independent Socialist.[8] His acceptance of the Kapenguria brief made it certain that Kenyatta's case would receive wide publicity. If the Kenya Government hoped to get away with a hole-and-corner affair to cover their blunder in arresting Kenyatta, they badly miscalculated. Their attempt to make Kenyatta out to be an ordinary criminal came unstuck the moment Pritt arrived on the scene. As became clear during the trial itself, the prosecution soon shifted the base of its attack from Kenyatta's alleged criminal activities as manager of Mau Mau to the politics of African Nationalism.

But to the settlers of Kenya, Pritt appeared as the communist Beelzebub himself. His welcome at Nairobi airport by a crowd of several thousand Africans was enough to damn him in European eyes as a traitor to the white man's cause. His defence of Kenyatta also tended to confirm many Europeans in their belief that Kenyatta was a communist agent. Insults, libels, personal harassment and threats to his life followed Pritt throughout his time in Kenya. The prosecution estimated the case would last no more than a fortnight. In the end Pritt stayed for three months, having waived any additional fee, as the trial itself was more drawn out than he or anyone else imagined. In part this was due to legal complexities, largely of the prosecution's making, and in part to the government's vendetta against Pritt himself which took the form of their bringing a contempt of court charge against him which necessitated an adjournment of the main trial from 15 December to 2 January 1953. The contempt of court charge failed ignominiously, but the government was always on the look-out for any excuse to expel Pritt from Kenya.

Kapenguria was then no more than a small administrative post for the Suk pastoral tribesmen in the restricted area beside Mount Elgon to the north-west of Nairobi where Kenya borders Uganda. It consisted of two prisons, a district commissioner's house, and a building intended for use as an agricultural school, which became the courtroom. It was a pleasant enough location in itself, but its inaccessibility created serious difficulties for the defence. It was thirty miles from the railhead township of Kitale, the nearest place where hotels, telephones, restaurants, transport and drinking water were available.

Pritt and his team had to drive the thirty-odd miles to the court and back each morning and evening along bad dirt roads and often through choking dust thrown up by police vehicles. Being a restricted area, the local District Commissioner tried at first to limit Pritt's time with his clients to ten minutes before the case began in the morning and ten minutes after it finished in the afternoon.[9] Added to these difficulties, Kitale was a settler town and Pritt's international team were constantly faced with the colour bar which made eating and consulting together difficult, and which produced a lack of co-operation in the local population in such essential matters as typing. Police frequently searched their rooms and interrogated their friends.

On 3 December 1952, all was ready for the trial proper to begin. The government provided window-dressing in the form of armoured cars, barbed wire and helicopters circling overhead. Troops were everywhere in evidence. The six accused men were brought from their prison a mile away by army truck and marched in handcuffs by armed *askaris* to the door of the court. Only then were the handcuffs removed. The 'public' consisted of wives of settlers and of government officers who applauded every point which seemed to go against Kenyatta. But Nairobi journalists and half a dozen of the best foreign correspondents of the English Press were there, along with government photographers. The government intended, no doubt, to humiliate Kenyatta and impress such Africans as were present with the power of the colonial regime. In the long run the steps taken to destroy him in the eyes of his people ensured his resurrection as their suffering servant.

Kenyatta still wore the clothes in which he had been arrested. The police had removed his stick and ring. He was to spend fifty-eight days in court before judgement was passed, but everyone who was present at the trial felt that his was the dominating personality at Kapenguria.

On 3 December 1952, then, Deputy Public Prosecutor Somerhough opened for the Crown:[10]

'May it please your Honour. The charge is that of managing an unlawful society . . . The Crown cannot bind themselves to any particular place in the Colony where this society was managed. The Society is Mau Mau. It is a Society which has no records. It appears to have no official list of members. It does not carry banners. Some details of its meetings and rites, the instrument of which are got from the local bush, will be heard later in the proceedings. Arches of banana leaves, the African fruit known as the Apple of Sodom, eyes of sheep, blood and earth—these are all gathered together when cere-monies take place . . .

The Crown case is going to be that Mau Mau is part of KAU—a mili-tant part, a sort of Stern gang, if I may borrow a phrase from another country. It is possible to be a member of KAU and have nothing to do with Mau Mau; yet Mau Mau itself is a definite limb or part of KAU as it existed in 1952 when all the accused were closely connected with KAU as high office bearers.'

The Crown proceeded confidently to its first witness, a certain Rawson Macharia. Rawson Macharia was a young man still in his thirties and Kenyatta's neighbour at Gatundu. His evidence con-tained obvious untruths which the defence exposed, but its main significance was that it was the strongest of only three statements that implicated Kenyatta directly with oath-giving ceremonies. Macharia claimed to be a drinking friend of Kenyatta's, and to have been present when Kenyatta personally administered a 'Mau Mau' oath to several people and tried to make Macharia take it also.[11] He gave convincing details—a goat's head from which the eyes had been removed and placed on thorns and the tongue cut out, cere-monial arches, a brew of blood and earth. Kenyatta, he alleged, made the oath-takers repeat the words:

"When we agree to drive the Europeans away you must take an ac-tive part in driving them away or killing them."

MAGISTRATE: Jomo Kenyatta said this?

MACHARIA: Yes, Mr. Kenyatta said this: "If you see any African killing anyone, you must not disclose it or tell anyone. If you shall see an African stealing, you must help him. You must pay sixty-two shil-lings and fifty cents to this society." Then he said: "And that is Mau Mau, and you must not ask how this money is used, and if you shall be asked whether you are a member of this society you must say you are a member of KAU."'

Macharia said this incident took place on 16 March 1950, which was before Mau Mau was proscribed and so, even if proved, it was not an offence in itself. Pritt argued that the evidence should be disallowed. Thacker, however, accepted it on the grounds that it was a strong indication that Kenyatta must also have engaged in similar oath-giving ceremonies after the banning of Mau Mau. But the prosecution could produce nothing to substantiate this.

Thus began a long and confused presentation of evidence remarkable for its weakness in the judicial sense. Readers interested in the technical aspects should consult the full accounts given by Pritt himself and in Montagu Slater's book *The Trial of Jomo Kenyatta*. They will not be analyzed here as no lawyer would now seriously challenge the defence view that there was no criminal case to answer. As Pritt said in his final speech: 'Managing Mau Mau. Well, where? Not why, of course, but how? In what fashion, with what assistance, in what office, with what policy, with what documents? Never, never anything.'

It was only as the prosecution developed its case that Pritt and his clients learnt for the first time what was the detailed evidence against Kenyatta. He frequently had to postpone cross-examination while Kapila and his Indian colleagues searched for witnesses to refute it.[12] The government's choice of Kapenguria for the trial now materially added to the difficulties of the defence as members of their team had to be constantly telephoning and travelling between Kitale and Nairobi, 300 miles away. They found that many potential defence witnesses had already been taken off by police for questioning.

It was this atmosphere of suspicion, intrigue, intimidation and fear which made the Kapenguria trial seem more like a political frame-up than something in which the British imperial mission could take any pride. Pritt's clients repeatedly protested that the room allocated to the Crown Counsel was connected by a door to the judge's room. Both Somerhough and Thacker periodically retreated to Nairobi where they presumably consulted with government officials. The court interpreter was none other than L. S. B. Leakey, Kenyatta's old opponent, to whom Pritt was forced to object, after five weeks of pressure by his clients: 'Here we have an interpreter who is biassed and has written a book against my clients . . . He puts things in and he puts things out. He is a partial interpreter.'[13] He was eventually replaced by a Scottish missionary, Robert Philp, son of old Dr Philp of Tumutumu. Thacker's remarks betrayed his racial sympathies. In the tensions of the Emergency any hint that a man might have links with Mau Mau was enough to condemn him. At Kapenguria Kenyatta was already cast as the villain by the government, and anything he had done or had said, anything which he now said in court, took on sinister meaning in the eyes of the Europeans.

It was for this reason that Rawson Macharia's evidence was so significant. It set the tone for the prosecution case, and put the judge in a receptive frame of mind. Despite the fact that Macharia's story was refuted by no less than nine witnesses whom the defence were able to bring to Kapenguria, as well as being denied by Kenyatta himself, the judge in his summing up said: 'Although my finding of fact means that I disbelieve ten witnesses for the Defence and believe one for the Prosecution, I have no hesitation in doing so. Rawson Macharia gave his evidence well.'

Rawson Macharia had reason to do so, knowledge of which was denied to Pritt at the time, though not to the government. The reader should now be made aware of it, as it is an important illustration of the peculiar circumstances in which Kenyatta's trial was held.

Almost six years later, towards the end of 1958, Macharia signed an affidavit swearing that his evidence against Kenyatta was false. He was then prosecuted himself for perjury—but for what the government said was a perjured affidavit, not for the perjury at Kapenguria to which he confessed. At his trial in 1959 a copy of a letter was produced which purported to emanate from the office of Kenya's Attorney-General and in which were set out the terms of a government offer to Macharia to pay for his air fare to England, for a two years' course at an English University and two years' subsistence for himself and his family, and a government post on his return. The value of the offer amounted to over £2,500. The letter included the sentence: 'In the event of the above named [Rawson Macharia] being murdered for providing evidence, Government will undertake the maintenance of his family and the education of his two sons.'

It carried the date 10 November 1952.[14]

During his cross-examination, Macharia said he 'came under police protection' on 11 November 1952, and that between then and 4 December he was interrogated four times by the police. He was the first prosecution witness, which showed the great reliance the Crown placed on his evidence.

The decision to charge Kenyatta with criminal activities can have been taken only shortly before 18 November. Thacker's appointment dated from 17 November. It is reasonable to suppose, therefore, that what Macharia told the police on 11 November played an important part in the government's decision to bring Kenyatta to trial. After

8 December 1952, Macharia was no longer required at Kapenguria, and by 1 January 1953 he was already in England.[15]

With the delay caused by the contempt of court charge against Pritt, it was not until 19 January 1953 that the prosecution completed its evidence. Pritt then argued at length that there was no case to answer: 'I would submit that it is the most childishly weak case made against any man in any important trial in the history of the British Empire.' The Crown disagreed and Thacker adjourned for a weekend to ponder the arguments in Nairobi. He ran into the most dramatic confrontation between the settlers and the colonial government of the whole Emergency.

On the evening of Saturday 24 January occurred the murder of the Ruck family. The Europeans heard the news on the Sunday and at once gave vent to their feelings. On Monday several hundred of them gathered in Nairobi and marched in a body to Government House brandishing their weapons and shouting for the Governor. They demanded a greater say in the running of affairs; the government seemed on the verge of collapse; whole districts of the Kikuyu reserve appeared to be in the hands of Mau Mau and their passive supporters, Fort Hall being described as virtually a Kikuyu Republic. The Europeans complained that Chaman Lall was able to address public meetings, at one of which he advocated civil disobedience. At a settler meeting in Nakuru a demand was made for the immediate shooting of 50,000 Kikuyu. In their angry and frustrated state of mind the settlers would surely have lynched Kenyatta had he been within their reach.[16]

Thacker returned from Nairobi to rule that there was a case to answer. The trial resumed under the shadow of increasing settler discontent. A Kenya newspaper warned the judge against acquitting Kenyatta. An article by Elspeth Huxley comparing him with Hitler was reprinted in a settler periodical. Inaccurate information about his life was circulated by men like W. O. Tait who had known him in the past. Kenyatta was the universal scapegoat.[17]

After lunch that Monday, 26 January 1953, Kenyatta at last entered the witness-box himself. He was taken through his evidence in chief by Chaman Lall, Nehru's emissary.

LALL: In what language do you wish to speak?
KENYATTA: English.
Q. What is your age?

A. Over 50. I do not know when I was born—what date, what
    month or what year—but I think I am over 50.
Q. Where were you educated?
A. First in the Church of Scotland Mission, Kikuyu, and after that
    I had what you would call self-education. I educated myself.
Q. What is your religion?
A. Christian.
Q. Will you tell us something about your own personal history,
    such as your development into a political leader?
A. I started political activity in 1922, but I took it up as a whole-
    time activity from 1928.
Q. What sort of political activity did you indulge in in 1922?
A. First it was the East African Association, but after 1922, when it
    was not functioning, I was not an active member in it—I was a
    supporter or sympathiser with the organisation. The next organi-
    sation started to function soon after, I think, 1922/23 and so on,
    but actively from 1925 and I became a full-time worker on the
    Association, that is, The Kikuyu Central Association. From 1928
    I took up political work as a full time job.

Kenyatta spoke of the growth of the Africans' early political associations and his own role in them. He described the grievances for
which they sought redress and the aims of KAU and how its meetings
were conducted. He gave his views of the Mau Mau picture and explained how he had publicly cursed it at the famous Kiambu meeting
of August 1952. As to himself, Kenyatta said he was 'just an ordinary
man striving to fight for the rights of my people and to better their
conditions without necessarily hating anybody.'

LALL: Is it a part of your policy to drive the Europeans away
    from Kenya?
KENYATTA. No. My policy is that we should live together, that is
    if we could get away from greed, selfishness, we can all live together
    happily as brothers and sisters.

The defence was not going to let the opportunity slip of drawing
attention to Kenyatta's work during the war:

LALL: One last matter. You were in London during the war?
KENYATTA: Yes, throughout the war . . . I was doing many
    things, but one of my jobs as war work was to lecture to British

soldiers. I lectured for, I think, over 5 years in different parts of England, in various searchlight units as well as in barracks from the south of England to the north, around Manchester and so on. I was sent to the north after D.Day to lecture to sick soldiers in hospitals, and in rest homes. Before D.Day I was lecturing in the south coast of England.

This last answer illustrates an important characteristic of Kenyatta's evidence, the force of which only comes from reading the original transcript with close attention to the details of his career which have been recounted in earlier pages. Kenyatta always implied rather more in his answers than strict accuracy required. It was a simple point, but why should he have said he was in London for the whole of the war? He gave the impression that he had been sent north 'after D.Day' by the War Office and throughout was enrolled in some kind of government service. The account given in previous chapters of his time at Storrington and his preparation for the Pan-African Congress in Manchester could hardly justify this interpretation. The explanation lay in his deep-rooted vanity. Under the hostile interrogation of the prosecution it was to show up as a real weakness.

Kenyatta's evidence in chief had taken until mid-afternoon of his third day in the witness-box. It was then that Deputy Public Prosecutor Somerhough rose to begin a cross-examination that was to continue for a further seven days.

SOMERHOUGH: What is your real name?
KENYATTA: Jomo Kenyatta.
Q. Son of who?
A. Son of Muigai.[18]
Q. And you were christened Johnson when you became a Christian?
A. Yes.
Q. You no longer call yourself Johnson?
A. No.
A. I think you told us that you are over 50 years of age, but that you do not know the day, month or year of your birth?
A. Yes.
Q. I think in your passport it is given as 1893?
A. Yes.
Q. Was that on information supplied by you?
A. Yes. When I wanted to get a passport, it was suggested what my approximate year of birth would be and that date was inserted.

Q. And that makes you nearer 60 than 50?

A. Yes.

Q. You were educated at the Church of Scotland Mission—where was that, at Dagoretti?

A. No, Kikuyu.

Q. When did you leave school?

A. In 1914.

Q. Did you continue your education, or did you start work?

A. I started working.

Q. With whom?

A. With various people. I have done lots of things: worked for the settlers on farms, and finally I worked in the Supreme Court in Nairobi.

Q. What were you there?

A. An interpreter.

Q. When?

A. 1919 or thereabouts; I also worked for a short time in the D.C.'s office, Nairobi. Then I was transferred to the Municipal Offices.

Q. Were you working in the Nairobi Municipality about 1921?

A. Yes.

Q. What did you do?

A. I was in charge of the water works, that is, measuring for the pipes to be laid, supervising the employees of the Water Department, as well as reading meters and general inspection of water works.

Q. You were there until 1926?

A. Until 1928.

Q. About your education. You said that after leaving the Church of Scotland Mission you were self-educated?

A. I was educating myself all the time.

Q. Did you attend various universities?

A. Yes.

Q. Which ones?

A. In London I attended the London School of Economics, which is attached to London University. I was also for a time at Woodbrook College, Birmingham. I think that is all I can remember. I had a shot at an evening institute before I entered London University.

Q. What about abroad?

A. I travelled widely in various parts.

Q. Where?

A. Practically all over Europe.

Q. Where?

A. Belgium, Holland, Switzerland, Italy, France, Poland, Estonia, Bulgaria, Denmark, Sweden, Norway, and finally—what you have been wanting me to say—Russia.

Q. Did you attend any educational institution on the Continent?

A. A bit in Russia.

Q. What institution there did you attend?

A. Moscow University.

Q. How long were you there?

A. I think about two years.

Q. What years?

A. It must be between 1932 and 1934. I have been there twice.

Q. Twice to Russia, or twice to the University?

A. Twice to Russia: once in 1929, and again in 1932.

Q. And both times to the University?

A. Not University; but I was learning all the time. The first time I spent most of the time seeing the country as part of my education. I was not confined. I was my own master.

Q. When did you enter the University?

A. I cannot remember the date.

Q. The year?

A. I have told you—about 1932.

Q. When did you finally leave the University?

A. I cannot remember whether it was the beginning of 1934 or thereabouts.

Q. And then you came back to England in 1934?

A. Yes.

So it went on. For the first time the Europeans of Kenya, in the person of their prosecuting counsel, felt they had Kenyatta in their sights. His evasiveness, at this early stage in his evidence, gave Somerhough lead after lead.[19]

They came to *Facing Mount Kenya:*

SOMERHOUGH: That was serious scientific study?

KENYATTA: Yes

Q. Based on your personal knowledge and observations?

A. Yes.

Q. Looking back on it, does it still represent your views on the Kikuyu Tribe?

A.   The book cannot necessarily be my guide during my whole life.

Q.   Do you still regard it as a serious scientific work? Does it represent your opinions?

A.   It depends on what you mean.

Q.   I ask you, is it a serious scientific work? Does it represent your opinions, and have you changed your opinions since then? Do you adhere to it?

A.   The book is not my opinion as such, but it represents the habits and customs of the Kikuyu people.

Q.   Have you ever published a correction of the book or anything like that?

A.   No, because I wanted to revise it when I came back, but having so many things to do, I did not have the time.

Q.   And would you accept the description that the Crown applied: that you are an exceptionally wide travelled and exceptionally well educated African?

A.   That is the Crown's opinion and you are entitled to your opinion.

Q.   Would you accept that as being a proper description?

A.   It all depends.

Q.   Depends on what?

A.   On what you mean by 'exceptionally'.

Q.   Not many have travelled as widely as you or have been educated at such widely different institutions—would you agree with that as a description of yourself?

A.   If that is your opinion.

Q.   You have described yourself as a Christian?

A.   Yes.

Q.   What Church and denomination?

A.   I do not believe in denominations. I am a true Christian believing in God.

Q.   You do not follow any of the Churches?

A.   I do not follow any particular denomination. I believe in Christianity as a whole.

Q.   And you have left the Church of Scotland?

A.   I have not left it. I respect Christianity as it is, but not as it is preached by one particular denomination. I said to Dr Arthur that, from my scientific study, I could not tie myself to any particular denomination.

Q.   Do you or do you not still regard yourself as a member of the Church of Scotland?

A. Yes, of every Church—the Church of Scotland, the Church of England, the Catholic Church, in fact, wherever I happen to be at the time. I belong to all these religions.

Q. Do you practice polygamy?

A. What do you mean?

Pritt protested at this last question, saying that it was irrelevant to any of the charges, and that it had not been given in evidence that polygamy was one of the characteristics of Mau Mau. His objection was overruled.

SOMERHOUGH: Do you practice polygamy?
KENYATTA: Yes. But I do not call it polygamy.

The Court rose. It was 4 o'clock in the afternoon.

The succeeding days followed the same pattern. Something from Kenyatta's past—the record of a speech or an article, the course of his political career, his own personal beliefs—one by one these items were subjected to ironic questioning. Tempers in the courtroom rose; Somerhough complained he was being barracked by Pritt; the judge grew restless at their quarrels and threatened adjournment. They spent hours arguing over the precise meaning in English and Kikuyu of words like sect and association, about the significance of oaths to Christian and non-Christian Africans, and about the racial implications of Kenyatta's speeches on land. Somerhough appealed to the judge that Kenyatta's answers were long and incomprehensible and the judge himself complained at 'the workings of the African mind.' On many issues Kenyatta said he could not remember; there were long pauses in which he and Somerhough stared at each other; flies buzzed about the courtroom and distracted counsel.

Once again the attentive reader of the original record who knows the details of Kenyatta's life cannot fail to be struck by how accurate his memory proved to be on certain matters—such as the date of his baptism in August 1914—and how vague it became on political questions. Somerhough pressed for details apparently quite irrelevant to Mau Mau, as Pritt time and again protested. But the prosecution case grew out of this cross-examination. Put on the spot in this way, Kenyatta made a poor impression. The prosecution's methods might not have got by in a properly conducted criminal trial, but they proved of devastating effect as political propaganda.

As the days wore on, Kenyatta's evasiveness appeared increasingly incriminating. On more than one occasion he betrayed the wound to his pride he suffered at being subjected to this treatment. There is little doubt he would have made a bad impression on a jury.

Yet nothing proved Kenyatta had engaged in any actual criminal activity. It was all circumstantial and, as has been indicated, highly questionable in law. The thrust of the prosecution's case was to portray Kenyatta as the leader of African Nationalism pledged to drive the Europeans from Kenya, by violent means if necessary. In the Kikuyu 'hymn books' Kenyatta's name was substituted for that of Christ. Mau Mau oaths included a pledge of loyalty to Kenyatta. The KAU was Kenyatta's instrument. Therefore, argued the Crown, Kenyatta was really behind everything, including the Mau Mau terror. Somerhough produced a series of newspaper reports of Kenyatta's speeches in which, he argued, no denunciation of Mau Mau appeared. Kenyatta grew irritated.

KENYATTA: It all depends, Sir, what you mean by denunciation. You have your own idea of denunciation and even if I go to heaven or hell, perhaps you would not say I denounced Mau Mau. I have done my best to denounce Mau Mau, and I do not know what words you want me to denounce it.

The meaning of Kikuyu words was questioned, for example, a *baraza* report of a meeting in Kiambu, which quoted the phrase: 'Kenyatta does not want the name of KAU to be mixed up with Mau Mau.'

KENYATTA: Is that not enough? If you do not want to mix up with somebody, are you still like him?
SOMERHOUGH: You say that that is a denunciation?
KENYATTA: That is denunciation. Yes.

Later after further Press accounts had been read out, Kenyatta explained that he was more concerned with the meetings themselves than with subsequent reports, as the majority of his supporters could not read anyway. 'I mean in this meeting, many other meetings, I went on explaining to the people that Mau Mau was an evil thing and that people should not associate themselves with it.' The paper, he went on, had not reported that part of his speech. But, Kenyatta pointed out, there was one simple way of checking on what he had actually said. At the meeting at Kiambu the government information services had themselves made a recording. 'So do not beat about the bush, bring the record and you can hear what I did say.' It was a fair point. What had happened to those recordings? Why, if the government were satisfied with the strength of Kenyatta's curse to have sent a report to the Colonial Office to that effect, were the tapes never used? Pritt at once asked that they be produced in court. The Director of Information Services was ready to oblige. But Thacker ruled they were inadmissible.

Kenyatta had now been cross-examined for over a week. After the second weekend Somerhough finally recapitulated the Crown's case to the witness. It was, essentially, an accumulation of evidence which linked Mau Mau with the KCA, the KCA with KAU, and everything, hymn books, oaths, politics, with Kenyatta.

SOMERHOUGH: The Crown case is that at no time have you denounced Mau Mau at all with any intention to be effective.

KENYATTA: That is not true. I have denounced Mau Mau in the best way possible. I do not think there is anyone who has done more than I have done.

Q. And that in general the most that you did, the Crown says, is to deny the connection of Mau Mau with KAU which of course you had to do as Mau Mau was a proscribed society.

A. That is not true, I have denounced Mau Mau in the most strong terms I could use.

Q. And that when on occasions such as at Kiambu you were forced into when a position where you had to say something more definite than a denial of the connection of KAU and MAU MAU, you used such terms and with such double meaning and in such form that—

A. That is a lie.

Q. Let me finish my sentence—that your hearers were not deluded or deceived for one moment as to your true views.

A. If you are doubtful I ask you to call this 40 to 50,000 people to come here and tell you if they did not understand what I said: and at Kiambu I was not forced, I was one of the organizers of the meeting, therefore I could not have been forced to say what I said.

Q. You will agree will you not that your so-called denunciation had very little effect at all?

A. That is a lie.

Q. You think it has?
A. It has, yes.
Q. You think Mau Mau is much better since you started denouncing it?
A. You people have audacity to ask me silly questions. I have done my best and if all other people had done as I have done, Mau Mau would not be as it is now. You made it what it is, not Kenyatta.
Q. What—'you Europeans', the Crown, or who made it what it is?
A. The Government is not handling Mau Mau in the proper way, and you blame it to me.
Q. It is the Government's fault that Mau Mau exists and goes on?
A. Well I say yes.
Q. I will take that answer. Thank you.

Kenyatta's ordeal by cross-examination was over. It was now Monday, 9 February, a fortnight since he first entered the witness-box.

Pritt put the opposite interpretation on the political motivation behind African Nationalism. In an incisive closing speech he dealt with a register of the various incidents on which at one time or another the prosecution had seemed to rely, which he had prepared earlier and got the prosecution to accept. Item by item he disposed of their weakness. On 3 March he had to leave Kenya at last. Better than most, he knew that in political trials the verdict has been arrived at in advance. He had sought to achieve the greatest political advantage for his clients, and he was confident he could win the case on appeal whatever happened. Kenyatta and his fellow accused were deeply appreciative of all that he had done and endured on their behalf. They knew, too, what the verdict of Kapenguria was going to be, and they were heartened by Pritt's confidence in the appeal mechanism.

Somerhough's concluding speech took until 10 March. Thacker then adjourned to consider his judgement. He was ready to give it on 8 April.

In the interval the situation with Mau Mau underwent a dramatic deterioration. Two incidents, both on the night of 26 March, shocked all races in the colony.

The first was a daring raid on Naivasha police station, in the Rift Valley. With only five guns between them, the attackers rushed the post in the dark and got away with weapons and ammunition which they loaded on to government trucks and drove off to the forests. It showed the Mau Mau bands were capable of military planning and discipline, and it gave them essential supplies for guerrilla warfare.

The second incident had greater repercussions. For reasons which in part stretched back into the troubled history of the Tigoni removal, all the villagers of a location called Lari who were loyal to their government-appointed chiefs were marked for destruction by rivals. On the night of 26 March some 3,000 embittered men, most of whom had taken the stiffest Mau Mau oaths, swept through the location burning huts and hacking wildly at humans and animals. At least ninety-seven men, women and children in the village died. Half a century before, men like Francis Hall would have thought little of it, as it was a natural part of the African scene before the arrival of the colonial power. But in the tense atmosphere of Kenya in 1953, Lari became a symbol of Mau Mau terror. Few Europeans in the colony paused to consider what could have caused such a return to the habits of past centuries; most attributed it to a breakdown in tribal morale. Very few saw it as a tragic indication of the failure of the colonial mission.

After Lari the Europeans became convinced that the Mau Mau were capable of any imaginable atrocity. There now developed what can best be described as the pornography of violence. European propaganda against Mau Mau dwelt on the worst of the atrocities and the worst of the oaths. These seemed to grow in obscenity and bestiality as though in response to this propaganda. Home Guard units —the 'loyalists'—sometimes indulged in their own atrocities. The inefficiency of the government led the settlers into demanding that they be allowed to run things their own way. The police were ill-organized, under strength and suffering from poor morale. Intelligence appeared unco-ordinated and at first directed as much against European activities as those of the Mau Mau. The army was at a loss to know how to operate against tribal rebellion on such a scale and spoke of having to detain up to three times the 80,000 or so Kikuyu who eventually passed through the camps. While gradually there evolved a system of counter-terror within these camps and in the reserve which led the missionaries to protest against the indiscriminate use of violence as a government weapon.

Lari and the beginnings of the spiralling descent into nightmare coincided with the closing stages of Kenyatta's trial. They placed him in an impossible situation. The leader of a nationalist movement must always expect to find himself in the dock sooner or later. What he then says will decide his future standing with his people. For Kenyatta to deny the springs of nationalism would have been to deny his whole political life. The judge at Kapenguria could only sentence him to a term of imprisonment; but if he said anything against his own people, who could say what might happen to him. Some of the other accused who played such a subordinate role at Kapenguria were not above murder for their cause. It is not beyond a possibility that he was placed among them by the government with the deliberate intention of provoking personality clashes. Events were to show that he could have had reason to fear his fellow prisoners.

On 8 April 1953, the court reassembled at Kapenguria for the last time. In the situation just described, an acquittal was politically unthinkable. The judge duly found them all guilty. He dwelt upon Kenyatta's evasion attitude, implying that Kenyatta had virtually condemned himself. Kenyatta then addressed the court. For all he knew it was to be his political testament. In the circumstances it was a remarkable statement.

'May it please Your Honour. On behalf of my colleagues I wish to say that we are not guilty and we do not accept your findings and that during the hearing of this trial which has been so arranged as to place us in difficulties and inconvenience in preparing our cases, we do not feel that we have received the justice or hearing which we would have liked.

I would like also to tell Your Honour that we feel that this case, from our point of view, has been so arranged as to make scapegoats of us in order to strangle the Kenya African Union, the only African political organisation which fights for the rights of the African people. We wish to say that what we have done in our activities has been to try our level best to find ways and means by which the community in this country can live in harmony. But what we have objected to—and we shall continue to object—are the discriminations in the government of this country. We shall not accept that, whether we are in gaol or out of it, sir, because we find that this world has been made for human beings to live in happily, to enjoy the good things and the produce of the country equally, and to enjoy the opportunities that this country has to offer. Therefore, Your Honour, I will not say that you have been misled or influenced, but the point that you have made is that we have been against the Europeans, and sir, you being a European, it is only natural that perhaps you should feel more that way. I am not accusing you of being prejudiced, but I feel that you should not stress so much the fact that we have been entirely motivated by hatred of Europeans. We ask you to remove that from your mind and to take this line: that our activities have been against the injustices that have been suffered by the African people and if in trying to establish the rights of the African people we have turned out to be what you say, Mau Mau, we are very sorry that you have been misled in that direction. What we have done, and what we shall continue to do, is to demand the rights of the African people as human beings that they may enjoy the facilities and privileges in the same way as other people.

We look forward to the day when peace shall come to this land and that the truth shall be known that we, as African leaders, have stood for peace. None of us would be happy or would condone the mutilation of human beings. We are humans and we have families and none of us will ever condone such activities as arson that we have been guilty of.

Without taking up much more of your time, I will tell Your Honour that we as political bodies or political leaders stand constitutionally by our demands which no doubt are known to you and the Government of this country, and in saying this I am asking for no mercy at all on behalf of my colleagues. We are asking that justice may be done and that the injustices that exist may be righted. No doubt we have grievances, and everybody in this country, high or low, knows perfectly well that there are such grievances, and it is those grievances which affect the African people that we have been fighting for. We will not ask to be excused for asking for those grievances to be righted.

I do not want to take up more of your time, Your Honour. All that I wish to tell you is that we feel strongly that at this time the Government of this country should try to strangle the only organization, that is the Kenya African Union, of which we are the leaders, who have been working for the betterment of the African people and who are seeking harmonious relations between the races. To these few remarks, Your Honour, I may say that we do not accept your finding of guilty. It will be our duty to instruct our lawyer to take this matter up and we intend to appeal to a higher Court. We believe that the Supreme Court of Kenya will give us justice because we stand for peace; we stand for the rights of the African people, that Africans may find a place among the nations.

That is, in short, is all that I shall say on behalf of my colleagues; that we hope that you and the rest of those who are in authority will seek ways and means by which we can bring harmony and peace to this country, because we do believe that peace by force from any section is impossible, and that violence of any kind, either from Europeans or from Africans, cannot bring any peace at all.'

Thacker turned to sentence him.

'You Jomo Kenyatta, stand convicted of managing Mau Mau and being a member of that society. You have protested that your object has always been to pursue constitutional methods on the way to self government for the African people, and for the return of land which you say belongs to the African people. I do not believe you. It is my belief that soon after your long stay in Europe and when you came back to this Colony you commenced to organize this Mau Mau society, the object of which was to drive out from Kenya all Europeans, and in doing so to kill them if necessary. I am satisfied that the master mind behind this plan was yours.

I also believe that the methods to be employed were worked out by you and that you have taken the fullest advantage of the power and influence which you have over your people and also of the primitive instincts which you know lie deep down in their characters. When they have made so much progress towards an enlightened civilisation, you have successfully plunged many of them back to a state which shows little of humanity. You have persuaded them in secret to murder, to burn, to commit evil atrocities, which it will take many years to forget. Some small part of the Mau Mau plan to kill Europeans has succeeded, but perhaps the greatest tragedy of all is that you have turned Kikuyu against Kikuyu. Your Mau Mau society has slaughtered without mercy defenceless Kikuyu men, women and children in hundreds and in circumstances which are revolting and are better left undescribed. You have let loose upon this land a flood of misery and unhappiness affecting the daily lives of all the races in it, including your own people. You have put the clock back many years and by your deeds much of the respect for your tribe has been lost, at least for the time being.

You have much to answer for and for that you will be punished. The maximum sentences which this Court is empowered to pass are the sentences which I do pass, and I can only comment that in my opinion they are inadequate for what you have done. Under Section 70 and on the first charge the sentence of the Court is that you be imprisoned for seven years with hard labour, and under Section 71 and on the third charge for three years with hard labour, both

sentences to run concurrently, and I shall also recommend that you
be restricted.'

Thacker was immediately flown out of Kenya. The settlers were
satisfied: Kenyatta was out of the way. There was no question in the
minds of nearly all Europeans that his was the master mind behind
Mau Mau. All the hatreds and fears and suspicions of the last few
years found expression in this one belief. It became an article of faith
which permanently affected European thinking, for it was now
sanctioned by the most sacred text in colonial scripture, namely that
truth and justice will always result from a British court of law. It is
for this reason that Kenyatta's trial assumes a historic importance.
At the time it seemed to the settlers like the ace of trumps; in retro-
spect it can be seen as a deliberate revoke.

Seven years' hard labour, to be followed by indefinite restriction.
For a man of Kenyatta's age it might have been a sentence of death.

CHAPTER 21

Lokitaung

Lokitaung lies in a range of low hills on the western shore of Lake Rudolph and close to its northern end where the Sudan, Kenya and Ethiopia all meet. The surrounding country is a desert of sand and lava stone, of barren hills and dried-up water-courses which from the air looks like veins in a dead leaf attached to the stem of a dead branch, which is the River Turkwell.

Some fifteen thousand years ago the whole region formed part of the Nile system, of which the Nile perch in Lake Rudolph are now survivors. Further north, in remote passes, petrified trees testify to the great forests which once covered the landscape and ensured plentiful rain, fertile soil and, perhaps, contacts with earlier civilizations. Now, its blighted condition puts the traveller in mind of the psalmist's words of 'the dry and thirsty land, where no water is'. There is something very old and very basic about it, which brings a man close to the earth and the sky and a sense of his own insignificance.

The local people are Turkana: tall, fine-looking tribesmen of Nilo-Hamitic stock who live off meat and berries, milk and blood, and graze their herds of camels, goats and donkeys over vast distances. The men often carry an ivory plug under the lower lip, but otherwise are naked; the women wear skirts and necklaces made up of hundreds of coloured beads. They are a people of great endurance who preserve still a simplicity of life which matches their primitive surroundings.

The station of Lokitaung owes its existence to a spring of water oozing from a hole in the rock at the head of a dried-up river bed which runs through a deep canyon towards Lake Rudolph, some twenty miles away. It is surrounded by hills of a uniform greyish colour, which are covered with stones and thorn trees. In these arid regions water has always been a cause of fighting between tribes; and the spring at Lokitaung was the scene of constant raids of the more northerly Merile upon the Turkana, with consequent reprisals and blood feuds. For this reason, the British constructed a large police post near to the water-hole, and a district officer's bungalow on a ridge overlooking the canyon. For most of the colonial period the whole Northern Frontier District was closed to outsiders. Lokitaung was as isolated a place as could be found in Kenya.

When Kenyatta was first brought to Lokitaung, he was placed in a small house which stood on a plateau on the edge of the dried-up river, some distance from the water-hole and the police lines, but under the eye of the District Officer's bungalow. It was the building where Makhan Singh had begun the eleven-and-a-half years of his detention, following his arrest in May 1950. At the end of their trial at Kapenguria in April 1953, Kenyatta's fellow prisoners joined him in these temporary living quarters, which they called Red House because of its red corrugated-iron roofing.

While his appeal was being heard, Kenyatta had the option of either being treated on remand status, or of starting at once to serve his sentence. He chose remand status. It made little difference to the curtailment of his freedom, but at least he could still think of himself as an individual. The five others followed his example. They all had great confidence in Pritt and the appeal process. This now turned into a Kafka-like game of cat-and-mouse between the defence lawyers and the colonial government which lasted for more than a year.

The first move was a straightforward appeal against the decision of the magistrate at Kapenguria. Like the main trial itself, this appeal should have been heard in Nairobi, where law books and other documents required by counsel were at hand. Once again, however, the government decreed the case should be heard at Kitale, and once again Pritt came out from England to meet the murderous glances of the settlers. But at least Kenyatta had a right to be present, and this gave him a break from Lokitaung.

A second legal farce now took place. Kenyatta's advisers discovered that the Kenya government lawyers had slipped up by originally appointing Thacker as magistrate for the wrong district. The whole trial at Kapenguria was therefore void. Sitting at Kitale, the Supreme Court of Kenya agreed with this defence claim and on 15 July 1953, Kenyatta was technically a free man. By now the atmosphere at Kitale was very bad. The settlers were threatening to shoot Pritt, let alone the African prisoners. It was market-day; many of them had been drinking and they all carried guns. The police quickly served new detention orders on Kenyatta and his colleagues and smuggled them away, while they got Pritt out of his hotel in a hurry by the back door, and even packed his luggage for him.[1]

Now it was the turn of the Kenya government to appeal against the Kitale decision to the East African Court of Appeal, which sat in Nairobi. On 22 August 1953, this court reversed the Kitale judgement on the technical point of Thacker's jurisdiction.

Pritt now carried this decision to the Privy Council in London. Criminal appeals to that court can only be brought by leave of the court, which is applied for in open court by petition. This course was followed here, and when the petition came up for hearing, Pritt found that Lord Goddard, the Lord Chief Justice, made a point of attending, which indicated that an important matter of state was at issue. The Privy Council considered it privately for only twenty minutes and then dismissed the petition without giving any reasons. Pritt was shocked. He wrote to Kapila in Nairobi: 'I fear I was wrong in thinking that when it came to politics the Privy Council would behave any better than anyone else.'

It was now 28 October 1953. Kenyatta had been in custody for over a year and the appeal apparatus was resumed at the stage it had reached at Kitale when the defence successfully raised the technical point about Thacker's lack of proper juridical authority. The Kenya Government flew out a pugnacious English silk to lead against Pritt.

On 15 January 1954, the Supreme Court of Kenya ruled against Kenyatta and all his colleagues except Oneko, against whom they declared there was no case. Oneko was accordingly transferred from Lokitaung to a special camp for political detainees.

Kenyatta had one last card to play. He could appeal either to the East African Court of Appeal or to the Privy Council. Knowing that he would have little chance of a fair hearing in Nairobi, he opted for the Privy Council.

The petition for leave to appeal did not come up in London until the summer of 1954. Pritt was supremely confident. He prepared the case with great care in what he described as one of the two best bits of 'paper work' he ever did. Clearly and systematically he reviewed the weaknesses of the prosecution's case against Kenyatta and gave telling examples of Thacker's prejudice and perversity in assessing the evidence. In July the Privy Council met for the second time to decide Kenyatta's fate and Goddard again attended in person. The petition was refused. Pritt later wrote of this:

'In the forty years in which I practised before the Privy Council, during which time I presented hundreds of petitions for special leave, I never had another which was as strong as this one of Kenyatta and his colleagues, and when I came to present it I did not believe that any consideration of any kind could prevent my obtaining leave. But I was wrong; after listening to my arguments for a day and a half, the Privy Council rejected it without giving any reasons.'

Again, it seemed, political considerations had counted for more than legal arguments. Five thousand miles away in the heat of Lokitaung, Kenyatta was told of the final decision against him. Only now, technically, did he become a convict; only now did he start serving his sentence of seven years with hard labour. There was nothing further Pritt could do. But a few months later he received a handwritten letter from Lokitaung signed by his five clients thanking him for all the efforts he and his team of junior counsel had made on their behalf: 'the best we could get'.[2]

While the appeals were being heard the government undertook the construction of a special prison compound at Lokitaung on the plateau between Red House and the District Officer's bungalow. It measured 100 yards by 100 yards and was surrounded by a 20 foot high barbed-wire fence. Barbed wire separated the compound into two sections, one for prisoners, the other for their guards. The buildings were of local stone, grey and functional. One large block ran down the length of the prisoners' side of the compound facing inwards. It was divided into two large cells on either side of a smaller central one, with an office at one end and a store room at the other. The roof was of corrugated iron and carried on high wooden rafters. There was no ceiling.

This was to be their home for the next five years. As soon as their sentences were confirmed, the five prisoners were moved in—Kenyatta into the central cell, the four others into one of the two larger ones. The second was kept for eating, reading and odd jobs. Two blankets each were provided. They slept on mats on the stone floor.

The Privy Council decision gave the Kenya Government the go-ahead with its purpose of destroying Kenyatta—making him, in communist jargon, an 'unperson'. He was now just a convict, known only by a number. He lost his name and identity. The stick and ring had gone long ago, now his clothes were removed and he had to wear convict's uniform—white shorts and white sweat-shirt with two broad horizontal bands around the chest. He had to shave off his beard and keep his hair short. For several months, along with the other prisoners, he wore chains around his ankles. His diet became a monotonous repetition of beans and mealie meal, with occasional bits of meat.[3]

Because of his age, Kenyatta was released from the hard labour his fellow convicts had to serve. For them it consisted of breaking stones, digging holes and then filling them up again. Kenyatta was cook. He rose before the sun was up to prepare breakfast and then faced an empty day contemplating the sky and the grey prison compound. Turkana children stared in from outside the barbed wire, the *askaris* were under orders not to converse with the prisoners, and the few Europeans passed by indifferently. Ahead the days stretched to eternity. Around lay only the skeletal debris of life—animal bones bleaching in the sun, goats' dung baked into little hard white balls, rusty tins and cast-off shoes.

The heat smothered sounds of life. About Lokitaung there was a silence of death, broken by day only by the wind sighing through the thorn bushes and the crickets and the occasional buzzing fly; by night, by the disturbing noises of men deprived of freedom crying out in their sleep and rarely, very rarely, by the sound of some wild thing beyond the barbed wire, a leopard or a bush-buck making its way to the waterhole.

For Kenyatta human contact was reduced to shadows and dreams. His guards were from other tribes, like the Kamba, who had no sympathy for the Kikuyu. The Turkana were told that if anyone escaped, he was fair game for their hunting instinct, and the Turkana were the best trackers in the northern deserts. No one could survive alone in those waterless wastelands. The tribesmen killed strangers as a matter of course. The chains, the sentries and the barbed wire were an unnecessary precaution against only five men, one of whom was elderly. They were all designed to destroy the soul.

As had happened during his trial, so the long-drawn-out process of Kenyatta's appeal continued alongside dramatic moves in the Mau Mau rebellion. These seemed to override the necessity for those legal refinements on which Britain traditionally prided herself and they may have accounted for the attitude of the Privy Council in London.

For some time following the declaration of the Emergency the hold of Mau Mau over the Kikuyu population seemed complete. In Nairobi they were able to enforce a ban on smoking, beer drinking, the wearing of hats and the use of municipal buses. Their agents collected contributions to funds according to their own assessment of the victims' wealth which few dared to resist. Failure to pay up led to beatings and death. Mau Mau appeared to operate a network of secret 'courts' with impunity, and the number of Africans sentenced and executed without trace will never be properly known—perhaps they amounted to over 3,000.[4] Security forces often came upon corpses buried outside what they took to be Mau Mau centres. Sometimes several dozen were unearthed at a time. One such 'trial' of two African nurses was held in a barber's shop in broad daylight. They were accused of collaboration with government and sentenced to have their fingers chopped off and fed to dogs, after which they were to be strangled. Fortunately for them, as they were being led away for execution they succeeded in attracting the attention of a street patrol, whom they promptly guided back to the barber's shop where the members of the 'court' were arrested.

The effectiveness of the Mau Mau communications and intelligence systems took the government by surprise. By using the railway and regular bus routes, until these were curtailed, Mau Mau supporters maintained an efficient courier service with the Kikuyu reserve, and so with the forest bands. Women played a key part in this respect as emissaries and sources of information; and Kikuyu employees in the Post Office were heavily implicated in passing messages. The Kikuyu were masters of code language, and no one could tell when an apparently innocuous shout across the ridges was not, in reality, a warning of an impending police raid. The government was so uncertain of the reliability of the Kikuyu, even those in the administration, it asked Barlow to return to Kenya for a time to monitor Kikuyu broadcasts on its own Voice of Kenya radio network for hidden meaning.

At night Nairobi became a dead city, with only the occasional police car patrolling down its deserted streets. Wire barricades were erected around the African locations in the city, but there could be little control over what went on in their warren-like shacks and godowns, and at one time assassinations of Africans averaged four a night. Steel mesh covered the windows of houses and flats in the European quarters. At the Norfolk and New Stanley Hotels Europeans sipped their drinks with guns on their knees. Many who forgot to take their weapons out of their cars would return to find the doors forced and their revolvers gone. Heavy fines were imposed for firearms lost, but despite these many were reported missing. Because they thought it made them vulnerable if they carried guns, many people preferred to go without them altogether.

On their farms the Europeans were left to organize their own protection. Barbed wire usually surrounded their homes and arc lamps lit the exteriors at night. Their owners were careful to be indoors by dusk and to see that their Kikuyu servants were out of the house by the same time. With loaded revolvers beside their plates or on the arms of their chairs they watched their servants closely whenever they were in the room with them, as there were cases where they were known to have given the signal for attackers from outside. After dinner, doors were locked, sofas and chairs were pulled against them as additional barricades, and the inmates settled down as calmly as they could to listen to the noises of the African night. They were advised to have one room ready as a kind of inner keep, complete with fire extinguishers and iron rations and signal rockets to summon assistance. Two elderly ladies living alone and armed with a pistol and a shotgun successfully drove off one gang and did much to restore morale among the farming community. They were decorated accordingly. Prominent men were given Special Branch bodygaurds; their insurance premiums soared, and threatening messages became part of their daily lives.

In these tense conditions feeling remained strong following the march on Government House, Nairobi, of January 1953 and the Lari massacre of March. The settlers blamed the government for inaction and unpreparedness. Murders of Europeans continued—four in April 1953, one in July, two in September, and throughout 1954. The last ascribable to Mau Mau was in April 1955. But the total was then only thirty-two. The small number killed made each one no less tragic for the families concerned, but it was fewer, as it happened, than the number of Europeans killed in traffic accidents in Nairobi during the same period.

This aspect of the Emergency needs stressing. The Mau Mau 'rebellion' was soon diverted from whatever coherent anti-European plan it may once have had. Why this diversion took place is still not clear. The settlers were pitifully exposed on their farms, which mostly lay outside the field of military operations and lacked any possibility of serious military defence. Determined efforts by Mau Mau guerrillas could without difficulty have claimed many more European victims. The sudden removal of the African political leaders may partly have accounted for this incoherence of plan, but explanations must also be sought in the nature of tribal societies placed under the extreme social and economic pressures from which the Kikuyu suffered. One obvious cause was the ever-present problem of land.

As the Emergency developed many Europeans were driven to evict the Kikuyu who were working as squatters on their farms, feeling they could no longer trust any member of the tribe. Other Kikuyu families left of their own accord rather than submit to Emergency regulations requiring all those living outside the reserve to be photographed. Stiff controls were imposed on the movement of Africans in Nairobi and led to a further Kikuyu exodus from the city. Thus a stream of Kikuyu families flooded back into the Kikuyu reserve where theoretically they still claimed a share in ancestral land rights. But many were by now second or third generation squatters on European farms and their connection with the original Kikuyu land unit had grown tenuous. They returned without any means of support and were not made welcome by relatives on land that was already overburdened. The situation naturally produced extreme tensions, and there are grounds for attributing much of the bitterness of Mau Mau to a fundamental struggle over land tenure.

On top of this the Emergency also precipitated a clash between rootless urban elements who had nothing to lose and who felt little respect for tribal authority, whether it was expressed through their elders, chiefs and headmen, or through ancient tribal custom, and rural conservatives who stood to gain by co-operating with government and the confiscation of the property of terrorists.

It soon became obvious that most of the Kikuyu at one time or other had taken an oath according to the early formulae, for the great majority of them broadly agreed with the long-term nationalist objective, as Kenyatta had expressed it before his arrest. Indeed, it is difficult to identify the precise ideological dividing line between 'Mau Mau' and the remainder of the Kikuyu. Many headmen found it wisest to keep in with both sides, helping Mau Mau activists by night, and working with the security forces by day. Boys from the Alliance High School often found, on returning to their homes for the holidays, that their fathers and mothers had taken Mau Mau oaths. Should they denounce their own parents? And now that political activity was outlawed, what did Mau Mau actually stand for?

Suddenly the question of oaths took on new significance. Hitherto, oath-taking had not appeared unduly sinister in itself to those who knew Kikuyu customs. But according to the special teams investigating Mau Mau suspects, oathing ceremonies now included elements of a most degrading obscenity. Forest leaders appeared to vie with each other in devising new and more horrible versions, which might involve bestiality, cannibalism, and menstruating girls, or a combination of all three. The explanation given by those reporting these developments was that the Mau Mau leaders were desperate to undermine the effect of government propaganda which included a campaign of 'cleansing' ceremonies for those who had already taken a Mau Mau oath in which use was made of the most powerful counter-oaths known to Kikuyu tradition. Mau Mau, so this explanation ran, were forcing their adherents to depart so far from normal tribal behaviour that no further cleansing would ever be possible. So conditioned, they would be beyond the reach of the old magic and ready for any demands made of them.

But the evidence must be treated with caution. Even if extreme degradations did take place, they can hardly have done so on a wide scale. And it is doubtful if the existence of these new style oaths alone could have accounted for the internal divisions in Kikuyuland which the Emergency provoked. Clearly the attempt to induce confessions, to which reference will shortly be made, led to the invention of many bizarre 'confessions' which included obscene details as a form of verbal violence. When used consistently as a deliberate weapon violence, as has already been suggested, is closely linked with pornography in its morbid sexuality. Hate, bitterness and murder in the heart were growing on all sides; the imaginations of all were inflamed; human bodies struck by pangas made a horrifying sight, both to those attacking and those witnessing the aftermath. In these situations men are often driven to excesses, in description and in deed, and the African context made Europeans ready to believe everything they heard. Accounts of atrocities were repeated with an emphasis on these gruesome details, which suggests a sadism in the reports as much as in the acts. Thus frequent references were made to stories of pregnant women being disembowelled and the foetuses being stuffed down their throats; of men being strangled with their own intestines or slowly decapitated with pangas; of eyes being gouged out and the liquid from them drunk.

Yet far from such incidents being part of a systematic and well-thought out campaign of terror, as many observers implied at the time, they must rather be judged the acts of men so frightened they were driven to a wild and unnatural blood-lust, often induced by drugs. No doubt there were some particularly cruel terrorist leaders; nonetheless responsibility for the deterioration of standards must rest primarily with the colonial power and with its record in the decades before the Emergency.

These sensational aspects have thrown a lurid colouring over the whole subject of Mau Mau. It is still difficult, if not impossible, to arrive at a dispassionate view of what actually happened during the first years of the Emergency. At first the government itself had no clear idea of what it was facing and no clear plan of how it should proceed. For many months there was an atmosphere of confusion and indecision which contributed to the frustrations of the European community. It was the Governor, Sir Evelyn Baring, who realised sooner that his advisers on the spot that it was not a simple police operation that was required, but something much more fundamental. In London Baring received invaluable advice from General Templer, whose experience in Malaya showed that the problem of guerrilla warfare, which was what Kenya really faced, was essentially one of information. To secure an effective supply of information from the Kikuyu reserve meant that the government would have to trust and give material backing to 'loyal' Africans. Accordingly those sections of the tribe which, for self-protection, had grouped themselves around strong chiefs and headmen were issued with arms and assigned European officers, and these became new local power centres. They formed the basis of the Kikuyu Home Guards and were an essential part of the government's security forces.

Instead of the Mau Mau rebellion being directed against Europeans, then, or even against the colonial system by way of sabotage of important installations like the railway, it became something more like a civil war within Kikuyuland itself. Initially the full brunt of Mau Mau terror fell upon African Christians, many of whom were deeply affected by the East African Revival which swept into Kenya from Ruanda in 1949. They now stood up to the threats and cruelties of the Mau Mau gangs with a bravery which humbled and inspired their European missionary colleagues. A few of these missionaries were themselves attacked, but most were protected by their congregations, among whom there were usually some who had contact with the terrorists, and they continued to live and work in the reserve throughout the Emergency.

From their vantage point the missionaries were the best placed to see just how corrupting the atmosphere of hate and violence was proving. The security forces often went on a rampage of killing and torture of their own. There were tales of oaths being taken in prison camps involving urine and faeces and causing serious infections; but there were also tales of torture, castrations, beatings and wanton killings on the part of government forces. Hooded men or women accompanied the security forces to identify enemies against whom they might have any number of quarrels; opposite them sat rows of prisoners with sullen faces, blank eyes, expressions of utter hostility. More disturbing than the actual rebellion was the danger that the whole colony would be demoralized through the struggle, and the civilizing work of half a century swept away in a flood of racial hatred. In April 1953 the situation appeared so serious that Carey Francis, the immensely respected Headmaster of the Alliance High School, wrote a confidential note to a senior government official expressing in forceful language the fears of many members of his Church:

"I have no doubt whatever that the Security Forces, and particularly the Police, have been involved in many acts of brutality to prisoners (sometimes amounting to deliberate and despicable torture) and of callous ill-treatment of innocent Africans (usually, but not always, Kikuyu) and of looting and destruction of private property. These acts have not been 'occasional errors of judgement . . . inevitable on the part of junior leaders and the rank and file'. They have been widespread, so widespread as to be regarded as the normal policy of the Security Forces; European officers have often taken part and still more often connived at them. The Police are feared and loathed, and never trusted, by the great bulk of Africans, not least by those who are well-disposed. . . .

The essential trouble is one of attitude. So many of the members of the Security Forces seem to understand nothing about Africans, do not even regard them as fellow human beings. They shout at them, demand that they take off their hats at their approach, speak contemptuously of them in their presence, have no respect for their feelings or their convenience. Some even speak as though they enjoyed killing Africans, and I fear that it is true. Why do so many Africans attempt to escape? Why are they almost invariably shot dead?

I know the other side. Security Forces have a most difficult, dangerous, unenviable task. Africans are hard to understand and can be desperately aggravating. Full allowance must be made for these things. And yet that does not account for or excuse what is happening. The unjust attitudes and unjust actions which are commonplace today are building up a legacy of hatred which will be far harder to overcome than are the bands of terrorists."[5]

Through the Christian Council of Kenya the missionaries continued to protest vigorously at abuses of power by the forces of law and order and they earned much official opprobrium as a result.

African Christians were also victimized by government security forces who often took the easy view that 'the only good Kuke is a dead Kuke'. A man who refused to join the Home Guards for reasons of conscience automatically qualified in loyalist eyes as a terrorist. But many of these African Christians had already been through the female circumcision controversy with Dr Arthur and preferred to stand by their principles, even if it meant being beaten up and killed, than be implicated in the hate that was raging through Kikuyuland. That Kenya was able to recover at all from the Emergency was largely due to their steadiness. The figures of deaths during the Emergency reveal the wholly disproportionate emphasis that was placed on violence as a quick solution: up to the end of 1956, 11,503 'terrorists' were killed, against only 167 members of the security forces. During the same period 1,819 'loyal' Africans also died.

Yet for most of this time life outside Nairobi and the Kikuyu reserve went along normally. The other tribes were scarcely affected by Mau Mau, and willingly took over jobs from evicted Kikuyu. Many were enrolled as auxiliaries in police or army units and seemed to enjoy working against the Kikuyu. At Mombasa, 350 miles from the trouble, and other distant centres, it was hard to believe in the reality of the Emergency. Even in Nakuru, at the time of the Ruck murders, an African on the run was able to escape by slipping into a cinema, which happened to be showing *King Solomon's Mines*.[6] European families could still holiday on the coral beaches of Malindi or fish in their favourite spots in the highlands unaware of the danger felt by their friends on their lonely farms. Industrial development, held back by the war and the austerity that followed, flourished; Nairobi continued to put up fine buildings, and work proceeded without interruption on the new international airport at Embakasi (opened in 1958). The tourist trade showed no falling-off and a steady number of Europeans entered Kenya in business or other permanent or semi-permanent occupation, so that in the period of the Emergency the total white population rose from an estimated 40,700 in 1952 to 66,400 in 1959, an increase of 63%. Royal visitors came and went throughout, and generally speaking Kenya advanced steadily in 'development' fields such as education, where the numbers of African pupils in all schools more than doubled in the same time.[7]

Though the struggle within Kikuyuland was murky and stained, the military aspect was more clear-cut. Largely thanks to Baring's insistence the British government appointed a full General, Sir

George Erskine, as Commander-in-Chief in June 1953, and after his arrival the military problem was soon clarified. It is thought that some 15,000 terrorists in all found their way into the forests. They dispersed into the two main forest ranges of Mount Kenya and the Aberdares, where they organized themselves loosely on British Army lines and their leaders took British officer ranks and code names. Against them Erskine deployed 11 battalions, including African units of the King's African Rifles and many National Servicemen from Britain, and he had the support of an enlarged police force, some 21,000 strong, and the Kikuyu Home Guards, whose numbers grew to a maximum of about 25,000.[8] In addition to these ground troops the RAF provided squadrons of bombers, whose effectiveness, however, was questionable.

To contain the terrorists in the two forest areas a strip a mile wide was cut along the forest boundary at 7,000 feet where it bordered the Kikuyu reserve. Movement in this strip was forbidden and anyone found in it could be shot on sight. Patrols were set up and bases established in the forests. Nairobi and the Kikuyu reserve were declared Special Areas where the military acted in concert with police.

The superior organisation and fire-power of the British forces were certain to tell in the end, but the terrorists posed a real threat because of the exceptionally difficult terrain. The forest provided them with perfect cover, shelter, and opportunities for ambush. They could swiftly retreat into the bamboo belt, which began at about 8,000 feet, where the sounds of their pursuers could be heard for miles distant, giving them ample warning to escape to new hide-outs. The thin air of the high ground also made strenuous operations difficult.

Inside the forests the rebel forces developed an extraordinary sense of woodcraft which made nature their ally. Birds and animals became additional eyes and ears for them, and rhino, elephant and buffalo were a serious hazard to the attacking troops. The guerrillas also showed great versatility in manufacturing their own weapons from wood, iron piping and rubber tyres, and in adapting whatever they could capture or steal. Their courage and endurance proved remarkable and gave the lie to those who said the Kikuyu would never put up a fight. Men were known to cover seventy miles in a single day on bare feet across the roughest ground to escape army sweeps.[9] Ages ranged from men in their seventies to teenagers, though the majority were of the warrior grades, and women made up perhaps a fifth of their total number. Among them also were many elders performing traditional magico-religious functions.

The turning point in military operations came on 24 April 1954. In what was called Operation Anvil, the entire African population of Nairobi was screened by the Army and no less than 30,000 Kikuyu removed to special camps. Kikuyuland was sealed off from the rest of Kenya and within the reserve every member of the tribe was moved into newly constructed and specially fortified villages. Curfews were imposed and movement restricted, in some cases to only one hour a day of work in the fields. These measures finally cut off from the forest guerrillas what the government called the 'passive wing' of Mau Mau, sympathizers who went about their normal lives on their farms by day, but at night supplied the forest fighters with food, clothing and other needs. The fighting wing, who called themselves the Land Freedom Army, retreated further into the forests where it was almost impossible to combat them. By the end of 1955 all but 1,500 or so were accounted for and the army began to withdraw, leaving the security forces to hunt down the remainder by the technique of 'pseudo-gangs'—security officers in disguise acting alongside captured terrorists who had agreed to turn against their former colleagues. In October 1956 the most elusive and notorious of the gang leaders, Dedan Kimathi, was captured and hanged, but others were still at large on the eve of Kenya's independence. As a military threat, however, Mau Mau was defeated by the end of 1954.

But as General Erskine himself said in a radio broadcast, to the dismay of the settlers, Mau Mau was not solely a military problem. There remained the deeper issues of economic and political reform. These were put in hand.

In the economic sphere they amounted to a revolution in the Kikuyu method of farming. The forcible grouping of all the Kikuyu in the reserve into villages gave protection to loyal members of the tribe and control over the others. With villagization went consolidation of land, and a great increase in cash crop farming. Where the traditional Kikuyu system of agriculture led to many small plots being scattered over wide areas, to which each member of the extended family had a claim, family holdings were now consolidated under individual ownership in single large units, with the offer of a freehold title. Government aid helped towards transforming this high potential land from what had been hardly more than subsistence usage to an efficient industry producing substantial surpluses.

The growing of cash crops was encouraged, and particularly those that had earlier been reserved for Europeans, such as coffee, tea and sisal. In the five years between 1954 and 1959 African coffee planting increased from about 4,000 to 26,000 acres, and a considerable number of the Kikuyu were now engaged in large-scale production.[10] Against all precedents, smallholder tea production was tried out at high altitudes where traditional Kikuyu farming was unsuitable, and it proved so successful that it formed the basis of future important development projects by the World Bank and the Commonwealth Development Corporation. Irrigation schemes and experiments with grade cattle also paved the way for an expansion of the rural economy which has gone forward steadily in Kenya ever since.

The result of these economic measures was virtually to create a new system of agriculture and to confirm the loyalists as a new land-owning class. But large numbers of Kikuyu were displaced from the land altogether, among them many members of the Land Freedom Army, and this was to give rise to problems in the post-independence era.

Constitutional reforms went forward at the same time and these marked the end, as a politically significant force, of the diehard settlers. In March 1954 the British Colonial Secretary, Oliver Lyttelton, on Baring's advice, offered them two choices: either they must accept a mixed government with both African and Asian ministers, or a suspension of the constitution followed by the appointment of a military governor and no guarantees for the future. They agreed to the constitutional reforms. These led within a short time to the enfranchisement of Africans and the first elections of eight African members to Legco in May 1957, later increased to fourteen giving them parity with European elected members. Meanwhile the settlers were given a War Council, for which they had been pressing since the Emergency was declared, but the man chosen to represent them in the Council, Michael Blundell, did not share their rigid outlook. Courageous and imaginative, Blundell saw the need for multi-racial advance if Europeans were to retain any sort of future in Kenya. Even his brand of liberalism was to prove too slow for the African Nationalists, but in the troubled days of the Emergency it was a lead that was badly needed.

Thus although the total cost of the Emergency was put at over £55 million, half of which was borne by the Kenya government, it is not primarily in economic terms that Mau Mau must finally be evaluated. Its principal effect was to provide legends for the future, and as it turned out it formed the prelude to political independence.

There was one concession to European feeling which the British had no qualms over making. On 7 September 1954, the Governor announced that a Restriction Order had been made against Kenyatta to come into effect at the end of his sentence and requiring him to live 'in a remote place'. He would never be allowed to return to Kikuyuland.[11]

One unforeseen effect of Kenyatta's lengthy appeal procedure was that the critical period of the Emergency passed while his case was technically *sub judice*. It was thus only after July 1954 that his name could again be openly linked with the terrorists. But Mau Mau then stood for something very different from what had been suggested at his trial. Indeed, when Pritt first arrived in Kenya to defend Kenyatta he had some difficulty finding out what Mau Mau meant, as the word had hardly impinged on the consciousness of most Europeans and Indians. But by the summer of 1954 versions of the worst atrocities and the most obscene oaths were uppermost in people's minds. To most Europeans the rejection of his appeal implied confirmation in his guilt with 'Mau Mau'—Mau Mau as they now understood it. They did not bother with the fact that the Privy Council decision was based on legal arguments only and not on a review of the evidence; nor did they pause to consider that he had already been in custody since October 1952, a period of 21 months, and that it was only during this period that the excesses of violence and oathing took place.

There was another possible reason why the Governor's announcement of the Restriction Order came at this time. By the end of 1954 the government had something like 17,000 convicts and 50,000 detainees in its prison camps. Nearly all of them were Kikuyu and it now faced the problem of what to do with them. Earlier in the year a psychiatrist who from 1938 to 1950 had been in psychiatric charge of Nairobi prison and of a large mental hospital outside Nairobi, J. C. Carothers, had flown out to Kenya at the government's request to investigate the psychology of Mau Mau. His conclusion coincided with the views of anthropologists and Kikuyu experts working with the teams 'screening' Mau Mau prisoners, to the effect that Mau Mau was a form of religion, analogous to the Black Magic of Europe's Middle Ages, and that adherents, if not the whole Kikuyu tribe, would have to be 'rehabilitated' into normal society as if they were suffering from some mental disease.[12] The theory was accepted by the government and used as justification for a calculated campaign of counter-terror. The argument ran as follows: the Kikuyu are in mortal dread of Mau Mau; the only way to break their fear of Mau Mau is to make them more afraid of government. The crucial test was whether they would 'confess' to Mau Mau. Once they had confessed, a gradual 'rehabilitation' was possible during which they passed down a 'pipe line' until ready for release.

In accordance with this theory elaborate measures were taken to terrify Mau Mau suspects in the camps. Long lines of gallows were erected. In one camp men who refused to answer questions were taken away outside the camp and shots were fired. They were then transferred quietly to other camps, while the officer returned to start questioning others with his revolver still in his hand.[13] Counter-oaths were sometimes administered of a supposedly more fearful nature than those adopted by the Mau Mau. Above all, strong emphasis was placed on physical labour such as land conservation, irrigation work, building roads, airports and other projects.

The complex psychological and anthropological explanations of Carothers and others later formed the kernel of the argument in the official *Corfield Report* on Mau Mau. The argument required an instigator of intelligence and sophistication. Only Kenyatta fitted the description, and the whole theory therefore hinged on the presumption that Kenyatta had personally master-minded Mau Mau, for which, it was honestly believed, he had been found guilty in law and justly sentenced. It may have been the adoption of this new policy of 'rehabilitation' which partly accounted for the harsh treatment the prisoners at Lokitaung received as they commenced to serve their actual sentences.

It was long before Kenyatta heard of all these developments and many of them, of course, still lay hidden in the future. Prison regulations were strictly applied and outside contact cut to the minimum. But one morning, as he was preparing lunch in the cook house, he heard a voice singing in Kikuyu from a newly occupied cell. 'Oh Kenyatta, my Mzee, I am here, I have arrived and if you hear me, signal with a cough.'[14] None of the African guards could speak Kikuyu, and they only yelled to the prisoner to be quiet. Kenyatta coughed discreetly, and the voice picked up again:

'We have suffered a lot, Mzee, for our country, but that does not matter for it is our duty. I have escaped death, but our brothers have been killed and even today many are dying or await the gallows. But wherever we are and whatever we do, be sure that the people of Kenya support you and keep their thoughts with you. In the forests we remember you day and night.'

'Be patient', Kenyatta sang back, 'for now that we are together there is nothing to worry about.'

The voice turned out to belong to Waruhiu Itote, or 'General China' as he was better known, the man who came to Gatundu in August 1952 to seek Kenyatta's blessing before taking to the forests. China had been one of the most effective Mau Mau commanders in the Mount Kenya area. On 15 January 1954, he was captured with a bullet wound in the throat. He was then tried and sentenced to death.

China maintained that he had been looking for a way to surrender in response to a government offer to the forest fighters. This defence was not accepted at his trial but, shortly after, his sentence was commuted to life imprisonment and the government asked him to help negotiate the surrender of other Mau Mau forces. The attempt failed and in April 1954 China was sent to Lokitaung where he was placed in solitary confinement. He, too, had to wear chains for a time.

Kenyatta was not able to speak properly with China until some time in 1955 when after a year of solitary confinement China was at last permitted to join the other prisoners. Conditions for them all improved that year with the arrival of a new District Officer, Lt. Col. P. de Robeck. He was a soldier who had mostly served in the Sudan and, like China, had been in Burma during the war. de Robeck did not share the prejudices of most Kenya officials against the Kikuyu nor did he think of all Mau Mau supporters as evil. He allowed the prisoners to wash and iron their civilian clothes regularly so that they would be wearable at the end of their sentences. It was a small gesture, but important psychologically as it restored to them the feeling that they had a future beyond the compound of Lokitaung.

de Robeck also got permission to use the prisoners on more constructive work than breaking stones. He provided them with vegetable seeds and allowed them to cultivate small gardens in the compound. And he allowed China to ask Kenyatta to give him lessons in English.

Kenyatta responded warmly to the idea. 'You've done much for our country,' he said. 'If I gave you money in return, no matter how much it was, one day it would all be gone. But if I give you education, it will serve you for the rest of your life.' Kenyatta spoke from the heart. He knew how much the African yearned for education, that white man's magic which had drawn him, when he was a boy, so many, many years ago, away from his ridge and his family into the mission at Thogoto. As the Scottish missionaries had found with Kikuyu children fifty years before, teaching China English was slow work. They began with only two words a day. Kenyatta explained their meaning and usage, their spelling and pronunciation, and gradually China picked up the vocabulary.

From China Kenyatta learnt for the first time and at first hand what had really happened in the forests. Though newspapers were by now permitted, they contained only government-vetted information. China was able to describe events up to the moment of his capture and, equally important, the course of the surrender negotiations.

The arrival of China and his new interest in teaching revived Kenyatta's spirits. He began to think again of the outside world. He found that his old friends in England had not forgotten nor turned against him.

Dinah Stock was now teaching in India. She had been worried about the reports from Kenya and conflicting Indian attitudes. While Nehru was prompted by emissaries like Murumbi into backing the nationalist movement, local Indian leaders in Nairobi spoke of the African still as a 'wolf-child' in need of firm handling by his father, the European, and his mother, the Indian. Stock paid a visit to Kenya herself in 1953 and reported fairly on the government's blockade of Kikuyuland and policy of counter-terror. Perhaps word of her support reached Lokitaung. On 15 March 1955, Kenyatta wrote to her a brief, cautious, appeal for contact.

'Dear friend,

Just a few lines to send my salaams and to let you know that I am keeping well. I live hundreds of miles away from my home, the prison is built in a small village called Lokitaung—an isolated kind of place in the heart of Turkana. The surrounding country is very dry and is totally useless for cultivation—it is in fact a desert.

I have five companions with me, my duty is to prepare the food for the group. We have a few books which we read in our spare time, the reading helps to break the monotony of the prison life.

I would very much like to hear from you and to know how you are. I hope you are well and enjoying life.

Give my kind regards to all. Yours, Jomo'

Dinah Stock knew how to cater for Kenyatta's intellectual interests and to remind him of those days of 'hallelujahs' when they had talked of revolution and of the spear and diplomacy. She sent him a grammar for teaching China English and books for himself. They were, Kenyatta replied, 'the only means available to satisfy intellectual hunger'. At his request, she sent him works on the world's great religions. Kenyatta read them attentively.

'I am finding them enlightening as well as entertaining,' he wrote in January 1956.

'Through these books I feel that I am slowly getting acquainted with some of the religious and moral aspects of the Indian people as represented by various sages. I have not yet come to any section dealing with the doctrine of non-violence, what I have read so far is full of glorifications of warriors fighting great battles under different circumstances. I would like to compare this with the Islamic ideas of "holy wars", and for this reason I would be grateful if you could get me a good English translation of the Holy Koran.'

The Koran duly arrived. Kenyatta went on from it to Indian philosophy in which he found much which,

'if adopted as a code of moral behaviour, could guide human beings in their contact between man and man.
In my opinion, Hinduism seems to put more emphasis on renunciation or abnegation and rebirth, rather than on non-violence. I think that the doctrine of non-violence is one of the things that are embraced in the moral code of Buddhism.'

Cautiously he put out a feeler to Edna. They had not been in touch since his departure from England in 1946 and she had been having a difficult time from reporters out for a story of what it had been like to be the wife of the man whom everyone assumed was behind Mau Mau. He addressed his letter to Mrs E. Kay.

He learnt that she had remained loyal to him and that with their son, Peter, she had spent a night at Woodbrooke at the invitation of Mrs Cadbury, wife of his old warden, who was taking a personal interest in Kenyatta's welfare. Peter had played ping-pong in the same room as his father had done twenty-five years before.

Momentarily, the last ten years in Kenya dissolved and reminders of his life in Europe came to him like mirages in the Turkana desert.

His son was now at a grammar school. Dinah Stock suggested that he should use his royalties from *Facing Mount Kenya,* which had been reprinted to meet the interest aroused by Mau Mau, on Peter's education. He responded warmly to the idea.[15]

From Dinah Stock, too, he heard that Prince Peter was completing his anthropological studies in Nepal. Her descriptions of the Himalayas seemed to Kenyatta 'heavenly, in fact it reminds me of Kere-Nyaga—the abode of gods—which makes Turkana look like Gehenna'. Was it possible, he might have asked himself, that those hidden forces were still working on his behalf?

Geoffrey Husbands, the insurance clerk, had also remained true and was sending him Christmas cards regularly. At the end of 1956 Kenyatta wrote to his old friend, thanking him for his concern: 'I very often think of you and recall to mind the happy memory of how we used to get together and how we used to have lively discussions on various topics.'

There was no chance of picking up those lines now. Apart from the censors, the heat and monotony provided no stimulus for political ideas. There was little of interest to be seen from the barren plateau of the prison compound, but Kenyatta, as always, found illustrations in the animal world to express his feelings:

'We get our water supply from a well which is not far from this prison camp where six of us live. Every morning the water is brought in drums carried by the camels. It is interesting to see these animals swaying their humps rhythmically as they march along the road. They move leisurely swinging their long necks back and forward as though they do not feel the weight of the heavy burdens on their backs. But sometimes when they are annoyed, one of them gets in such a temper and starts making terrible sounds protesting against their being enslaved by man.'[16]

Kenyatta was being forced in on himself in a way he had never before experienced. Though he had always kept his thoughts to himself, he liked company and being the centre of the stage. But at Lokitaung the only stage was the prison compound, and the only action was the daily routine of preparing food in the open stone kitchen which stood a few yards from the prisoners' block. Kenyatta's cell measured twelve feet by twenty, with a bare stone floor and bare stone walls. A window was high in the wall opposite the door, too high for him to look out of—but what was there for him to look out on to, except those stony, thorn-covered hillsides the same grey colour as the prison itself?

The letters he received from his old friends were Kenyatta's life-line with his past and the world outside. The letters he wrote were part of the battle he fought to keep himself under control and his mind sane.

Early in 1956 Kenyatta heard at last from his daughter Margaret Wambui. The relationships between the different members of Kenyatta's family had always been uneasy, and his arrest left them dispersed and unsure of themselves. He could not be certain how they were reacting to his situation. But Margaret had been with him at Githunguri and was closer to him than anyone else. After considerable trials she had found shelter with an Indian book-binder in Nairobi who supported the nationalist movement and hid occasional Mau Mau fighters on the run.

In January 1956, Margaret was able to write to her father. He replied at once:

'My dear child Wambui
. . . When I got your letter my heart was filled with joy to know that you are in good health. As you know it's a long time since I had a letter from you, the last letter I sent you was about the end of 1954. When I didn't get an answer I didn't know what to do, and to tell the truth I was full of fear, not knowing what had become of you; but I just put my hope in Almighty God, for he knows all. Every day I sat remembering in my heart. Now I have many thoughts, since I got your letter . . .'

Gradually he put the pieces together—his son was in a detention camp, his wife Ngina and the children had been removed from his home at Gatundu and the farm taken over by the government.

'All this I place in the hands of God who is the Father and protector of all his creatures.
As for me, I have nothing to say, I am very well and have no trouble whatsoever. I still live quietly, as I have done for a long time . . .
Let us thank God to guard us and keep us in his grace, with mercy and kindness.
Au revoir. I am your loving father, Jomo Kenyatta'

Kenyatta and his daughter were at once on each other's wavelength.

'My dear child,

. . . As you say, I know it is very hard for the children to be separated from their parents, and to be left desolate and orphaned to face the troubles of the world, and especially in this time of great danger. Things like this show that the world is full of cruelty of many kinds. When things are in this state each one tries to ensure that his side is the one in the right. This is because men have not yet learned how to act rightly towards each other, dealing with each other as brothers, like the love of God.

Indeed, my child, many things have been done to astound and frighten the heart, yet although this is very sad, I feel that it is not right for a man to be filled with anger and disquieted in his heart, because to do this is sheer folly. In my opinion it is better to be calm and to forget evil, and to look forward to the good which will follow when all these troubles are at an end. I have no doubt that all this has happened according to God's plan to teach his children to forsake the evil of hatred, and to follow goodness according to the righteousness and faith in God.

For my part I rely most upon the teaching of the 23rd psalm ('The Lord is my shepherd, I shall not want'.) If you like, you can read it yourself and see how full of good sense it is.

Greet all those at home, and the children and the womenfolk. If you write to Muigai give him my greetings. I trust Almighty God to keep and guard them, leading them towards the light, and a life of long-suffering and faith. Grace and peace be upon you always. God willing we shall meet again.'[17]

Kenyatta's correspondence with his daughter was the most intimate and most regular link with normality he possessed. Much of the time he wrote about things he needed and family news. There were frequent requests for vitamins, food and special items to improve his diet and help his body; and for papers and books and the latest publications about Kenya. But there was greater communication between father and daughter than his words could convey: 'Your great love for me consoles my heart . . . may we see each other with the eyes of the spirit.'[18]

Both Kenyatta and Margaret knew their letters were being scrutinized by the police, and so no mention of politics passed between them. But Kenyatta was far too cautious a man, in or out of prison, to put anything in writing which was likely to compromise him.[19] Somewhere in the past, in Moscow perhaps, or from Ross, he had learned the importance of discretion. The failure of the police to produce anything incriminating against him at Kapenguria, after their three weeks' intensive search of his papers, proved the value of that lesson. Kenyatta, of course, would deny that he had anything to hide.

None but the most sceptical reader can fail to be struck by the absence of any form of recrimination in Kenyatta's words. When later he authorized an official account of his life to be written on his behalf, he called it *Suffering Without Bitterness*. It was at Lokitaung that Kenyatta worked out the underlying philosophy behind that book, and every letter he wrote to Margaret reflected it. In the solitude of prison he returned to those inner feelings he had hinted at on a few earlier occasions, as in the log at Woodbrooke in early 1932. The conclusion he reached was that 'Almighty God is the giver of all things which are good and righteous'.[20] It was a profound religious experience.

Though his spiritual loneliness was eased by these contacts with his own family and the outside world, Kenyatta suffered from almost constant bodily torment. The trouble was his skin. All the prisoners experienced severe chafing around their ankles from their chains, and though these were removed after a few months, Kenyatta's skin remained sensitive.

The poor diet and the climate combined to poison his system. Early in 1956 he came out in eczema. It began with the sole of his foot and produced suppurating and itching. Margaret sent what medicines and vitamins she could, and government doctors attended him. Incredibly, for one suffering from this skin condition, he was then vaccinated against smallpox. As might have been expected, his system reacted violently. Sores and swellings broke out all over his body and he fell seriously ill. He kept it from his daughter until the danger had passed:

'My whole body was filled with much pain and constant itching, as if someone were covered all over his body with "stinging nettles". The whole time my body was filled with a strong desire to keep on scratching . . . My right leg swelled up right to the knee. The pain was very severe.'

The 'intense itching nearly drove me crazy' he wrote later to Husbands.[21]

Kenyatta met his hardship with the same detachment as he met whatever else life brought his way. He often refused medicine from the government doctors but gave it to China or one of the others to throw down the latrine. He preferred what Margaret sent him. It was the same reaction to European doctors as had made him, years back in 1915, stumble to his friend Charles Stokes at Tumutumu rather than return for treatment to Thogoto. He bore his illness with resignation: 'As you know', he wrote to Margaret,

'it is very easy for any illness to get into the body, but hard to get it out again. So I have no doubt that the illness itself will come to an end, by the use of the medicine together with the help of the Lord. Remember, that in this world God sends to men trials of various sorts, and he who overcomes is he who endures with a pure heart free from anger and complaining.'[22]

But the sickness depressed him and the spring of 1957 was one of his lowest points. A letter from Edna then cheered him up more than she could realize. 'The news from you gave great comfort and consolation to my soul', he told her. He would read it over and over again till it cast its spell over him and carried him back in spirit to Storrington. A letter from Husbands describing the winter scenery of England brought another flood of memories:

'Christmas time in England is something one cannot easily forget. Sometimes I used to think that the weather would be too cold, but log fires and congenial friends made it warm and cosy for me. Sometimes I think that perhaps after years of perpetual grilling sun, I shall have an opportunity of enjoying sitting around a log fire with congenial friends once again!'[23]

Gradually the swellings and the sores got better. But he was ageing. Perhaps he was already past sixty. In 1958, the doctors warned of high blood pressure; 'this is one of the ailments that come to people who are entering upon old age,' was his reaction.[24] But he did not despair. The sense that his destiny was still before him, and that Lokitaung was not to be his grave, kept him quietly confident. He spoke of death with equanimity:

'Death is one of those things which are beyond our control, and which, whether we like it or not, must follow the natural cause. All we can do is to be ready to take calmly any news of such happenings. Naturally everyone of us must, soon or later, pass through this unavoidable gate.'[25]

Margaret also received a letter from one of Kenyatta's fellow prisoners. He had discovered her address from her father, whom they called simply Mzee—'the old man'.[26] The younger man asked for news of his own friends and it led to a brief correspondence. His was a flowery and passionate language, full of neat Swahili phrases and expressing the intense loneliness induced by what the writer described as the rules of 'St. Lucifer's Monastery of Lokitaung'—a total absence of women, drink and tobacco.

It led to one incident which is best described in the writer's own words:

'I will not conceal from you that there has been a very unpleasant incident, for even as I write I am more upset than I can say; and what upset me is as follows: I am sorry, and it was bad luck that when the DC was handing out our letters he mistakenly thought your letter was for Mzee! and gave it to Mzee! and Mzee didn't look at it, he too didn't see that it was for me, and when he saw your name he didn't bother to look for his name—immediately he went to his room and put on his glasses! and he read! and he read! and he read it! yes indeed! he read it. But then suddenly I heard him moaning and groaning and then I heard him saying "Aaallah! whose letter is this?" and he called out for *me* "Hey, hey, Aaallah! this is your letter, take it!" and he gave me the letter and when I looked at it and saw your name I was taken aback—Loco! Subahana! the rabbit fried in his own fat! and I nearly fell over, for every joint froze and my wits deserted me! "Hi, what're you going to say now, I've caught you, ehee, you've kept mum for a long time and you're a son in law and never said a thing, hey?" That's what came out of the old man's mouth. Sister, the old 'un's found out the secret and every one of my friends here nearly passed out when I told them the story . . .'

Whether because of this incident, or arising from some other—some quarrel, perhaps, over the sharing of food or the distribution of tasks—divisions grew among the prisoners. Kenyatta's age set him apart from the other prisoners. While he sat around preparing their lunch they worked outside in temperatures usually over the nineties. Bickering could only be expected in these conditions, and Kenyatta was often the butt of their resentment. They would ridicule him and shout obscenities when he went to the latrines.

These personality clashes were in part a legacy of a deeper rift. It had already been revealed in the tensions which preceded the Emergency.[27] In discussions at Lokitaung, Kenyatta's age and experience, his extraordinary sense of political detachment, gave him a totally different perspective from that of the younger men.

By the beginning of 1957 the division of the prisoners took on regular form. On one side were Kaggia, Kubai, Ngei and Kunga Karumba; while China, who also had seen the need for an end to fighting and pointless violence, sided with Kenyatta.

Then in March a new prisoner arrived. He was Kariuki Chotara, a young Mau Mau fighter. He naturally sided with the majority group. They now gave themselves the status of a party, which they called the 'National Democratic Party', for which they held elections and distributed offices among themselves: Kaggia as President, Kubai Secretary, Chotara Treasurer, Karumba Vice-President, and Ngei Assistant Secretary.

In August that year the prisoners received a Kikuyu visitor, the first they had been allowed to see since they arrived at Lokitaung in April 1953. He was Obadiah Kariuki, one of the leaders of the Anglican Church who had shown great bravery in his work as rural dean in the Fort Hall district during the worst Mau Mau period. Now a suffragan bishop, Kariuki was entrusted by the government to help the work of rehabilitating Mau Mau detainees in the camps.

Kariuki was married to another daughter of old Koinange, and so enjoyed a family relationship with Kenyatta. No doubt he was alerted to Kenyatta's spiritual hunger by reports of what the prison censors had read in his letters. Accordingly he took with him to Lokitaung an English Bible, a Kikuyu New Testament and an Anglican Book of Common Prayer.

Kenyatta was moved to see him. He always responded to the affection of others, as his letters to his daughter showed, and this proof that some of his own people were thinking of him and praying for him made a deep impression. He took Kariuki to his cell and they talked alone about the state of their country, and about God's love and mercy for the individual. Kenyatta learned how the Christians had met the Mau Mau and loyalist terror with equal courage. He asked if he could keep the Bible; it was what he wanted most of all, he said, and he planned to read it right through from beginning to end.

Kariuki then went to one of the larger rooms to meet the other prisoners. Here his reception was very different. He had journeyed up to Lokitaung with the European prison chaplain. Kaggia at once attacked him for this; Kaggia, the one-time leader of his own sect, declared that there was no point in praying to God. There is no God, he said, Christ is only for Europeans. Kenyatta tried to quieten them, but without success. One by one they all trooped out of the block, leaving only Kenyatta and China to receive Kariuki's farewell prayers.

It was an unpleasant scene, typical of what many Kikuyu felt at any suggestion of co-operation with the white man. The same reaction could be found among Mau Mau detainees—an expression of blank hatred and a refusal to look a European in the eye. Conditions in these camps were often appalling enough, with Mau Mau and anti-Mau Mau forces contending for each prisoner's loyalties and the government pursuing a deliberate policy of making suspects more terrified of the colonial power than of Mau Mau. The Emergency apparently divided the Kikuyu into two implacably hostile camps, just as, in a lesser degree, the female circumcision controversy had done. Men took the opportunity of paying off many old scores dating back to the twenties. The likelihood of any future reconciliation between them, and between the Kikuyu tribe as a whole and the rest of the peoples of Kenya, seemed remote indeed.

The African bishop's visit was an important episode in Kenyatta's life at Lokitaung. Now he could see more clearly than ever before where his destiny lay. Only he could bridge this divide of bitterness which at present seemed as wide and deep as the Rift Valley itself.[28]

The year 1958 was one of the driest on record. In April an incident occurred at Lokitaung which was to have far-reaching consequences. It prompted the writing of a letter which eventually found its way out of Kenya and was published in the London *Observer* on 8 June 1958:

'We political prisoners of Lokitaung', the letter began, 'are desirous that the world and Her Majesty's Government in the United Kingdom should know that we are being subjected to treatment which we think is not given to any other human beings in any part of the world.'

The letter then went on to make a number of allegations. Letters were being restricted and delayed. 'We have been beaten in the most brutal manner. Our rations are inadequate, we do not get vegetables or fruits. We live on mealie meal and beans of the worst quality.' They were all suffering from illnesses as a result; 'some have almost lost their eyesight', there was 'no adequate medical treatment'. Then the letter went on to describe the current water shortage and how the prisoners had been ordered to draw their water from an old well in which a dog's carcase was floating. They refused and demanded the use of a clean well which the government later claimed was in need of repair. 'The DO told us the clean well is for Europeans only,' the letter continued.

'Now as we write this letter we are entering our fourth day without water in a desert while the new "European" well is full of clean water . . . It now appears to us that it is the intention of the Kenya Government to starve us to death . . . We consider this the most brutal and inhuman treatment ever compared to that of the Nazi concentration camp. As we have nowhere to appeal we now appeal to the High Court of the World Public opinion.'

The allegations brought an instant rebuttal from the Kenya government. On 11 June the Chief Secretary denied the charges in Legco. In the course of his statement he said:

'In making these allegations the convicts concerned described themselves as "political prisoners". That is quite incorrect. All of them are serving sentences following convictions in court for criminal offences. They include some of the most dangerous leaders of the Mau Mau organisation . . . men who were responsible for the collapse of law and order in Kikuyu country which resulted in the need for the Emergency to be declared. These were men who inspired superstition and fear among the masses of the Kikuyu . . . We know from our experiences during the month just before the declaration of the Emergency how expert these men are at the use of "double meanings". In order to obtain the greatest possible security it has been necessary to keep them in a very remote spot . . .'[29]

This represented the view of nearly all the people of Kenya at that time. Too much had happened between Kenyatta's midnight arrest in October 1952 and the summer of 1958 for Europeans to unthink their convictions that he was responsible for everything that had taken place during the Emergency.

Most of the new generation of African politicians, brought into prominence through constitutional reforms, took the same line. Perhaps they did not express it so strongly. It was enough for them if Kenyatta's name was never mentioned. They saw themselves as the future leaders of the country, and they saw no need to raise the living ghosts of the past.

But one man remained loyal to Kenyatta, and he was not even a Kikuyu. In June 1958, following the government's statement about the prisoners at Lokitaung, Odinga rose in Legco: 'These people', he said, 'before they were arrested were the political leaders of the Africans in the country, and the Africans respected them as their political leaders, and even at this moment, in the heart of hearts of the Africans, they are still the political leaders—' He could get no further. He had mentioned the unmentionable. Pandemonium broke loose in the chamber, and the Speaker hurriedly adjourned. But next day Odinga returned to the subject:

'These people are the leaders of the people. Just as when Archbishop Makarios was arrested by the British Government, he was taken to the Seychelles and he was put in the Governor's lodge there. Nearly every day there was a report of his health, of his activities, in the press. The same thing should be done with Mr. Kenyatta . . .'[30]

Again he was shouted down. There were cries of 'Mau Mau'. The other African members tried to correct the impression Odinga had made. Next day the press urged that the only thing to do was to 'hound Odinga out of political life forever'.

News of what had happened reached Lokitaung. The papers were a long time coming, but 'this doesn't matter, for news is new when a man gets it, even if it's a whole year old.' 'When you see Oginga Odinga give him my greetings and many thanks', Kenyatta wrote quietly to his daughter.

Kenyatta's future was also of interest to the new five-man political party at Lokitaung. It was noteworthy that he and China had not signed the letter to the *Observer*. The split between the prisoners now erupted into what could have been tragedy.

One day China overheard what he understood to be a plot by the others to kill Kenyatta. He warned the District Officer and nothing came of the attempt. But neither was anything done to isolate the danger, except that China himself was moved into a room on his own at night. He constituted himself Kenyatta's bodyguard. A few months later he was called on to save the older man's life when a scrimmage suddenly broke out at breakfast.

As Kenyatta came to get some water, one of the prisoners went for him with a knife. Fortunately for Kenyatta, his attacker's trousers caught in a splinter of wood in the table. Kenyatta had just enough warning to catch the man's arm with the knife in it. He shouted to China. The others tried to hold China back but he threw them off and grabbed the knife. With their table upset and their breakfast 'porridge' spilling over them, the men struggled on the ground, until the warders ran up to separate them.

After this second attempt on Kenyatta's life, his assailant was moved to another camp. But word of the attack on her father reached Margaret. She cabled anxiously for news and a few weeks later Kenyatta was able to write calmly of the incident:

'Envy and hatred have no mercy . . . Now calm your heart, for although the attack was planned secretly and craftily it did not achieve its aim. Almighty God brought me out of this great danger . . . I was not badly injured, because although the attacker had a knife, I managed to get hold of the hand that held the knife, which was then snatched from him. So a serious accident was averted. I don't want to go into any more details, but I think you are well aware that envy, desire and ignorance are a trouble to many people in this world. I have no doubt that you remember all the things that can lead you into the light. This is all of God.'[31]

The government had done its best to erase the memory of Kenyatta from Kikuyuland. His college at Githunguri had been destroyed, his home at Gatundu pulled down and his farm given over to an agricultural college. For years his old Hudson car was left rotting in the bushes. Mau Mau detainees were forced to abuse his name in the camps. His family were split up.

Kenyatta took it all philosophically. When his daughter told him what had happened at Ichaweri, his Gatundu home, he replied:

'Everything that is being done there is according to the will of Almighty God, so I see it all as good, especially the way the shambas are being used for teaching agriculture and animal husbandry, this is very useful for those who are learning to help improve the life of the people.'[32]

Whatever the government might do, Kenyatta would not let it crush his spirit. On the contrary, when European officers visited his prison Kenyatta was at the gate to meet them and he escorted them round as though it was his estate at Ngenda, even providing them with tomatoes from his small vegetable plot by the wire, where the prisoners' washing hung bleaching in the sun.

And now that his name had been mentioned again in public, his future was once more a political issue.

CHAPTER 22

Uhuru and Dust

On 14 April 1959, Kenyatta completed his prison sentence. He had been more than six years at Lokitaung, fifty-eight months of them as a convict. But the restriction order passed by Thacker and confirmed by Baring in September 1954 was immediately applied, and he was simply moved ninety miles south to Lodwar, the administrative headquarters of the Northern Frontier District where bungalows had been specially built for the men from Lokitaung.

Here Kenyatta had to report twice a day to the District Commissioner. He was free to move around in an area confined to about 800 yards of sand dunes and forbidden to enter any private buildings. He was given an allowance of £6 a month and on three days a week, for two hours each day, was permitted to visit two specified shops. They were typical Indian *dukas* (stores) selling everything from zinc tubs to beads, kettles to curry powder. But Kenyatta was not allowed to discuss political matters with the shop-keepers or other customers. There was a curfew from 7 p.m. to 6.30 a.m. As he told Dinah Stock, it was 'a different type of imprisonment'.[1]

Lodwar was the centre of Turkanaland. It boasted a geological station and sizeable police lines. When Kenyatta arrived there was also a hospital, newly built by 400 Mau Mau prisoners held there. A runway for light aircraft lay in the plain and within a few hundred yards of Kenyatta's house. On a slight eminence above were the administrative offices, which had formed the headquarters of forces operating against the Italians in Ethiopia during the Second War. Here was the District Commissioner's bungalow—a spacious building designed to catch whatever breeze there might be and so that his sink and bath water would drain into small vegetable plots. Bougainvillaea graced the veranda and fresh lettuces from his garden the DC's table. Some distance away, where the dirt track from Kapenguria and Kitale entered, was a square of ramshackle 'shops', a petrol pump, and huts in which lived the few Indian families. Police, local officials and the naked Turkana all came here for their needs and it was here that Kenyatta was permitted to do his shopping.[2]

Being in the valley of the River Turkwell and at a lower altitude, Lodwar was hotter and more humid than Lokitaung. The temperature seldom dropped below the nineties and there was no need for blankets at night. Sand-storms were frequent and Kenyatta's bungalow was also plagued with snakes which dropped down suddenly from the roof beams and could be heard slithering across the floor in the dark. The five bungalows were grouped together, with communal lavatories and washing facilities. They stood on the edge of the township, with nothing but lava-rock mountains and sand-dunes at the back.

'Life here is one continuous monotony, heat and dust shout their hallelujahs daily,' Kenyatta wrote to Geoffrey Husbands; and to Dinah Stock: 'Here the weather is as usual, it is terribly hot and I am sweating like the dickens, so I say hallelujahs for now.' The hallelujahs expressed hope, the hope of freedom not just for himself but for all Africans. To his own people he expressed it in the phrase *Uhuru and Dust*.

But at least their wives could now join the detained men. Kenyatta had not seen Ngina and his two young daughters since October 1952. They arrived a month after his own arrival; there was a great outburst of feasting and dancing.

That Christmas Kenyatta was at last able to enjoy the company of his family. His brother James Muigai and Margaret Wambui were allowed up for it with a fresh supply of gifts and provisions. There was another warm reunion, this time between father and daughter. Kenyatta wrote afterwards to her that her visit made it 'the first really happy Christmas for 8 years . . . This teaches us that nothing lasts for ever; events come and go as night succeeds day.'

Kenyatta was to spend two years in the heat trap of Lodwar. He needed all his sense that his destiny awaited him. The world was changing with bewildering speed—satellites in space, jet aircraft, and the idea of nationhood coming to people who were living in the Stone Age at the time of his own birth. Could he expect to see his destiny fulfilled in his life-time, or was he to be a martyr for the future, remembered in legend only like Waiyaki and Wangombe and the heroes of the past?

Kenya was fortunate in having as her Governor throughout the Emergency a man of Sir Evelyn Baring's distinction. Born in Cairo, where his father, Lord Cromer, ruled the Eastern Mediterranean for

Britain, educated at Winchester and New College, Oxford, where he won high honours, Baring was heir to the best imperialist tradition. His previous service in India and southern Africa gave him a wide experience of the racial and constitutional complexities of the British Empire. Austere in his personal life, courteous towards all, cool, aristocratic, handsome, Baring was more than a match for the settlers. Thanks largely to his political and financial connections in London, Kenya made great progress during the seven years he was Governor. By the time he came to leave, in the autumn of 1959, the colony's agriculture was transformed, her economy revitalized, and her political institutions properly geared for increasing African participation. In 1959 the government at last threw open the White Highlands to all races in the colony. By then, events in Africa were changing so rapidly the decision went largely unnoticed. But in its way it marked the end of an era. Baring left Kenya as Britain prepared the handover of her East African colonies to African majority rule.

By the late 1950s it was clear to all but the most reactionary white men that history was moving against the old colonial philosophy of Western Europe. In its place was growing the new philosophy of 'one man one vote' and independence for any state which cared to claim it within the United Nations. Churchill's Atlantic Charter had opened the way for the dismemberment of the British Empire. The process gathered pace after the war: in Asia independence for India and Pakistan in 1947, for Ceylon and Burma in 1948; in the Middle East the end of the British mandate in Palestine in 1948, withdrawal from Egypt in 1953 and the Sudan in 1956; in South-East Asia independence for Malaya in 1957, soon to be followed, it was expected, by Singapore and Borneo; in the West Indies similar preparations for the early 1960s.

Africa could no longer be isolated from world history. On 6 March 1957, Britain's colony of the Gold Coast became the independent state of Ghana with Kenyatta's old colleague from Manchester, Nkrumah, as Prime Minister. Pan-Africanism now had a firm base within the continent of Africa. Accra rivalled Cairo as a centre of anti-colonial propaganda; in 1958 Addis Ababa became the headquarters of a United Nations economic mission to Africa. 'Scram out of Africa' was the new cry of African nationalists against their European masters. The French prepared to pull out of Algeria and their territories in West Africa and the Belgians from the Congo. Britain was ready to do the same from Nigeria and did not deny the claims of Uganda and Tanganyika. For Kenya, self-government could only be a matter of time.

In the British General Election of October 1959 the Conservatives were returned in their third win in a row. Having successfully retrieved the fortunes of his party after the Suez débâcle of 1956, Prime Minister Harold Macmillan determined to rid Britain of all embarrassing legacies of her Victorian Empire and instead to apply for membership of the European Economic Community. Early in 1960 he went on a tour of Africa and on 3 February 1960 addressed the South African Parliament. Overnight his speech became a journalist's catch-phrase: 'The wind of change', he declared, 'is blowing through this continent and whether we like it or not this growth of political consciousness is a political fact and our national policies must take account of it.'

The South African answer was to leave the British Commonwealth and impose stricter Apartheid laws. On 21 March 1960, at Sharpeville, South African police fired on a crowd of Africans demonstrating against the laws and killed seventy of them. The shock was world wide.

Kenya had already given Britain cause for shame. On 3 March 1959, eleven inmates died at a camp for hardcore Mau Mau supporters on the Tara River, called Hola. At first the Kenya Government tried to cover up what really happened, but an investigating committee revealed that the deaths had resulted from the deliberate use of violence against those who refused to co-operate with the administration's rehabilitation procedure. Anxious debates in Parliament followed in which at least one prominent Conservative member, Enoch Powell, attacked the Kenya administration. Hola was the grim epitome of the counter-terror employed against Mau Mau. It spelled also the end of white rule in Kenya.

Britain's new Colonial Secretary, Iain Macleod, later wrote in the *Spectator:* 'Hola helped to convince me that swift change was needed in Kenya.'[3] In January 1960, while his Prime Minister was in Africa, Macleod called the various groups interested in Kenya's future to a conference at Lancaster House in London. There he made it plain that Britain intended to give Africans majority rule in Kenya as soon as possible.

The white settlers were stunned. They had looked on the Emergency as a fight for their own future as the dominant race and had staked all on ensuring the victory of the 'loyalist' Africans. It did not occur to them that 'loyalist' Africans were after the same ultimate goal as their brothers who had chosen to join Mau Mau and fight. Most of the settlers had braved out the worst Mau Mau years in long hours of isolation with tautened nerves and heightened imaginations which gave them unreal perspectives in the world outside. During the Emergency European men and women could be seen on the streets of Nairobi with pistols in their belts or handbags like characters from a Western. Ostrich-like they continued to hide themselves from the realities of world politics long after the Mau Mau danger had passed. They still played polo on their farms, grew asparagus for London restaurants, and flew around East Africa in their private aeroplanes. But they were impotent to resist the will of the British Government since Britain, thanks to the Emergency measures, possessed the troops on the ground to impose it.

With great courage Michael Blundell again took the lead in accepting Macleod's proposals. He formed his liberal group into the New Kenya Party, and pledged its support of an African government. Momentarily he played an important role in bridging the gap between the past and the future.[4] The pace of decolonization quickened. Tanganyika's independence was due on 9 December 1961, and Uganda's on 9 October 1962.

Kenya's new Governor was Sir Patrick Renison, who was sworn in in the closing days of 1959 and on the eve of the Lancaster House conference. He was hard-working, but new to Africa. Upon him fell the difficult task of guiding Kenya towards independence. The heart of his problem was what to do with Kenyatta.

On returning from the 1960 Lancaster House conference, the Africans divided into two main political parties. The first to be formed, in May that year, was the Kenya African National Union, or KANU, named in obvious imitation of the old KAU whose loyalties it inherited. It was composed of the two biggest tribes, the Kikuyu and the Luo who, though traditionally despising each other, were drawn into alliance chiefly through the support of their leaders for the goal of immediate independence, an imprecise belief in what they called African socialism, and the return of Kenyatta.

A few weeks later a second party appeared called the Kenya African Democratic Union, which took in the smaller tribes. Their leaders were fearful of a Kikuyu/Luo domination of an independent Kenya. They sought instead greater regional autonomy and were prepared to wait longer for national independence while enjoying their new-found influence. They were much less keen to see Kenyatta return to political life.

On 14 May 1960, KANU nominated the absent Kenyatta as their President. The government at once vetoed the idea.

To most Europeans the return of Kenyatta was unthinkable. On 31 March 1960, Renison issued a statement 'that in prevailing circumstances the release of Jomo Kenyatta would be a danger to security'. He then went to London where he discussed Kenyatta's future with Iain Macleod. Immediately on his return, on 9 May 1960, Renison called a press conference and issued another statement. It dealt with Kenyatta to the exclusion of everything else. Renison reaffirmed that in his judgement Kenyatta's release would be a danger to security.

He gave his reasons in terms which appeared to put Kenyatta beyond the pale of civilization for ever:

'Jomo Kenyatta was the recognised leader of the non-co-operation movement which organised Mau Mau. Mau Mau, with its foul oathing and violent aims, had been declared an unlawful society. He was convicted of managing that unlawful society and being a member of it. He appealed to the Supreme Court and the Privy Council. In these three separate courts his guilt was established and confirmed. Here was the African leader to darkness and death. He was sentenced by due process of law to seven years' imprisonment (the maximum punishment then prescribed for his offences) . . .'[5]

Renison continued with a statement which can only be described as official blackmail. Self-government according to the Lancaster House formula, said Renison, depended on the co-operation of all races in Kenya. To secure that of the European community, Africans must accept the government's view of Kenyatta:

'Their readiness for self-government will be measured by the readiness of their leaders to acknowledge those facts and their ability to carry their followers with them. I have at present no evidence whatsoever that Jomo Kenyatta will help Kenya in these aims. I have much evidence to the contrary . . .'

The evidence that Renison was referring to came from a document which had been some time in preparation and was published later that May, entitled 'Historical Survey of the Origins and Growth of Mau Mau'. It was compiled by F. D. Corfield, a soldier and political adviser with wide experience of the Sudan, Palestine and Ethiopia. He had retired to Kenya in 1954 and served on the Secretariat of the War Council. He had been working on the report since October 1957.

Corfield took as his premiss that Kenyatta was rightly found guilty at Kapenguria and therefore was the man primarily responsible for all that had happened in Kenya during the Emergency. He evaluated all his material on this premiss. His conclusion was that Mau Mau was the product of none but Kenyatta's sophisticated mind and foisted by him on to the Kikuyu in a deliberate throw-back to the savage ways of Africa's dark past.[6]

Corfield and Renison were both honest men. They came from a tradition which believed the colonial mission represented the forces of light, and African Nationalism—any nationalism—those of darkness. Renison found confirmation in this belief in words spoken by the Archbishop of Canterbury in the House of Lords on 28 March 1960, in which he described the role of the Christian Church in the 'African struggle of light against darkness' being 'throughout the continent from one end to the other . . . to create realms of trust and reconciliation'. Corfield ended his report with the words: 'Without the light of some basic religious belief to replace the darkness of witchcraft, there would appear to be no real future for the African state.'

Renison accepted Corfield's premiss and his conclusion and so, it must be assumed, did Macleod.[7] The Governor took at its face value all that his advisers told him. There had been no impartial review of Kenyatta's case. Yet the facts of Macharia's perjury were now available, and any lawyer could have told Renison that Kenyatta's guilt had not been 'established and confirmed' by the Privy Council. That court had simply refused to allow him to appeal to it. Nor did Renison inform himself of Kenyatta's present outlook, but based his judgements on what supposedly had taken place ten years before.

Both Renison and his advisers, and Macleod and the Colonial Office, must have had strong reasons of their own for insisting that Kenyatta was not the man to lead Kenya to independence.

One possible explanation is that there was an overwhelming weight of African 'loyalist' opinion against Kenyatta. It would not have been surprising. Kenyatta had made many enemies among his own people and particularly among those well in with Europeans.[8]

Furthermore the attitude of the new generation of African politicians who had risen during the Emergency was equivocal. The suppression of the Kikuyu, the ablest tribe in Kenya, brought other men into prominence. Notable among these was a young Luo, Tom Mboya, who had received special training in trade union affairs in Britain and was strongly backed by the Americans as a counter, they hoped, to the support given his fellow Luo leader, the flamboyant Oginga Odinga, by the Soviet bloc. Uncommonly gifted intellectually, Mboya was a fluent debater and a shrewd politician. He was naturally ambitious and his trade union base gave him wide intertribal support. He could have felt he was being groomed for national leadership. There was no one to touch him provided he could outmanoeuvre Odinga, and Kenyatta was out of the running.

Among the Kikuyu, too, younger men had taken over from the old guard. Old Koinange had died, one son, Peter Mbiyu, was still denied re-entry, another was a loyal government servant. Mathu had lost his seat in a recent election and was out of things. The new men's 'loyalty' to government had been proved by special 'loyalty certificates' which they had to obtain from the administration before they were allowed even to enter politics. They may also have thought that their own best interests coincided with European determination never to allow Kenyatta to return to his own people.[9]

To African 'loyalist' opinion was added the long-nurtured vendetta of the settlers, some missionaries, and certain officials, against Kenyatta personally. They still saw African Nationalism in terms of individual 'agitators', in the tradition of Grigg in the late 1920s and of the Electors' Union in the 1940s. They were unable to adjust to the sudden collapse of the British Empire and their own imminent disappearance from the stage of history. Instead they looked for psychological arguments to explain Mau Mau and the liberation movements that were sweeping the world. Corfield placed his facts and documents in this context. Anyone who tried to get rid of the British must be mad. But they could not say this of Kenyatta. So, they believed, he must have more sinister ambitions. Having failed to destroy him legally at Kapenguria or physically at Lokitaung, they sought to destroy his place in history.

The possibility must also be considered that English men and women were increasingly being influenced by visual impressions induced by television, newsreels and advertising. Photographs of Kenyatta taken when he emerged briefly from Lokitaung, in March 1959, to attend Macharia's trial at Kitale, showed a somewhat remote figure dressed in a brown leather jacket, with sunken cheeks and hooded eyes. Government propaganda exploited this visual aspect of Kenyatta's personality, as they had done with Mau Mau atrocities. Kenyatta could look, and be made to look, sinister.

Finally, mention must be made of the stories which were widely circulated that Kenyatta was drinking himself to death. The origin of these stories has not been established, though they bear a strong resemblance to those put about by the missionary informants of the Electors' Union in the late 1940s. But they were believed with an astonishing credulity by people who should have known better. It was also commonly said that the British were encouraging Kenyatta in his supposed vice, the work, it was assumed, of secret agents.[10]

The settlers applauded Renison's statement. It was their last ditch stand against the currents of history. Even Blundell thought they had ten years before the handover would take place. Kenyatta must surely be dead in that time. Overnight the phrase 'the leader to darkness and death' became their answer to Macmillan's 'wind of change'.

The phrase boomeranged. In African eyes Kenyatta's release and independence went together. From the *Uhuru and Dust* of Lodwar the slogan became *Uhuru na Kenyatta*. KANU declared they would not take part in any government until Kenyatta was freed. In the elections of February 1961, the first held under the Macleod constitution, KANU campaigned on this issue. Though Kenyatta was still in detention, his face was on their posters, his name on their lips, and his legend won them a convincing majority of the votes. Despite strong pressure, they refused to form a government and Renison was driven to offer ministries to the minority party, KADU. Having pledged his New Kenya Party to support an African government, Blundell joined them. But the KADU leader, Ngala, whose official title became 'Leader of Government Business', required official nominees to secure a majority in Legco. Without Kenyatta, the constitution was a fiasco.

Kenyatta waited and listened at Lodwar. He now had his radio and regular newspapers, his wife and children were with him and he received occasional visitors like Bishop Kariuki. Renison's statements and the Corfield Report appeared not to distress him unduly. In July 1960 he wrote to Edna: 'It is comforting to see that there are clear signs everywhere that Africa is slowly and surely marching to her freedom.'

But time was against him and the government's stalling tactics tested his nerves during this period more than at any time in his long exile. In January 1961 his remaining sixteen teeth were extracted. Doctors seemed satisfied with his health, but no one really knew how old he was. Still less was there any certainty over his state of mind. The administration allowed a few of the new leaders to visit Lodwar, perhaps in the hope they would return believing him senile, perhaps to try and draw him into a clear statement of his political beliefs.

Kenyatta refused to oblige on either score. He appeared fit and abreast of the situation, glad to see Odinga, and talking about the future, not the past. He would not declare himself for either party, KANU or KADU, but threatened to form a third if they could not resolve their differences. He stood, he said, for all Kenyans, and unity was the only important thing. It was the old formula: 'we want to rule ourselves'. The rest was no business of what he called 'the colonial sahibs'.

On 4 April 1961, Kenyatta was at last flown out of Lodwar. For the final stage of his exile the government brought him to Maralal, an attractive hill station at the northern tip of the Laikipia plateau and the headquarters of the Samburu district.

A week later, on 11 April 1961, the government decided the time had come when Kenyatta should again meet the world's press. It was eight years since Thacker's judgement at Kapenguria—the last occasion reporters had seen him. For most white men he was the personification of the sinister forces conjured up by the words 'Mau Mau'. They now measured him, through the eye of the newsreel cameras, against the Governor's description of 'the leader to darkness and death'.

Kenyatta wore his leather jacket. His face was thin, almost harsh, his voice slow but controlled. He spoke in English, choosing his words with care. He began with a brief prepared statement of his own in which he reminded them that he was speaking at a disadvantage after eight years of being 'bottled up in remote districts away from public life and world affairs'. 'During that time', he continued, 'I have been greatly misrepresented by some of you, but today I hope you will stick to the truth and refrain from writing sensational stories about me.'

Kenyatta took the opportunity to dispose of the Corfield Report, which he said he had seen, as 'a pack of lies, collected from needy informers. If I had my way I'd put it in the fire.' But, he said, he bore no one any grudge. The Governor had been poorly advised and he, Kenyatta, could borrow from the words of Jesus: 'Father forgive them, for they know not what they do.' 'I have never been a violent man. My whole life has been anti-violence. If I am free I will continue to be so.' But he was for immediate independence—*uhuru*—the slogan with which the Africans prefaced meetings and greeted one another. 'I shall always remain an African Nationalist to the end.'

As to his past in Europe, Kenyatta denied any sinister connections: 'I have never had any Communist affiliations at all. I visited Russia just like anyone else . . . for educational purposes.'

As to the Cold War between East and West, after recent events in the Congo much in the minds of foreign correspondents, Kenyatta described both world blocs as 'hungry dogs' after a bone. It was the Africans who suffered, he said, as grass suffers when two elephants fight.

As to the future, no one had reason to fear. All citizens of an independent Kenya would be protected in their persons and their property by an African government—both forest fighters and loyalists 'since they are all of them brothers and sisters', and the Europeans who chose to stay in the country, provided they gave up their 'big boss' mentality.

It was a performance which left many observers sceptical. They were unable to adjust to the idea that Mau Mau represented a legitimate national liberation struggle. Anything short of outright abuse of Mau Mau, along the lines of the Corfield Report, seemed to them equivocal. Many ordinary people who saw the newsreel of Kenyatta were reminded too of a similar line of questioning addressed to Archbishop Makarios of Cyprus, whose answers, framed with Greek subtlety, seemed equally unconvincing. In all, the scene at Maralal was aptly described as 'a publicity circus' in the *East African Standard,* 'second only to that in which Eichmann was the central figure in Jerusalem.' The concurrence of these news stories must have led to an association of ideas in the minds of many readers at that time.

Maralal was still 180 miles from Nairobi and out of reach of Kenyatta's own people. But on clear mornings he could see the jagged outline of Mount Kenya to the south, with its glaciers alternating with black rock. Kere-Nyaga, the abode of gods, had always meant much to him as the possible source of those supernatural powers his grandfather knew how to invoke. Maralal was known chiefly as a safari centre, but for the four months that Kenyatta spent there it became an African Delphi. Representatives of different political parties, of Christian denominations and of other religions, of racial communities and of world powers, lawyers, photographers, doctors, foreign visitors, friends, relatives, priests, all came to see Kenyatta at Maralal and returned able to reassure their friends that, after all, he was the man to safeguard their rights in an independent Kenya. Kenyatta could have had no better build-up to his return to the political scene. On the eve of his release the government even made it possible for him to broadcast to the people of Kenya, appealing for calm.

Among the pilgrims to Maralal was Michael Blundell. Again in advance of most settlers, he was prepared to see Kenyatta released before independence. They talked, among other things, of land problems for the poorer Kikuyu, one of the economic factors which lay at the heart of Mau Mau. Land had always been the central issue of Kenya politics. Kenyatta's relationship towards the European community—especially the farmers—was the key to the future. Some senior British officials still saw him in terms of an African Hitler. They could no more hand over power to such a man than collaborate with the Nazis.

As Blundell was about to leave, Kenyatta suddenly turned to him and asked: 'Why do Europeans hate me so?' The two men faced each other, the white and the black politician. Blundell spoke frankly. He told Kenyatta that Europeans felt *he* hated *them,* and had started Mau Mau to get rid of them.[11]

Kenyatta grunted. It was a characteristic of his when thinking. He was determined that Africans should not be second-class citizens in their own country. For him independence was not just a question of Africans ruling themselves, though that was the first thing, it must also mean an end to the colour bar, to the racist slang of the settler clubs, to the white man's patronizing attitudes of half a century and more. Kenyatta could not afford to wait ten years. The Europeans must be brought to accept his leadership of independent Kenya, not an interim period under a white liberal like Blundell.

The time at Maralal passed quickly. The government had failed in every way to destroy Kenyatta, and it was now trapped by the publicity it had given him. For it had made it known it was building a new house for him on his old plot of land at Gatundu. Renison accepted the inevitable and on 14 August 1961 the day arrived when Kenyatta was at last allowed to return to Kikuyuland. Ngina, now expecting a baby, accompanied him. Margaret and other members of his family, with Ambu Patel, Margaret's Indian protector and now Kenyatta's private photographer, were waiting at the new house.

150 police were on duty. Alerted by their own system of communication some 10,000 Africans had gathered at Gatundu. A short flight from Maralal, a brief meeting with Ngala and other African politicians, and Kenyatta led a procession of land-rovers back to his birthplace. The crowd chanted his name; women danced and trilled. Reporters pressed close to Kenyatta. He told them: 'I do not feel bitter towards anyone at all because I know my cause and my activities were just. I regard everybody as my friends; you know the commandment "Love thy Neighbour", well the world is my neighbour.' It was almost nine years since his arrest.

For a week Kenyatta was restricted to his home, which was surrounded by wire and patrolled by *askaris*. But every day and throughout the night singing and dancing continued as delegations came from all parts of Kikuyuland to greet their leader. Kenyatta spent much of the time walking around the compound waving his fly-whisk. He saw journalists, received gifts, and considered his future.

Renison was silent and withdrawn at Government House. Then, on 22 August, he at last agreed to meet Kenyatta. The venue was not Government House, seat of power, but the bare DC's office at Kiambu, where years ago Kenyatta had had to go to beg permission to hold meetings. It still symbolized colonial authority. Renison was tense, unsmiling; Kenyatta inscrutable. A brief communiqué was issued to the Press. Kenyatta received back his ring and his black, carved stick. He was now a free man again.[12]

Triumphal appearances throughout Kenya followed. On 25 August a crowd of many thousands saw him drive to Legco offices in Nairobi. It was Kenyatta's first sight of the new buildings which now graced Nairobi's city centre. On 3 September he was at Mombasa for a welcome from the coastal people where he affirmed his faith in the territorial integrity of Kenya. He would be no party to the idea of autonomy for the coastal strip, any more than he would to the loss of territory to the Somalis.

On 26 November the BBC screened a full-scale interview with Kenyatta in a television series called *Face to Face*. For forty-five minutes the British public were gripped by the appearance in their living-rooms of the man who years of propaganda had led them to believe was the embodiment of Mau Mau. Kenyatta wore a Luo hat to symbolize his national status, the ring gleamed on his finger and he clasped his stick between his legs. The programme dealt with the familiar subjects of Mau Mau and violence, Russia and communism, for which he had by now a standard answer. He was as enigmatic as ever. There was an edge to his personality which no European could define.

Though dying, the colonial regime still represented the only legal machinery through which independence could be granted. There were countless details to be worked out, safeguards to be built into the independence constitution, and problems to be decided of national security, of military bases, of treaties undertaken by the colonial power (for example with the Masai), of frontiers (with the Somalis in the north-east), of service conditions for Europeans who remained in the civil service. Only properly constituted African leaders could negotiate these matters. Kenyatta had no option but to join the struggle for political power. On 28 October 1961, he accepted the Presidency of KANU. The rules were changed to allow him to enter Legco, and on 12 January 1962 he was returned unopposed for the Fort Hall constituency, where a KANU man vacated his seat for him. On 10 April 1962, he agreed to serve in a coalition government in the relatively minor post of Minister of State for Constitutional Affairs and Economic Planning. But he accepted the Governor's veto on Odinga's entering the government with him. On 21 March 1963, Legco sat for the last time in its traditional, colonial, form in which, through fifty-five years, it had changed from being a small group of settlers and colonial officials meeting in the railway institute to an imitation of the Palace of Westminster in fine new buildings with Africans ready to crowd out the Europeans. The elections that followed were to decide who would lead Kenya to independence.

Kenyatta had not shown himself to be notably effective either as a party leader or as a government minister and there were some who questioned his future usefulness. The struggles of the past, the long years of isolation from African politics—first in Europe, then in prison—his supposed drinking habits, all these, it was argued, had exhausted his powers and brought him near to senility. He had made little impact in parliamentary debate and appeared to lean heavily on his younger colleagues for guidance on policy. It was they who seemed to supply the drive and to be making the important decisions.

But a European political style had never been Kenyatta's. Though KANU accepted the agricultural reforms of the Baring era and incorporated them in its electoral manifesto, Kenyatta himself kept away from ideological issues. He was at his best in the open air, at

huge meetings reminiscent of the old tribal *barazas* where his use of
proverbs, tribal lore, and spell-binding words was unmatched. He
deployed these skills now to the full.

A few prominent settlers threw in their lot with KANU, and
notably Bruce Mackenzie, a South African-born farmer with an
air-force-type moustache, whose opportunist approach to politics was
similar to Kenyatta's own. The support of these Europeans was an
important factor in KANU's campaign funds and offset the covert
backing of KADU candidates which European government officials
had earlier been giving. With Kenyatta's name to draw the crowds,
Mboya's organizing ability and Odinga's loyalty, KANU overcame
the complicated electoral arrangements of the new regional constitution and swept the polls.[13]

Kenyatta joined his younger colleagues in a victory dance in the
street. On 28 May 1963 he was invited to form a government, and on
1 June he became the first Prime Minister of a self-governing Kenya.
His cabinet was a careful balance of African leaders. He could now
reward Odinga, who became Minister of Home Affairs; Mboya was
made responsible for Justice and Constitutional Affairs. Mbiyu
Koinange and Joseph Murumbi, who had laboured for the independence movement outside Kenya, both became ministers. Kubai
and Kaggia received junior posts and Oneko held an influential port-
folio. Kenyatta gave his country a new rallying cry: *'Harambee!'*,
an old work chant at the coast meaning 'pull together'. Full independence was set for the end of the year.

Two scenes stand out from the excitements of those months.
Remembering, perhaps, what Blundell had said to him at Maralal,
Kenyatta had done his best to reassure European farmers about their
future. On 12 August 1963, he met some 300 of them at Nakuru.
The settlers of Kenya had always carried an influence disproportionate to their numbers, but they rightly felt that it was they and
their predecessors who had made Kenya what it was. The colonial
mission in East Africa was founded on white settlement, and it was
fitting that Kenyatta should now meet them in Delamere's old
stronghold. He won them over in a notable appeal to forgive and
forget the past. The support of these hard-bitten and tight-lipped
men and women was important psychologically. For they provided
a barometer of European confidence in the new Kenya. Kenyatta
needed that confidence to ensure that Western capital would remain to underpin the new nation's economy.

The second incident was a piece of theatre which only Kenyatta could contrive. On the eve of independence and to the astonishment of newsreel viewers throughout the world, Kenyatta appeared in public with his arm around a man with rolling eyes and matted hair reaching down to his shoulders who styled himself a Mau Mau Field Marshal. Kenyatta jovially showed him off to the world's press. In an ironic reminder of Renison's broadcasts, Kenyatta assured questioners that the 'Field Marshal' and his kind were no danger to security as all they wanted to see was a Kenya flag flying over their country. It was part of Kenyatta's attempt to bring the remaining freedom fighters out of their forest lairs. Many of them looked for an easy future from an independent African government. Behind Kenyatta's joviality lay tough talk and a legacy of bitterness which his independent government would inherit.

12 December 1963, the day of Kenya's independence arrived. A huge crowd assembled in a specially constructed independence stadium. The Duke of Edinburgh represented the British Crown; Duncan Sandys, whose Commonwealth Office now included the old Colonial Office represented the British Government.

Kenya was the thirty-fourth state in Africa to achieve independence. All over the world the Union Jack was coming down and 'Auld Lang Syne' being sung, but nowhere was the scene played with greater poignancy than in Nairobi that December day. Kenya was the only British colony, except Southern Rhodesia, with a sizeable settler population, and the only one which had staged a rebellion of sorts. Like Nehru and Nkrumah, Kenyatta had graduated to national leadership through a British prison, but no other African had aroused such strong emotions.

The day began with an impressive ceremony in which the Duke of Edinburgh handed over Kenya's instruments of independence. Kenyatta delivered a carefully prepared speech in which all the decencies were preserved. There were no recriminations, nothing outrageous. He repeated his theme, impromptu in Swahili. It was summed up in his one-word rallying cry *'Harambee!'*. All stood and cheered.

Beside Kenyatta on the dais was Kenya's last Governor, Malcolm MacDonald, a small, cheerful politician turned diplomat who had earned distinction as a charming and unconventional decolonizer of Britain's possessions in South-East Asia.[14] MacDonald had taken over at the beginning of 1963 after Duncan Sandys had abruptly retired Renison in late 1962. A man who mixed easily with members of all races, MacDonald had brought to Kenya an open mind and an optimism in the future as persuasive as Kenyatta's. Like Charles

Eliot at the dawn of the century, MacDonald was the antithesis of the settler type. If it was largely thanks to Eliot that the colonial enterprise was launched in Kenya, it was largely thanks to Mac-Donald that it was laid to rest with such lack of rancour.

Harry Thuku spent the day on his farm planting out new coffee trees. He was ageing and almost forgotten in the press of new men fighting for positions at Kenyatta's court. But he had his farm, a happy marriage and the confidence of his lately won Christian faith. He could be forgiven for his seeming betrayal of the cause of national liberation for he had carried the torch for Kenyatta and had suffered for it.

'General China' was in the forests. Kenyatta had retained a fatherly interest in him since their ways parted at Lokitaung. He had secured China's release from prison and had arranged for him to receive secret paramilitary training in Israel. At Kenyatta's request he was on a mission to one of the last Mau Mau headquarters on the slopes of Mount Kenya.

Among Kenyatta's guests for the celebrations were Edna and their son Peter, who were flown out at the expense of Kenyatta's government and given special treatment. Kenyatta had met them both when he first returned to London for constitutional talks after his release. Son and father had taken intuitively to each other after the long separation. Edna had shielded Peter well from the vicious white reactions to the Kapenguria verdict. Kenyatta was proud of her loyalty, and in Kenya Edna was warmly welcomed into the Kenyatta family by Grace Wahu, Margaret Wambui and Ngina.

Other specially invited guests included Dinah Stock and D. N. Pritt. They had been with Kenyatta in the bad times and deservedly shared in his triumph. It was the day for which European friends and old KCA leaders had worked, and for which Mau Mau fighters had died. MacDonald insisted that representatives of the old animist faiths should join other religious leaders in blessing Kenya's future. As they performed the ancient tribal rituals, Britain finally washed her hands of her civilizing mission. The Christian churches were now on their own.

'This is the greatest day in Kenya's history and the happiest day in my life,' said Kenyatta in his speech. At midnight, the climax of the celebrations, the colonial flag at last came down picked out by searchlights. For an instant there appeared to be a hitch when the guyrope stuck and Kenya's new flag hung unfurled. The Duke of

Edinburgh whispered to Kenyatta: 'Do you want to change your mind?' Kenyatta grinned. It was the supreme moment of his life.

The new flag broke open and all the tensions of half a century and more disappeared into the dark. Marching and counter-marching followed; there was dancing African-style in the stadium, Western-style at Government (now State) House; there were fireworks, drinking and laughter, and not one act of recrimination.

Kenyatta's destiny had prepared him for this moment. But no one knew what really lay in his mind nor what the future held for Kenya.

CHAPTER 23

The President

With independence all terms of reference changed. 'Terrorists' became freedom fighters, 'nationalist agitators' were liberators of the people, and the 'leader to darkness and death' was now seen as chief guarantee of light and liberty.

Kenyatta had always kept himself free from ideological commitments. He had sought power according to the simple formula 'we want to rule ourselves'. It was an absolute right and did not depend on any political theories originating in Moscow or Westminster. He had educated himself in these models, as he often said, but he was not tied to them. He remained free to exercise his own style of leadership in that earthy and undoctrinaire manner which had always been his characteristic.

Everything will come when we have political power, was how he had expressed this practical approach to Oginga Odinga when the Kikuyu nationalists were seeking allies among the Luo in the 1950s.[1] But there was to be no revolution after power as some of the old Pan-Africans hoped and many of the old colonials feared. From the moment he became Prime Minister, on 1 June 1963, Kenyatta began to assert his own will in the way Kenya was run. The achievement of personal power unstopped reserves of self-confidence and authority which many had previously doubted he possessed.

Kenyatta preserved what he most needed from the colonial structure, and particularly its law and order aspect. Institutions like the police and army were taken over intact. For a time he retained the services of European officers like Ian Henderson, the police inspector who had prepared the case against him at Kapenguria, and Whitehouse, the DC of Turkanaland and his chief gaoler at Lokitaung.[2] When an army unit threatened mutiny within a month of independence, similar to more violent outbreaks in neighbouring Zanzibar, Tanganyika and Uganda, he did not hesitate to ask British troops to put it down for him.

In the same way the judiciary, civil service and Parliament continued to function according to their British models and with white men still in senior posts. A settler, Bruce Mackenzie, held the important Ministry of Agriculture in Kenyatta's Cabinet: another, Humphrey Slade—once a bitter opponent of Blundell and his liberal approach—remained as Speaker of the National Assembly. Blundell himself stayed on to farm his extensive estates overlooking the Rift Valley and as director of several businesses.

Kenyatta's call to forgive and forget the past turned out to be no empty phrase; it was the keynote of his government. Youth wingers and old nationalists who spoke of revenge were sharply rebuked; Mau Mau fighters who had grown accustomed to the ways of the forest and refused government resettlement schemes were quietly rounded up. White men and women who only a few months before had thought of Kenyatta with fear and revulsion now took Kenyan citizenship. 'Everything will be all right so long as the old man is there', they said to each other, and life in the Rift Valley Sports Club and other bastions of the old White Highlands went on much as before, though without the racist talk and without the colour bar.

Principle and expediency both dictated this policy. He had always said that he harboured no prejudice against the white man as a person and had no wish to drive him out of Kenya. Equally he knew that white farms were vital to Kenya's economy and that Africans, as yet, lacked the capacity for such large-scale agriculture themselves.

But two practical measures of restructuring were undertaken without delay. First the regional set-up of the independence constitution was scrapped and Kenya reverted to the central administrative system of the colonial period.

Then, in December 1964, Kenya became a Republic within the Commonwealth, with Kenyatta as President. He was stepping into a role he had watched many a plumed-hatted governor fill in the past. Malcolm MacDonald, who had remained as Governor-General for the year after independence, vacated State House and became Britain's High Commissioner. It was an unprecedented succession of appointments for one man to hold. Much of the goodwill generated for Kenyatta's government from old colonial figures came from MacDonald's unpretentious manner as representative of the old colonial power. His personal charm and easy manner with all races, and his close personal relationship with Kenyatta, were welcome changes from the ways of the past.[3]

With the tensions caused by Rhodesia's unilateral declaration of independence in November 1965 it was Kenyatta and MacDonald between them who helped preserve Commonwealth ties. Where he could, Kenyatta helped the British Prime Minister, who flew out specially to Africa, while remaining free to attack the racism that flowered south of the Zambezi.

Under the Republican constitution Kenyatta was executive head of state, and he ruled Kenya with a ministerial team of great ability. Closest to him were members of the Kikuyu inner caucus from southern Kiambu such as Peter Mbiyu Koinange, Charles Njonjo and Dr Mungai, the son of Kenyatta's aunt (his father, Muigai's, sister in whose homestead he had often stayed as a young man). Dr Mungai was both Kenyatta's first cousin and his personal physician, a relationship indicative of the close family and tribal ties between some of these younger colleagues and their President. The two Luo rivals, Oginga Odinga and Tom Mboya, balanced and watched each other.

This balancing of forces was typical of Kenyatta's approach. Throughout his life he had remained detached from other men's passions, and he did as much now between the ideological differences of the Cold War, as between the ideological differences of the Christian churches and between the loyalists and freedom fighters of the Emergency. He preached unity to his people and pointed out how the British had won their empire through a policy of divide and rule; but he showed he had learnt enough from them to apply the same technique to his own government. Capitalist and communist aid were duly forthcoming and Kenya took the lead in development in East Africa; but Kenyatta came down heavily on any signs of communist infiltration. He had learnt enough of their techniques too.

As far as African Socialism was concerned, it remained a vague concept. In the thirties Kenyatta had been closest to the Independent Labour Party, but he had not embraced their economic doctrines with the same conviction as other, younger, members of the nationalist movement. His government made some attempt to provide land for the landless, but he saw more potential from practical experiments in co-operative ventures and schemes backed by the World Bank and the Commonwealth Development Corporation. The latter was headed by Lord Howick who, as Sir Evelyn Baring, had locked him up in 1952. In keeping with his lack of ill-feeling towards those who, as he used to say, were only doing their job, Kenyatta always made the former Governor welcome in his old home, now State House.

Again principle and expediency counted equally in this policy. Unlike Zambia, Ghana and Nigeria among Britain's former African colonies, Kenya has no raw materials required by the West. The sanction of the World Bank assured her of foreign investments. The results were visible in Nairobi's changing skyline where a new Hilton Hotel symbolized American faith in Kenyatta's regime.

Republican status made possible a further restructuring of Kenya's political institutions. Kenyatta was a believer in the one-party state. It was, he said, the expression of the people's new-found unity. KADU, the opposition party, bowed to the inevitable and in November 1964 went into voluntary liquidation. Kenyatta showed no recrimination to its leaders who were welcomed into KANU's fold and given government posts.

KANU was the natural heir to the independence movement. Like every other newly independent African state, Kenya was a colonial concept. The party was the crucible in which could be forged a new national idea out of the raw tribal, social and economic materials which were the colonial legacy. Within it personal and policy differences could be worked out without dividing the country, as in the old tribal council of elders—Kenyatta drew the parallel himself in one of his rare references to *Facing Mount Kenya*.[4] Political theorists might be sceptical of the parallel, but overseas investors with interests in Kenya found it prudent to channel funds into KANU and the party's headquarters in Nairobi joined the Hilton Hotel in its architectural boast in Kenya's future.

The building of a one-party state places emphasis on the personality of the leader. Through him nationalism is transformed into patriotism. Kenyatta was admirably suited to this role. For the Kikuyu he was the resurrected Waiyaki, the reincarnation even of Gikuyu, the Adam of the tribe;[5] for other tribes he was the one man who seemed to stand above tribes; for other races he was surety for a multi-racial society. As President of a one-party state Kenyatta was all things to all men. He was simply Mzee, the Father of the Nation.

It matched his temperament. Ever a showman he could appear one moment in gaily coloured shirts, decorated with the cock of KANU, and the next in elegant suits from Savile Row, seldom without a rose in his buttonhole; he could be photographed in leopard-skin hat and cloak waving a silver fly-whisk or in old slacks on his farm tending his shrubs; he was equally at home in academic robes at a university function and in sandals and shorts on the beach at Mombasa. African exuberance and love of display found perfect expression in

Kenyatta's flair alongside the dignity and respect due to 'His Excellency, the President, Mzee Jomo Kenyatta'.

This attention received legislative sanction. In November 1963 disrespect to the person of the Prime Minister (as he then was) was made an offence and any sign of it from old colonials, even in jest, was met with instant expulsion from Kenya. On 4 December 1963, Delamere Avenue was renamed Kenyatta Avenue and the statue of the pioneer settler on its plinth opposite the New Stanley Hotel was unceremoniously removed. Instead a bronze of Kenyatta with his fly-whisk was installed beside the National Assembly.

The President's apotheosis gathered momentum as all bid to do him honour and, perhaps, for his favour. Kenyatta's photograph appeared in every shop window; his face was on Kenya's new currency; radio broadcasts and newsreels featured his daily activities. A special Presidential film crew accompanied him everywhere. Wherever he drove he would be preceded by police outriders with wailing sirens and limousines filled with bodyguards; other road users had to stop, in the ditch if need be. Special red-beretted paramilitary units under 'General China' and other trusted men provided additional protection.

Kenyatta enjoyed it all. He revelled in a collection of bigger and better cars—a Rolls Royce from London's Motor Show, a Lincoln Convertible from American businessmen, a Mercedes 600. Gifts from Asian well-wishers and investments in land and property swelled his personal and his family fortune. He extended his farm at Gatundu where the founder of his family, his great-grandfather Magana, had first established his estate and where Kenyatta had been born. The area was closely guarded now against intruders, for Kenyatta, like all such leaders, was a target for assassination.

The highly personal style of government which Kenyatta's unique position created could be justified as giving confidence and stability to the new nation. But to some it began to look as though the old colonial power had simply transformed itself into one where Kenyatta was a new-style Governor and the Kikuyu had replaced the Europeans as top dogs. There was a constant problem of unemployment, many of those out of work being former members of the Mau Mau forces. Old KCA leaders looked enviously at the smart cars and European secretaries enjoyed by younger men, the fruits, their elders felt, of their sacrifices.

As the euphoria of independence wore off and Kenyatta's annual exhortations to work hard and pull together began to lose some of their appeal, opposition to his style of government was heard. The apparently pointless assassination of Pio Pinto in February 1965 spread this uneasiness. Joseph Murumbi, one of the ablest members of Kenyatta's Cabinet and for a time Foreign Secretary, resigned and abandoned politics altogether for business.

Then pressure fell on the Asian community.[6] Africans had always accused Indians of exploiting them, and despite the help many Indians from all walks of life had given to the freedom struggle, Kenyatta too, shared in a feeling of resentment towards them. Asians who had not taken up Kenya citizenship found their work permits were not renewed; Africanization put the trade and property of all at risk. Many tried to leave Kenya, only to find Britain refused to allow them the right of unrestricted entry which they believed their British passports gave them.

In 1969 the first elections under the Republican constitution—the first since independence—fell due. Kenyatta was now seventy or over. The Kikuyu, about 20 per cent of the population, filled most of the important posts in government and administration. This was in large measure justified by their natural ability. But from 1966, when Oginga Odinga formed a new party called the Kenya Peoples Union (KPU), opposition was growing. With Odinga were Bildad Kaggia and Achieng Oneko, both of whom had been in the forefront of the independence struggle, Oneko for a time being especially close to Kenyatta. It recalled the ganging up of the other prisoners against him at Lokitaung.

Odinga complained that economic independence had still to be won, that the KANU machine was running down and subject to Mboya's manipulations, and that his own position was being systematically undermined by a clique around the ageing President. There seemed to Odinga to be two governments functioning in Kenya: the official one in Nairobi to which he belonged, and the real one at Gatundu run by the Kikuyu inner caucus from which he was excluded.[7]

Odinga commanded the following of the Luo tribe and thanks to him the Luo had joined the Kikuyu in KANU in the independent struggle. Should the Luo desert KANU and take some disgruntled Kikuyu with them to combine with the other tribes, it was possible that the governing party would collapse, the Kikuyu caucus be outvoted and Kenyatta's own position, even, be at risk. The prospect was unthinkable to those in Kenya and without who were committed to the President, and it would have nullified his work of the previous five years.

The Kikuyu reacted to the threat as they had often done in the past. From early in 1969 Kenyatta and his advisers persuaded themselves that in the interests of tribal solidarity they should restart oathing. The forces which guarded the destiny of the tribe would again be invoked in this new trial. On the understanding that it would be peacefully conducted, Kenyatta persuaded the churches in Kenya to go along with the programme. People were to be invited, they were told, simply to express their love for their President and for the constitution. The fees charged would build up party funds for the election. It was all to be 'voluntarily' done.

As might have been expected, the campaign got out of hand. Once again the ridges of Kikuyuland seethed with activity as lorry-load after lorry-load made its way to Gatundu to 'have tea with the President', the euphemism for the oathing ceremonies. There they swore that 'the flag of Kenya shall not leave the House of Mumbi'. Often participants took the oath on a flag of Kenya spread out on the ground.

The outside world might have known little of this. Journalists were discouraged from reporting it and some were deported. But in the course of the summer an event took place which could not be concealed. On 5 July 1969, Tom Mboya was shot dead outside a chemist's shop in Nairobi's busiest quarter. The assassin, a Kikuyu, was arrested and eventually hanged. Coming at a time of rising tension, the murder threatened to smash Kenya's precarious unity. Luo resentment flared. There were riots in Nairobi and threats against the President.

Kenyatta appealed for calm. He resorted to television in a bid to avert tribal warfare.

'Brothers and sisters, I know that every one of us is very much grieved, but what I appeal to you my fellow citizens at this unfortunate time—for as you all know death is inevitable and it is a path which everyone will pass, whether he likes it or not—I appeal to you to identify yourselves as Kenyans, to unite together as one people, and one big tribe of Kenya. As we know, it is only love and unity that can rid us of the disease of separation and disunity. We should not be thinking in terms of "I come from that place or that district or that tribe" because all of us are of one tribe, and that tribe is Kenya.'

It was not the incisive performance of a de Gaulle and it did not still the voices which asked who had been behind the murder, and why it had been committed.

Nor did the oathing stop. Kikuyu and Luo reacted against each other. The latter rallied to Odinga and KPU, the former stepped up their oaths. Many Christians refused to join the 'tea-parties' which after a time were no longer held at Gatundu but in the countryside. Intimidation grew, the local authorities being unwilling to intervene. Government servants themselves often took a lead in the oathing arrangements. Threats produced stiffer resistance which in turn led to increased violence. Some church services were broken up, a few leading Christians were badly manhandled, many lost their jobs, and one Presbyterian elder was beaten to death.

At first Kenyatta refused to concern himself. For much of the time he was at the coast. When a deputation of African clergymen visited him he declined to be cross-examined on his conduct of affairs. The churches then came out openly against forcible oathing. The Presbyterians had borne the brunt of these campaigns in the past and they did so again. To Kenyatta's fury their leaders, African Christians brought up in the tradition of Arthur and his successors, drew up a covenant and resolutions challenging the Kenya Government to abide by the constitution.* In the same breath they affirmed their loyalty to the President. At huge public gatherings the mass of their followers, many of whom had been intimidated into taking the new oaths, gave them solid backing. One Sunday in September, 50,000 Anglicans assembled at Fort Hall to hear their bishop, Obadiah Kariuki, take the same line.

The Christian periodical *Target* publicized the actions of the churches, and other newspapers then felt free to pick up the story. Questions were asked about oathing in Kenya's National Assembly. The dossier on events in Kikuyuland could no longer be belittled. KILLING OUR UNITY read *Target*'s September headline to an article criticizing 'a few of our leaders'. In the middle of the month Kenyatta returned from the coast and abruptly the oathing stopped.

On 25 October Kenyatta went to Kisumu in the heart of Luo country to open a hospital which had been built with the aid of Odinga's Soviet contacts. He was greeted by Odinga's supporters chanting their KPU slogan. On such occasions in the past and against men like Ngei and Kaggia, Kenyatta had used his unrivalled rhe-

* See Appendix C.

torical technique of banter, sternness and local aphorism with devastating effect. But the Luo insults at Kisumu so ruffled him that he lost his temper.

Such at least was the impression given by the reports in Kenya's newspapers. *'I'll crush you', a furious Mzee tells KPU* read one headline. 'These stupid people must stop their nonsense and unless they do we will deal with them severely,' he was quoted as saying. Blazing with anger, he rounded on Odinga, sitting uneasily a short distance away: 'If it was not for my respect for you, Odinga, I would put you in prison now and see who has the power in this country.' He warned that anyone who played on tribal feelings would be 'crushed like locusts'. He taunted Odinga with the poor achievements of the Nyanza region. 'Why don't you help your people to do something instead of feeding them with propaganda about Utopia?'

It was possibly the roughest dressing-down he had ever delivered in public. As he left Kisumu, some of the crowd began pelting his car with stones. The President's bodyguard fired back with their automatic weapons. Exactly how many were killed and wounded was not made known. Photographers had their film confiscated and in some cases their cameras smashed. For a fortnight a dusk-to-dawn curfew was imposed. The leaders, including Odinga, were removed from circulation and the KPU banned.[8]

In the elections which followed, many members of Kenyatta's government were defeated, and though the inner Kikuyu caucus survived the crisis, Kenya was badly shaken. After more than a year in detention, during which time there were rumours that he would be quietly disposed of, Odinga was allowed to return to his home. But the Luo remained sullen. Alleged plots by senior army men were uncovered which contributed to an uneasy feeling that Kenya enjoyed a surface calm which could be preserved only so long as Kenyatta himself remained alive.[9]

The events of 1969 demonstrated how far Kenyatta was still a prisoner of his situation. He knew he had little time to create a new Kenya and his pragmatic approach was the one for which his life had most fitted him. But he succeeded in giving Kenya a precious respite from the worst of the troubles which racked other newly independent states, and his age tempered ambition for wider glory. Unlike younger men such as Nkrumah, who aspired to a world role and brought about the bankruptcy of Ghana and his own downfall as a result, Kenyatta contented himself with the less grandiose part. As he had done throughout his life he concentrated on his own country. Apart from a visit to Britain for a Commonwealth Prime Ministers' Conference in 1964, he never left Africa.[10] The idea of an East African Federation, which had featured prominently in the negotiations preceding independence, was shelved, and when Obote was ousted from Uganda Kenyatta remained detached from the disputes between the partners in the East African Community which followed.[11] A mild stroke in 1966 made him unwilling to travel by air and gave added reason for him to spend some months each year at the lower altitude of the coast, where he availed himself of Grigg's Mombasa residence and his own beach house at Bamburi, a few miles north.

But his energy appeared undiminished. He undertook the exacting chores of a Head of State with vigour, together with party rallies, speeches and attending to domestic affairs. Delegations were always welcomed at State House for a brief reception; old friends and allies could rely on having their photographs taken with him; important visitors were treated in the style of the old colonial regime; parties of girls were seldom absent from the grounds to provide songs and dances for the evening's entertainment.

Yet Kenyatta was, in a special sense, a lonely man. As the prosecution had said at his trial, he was in a class by himself. He had always been a loner and sought the company of other outsiders like the half-caste Muganda, Charles Stokes, and Joseph Murumbi, the Masai/Goan. He had no cronies of his own age with whom he could relive his past, and he often showed nostalgia for London and Manchester, speaking at times of England as 'home' in the manner of old colonials. He was an avid collector of the scattered mementoes of his past—photographs, books and documents, the long-lost typescript of *Facing Mount Kenya* which Geoffrey Husbands had preserved, a chapter of his autobiographical novel left behind with Edna, and copies of old and unimportant letters between former correspondents like Barlow.

He was surrounded by younger men over whom his hold was complete, but he knew that they were jockeying among themselves for succession. He took pleasure in his own children and grandchildren; a son, Uhuru, was born in October 1961, a daughter, Nyokabi, and another son, Muhoho, followed. And it was a source of great pride to him when his eldest daughter, Margaret Wambui, was elected Mayor of Nairobi in 1970.

His pilgrimage through life had left a trail of memories: a rotting zinc tub in the sands of Lodwar where he had planted a small shrub;

an empty cell at Lokitaung; some fruit trees at Dagoretti on the site of the old Kinyata Stores where the roads parted; a name in the first register at Thogoto. Behind him, too, he has left a mystique which no Westerner can penetrate but which belongs to the legends of Africa.

Kenyatta's basic philosophy remained remarkably consistent. It was that all men deserved the right to develop peacefully according to their own wishes. It was the underlying theme of *Facing Mount Kenya*. As President he defined it as valuing the spirit of family or communal loyalties; it was similar to the 'African Humanism' of Zambia's Kenneth Kaunda, which stood for togetherness or brotherly love. Kenyatta expressed it in the Swahili word *Ujamaa*:

'The ultimate ideal would be to extend this to all humanity, recognising that all men everywhere, although in their various ways, share the same basic wish to enjoy security, the fruits of endeavour and pursuit of contentment.'[12]

To Westerners it might not seem so far, after all, from the ideal of the founders of the American Republic. But in interpreting it in Kikuyu terms Kenyatta left himself free to invoke forces which belong to African experience and not to that of the Age of Reason. In the new terms of reference created by independence, the only challenge possible was, as it had been before the colonial episode began, from an absolute Christian ethic. The events of 1969 showed that this also was now firmly part of African experience. Kenyatta had never denied it, and those occasions in his life when the two conflicted were the times when his personality came under greatest strain.

Kenyatta's personal faith is rooted in the earth of Kikuyuland. Gatundu, where his life began, is where he most likes to spend time towards the end of it, as a farmer watches new growth spring up after the rains:

'In a life of close association with the soil of Kenya, I have found joy and humility in the seasonal rhythms both of plant and of animal life, and in the crafts of careful husbandry. But I have seen drought and flood, hail and tempest. I have seen locusts come, and crops destroyed by virus or fungus, and livestock striken by rinderpest or tick-borne disease. One must learn to suffer and endure, to replant and rebuild, to move on again. And as with farming, so with politics, the practitioner must never lose faith.'[13]

The tragedies of the past must not mar the future. The shadow of Mau Mau, which so haunts Western imagination, must not be allowed to darken the sky of independent Kenya. In farming terms, it was a thinning of the bananas, a concept which may affront Europeans but which is authentically African. For Kenyatta new growth would spring out of the past; and past, present and future hold to a single, united destiny. And through the destiny of the Kikuyu he could also serve the destiny of Africa. To him and his people the achievement of absolute power was proof that he had finally gained the approval and support of those supernatural powers of whose existence he was first made aware by his grandfather, the worker of magic.

But to many Kenyatta's message of reconciliation, 'to forgive and forget', was perhaps his greatest contribution to his country and to history. 'I have stood always for the purposes of human dignity in freedom, and for the values of tolerance and peace.'[14] Ideology and power, he knew, must always threaten to corrupt these ideals. The long months of solitude at Lokitaung, examining the secrets of his own heart and the ways of mankind, left him with no illusions about man's fall from grace and sinful nature. If to the outside world he could seem vain, in his inner being he sought communion with God with a vision that embraced all races and creeds. 'Should you people fail to uphold me with your prayers and advice what should I do?' he once wrote to a Kikuyu church leader.

A retreating Western civilization has no right to look at independent Africa in an accusatory spirit. No one can tell what seed, blown by the currents of history across the continent, will have taken deepest root. Kenya's problems, as Winston Churchill said in the heyday of the imperial mission, are still the problems of the world. To live under God in hope for the future, and not in regret for the past, is Kenyatta's legacy to mankind.

When Was Kenyatta Born?

There can never be a definite answer to this question but the different pieces of evidence may here be brought together. They broadly fall into two categories: (a) what Kenyatta said himself, and (b) what others have said or observed.

Readers will notice that Kenyatta gave two conflicting accounts of how he came to see his first white man.

1. The first was to the Carter Commission in 1932 (see p. 185). As Ross pointed out, the Dagoretti Boma was built 1902–3. But Kenyatta said he did not see it, as he would have been bound to do when taking his herd of goats from the Muthiga ridge to the Gitiba salt lick. To be about ten years old, therefore, before 1902 places his birth near to 1890.

2. The second was at the Seventieth Anniversary of the founding of the PCEA, in 1968 (see p. 45). Scott died in 1907 and the period in question must be *c.* 1905–7.

In the first case, the white man was a settler with a gun, in the second, a missionary with a Bible. Nothing could illustrate better the ambivalent nature of the civilizing mission and the divided reaction of the Africans to it.

For reasons partly connected with the early history of the Dagoretti area, and partly with the circumstances of his initiation and life at the mission, the earlier account must be rejected. Kenyatta's evidence to Carter was given at a time in his life when strict historical accuracy was not required. It belonged, rather, to the period when the young Kikuyu politicians were challenging the white settlers.

On the basis of the second account being nearer the truth, Kenyatta's birth may be placed *c.* 1897–8, with the following points borne in mind:

1. The white man's arrival in southern Kiambu took place, as is described in chapter 2, over the ten years 1890–1900, with two notable series of events—Francis Hall's 'pacification' programme, from 1892–5, and the railway work 1898–1901. A young boy growing up in the Muthiga area during these years could not miss these events, and if all the movements of his family took place before 1902–3 (the date of the new Dagoretti boma) with himself about ten to twelve years old by the end of the period, Kenyatta would have been right in the middle of them. Yet he never said anything to suggest he had witnessed them. It is much more likely that Kenyatta was born towards the end of these events and grew from infancy to boyhood in the calmer years that followed, when the Kikuyu were establishing themselves in the new border country and the missionaries were beginning their out-reach in the neighbouring villages.

2. In the close communal life of the dormitory at Thogoto, as in the special hut for unmarried boys which existed in every Kikuyu village, a boy could not conceal the physical signs that he was maturing or pretend that he was circumcized if it was not true. It was not unknown for village headmen to put off the initiation of their sons so as to delay their liability for tax which was partly assessed on the number of young men in the household. If Kenyatta was already in his early twenties by 1913 he would be subjected to ridicule and isolation by his fellows. He would be denied normal rights towards women and would risk losing his inheritance of his family lands. No Kikuyu was prepared to turn his back so drastically on his tribal past; and though there is a strong tradition that Kenyatta 'ran away from home', he was still very much within the circle of clan and family ties. It is possible that he was putting the moment of initiation off, for some reason best known to himself (and his selfish step-father, Ngengi, would certainly not press him to undergo it), and was taken in hand by Musa Gitau and the others who organized the peculiar initiation ceremony which then took place, according to the description given on page 62. But this somewhat devious explanation would not be required on the later birth-date. Kenyatta would, in this case, be approaching fifteen or sixteen, the normal age for initiation at that time.

3. The later birth-date also fits the accounts of the mission staff. Arthur, Tait and others spoke of Kenyatta's being a boy of less than twelve years old in November 1909. If, as seems likely, he was ap-

prenticed in July 1912, at the beginning of the school year, he would then be approaching fifteen and it would be another mark of his growing maturity.

4. The members of his tribe who were most closely connected with Kenyatta while he was at the mission all agree that he was a young boy (*Toto*) when he first came, and was definitely younger than them—sufficiently younger for them to be of a quite different regiment, or group of age-grades, from his (*Kihiomwere*). The older birth-date would open a wide gap between Kenyatta's birth and that of his stepbrother, James Muigai, and also between the relative ages of himself and his first cousin, Dr Mungai, though such age differences between members of a family were not impossible in a polygamous society.

5. There are, however, two substantial objections to the younger birthdate, and they come from two men who knew Kenyatta well at later periods of his life. Charles Kasaja Stokes was born in 1895 and came to know Kenyatta when he returned from Dundee in 1911, and even better during the end of the war and when Kenyatta was living in Nairobi. He thought Kenyatta was older than himself. Robert Macpherson, a Scottish missionary, who first met Kenyatta in 1928 when Macpherson was himself twenty-four, saw in him a man already in his late thirties. Later contacts with Kenyatta and great experience of the Kikuyu have strengthened Macpherson in this view.

These are formidable objections. But it must be said that Kenyatta's whole life was an exercise in persuading others to follow his lead. This would naturally make him seem older to men who did not come from his family or tribal background, and Kenyatta was adept at invention if it suited his purpose.

The Operation of Female Circumcision

The Church of Scotland memorandum on female circumcision included the following account of the physical aspects of the rite written in nonmedical language by four doctors working in Kikuyuland.

'This operation comprises cutting away the inner and outer soft parts lying round the birth canal. In its severest form, the cutting extends in front up onto the pubis and into the birth canal itself. The result is the replacement of much of the normal elastic tissues of these parts, and by an unyielding ring of hard fibrous tissue.

These parts are highly sensitive and the cutting causes great agony. The following results of this operation have been seen by one or other of the undersigned during medical practice in Kikuyu Province. [The four names were: Dr Arthur, Dr Irvine, Dr W. M. Brown, Dr Elwood L. Davis.]

Of lesser evils, infection of the bladder with danger of spread up to the kidney. Sterility owing to impossibility of sexual intercourse. Plastic operations have been frequently performed by us for this condition.

The most serious results, however, occur during childbirth. It should be remembered that at the birth of the child's head extreme stretching takes place, especially if there is some abnormality in the delivery. The hard fibrous ring resulting from circumcision hinders this stretching so that (1) the delay, especially in first birth, leads in some cases to the death of the child. (2) Such delay where skilled help is not sought, is treated in certain districts by incisions by the woman attending. These are sometimes made so that the bowel passage is cut into and the patient cannot retain her motions. In all cases the wounds become septic and increase the danger to infection inside which may be fatal or lead to prolonged suffering and sterility. We have treated many first births where owing to female circumcision the child could not have been born without either tearing or incisions.

Another evil result of the frequent delay at the outlet as described is that in certain districts, at the least suggestion of delay, the old women make deep and often unnecessary incisions.'

In *Facing Mount Kenya,* pp. 133 and 135, Kenyatta had this to say about female circumcision:

'The real argument lies not in the defence of the surgical operation or its details, but in the understanding of a very important fact in the tribal psychology of the Kikuyu—namely, that this operation is still regarded as the very essence of an institution which has enormous educational, social, moral, and religious implications, quite apart from the operation itself. For the present it is impossible for a member of the tribe to imagine an initiation without clitoridectomy. Therefore the abolition of the surgical element in this custom means to the Gikuyu the abolition of the whole institution . . .

The abolition of *irua* will destroy the tribal symbol which identifies the age-groups, and prevent the Gikuyu from perpetuating that spirit of collectivism and national solidarity which they have been able to maintain from time immemorial.'

Covenant and Resolutions by the PCEA, 1969

THE COVENANT OF UNITY AND LOYALTY

Believing that as members of the Church of Christ we are called to answer the challenges of any given hour, and in view of the troubled state of affairs and unrest in the country, we the people of God now subscribe to the following covenant of loyalty to God and our country.

a. We confess our supreme allegiance to Jesus Christ, Son of God, King of Kings and Lord of Lords as revealed in the Scriptures.

b. Recognising His command to render to Caesar the things that are Caesar's and the teaching of His apostles that the authorities that exist have been instituted by God and are due to be given such respect, service and obedience as is compatible with a God-fearing life, we pledge unfailing loyalty to the President, His Excellency Mzee Jomo Kenyatta and his government elected in accordance with the Constitution of the Republic of Kenya.

c. We pledge to serve the land of Kenya with our goods and our abilities and promote the national welfare of all its peoples, engaging to our utmost in the task of nation building.

d. Since the service of God involves loving our neighbour as ourselves, we stretch out the hand of brotherhood and fellowship to people of every other tribe and race, to foster unity and combat division, and to conduct our lives and work without discrimination or favouritism to any, accepting ability, experience, conduct and character as the sole criteria for public office or private position.

e. Believing the word of God that 'righteousness exalts a nation and sin is a reproach to any people', we affirm that we will conduct our responsibilities in whatever place we find ourselves, as loyal citizens and residents, not deviating from truth, honesty, decency, integrity and diligence and renouncing all acts of violence, lies, theft, murder, bribery, nepotism, intemperance, secret oaths or societies and any form of corruption as incompatible with our duty to God and our land of Kenya.

We shall support, uphold and defend the Constitution of the Republic of Kenya, allowing ourselves the right to criticise, when necessary only through constitutional means.

f. Believing that in all acts of conduct the word of God as revealed in Jesus Christ is our supreme rule, we admit that of ourselves we lack power to live righteously or to fulfill the demands of this Covenant, we call upon God to give us grace to live to these demands that we now make with Him and before Him, realising that we shall answer to Him in the day of judgment. God so help us.

DRAFT RESOLUTION

This extra-ordinary meeting of General Administration was summoned in order to show the views of the Church in conjunction with the oathing currently taking place in Kenya and particularly in the Central and Eastern Provinces.

The General Administration Committee after listening carefully to the concrete and substantiatable evidences concerning acts of beating, coercion, brutalised treatment and inhuman torture to people—Christian and non-Christian—being forced to take the illegal Kikuyu oath, it was unanimously agreed to state:

(a) that it is our strong conviction based on the understanding conscience and also the freedom provided under the Constitution of Kenya, that such an oath is contrary to the fundamental basis and belief of our Christian faith.

(b) that the only purpose that this oath can achieve in our judgment is the revival of sectional interests in conflicts which cannot build the unity of Kenya as a nation.

(c) That it is a contravention of the safeguards of religious and human freedom provided under the Constitution of Kenya.

The General Administration Committee on behalf of the highest Court of this Church now resolves:

(a) that the Presbyterian Church of East Africa cannot subscribe to such an oath, especially when one is forced against his conscience;

(b) that a confidential letter be presented to the President of the

Republic, His Excellency, Mzee Jomo Kenyatta on his return
from holiday giving a detailed account of some of the brutalities
that have affected members of the Church.

(c) that all members of the Church be invited to declare their
loyalty to the Government and to the Lord of the Church by
signing a document of Covenant to be signed by all Church
members in public worship, which document is shown [above].

(d) That the whole Church use Sunday . . . as the day of Special
prayer for our country confessing our failure and that of the
whole nation 'to love our neighbours as ourselves'.

(e) As a matter of great national importance, we urge that the
Parliament be convened immediately to discuss the situation.

ACKNOWLEDGEMENTS AND SOURCES

I am most grateful to the following.

For permission to use their private papers: Mrs J. W. Arthur and Mr David Arthur, Mrs Nan Barlow, Miss Margaret Bryan, Miss E. Buxton, Mrs Cicely Hooper and Mr Cyril Hooper, Mr Geoffrey Husbands, Mrs Edna Kenyatta and Miss Margaret Wambui Kenyatta, the late D. N. Pritt QC, Mr Peter Ross and Miss Dinah Stock.

For translating material from Kikuyu and Swahili: Canon Cecil Bewes, Miss Margaret Bryan, Revd Robert Macpherson, and friends in Kenya.

For reading portions of the manuscript and for averting a number of errors: Canon Cecil Bewes, Miss Margaret Bryan, Revd Robert Macpherson, the late D. N. Pritt QC, Mr and Mrs Peter Ross, Miss Dinah Stock.

The archives I have used are referred to in the notes as follows:
    Arthur Papers, Edinburgh University
    Barlow Papers, Edinburgh University
    CMS—Church Missionary Society, London
    COS—Church of Scotland, Edinburgh
    CO—Colonial Office Files, Public Records Office, London
    Colonial Project, Oxford—Oxford University Colonial Records Project, Rhodes House, Oxford
    KNA—Kenya National Archives, Nairobi
    PCEA—Presbyterian Church of East Africa, Nairobi
    University History Department, Nairobi

I am grateful to the archivists concerned for their assistance and patience.

I am greatly in debt to the many Africans who allowed me to question them about their experiences and so to add to the narrative the colour and detail I could never have found elsewhere. It will be obvious where these sources are reproduced in the text and I have not annotated them. I offer here my warm thanks to them all, but I should especially like to mention:

James Beauttah, Waruhiu Itote, Bildad Kaggia, Bishop Obadiah

Kariuki, Job Muchuchu, Gideon Mugo, Revd Charles Muhoro, the late Revd Musa Gitau, Canon Nathaniel Gachira, Samson Njoroge, Tiras Waiyaki.

I must also thank Mr Joseph Murumbi for allowing me to use his private collection of books and documents on Africa. They include many rare pamphlets. I have used his typed copy of Francis Hall's letters for chapter 2 and various important documents connected with the Electors' Union for chapter 19. Mr Ambu Patel was a never-failing fund of background information. His two publications *Jomo the Great* (Nairobi, 1961) and *Struggle for Release Jomo and His Colleagues* (Nairobi, 1963) contain much that I have not seen else-where. Mr Charles Kasaja Stokes gave me generously of his time and his memories in Kampala, as did Mr T. R. Makonnen in Nairobi.

While I was in Kenya I received help and hospitality from many British expatriates and Kenya citizens. I am sure they will understand if I do not name them and I hope they will respect my reasons if there are places where I have not followed their views. I must, however thank Mr Harold Gardner for taking me through the surviving glades of the Thogoto forest and interpreting for me the language of the trees as the Africans understood it before the arrival of the white man.

I am grateful also to Aziz Islamshah and his friends for their practical assistance. He has shown me how valuable a tool the camera can be in research work.

I am no less grateful for the help I have received in Britain in discussions or correspondence, from Professor David Abercombie, Mr Horace Alexander, Lord Brockway (Fenner Brockway), members of the Cadbury family, Professor Raymond Firth, Lord Hemingford, Miss Rita Hinden, Miss Dorothy Holloway, Miss Beatrice Honikman, the International African Institute, Mr C. L. R. James, members of the Korda family, Dr L. S. B. Leakey, Rt Hon. Malcolm MacDonald OM, Revd George Mackenzie in Dundee, Prince Peter of Greece, Miss Myrtle Radley, Save the Children Fund, Miss Charlotte Stone, Miss Mary Trevelyan, Professor A. N. Tucker and the School of Oriental and African Studies, the Lutterworth Press, University College London, Mr Frederic Warburg.

I can provide no comprehensive bibliography. The literature of the periods and subjects covered by this book is immense and growing. I have not read more than a fraction of it. A useful bibliography may be found in *The Myth of Mau Mau,* by Carl G. Rosberg and John

Nottingham (New York, 1966). I list below the published works on which I have principally relied. To them must be added newspapers, periodicals and pamphlets, always indispensable sources of detail. My thanks are due to the British Museum Newspaper Library, Colindale, London, the *East African Standard* Library and the Macmillan Library, Nairobi, the libraries of the Foreign and Commonwealth Office and of the Royal Commonwealth Society, London, the London Library, and the Library of Rhodes House, Oxford.

KENYATTA'S PUBLICATIONS

Facing Mount Kenya (Secker and Warburg, 1938)

My People of Kikuyu and the Life of Chief Wangombe, first published by the United Society for the Propagation of the Gospel in 1942. I have used the reprint by the Oxford University Press, 1966, for which page references are given.

Kenya: The Land of Conflict, published by the International African Service Bureau in 1945.

Suffering Without Bitterness, an officially sponsored work, published in Nairobi, 1968, containing some useful biographical information and a collection of speeches.

Chapters 25–29 of *The Phonetic and Tonal Structure of Kikuyu* by Lilias Armstrong (London, 1940), contain various texts written by Kenyatta relating to Kikuyu life, to which reference is made in the text.

Kenyatta's letters, articles and other newspaper material are referred to throughout.

GENERAL WORKS COVERING THE WHOLE PERIOD

Kenya: A Political History, by George Bennett (London, 1963), an admirable, concise study.

The Presbyterian Church in Kenya, by Robert Macpherson (Nairobi, 1970), a short, but scholarly and balanced survey by a missionary of great experience.

African Afterthoughts, by Sir P. M. Mitchell (London, 1954), an instructive autobiography by an enlightened Governor of Kenya.

The Myth of Mau Mau, by Carl G. Rosberg and John Nottingham (New York, 1966), a valuable guide which draws on African sources inaccessible to most researchers from the West.

History of Kenya's Trade Union Movement to 1952, by Makhan Singh (Nairobi, 1969) , a useful collection of documentary material, much of it from Kenya newspapers.

For the general political background in Britain I have mostly used A. J. P. Taylor's volume in the *Oxford History of England,* and for an economist's interpretation of British imperialism E. J. Hobsbawm's fascinating *Industry and Empire* (London, 1968) .

Mention should also be made of George Delf's *Jomo Kenyatta: Towards Truth about 'The Light of Kenya'* (London, 1961) . Written at a time when Kenyatta's future was still uncertain, this work is inevitably dated. But it was the first attempt to bring Kenyatta's whole life into perspective and for many years it was the only reference available.

Finally a word about the official paper *Historical Survey of the Origins and Growth of Mau Mau,* by F. D. Corfield (Cmnd 1030, 1960) . This is commonly called the *Corfield Report,* which is how I refer to it, and I have provided a separate note on it under chapter 20. No one interested in the subject should fail to read this document.

The use of other official reports, Blue Books and Command Papers is self-evident.

PART I

General works which I have found helpful include: Elspeth Huxley's two-volume biography of Lord Delamere, *White Man's Country* (London, 1935) , her evocative *The Flame Trees of Thika* (London, 1959) and *Red Strangers* (London, 1939) . Though she calls the latter a novel, no one has provided more sympathetic insights into the minds of the Kikuyu people as they watched the arrival of the white man. They match Karen Blixen's *Out of Africa* (London, 1937) as classics of the period. A useful balance to them is *Kenya From Within,* by W. McGregor Ross (London, 1927), a meticulous and powerfully argued indictment of the politics of white settlement from one who was closely connected with Kenyatta in London. *Kenya,* by Norman Leys (London, 1924) was the first book seriously to challenge the settler philosophy. M. F. Hill's *Permanent Way: The Story of the Kenya and Uganda Railway* (Nairobi, 1950) provides a wealth of detail on the opening-up of East Africa from the 'development' aspect; while *The Missionary Factor in East Africa,* by

Roland Oliver (London, 1952) is a penetrating study of an important aspect of the same theme.

For the Kikuyu background in chapters 1, 3 and elsewhere, I have drawn on *With a Prehistoric People,* by W. S. Routledge (London, 1910), *The Akikuyu,* by Father C. Cagnolo (Nyeri, 1933), *Kenya: Contrasts and Problems,* by L. S. B. Leakey (London, 1936) and the same author's *Mau Mau and The Kikuyu* (London, 1952), and *Kikuyu Social and Political Institutions,* by H. E. Lambert (London, 1956) in addition, of course, to Kenyatta's own writings. I have supplemented these authorities with reading from John Boyes's *Kings of the Wa-Kikuyu,* edited by C. W. L. Bulpett (London, 1911, reissued 1968), and in a wider context from John S. Mbiti's *African Religions and Philosophy* (London, 1969).

For the background to imperialism and the politics of white settlement in chapters 2, 5 and 6 I have relied on W. L. Langer's *Diplomacy of Imperalism* (New York, 1935). Margery Perham's *Lugard: The Years of Adventure 1858–1898* (London, 1956) and *Lugard: The Years of Authority 1898–1945* (London, 1960) are massive and authoritative. *Pax Britannica,* by James Morris (London, 1968) gives a vivid and perceptive impression of the British Empire at its height. The establishment of British rule in Kenya is well covered in G. H. Mungeam's *British Rule in Kenya 1895–1912* (Oxford 1966), with interesting material also to be found in *Kenya: From Chartered Company to Crown Colony,* by C. W. Hobley (London, 1929) and *The King's African Rifles,* by Lt.-Col. H. Moyse-Bartlett (Aldershot, 1956), and for credulous reading Colonel R. Meinertzhagen's *Kenya Diary: 1902–1906* (London, 1957).

Most of the early explorers wrote up accounts of their travels, and a useful collection of these exists in the single volume *East African Explorers,* compiled by Charles Richards and James Place (Nairobi, revised edition, 1967). African written sources are thinner. A helpful book is *Ten Africans,* edited by Margery Perham (London, 1936, second edition 1963) which includes an important chapter by Parmenas Mockerie on which I drew in Part II. Mockerie's own book, *An African Speaks for his People* (London, 1934), makes an interesting contribution.

To describe the growth of Nairobi I have used *The early history of Nairobi Township,* by Dr E. Boedecker, a typescript in the Macmillan Library, Nairobi, written in 1936; *Nairobi—Jubilee History 1900–1950,* also in the Macmillan Library; and *Nairobi: City and*

Region, edited by W. T. W. Morgan (Nairobi, 1967). *The Man from the Cape,* by Norman Wymer (London, 1959) is Grogan's biography. The official history of the First War is given in *Military Operations in East Africa Vol. 1,* compiled by Lt.-Col. Hordern (London, 1941).

The story of the Scottish Mission in chapter 4 is fully documented in the quarterly journal *Kikuyu News,* which starts in March 1908 but includes regular contributions on Kikuyu custom and the early history of the mission. Both *Kikuyu 1898–1923* and *Kenya 1898–1948,* the semi-jubilee and jubilee books of the Church of Scotland Mission, contain material from this missionary journal; Elizabeth Hewat's *Vision and Achievement 1796–1956* (Edinburgh, 1960) gives the wider context; *A Saint in Kenya: A Life of Marion Scott Stevenson,* by Mrs Henry E. Scott (London, 1932) is a moving account of the woman who probably first taught Kenyatta at the mission, written by the widow of the man in charge of it when he first came there; *A new day in Kenya,* by Horace R. A. Philp (London, 1936) is another eyewitness account from a man personally acquainted with Kenyatta both when he was a boy and later. To these Presbyterian accounts may be added *Kikuyu Conflict,* by T. F. C. Bewes (London, 1953), and *The Cross over Mount Kenya,* by Keith Cole (Nairobi, 1970), a short history of the Anglican Church in Kenya. For the wider context I have found Stephen Neill's *Christian Faith and Other Faiths* (Oxford, second edition 1970) helpful, particularly chapter 6, and John Taylor's *The Primal Vision* (London, 1963) full of insights. L. B. Greaves's *Carey Francis of Kenya* (London, 1969) covers the whole period and is important on the influence of the Alliance High School on the generation of African politicians who took over at independence.

For Harry Thuku and the beginnings of African politics in Kenya, in addition to the works already cited, I should mention *Kenya's Opportunity,* by Sir E. W. M. Grigg (Lord Altrincham) (London, 1955), and *East African Rebels,* by F. B. Welbourn (London, 1961), an important study of the relationship between colonial politics and the growth of independent African churches with substantial sections devoted to the Kikuyu. *Harry Thuku an autobiography* (Nairobi, 1970) consists of tape recordings edited by Kenneth King and is an invaluable, if tantalizing, source. I was unfortunately unable to see Thuku before he died in June 1970, but I am grateful to Kenneth King for his assistance.

PART II

The sources for Part II are largely unpublished and are of two kinds: first, what can be found in the archives of the Colonial Office and other bodies, and second, in private hands. Both are listed above. The Ross Diaries supplemented by the Ross Papers in the Colonial Project, Oxford, cover the period up to 1935 when Ross broke with Kenyatta. No detailed references to these are normally given since the date and location of the source are obvious from the context. Arthur, Barlow and their colleagues all kept detailed records. They are rich in material on Kenyatta up to his return to Europe in 1931. There are also notes in Barlow's hand of his meetings with Ross in May 1930, and with John Cook in August the same year. Copies of the same letters are often to be found in the PCEA archives, Nairobi, in the archives of the Church of Scotland, Edinburgh, and in the Arthur and Barlow private papers. The PCEA archives in Nairobi contain all the material from their old mission stations and are in the course of rearrangement. File references are therefore impossible. For simplification only the letter date, writer and recipient are given. The Anglican missionaries were less methodical in their records, but most of the relevant material can be found at CMS headquarters in London.

The report of the Kenya Native Affairs Department for 1929 included a strong criticism of the Church of Scotland missionaries. It accused them of launching an attack on 'the ancient Kikuyu custom' of clitoridectomy and on the Kikuyu Central Association 'to which they were fanatically opposed', and of provoking 'a state of public disorder'. Partly to answer these criticisms the Church of Scotland Mission Council late in 1931 produced its own memorandum. It runs to seventy-five pages, with seven appendixes, and is a masterly summary of the material and an invaluable source. No fair-minded reader can fail to be impressed by the force of the Scottish missionaries' case; nevertheless the popular view has long been the one expressed in the official report of 1929. I have drawn freely on this memorandum in chapter 11.

Two books should be mentioned. *Winter in Moscow* by Malcolm Muggeridge (London, 1934) has been described by A. J. P. Taylor as 'probably the best' book written about Soviet Russia by an eyewitness of Stalin's collectivization policy (Taylor, op. cit., p. 348). Muggeridge was in Moscow at exactly the same time as Kenyatta. *Black Revolutionary,* by James R. Hooker (London, 1967) gives as much information on George Padmore as the author could glean without seeing Padmore's own papers (presumably still in Ghana).

PART III

For the general picture special mention must be made of two autobiographies. First, Sir Michael Blundell's *So Rough A Wind* (London, 1964), a well documented and frank account from this attractive personality. I am grateful to Sir Michael for allowing me to look at his papers deposited with the Colonial Project, Oxford. Second, *Not Yet Uhuru,* by Oginga Odinga (London, 1967), a balanced and valuable account from the opposite point of view by an important figure in Kenya's politics. Its last chapter, dealing with the period since independence, is controversial. Tom Mboya's *Freedom and After* (London, 1963) adds to the picture.

Fenner Brockway's *African Journeys* (London, 1955) and Negley Farson's *Last Chance in Africa* (London, 1949) are both helpful for the period covered by chapter 19. *Mau Mau Detainee,* by J. M. Kariuki (London, 1963), and *The Hunt for Kimathi,* by Ian Henderson and Philip Goodhart (London, 1958) are useful for the Emergency. Three articles by Bildad Kaggia in *Drum* for January, February and March 1971 give his experiences; *'Mau Mau' General,* by Waruhiu Itote (Nairobi, 1967) is also important.

For the Kapenguria trial, I have referred in the text to D. N. Pritt's autobiography, Vol. 3 *The Defence Accuses* (London, 1966) and Montagu Slater's *The Trial of Jomo Kenyatta* (London, 1955). Both are essential.

Kenyatta's Country, by Richard Cox (London, 1965) is an eyewitness, if somewhat journalistic, account of the hand-over to an independent Kenya.

Malcolm MacDonald's *Titans and Others* (London, 1972) has a chapter on Kenyatta which is revealing in ways not altogether intended by the author.

In the notes that follow I have tried to strike a balance between the requirements of the specialist and what might add to the interest of the general reader. References to sources are therefore only given when these might otherwise be hard to place.

NOTES

CHAPTER 1

1. Kenyatta, *My People of Kikuyu*, chapter 1.
2. The first European explorers used Kamba guides who did not pronounce the 'r' and 'g' in Kere-Nyaga. Hence when asked the name of this mountain they answered 'Kenya', which is what the Europeans then called it.
3. Macpherson, op. cit., pp. 2–3. But if the Kikuyu had taken this route it is strange that it left their technology so retarded. Perhaps further comparisons between language and customs may provide new answers to the Bantu migrations.
4. Macpherson, op. cit., p. 4.
5. Ibid., p. 10.
6. Huxley, *Red Strangers*, p. 105.

CHAPTER 2

1. The year before, Rebmann had reported seeing snow on the top of Kiliman-jaro. But geographers in London refused to believe the missionaries. One wrote in 1852: 'With respect to those eternal snows on the discovery of which Messrs Krapf and Rebmann have set their hearts, they have so little of shape or substance, and appear so severed from realities, that they take quite a spectral character.'
2. Somaliland was brought under British Protection for strategic reasons in 1887.
3. The Chairman of the company, Sir William Mackinnon, had long enjoyed the confidence of the Sultan of Zanzibar. In 1872 Mackinnon's British India Steam Navigation Company brought Zanzibar into regular contact with India and Europe. In 1877 the Sultan offered Mackinnon a monopoly to run his trading activities for him with virtual commitment to British sovereignty. But the British government turned down the suggestion as they had done every attempt to involve Britain in similar East African adventures, and Mackin-non declined the offer.
4. This was the route used by Burton, Speke and Grant.
5. In 1881 a Swahili caravan of 300 men was annihilated by Masai near Lake Elmenteita in the Rift Valley. Only three men survived. The caravans were financed by Arabs but largely composed of Swahili. It is unlikely the Swahili organized them independently.
6. Ngongo Bajas was a corruption of two separate place names: Ngong, being the nearby hill, and Bagas being 'Mbagathi', the branch of the Athi River which rises in Ngong. It is preserved in Embakasi, the name of Nairobi's international airport.
7. Lugard appeared to think his method was in some way different from a 'writ-

[401]

ten compact' made on company treaty forms. It is hard to see where the difference lay. In much the same way Rhodes successfully bamboozled Lobengula, chief of the Matabele, and so justified his drive across the Limpopo. Lugard's 'treaty' would have served the same purpose if a man of Rhodes's will had been behind the IBEA Company and the Kikuyu had stood in his way.

8. According to Macdonald, the leader of the railway survey party who was instructed to report on Lugard's actions, Lugard 'chose the site more from political than military considerations, as he considered that there would be less chance of friction with the natives if the fort was not actually located amongst their clearings. By this means he also hoped to be able to influence the Masai, who could hardly venture to visit a station in the midst of their hereditary enemies, although they might go to Dagoretti with safety.' It seems as though Lugard considered the Masai to be the greater danger. Dagoretti was no-man's-land.

9. According to Lugard, it was actually where Lugard himself pitched camp on first arriving among the Kikuyu.

10. The disasters appear to have struck the tribes at different times. The worst period for the Kikuyu was from 1897. Ainsworth estimated that 15 per cent of the southern Kikuyu died.

11. Swahili scholars are sceptical of this explanation of the word's meaning. Originally it seems to have meant no more than 'white man', and its subsequent association with turning round and busyness may have come from an ironic observation of his activities. The Kikuyu word *Muthungu*, plural *Athungu,* is given in Kikuyu/English dictionaries as a meaning 'rough, overbearing and conceited', also as 'master' or 'boss'. This, too, may have come from observation, or it may be the true Bantu origin from which it passed into Swahili some time in the late fifteenth or sixteenth centuries when the white man first appeared off the coast of East Africa.

12. Justice cannot be done here to the forces of public opinion mobilized by the CMS in England. See Oliver, op. cit.

13. The Bill which gave the final go-ahead to the railway received its third reading in August 1896.

14. According to Sir Charles Eliot.

CHAPTER 3

1. See Routledge, op. cit., pp. 11 and 12. Routledge obtained the list from one of the first missionaries.

2. The railway's descent of the Rift escarpment was constructed between May 1900 and November 1901 and was the most spectacular of all the operations connected with the railway. Many Kikuyu were used for gang labour; they were regarded as the best of the tribes for this purpose. European planters at the coast also relied upon Kikuyu and Luo labour as local tribes were found to be useless. Kenyatta's description of the first Kikuyu travellers to the coast appears in *My People of Kikuyu and the Life of Chief Wangombe,* chapter 3 of the latter section. In this account he also wrote 'the Arabs tried, sometimes with success, to kidnap men and women, whom they lured with glittering promises to go with them to the coast, and then sold them into slavery.' Was this Kenyatta's own experience? He once told a close friend a story of

how as a young boy he had been attracted by Nairobi and the chance of more rewarding employment than tending his harsh 'step'-father's homestead. Arabs offered him work at the coast. He boarded the train. But something warned him of danger—perhaps a fellow tribesman on the platform. As the train made its way slowly across the plains he seized an opportunity and jumped down on the track. Seeing a party of Africans working along the line, he made his way towards them, only to be greeted with shouts and an arrow which narrowly missed his head, so he turned and ran all the way back in the dark.

3. Huxley, *Red Strangers,* p. 231.

4. The Revd David Clement Ruffell Scott, head of the mission from 1901–07. The Africans called him 'Watenga' from the Chinyanja word *tenga* used by Scott meaning 'to clear away'. His successor, Henry Edwin Scott, 1908–11, was called 'Chichia' because he wore spectacles. It was Watenga whom Kenyatta saw at Muthiga, Chichia who was in charge at Thogoto when he arrived there.

5. Kenyatta's account of the missionary's visit to his village is in a fragment of an autobiographical novel in the possession of Mrs Edna Kenyatta. He referred to it himself in a speech delivered on the Seventieth Anniversary of the Kikuyu Mission, 23 March 1968, a record of which is in the archives of the PCEA. The details of his questioning the paper are taken from this record. The date of his arrival at Thogoto also comes from the PCEA archives. The name Thogoto does not appear in the accounts of the first explorers who camped at Ngongo Bagas, four miles away. By 1910 it was applied generally to this part of the forest reserve and is still so used to this day. Possibly it was a corruption of the word Scotch. But there is a Kikuyu word similar to it which can mean 'to make faltering attempts to speak a foreign language', and 'Thogoto' may be a pun linking Scotch men speaking broken Kikuyu. The mission was sometimes called 'Kwa Thigochi', the place of the Scotch. The Scots at that time were not so sensitive about being called Scotch. But the latter usage has been avoided throughout these pages to avoid giving offence.

CHAPTER 4

1. Mungeam, op. cit., p. 132; for the frustrations of the early administrators, ibid., p. 140.

2. Ibid., pp. 197–8. For the Boma Trading Company, ibid., pp. 167–71.

3. *Kikuyu News* no. 19. Letter from Dr Philp, April 1910.

4. *Kikuyu News* nos. 21 and 22. Kamau wa Ngengi was in the 'Airdrie' bed from April 27 to May 28, 1910.

5. *Kikuyu News* no. 22.

6. On CMS stations Swahili was taught as a second language, being the *lingua franca* of East Africa, and the speaking of English was discouraged. But the Presbyterians made English their second language, which gave rise to disputes when the attempt was made to unite all the Protestant missions.

7. In February 1910 Kamau wa Ngengi was one of seven children attending their first term in Class 3 at Morning School.

8. Mrs Henry E. Scott in *A Saint in Kenya*, p. 122.

9. *Kikuyu News* nos. 36, where the date given is April 1912, 39 and 45. I am indebted to the Minister of St John's (Cross), Dundee, for corroborating this information in his church records. The date given there is December 1910. Two boys, both called Kamau, may have been involved; the *Kikuyu News* reference is to Kamau wa Ngengi and it may possibly have been connected with Kenyatta's taking his vows that Easter. Mrs Watson also had connections with Dundee.

10. This date is based on internal evidence supported by correspondence between the author and Macpherson. The photograph is in the Arthur Papers at Edinburgh University in an album marked 'Kikuyu 1911–1914'. The question of his age, for which this photograph provides a clue, needs to be treated with caution as appearances are so very deceptive, see Appendix A.

11. *Kikuyu News* no. 36. Easter 1912 was on April 7. Arthur refers to Kamau wa Ngengi as one of 'two schoolboys, both of whom have been with us for nearly three years.' The Revd J. Youngson, in *Kikuyu News* no. 38, describes the catechumens' class to which Kenyatta belonged as being encouraging 'for the earnestness of their attention'.

12. In much the same way the governments of independent African states now require university students to take up government-directed posts after completing their studies and as a condition of receiving grants.

13. At regular intervals the grades of up to eight consecutive years were grouped together to form a 'regiment' or age-set of a whole generation. These, too, were identified by some notable event or, often, by the same name as the first of the yearly grades within the set. Kenyatta belonged to the set known as *Kihiomwere*, which included men initiated in 1916 (L. S. B. Leakey was one) when the usual age was around sixteen or seventeen. The word *Kihiomwere* means 'the time the millet crop was blasted (by frost)'. Every twenty-five or thirty years, in a formal ritual called the *Itwika*, the ruling power within the tribe would be handed over from one generation of elders to the next, in an alternating pattern which stretched back to the legendary founders of the tribe. The last hand-over had occurred at about the time of Kenyatta's birth.

14. See church register, where the date has clearly been inserted later. For some reason he was not included in the mass baptism of his catechumens' class in June. It may have been that he was put back over some disagreement— perhaps the quarrel over his name, perhaps some problem over his failure to complete his apprenticeship. The record shows that two of his class, 'through insufficient attendance', and another for not knowing his catechism properly, were penalized in this way. Kenyatta may have been one of them. The names of all those coming forward for baptism were scrutinized by the church elders, fellow Kikuyu Christians, and sometimes candidates were put back at this stage.

CHAPTER 5

1. The railway survey placed Fort Smith as the centre of the line and thought the main station for the highlands would be in its vicinity. The Nairobi

swamp was chosen by engineers because the ground was flatter. See Hill, op. cit., p. 84. The depot was built by Sergeant Ellis whose name is preserved in that of one of Nairobi's streets.

2. Report of the Railway Survey, 1893, Hill, op. cit., p. 91. Portal concluded that the economic argument was poor and did not justify British occupation of Uganda, ibid., p. 113.

3. The exports which the railway was expected to carry were itemized as barley, wheat, coffee, cotton, ivory and rubber. Of these only ivory could be said to be a natural object of trade among the tribes, and then only because of Arab interest.

4. Service charges on the capital sum were finally discharged in November 1925. By then the total cost to the British taxpayer amounted to nearly £8 million. Hill, op. cit., pp. 242–3.

5. Cd 671 (1901). An important document setting out Johnston's evaluation of Uganda in its imperial context.

6. The mind boggles at the possibility of a confrontation between the Stern Gang and Mau Mau! The Zionists were put off by the rawness of the African continent. Ironically, many Jewish refugees from Nazi persecution sought to emigrate to Kenya in the late 1930s; many more were interned in special camps in Kenya during the Palestine troubles of the 1940s. The camps were occupied before them by Italian prisoners of war, and were to be used after them by Mau Mau detainees. The connection between East Africa and Zionism continues with Israel's providing special military advisers in the post-Independence era to several former African colonies.

7. Perhaps white settlement was implied from the start. The railway survey's report mentioned that the proposed route 'would enable the high-lying Guaso Ngishu plateau to be opened up by European enterprise' (Hill, op. cit., p. 89). Portal also referred to the suitability of the climate for Europeans (ibid., p. 100). By 1896 Lord Curzon defended the government's decision to go ahead with the railway by arguing that British colonists were already starting coffee plantations in the highlands (ibid., p. 136). Hardinge's report in July 1897 spoke of the suitability of the highlands for European settlement (ibid., p. 158). The term 'highlands' applied to all the country which ran from the Kamba hills north-westwards to Mount Elgon. It included the Athi plain and the Rift Valley, all of which lay at 5,000 feet and over.

8. Cd 671 (1901). The phrase 'white man's country' was evidently something of a formula for empire-building. Eliot used it in this sense in January 1902—see Mungeam, op. cit., p. 103. It suggests that racial feelings may have been the main source of inspiration to this new phase of imperialism. No one ever pretended that India was a 'white man's country'; but it was her possession of India that entitled Britain to call herself an empire.

9. Legal opinion in 1899 held that the state exercised sovereign rights over land, subject only to a recognition of existing private—i.e. Arab or European —rights. Hill, op. cit., p. 250.

10. Cd 2099 (1904), quoted by Mungeam, op. cit., p. 113. The Masai were thought to number about 50,000, while the Kikuyu were estimated at half a million. Hobley called the Masai the 'human scourges of Africa', Portal, 'an unmitigated curse'.

11. See Meinertzhagen, op. cit., p. 31. 'He's not my idea of a High Commissioner, he looks more like a University Don or priest. He is a scholar, a philosopher, and a very able man with great vision.'

12. Swahili headmen had provided the hard core of the IBEA Company caravans and they acted as intermediaries to slavers, missionaries and government officers alike. Many of the porters engaged were slaves, their masters receiving half the pay (Hobley, op. cit., p. 196 et seq.). The problem of ending slavery was complex. Freed slaves had nowhere to go and no means of supporting themselves. Missions found their presence an embarrassment as they diverted attention from missionary penetration to the tribal centres. Not until 1907 was the legal status of slavery abolished in Kenya; not until 1922 did it finally come to an end in East Africa.

13. Hill, op. cit., p. 265, quoting from Eliot's annual report for 1902.

14. In East Africa imperalism *was* white settlement, whether under British or German auspices. Those who genuinely looked forward to the time when Africans might take their rightful places among civilized men thought in terms of centuries and drew an analogy with the Romans in ancient Britain (e.g. Hobley, op. cit., p. 195). The missionaries, too, accepted Eliot's reasoning. It lay behind Clement Scott's purchase of the 3,000 acre estate at Thogoto, the development of which, he hoped, would make the mission self-supporting and give training to the natives in modern agriculture. In 1936 the mission handed much of the land back to local Kikuyu land-owners, after considerable opposition from the colonial government who, by then, were committed to a policy of *exclusive* white settlement—an idea which was absent from Eliot's thinking. Similarly, French Roman Catholic missionaries were among the first to establish coffee plantations near Nairobi and close to Kenyatta's family estate at Ngenda. Here, too, they developed into an *exclusive* European industry.

15. But the government changed its mind several times over whether civil servants should be allowed to buy land in Kenya. Many did so and retired in the colony, so becoming settlers themselves.

16. In Afrikaans *kaffir* originally meant 'heathen'. It came to be applied in a derogatory sense to all black men. *Sjambok* was a long rhinoceros hide whip used on Boer ox-teams.

17. In the bush of tropical Africa young government officers sometimes used their position to set themselves up with native concubines (Hill, op. cit., p. 303). See also Meinertzhagen, op. cit., pp. 9 and 12.
    'My brother officers are mainly regimental rejects and heavily in debt . . . On arrival here I was amazed and shocked to find that they all brought their native women into Mess . . . there is a regular trade in these girls with the local Masai villages'.

18. Ross, op. cit., p. 63.

19. See early copies of Nairobi's newspapers, e.g. *The African Standard,* for vivid insights into the fears and gambling instincts of the Edwardian pioneer. Wildlife fared no better than the 'niggers'.

20. Delamere's exuberant nature was a byword in Kenya. He bought his own hotel in Nakuru, the settlers' headquarters in the Rift Valley, in order that he

could beat it up periodically with friends after a party. They would buy oranges from an Indian trader and smash all the windows when the guests were asleep.

21. Wymer, op. cit., p. 134.
22. Ibid., p. 140.
23. Ibid., p. 162.
24. Huxley, *White Man's Country*, vol. 1, p. 81.
25. Churchill, *My African Journey*, pp. 21–2.
26. Ibid., pp. 64–5. They are both quoted in Mungeam, op. cit., pp. 188 and 189. The Grogan incident mentioned on p. 61 took place in March 1907. It was one of the factors which prompted Churchill's interest. Grogan's nomination to the first Legco was cancelled.
27. See Mungeam, op. cit., p. 261, for Leys's role.
28. When used as levies in punitive expeditions against other tribes the Masai were allowed to keep a share of the stock collected, the government taking the rest. By 1911 their possessions were estimated at about 200,000 cattle and 2,000,000 sheep (Mungeam, op. cit., p. 285).

    By 1907 anxiety was felt at the Colonial Office at the casualties inflicted by these operations which had resulted in the previous years in at least 2,426 Africans killed, and 28,693 cattle and 64,853 sheep captured, for the loss of only 179 Protectorate forces killed and wounded. In 1908 the use of levies was banned except in exceptional circumstances—Mungeam, op. cit., pp. 176 and 177, whose whole account of this period is very revealing of the underlying assumption that punitive expeditions and white settlement were linked. On page 164 he quotes an earlier Colonial Office minute: 'necessity for this slaughter is no doubt as much regretted by our brave and humane officers in Africa as it can be by anyone in this country.' But, the note went on, 'unless we are going to abrogate our civilizing mission in Africa such expeditions with their attendant slaughter are necessary.' Much the same arguments were still being made fifty years later at the time of the Mau Mau Emergency.
29. Quoted by Mungeam, op. cit., p. 195.
30. Ross, op. cit., p. 98. Ross was writing in 1927 by which time, he said, such 'negrophobe malevolence' would be impossible.
31. Ibid., p. 98.
32. The government of India stipulated that each coolie should be allowed to remain in East Africa if he wished to do so on completion of his contract. Hill, op. cit., p. 147.
33. East Africa was a natural outlet for the goods of the Indian sub-continent, as Johnston recognized. The monsoon trade winds have always brought dhows across the Indian Ocean to Lamu, Malindi, Mombasa and Zanzibar. By 1863 6,000 Indians were resident in the Sultan's territories and much of the slaving was thought to be financed by Indians. The IBEA Company was granted its Charter by Queen Victoria so as to facilitate the trade of 'our subjects in the Indian Ocean, who might otherwise be compelled to reside and trade under the government or protection of alien Powers'. When Britain established her Protectorate over East Africa, Indian warehouses already lined the harbour of Mombasa, beneath the rusting guns of Fort Jesus.

34. Jeevanjee did so well out of it all he presented the town with a marble statue of Queen Victoria.

35. Wymer, op. cit., p. 144.

36. The railway had later to be realigned due to the spread of the town. It was replaced by what is now Uhuru Highway. Survivors of Ainsworth's tin offices can be seen near the University. Victoria Street is now Tom Mboya Street.

37. It was called Station Road at first but changed its name to Government Road when Ainsworth moved across the papyrus swamp away from the unhealthy site first offered him by the railway company north of the Nairobi River.

CHAPTER 6

1. It was said later that these maps were deliberately falsified.

2. Unpublished thesis by B. G. McIntosh, 'The Scottish Mission in Kenya', p. 414, in Edinburgh University Library, quoting letters in PCEA Nairobi.

3. The Colonial Office refused permission to the Governor, Sir Percy Girouard, to build this railway. He thereupon changed its description to a 'tramway' and under this pretence secured the necessary sanction.

4. Elspeth Huxley, *The Flame Trees of Thika*.

5. A foolish attempt by the administration to dragoon them into service in September 1918 nearly led to full scale rebellion in the Narok district.

6. While in Scotland Arthur was ordained into the ministry of the Church of Scotland.
   It took three porters to keep one rifleman at the front. A machine-gun could fire off one porter's load of ammunition for the day in one minute. (Mitchell, op. cit., p. 40 et seq.) In *Kikuyu News*, no. 65, 3 November 1917, Arthur wrote from the front: 'It is a "Porters' War" that is being waged out here, and everything depends on them.' Mitchell, too, wrote of the sense of guilt which many British officers felt at the way African porters suffered.

7. Elspeth Huxley, *White Man's Country*, vol. 2, p. 41–2.

8. Jomo Kenyatta, *Facing Mount Kenya*, p. 210.

9. Fifteen rupees amounted then to about £1, a handsome gift in those days. K. N. Johnstone was the normal way baptized Africans styled themselves. K. N. represented Kamau wa Ngengi.

CHAPTER 7

1. Norman Wymer, op. cit., p. 190–1.

2. Elspeth Huxley, *White Man's Country*, vol. 2, p. 36.

3. *East African Standard*, 25 October 1919. 1,500 of them arrived at Nairobi, after Christmas in four special boat-trains. The hotels were so full that camps had to be set up outside Nairobi. The impact on the Africans must have been considerable. In 1925, of the 1,246 farms allocated only 545 were still occupied by their original owners (Hill, op. cit., p. 379 and Ross, op. cit., p. 82).

4. The government's brochure advertising East Africa included a short paragraph on 'Domestic Servants':

'African or Indian servants can be engaged. The wages vary, but they have a tendency to rise. The wages of a native servant were estimated in 1917 at from Rs 10 to Rs 15 a month. The African native always prefers a short highly paid job to permanent work at a more moderate rate.'

(General Information as to the East African Protectorate. HMSO Pamphlet issued by Oversea Settlement Office, 1919.) £1 was then worth 16 rupees.

5. Elspeth Huxley, *Red Strangers*, p. 185.

6. In 1911 Kioi possessed some 127 huts and there were 60 men, 116 women and 243 children living on his land. (Kikuyu District Political Record Book quoted in *Nairobi: City and Region* by W. T. W. Morgan, p. 60.)

7. Kenya Law Reports, vol. 8 p. 129 et seq. C.C. 132/1920. Kenyatta's role is not mentioned in the law report but comes from other sources. This is the origin of the legend that he was once an interpreter at the Supreme Court. The original papers relating to the case do not appear to have been preserved.

8. Kenya Law Reports, vol. 9 (part 2) p. 102. C.C. 626/1921. The matter did not rest there but was pursued in further cases involving complex legal arguments. The principal Kikuyu landowners of southern Kiambu were pleased with the judgement in Kioi's case, but worried about their own rights and they wrote accordingly, through the Kikuyu Association, to Grigg, 25 November 1925 (KNA PC/CP 8/5/1, and PCEA G1). The subject of Kikuyu land tenure was immensely complex, especially in this district where custom differed from elsewhere in Kikuyuland.

The Thogoto mission was involved because of the purchase of its 3,000-acre estate. Barlow made an exhaustive study of the question, and the whole subject formed the central body of the evidence taken by the Carter Land Commission in 1932–3.

9. Figures according to the official census for 1921 were: European males 5,800, females 3,851; Asiatic males 24,342, females 11,640. Europeans in agriculture numbered 1,893, Asiatics 498. But in all other walks of life the Indians vastly outnumbered Europeans, e.g. in Industry and Commerce: Europeans 1,496, Asiatics 9,765; in Government and Municipal offices: Europeans 1,082, Asiatics 3,390.

Though the European *rate of increase* was higher than that of Indians (29.8% as against 14.25% between 1921 and 1926), the total proportion of Indians remained overwhelming:

in 1921: 35,982 Asiatics against 9,651 Europeans
in 1926: 41,140   "   "   12,529   "
in 1931: 57,135   "   "   16,812   "

10. Report of Uganda Development Commission (1920). Quoted by Ross, op. cit., p. 325.

11. Thuku, op. cit., pp. 5–6 'The Arabs came selling that brass wire in exchange for elephant tusks. They called it *ruthuku*. So my grandfather took that name.' Kenyatta used the word *Thokomo* as the name given by the Kikuyu to the Arabs in the time of Wangombe. (*The Life of Chief Wangombe*, p. 54 et seq.)

12. Ross, op. cit., p. 191.

13. In June 1921 the rickshaw boys came out on strike for the weekend. They

all worked for Indian masters who, no doubt, encouraged them in this action. But many other Africans quit European employment in protest at the cuts.

The settlers also mounted a campaign against the imposition of an income tax upon themselves, in which they were successful. To their rage, Ross, Kenya's Director of Public Works, refused to sanction the cut in his department, which was a large employer of Africans.

14. Macpherson, op. cit., p. 73.
15. In imitation of the Young Baganda movement which attracted his interest. It was featured in the *East African Chronicle*.
16. *East African Chronicle*, 20 August 1921.
17. Cmd 1691 (1922).
18. Thuku corresponded for a time with Desai. Many years later he came to take a more sceptical view of the Indians and it may have been that during his long term of exile, during which he fell under the influence of an exceptionally wise English officer, he saw that they had been using him for their own ends. See Macpherson, op. cit., p. 82, note 78.
19. Sir Robert Coryndon was a life-long admirer of Cecil Rhodes whose private secretary he had once been (Hill, op. cit., p. 398).
20. Oliver op. cit., p. 250. Oldham was the first secretary of the Conference of Missionary Societies which established a permanent headquarters for the world-wide missionary movement.
21. The material is in the PCEA archives, Nairobi. It makes fascinating reading. The Kenya missionaries were near-unanimous in their opposition to Indian claims. But in London C. F. Andrews, of the Cambridge Mission to Delhi and a notable opponent of racial discrimination, who had suffered from settler abuse in Kenya, argued powerfully on behalf of the Indians. He had been included in *their* delegation. Oldham's task was to reconcile these conflicting missionary interests.
22. *Kikuyu News*, no. 85.
23. It was an ironic echo of what Northey had said when the racial trouble first began. He then told an Indian delegation: 'the principle had been accepted at home that this country was primarily for European development.' In a letter he confirmed this view by stating: 'European interests must be paramount throughout the Protectorate.'

CHAPTER 8

1. *Kikuyu News*, no. 58.
2. Thogoto Church Register.
3. *Kikuyu News*, no. 58.
4. It seems he never sought readmission to the church, though he was considered a member of it. See PCEA G/2—Statement by Dr Philp to Committee for the Protection of Coloured Women in the Crown Colonies, 10 April 1930, Appendix 2.
5. Philp in *Kikuyu News*, no. 145: 'Well I remember our young Kikuyu friend one day jumping off his bicycle in the streets of Nairobi in order to give me a cordial greeting.' Philp was reviewing *Facing Mount Kenya* unfavourably and was recalling his earlier impressions of Kenyatta.

CHAPTER 9

1. For a long time there was no church at Fort Hall. Hooper held Communion services in the DC's office for the few who cared to attend. In 1961 Fort Hall became the seat of the Anglican diocese of Mount Kenya and its Memorial Cathedral Church of St James and All Martyrs is one of the most beautiful churches in Kenya.
2. T. F. C. Bewes, *Kikuyu Conflict*, p. 19.
3. Thuku, op. cit., Document 8, p. 85. An official translation of the same prayer made at the time is in Cmd 1691, 1922.
4. Beauttah was an anglicized version of 'Mbuthia'.
5. The method of 'election' used in some areas was to place candidates in a field at intervals of about fifty yards and then get their supporters to line up behind them. A simple head count revealed the winner (see KNA PC/CP 8/5/1 letter of La Fontaine, 26 May 1931). The majority of LNC members, of course, were illiterate. (Official Report, 1931.)
6. One DC had to forbid the elders of his district from taking it by their traditional *thenge* oath, which consisted of beating a goat slowly to death.
7. Rosberg and Nottingham, op. cit., p. 97, quoting Kangethe. Being excluded from these practices, Europeans read into them sinister motives. The Scottish missionaries attributed the growth of the KCA in Kiambu to a particular initiation generation and Kenyatta's name came to be linked to this and others, and the secret societies which they were suspected of forming. See CSM Memorandum on female circumcision, Appendix 3, and Bennet, op. cit., p. 117.
8. Copies of KCA letters to the government were sometimes also sent to Indian leaders.
9. He may have been the same Macdermot who was once employed as an assistant treasurer by the IBEA Company. This Macdermot was the author of an official book on the IBEA published in 1893 which is quoted at length in a later KCA memorandum which probably originated during this period. See appendix to Mockerie, *An African Speaks for his People*, p. 78.
10. In line with the terms of the Brussels Treaty of 1892, Africans were forbidden to buy spirits. In Nairobi beer could only be sold and consumed at municipal beer halls.
11. Beauttah was writing from Uganda at this time urging the KCA to press for a paramount chief, following the pattern of the tribes in Uganda. Kenyatta went along with this line. But it was quite foreign to the Kikuyu, as the officials were quick to point out, since Kinyanjui's position arose from his close association with the British administration, not from Kikuyu tradition.

    A typed copy of the letter to the mission and drafts of letters about the casket are in the possession of Miss Margaret Kenyatta. Kenyatta's brother was at the mission school at this time, but there is no other indication that he had anything to do with the production of the letter. The letters to the Governor date from late 1926. The jingle is taken from the Hooper papers in the CMS archives, London.
12. The Aga Khan was blackballed from the Nairobi Jockey Club, ostensibly on the grounds that he was too rich.

13. The phrase is Taylor's, op. cit., p. 327.
14. Grigg, op. cit., p. 113. The phrase was coined by the Superintendent of the first English settlement in Canterbury, New Zealand.
15. According to a police report on Kenyatta sent to London on 4 April 1939, 'He was discharged in April, 1926 owing to neglect of duties.' (CO 533/513). The point was not taken up at his trial where Kenyatta said he was with the Water Department until 1928. There is no record of his leaving employment in the Municipal Archives, Nairobi. At his trial Kenyatta was somewhat ambiguous about his first involvement with the KCA. See p. 308 above. He went on to say, in reply to the question 'Did you become a member of the KCA?', 'Yes, in 1928—I think. After the visit of the Hilton Young Commission . . . At that time I was working at the Municipality . . . and so I was faced with two alternatives—to continue working or to join the organisation' (Verbatim transcript 3/879).

Later still, when cross-examined about his entry into politics, Kenyatta again referred to the Hilton Young Commission: 'I cannot tell you whether I gave evidence or I interpreted for those who were giving evidence.' (3/1038).

The pamphlet 'How Kenyatta was sent to Britain by the KCA', a copy of which is in the files of the University History Department, Nairobi, has Kangethe's account of the origin of the KCA and of Kenyatta's involvement. The details remain obscure and appear to relate to an aeroplane landing in a field; but the catalyst seems to have been the Hilton Young Commission.

16. Philp, Statement to the Committee for the Protection of Coloured Women in the Crown Colonies, 10 April 1930.
17. Rosberg and Nottingham, op. cit., p. 99.
18. Cmd 3234, (1929), pp. 92 and 185.
19. KNA PC/CP 8/5/3. Minutes of meeting at Kahuhia, 16 March 1928.
20. 'It seems to have been the first newspaper produced by Kenya Africans'—Rosberg and Nottingham, op. cit., p. 101.
21. CO 533/375, Governor's despatch no. 323 of 22 June 1928, enclosing evidence from witnesses and giving Grigg's comments thereon. Kenyatta's name was variously reported as John, and Johnson, Kinyatta. The government research officer mentioned by Grigg was Watkins, Kenyatta's interpreter. He did not sign the recommendations of the select committee, but put in a long minority report pointing out that what he described as the 'makeshift expedient' of the Crown Lands Ordinance of 1915, intended to control non-native lands, had now taken permanent form as a means of protecting native land rights. But the Africans, said Watkins, could not be expected to understand this legal fiction. Grigg ignored Watkins, another example of his passing over the views of his experts in the field.

The exchanges between the missionaries and the Governor over Grigg's Land Bill are revealing. See the report of the interview between representatives of the Kenya Missionary Council and the Governor on 19 June 1928, and Arthur's letters to MacLachlan, the secretary of the Foreign Mission Committee of the Church of Scotland, especially those of 21 May and 22 June 1928, in the Church of Scotland archives, Edinburgh. According to the report of the interview: 'His Excellency (Grigg) said he was really getting somewhat tired of the Kikuyu and their persistence.' Arthur to MacLachlan, 22 June 1928, pointed out that the Kikuyu who were pressing for title-deeds were concerned only for their own plots and 'are rather inclined to ignore the rights of the majorities who are landless, and the Government must protect these latter somehow, or they become a landless class'.

22. The government sub-station at Dagoretti was in charge of eighteen different officers between 1905 and 1928, during which time it was also closed for three years. The average was therefore about one new officer a year. KNA DC/KBU/3/7. See also Leakey, *Kenya Contrasts and Problems,* pp. 64–9 and Appendix pp. 185–9.

23. Rosberg and Nottingham, op. cit., pp. 100, 101.

24. CO 533/382, Governor's despatch of 26 October 1928. The translation from *Lamentations,* chapter 5, was made by Barlow. It is an interesting illustration of how ambiguous Biblical texts could sound when rendered in Kikuyu.

25. KNA PC/CP 8/5/3—Letter to Governor of 25 September 1928. Kenyatta suggested that Thuku be released as 'an amnesty' to mark the Prince's visit. The latter arrived with his brother, the Duke of Gloucester, at the end of September and Grigg put on the nearest thing Kenya could manage to a durbar.

26. Records of Alliance High School. James Muigai had previously been at the Scottish mission school. As his was the first name to be registered at the Alliance High School, he was known as 'James the First'.

27. CO 533/384. File no. 15540/29 no. S/F 'A'. This file contains all the details about Kenyatta's first visit to London.

28. Krapf's wife and infant daughter died within two months of their joining him in Mombasa in 1844. 'Tell our friends at home', Krapf wrote to CMS headquarters,
'that there is now on the East African coast a lonely missionary grave. This is a sign that you have commenced the struggle with this part of the world, and as victories of the church are gained by stepping over the graves of her members, you may be the more convinced that the hour is at hand when you are summoned to the conversion of Africa from the eastern shore.'
As the Swahili inscription on the cross puts it: 'Thus was the living Church of Christ discovered in this country.' In due course passing sailors used Krapf's wife's gravestone as a target for revolver practice. Crudely plugged with cement, the holes can be made out to this day. To the Christian missionary it is one of the most moving spots in East Africa.

CHAPTER 10

1. Hooper to Maxwell, 31 March 1930, CMS archives. For Solanke see Coleman's *Nigeria Background to Nationalism* (1958), Crowder's *Story of Nigeria* (1962), and Solanke's own *United Africa at the Bar of the Family of Nations* (1927, new impression 1969).

2. As Director of Public Works in Kenya, Ross had come across most of the advanced Africans. He knew Abdulla Taraira well and helped him and his wife when Taraira was arrested during the Thuku troubles. He also knew Thuku and tried to get him to join the Public Works Department when his

Treasury boss put pressure on Thuku to quit politics. Ross also offered James Beauttah a job, which Beauttah declined, preferring to work with the Post Office at Mombasa. After the war Ross was frequently out of Nairobi and when Kenyatta joined the Water Department it had come under the control of the municipal authorities. This was probably their first meeting.

3. CO 533/384. Grigg saw at once that Kenyatta's petition must have been drafted by a European: 'Petitions written by the Kikuyu themselves are very different in character'—Grigg to Shiels, 12 March 1930. This letter of Kenyatta's shows Indian, rather than European, influences.

   In *Kenya: The Land of Conflict*, pp. 12–14, Kenyatta reproduced the major part of his petition, but claimed it was the memorandum presented by the KCA to the Ormsby-Gore Commission. This was not the case.

4. Scotland Yard Report, 18 June 1929, CO 533/384. The police said Kenyatta was 'a representative of the "Universal Negro Improvement Association" and has come to this country to obtain justice for people of his race in Kenya'— an unintended insight! While in London Kenyatta has 'been in the company of Elinor Burns, and S. Saklatvala, the Parsee Ex-MP., prominent Communists. He has also been consulting R. Bridgeman, the Secretary of the British Section of the "League Against Imperialism," a Communist inspired movement'. Saklatvala was related to the Tata steel millionaires and represented North Battersea as a communist in the Parliament of 1924–9. Elinor Burns and her husband were also prominent anti-imperialists. See page 421 et seq. On 8/9 June 1929, the recently set up Imperialism Committee of the ILP 'received a deputation' representing 'the negroes of Africa' and 'promised all support'.

5. Hooper papers, CMS archives.

6. Ibid. Hooper to Miss Soles, 26 September 1929.

7. Kenyatta's articles in the *Daily Worker* 20 and 21 January 1930. Ross's letter is in the *Manchester Guardian,* 20 March 1929. In his *Sunday Worker* article, Kenyetta said, 'In 1922, when native discontent showed itself, bloody suppression was the result, no less than 200 unarmed Africans being shot down by machine gun fire.'

8. The police in Kenya were alerted to his movements through the innocence of Kenyatta's girl-friend, Conie Macgregor. While he was away the KCA cabled for news and she cabled back that he was in Moscow. No doubt it was a tip-off from this source that reached Ross in August and prompted him to look Kenyatta up in Victoria.

9. CO 533/395. Minute of 15 February 1930.

10. CO 533/384. Minute of 2 November 1929.

11. Ibid. Minute of 20 December 1929.

12. Both Shiels and Ross kept a record. Shiel's official note is in CO 533/384, Ross's in CO 533/395 enclosed in a letter to Shiels of 30 July 1930. I have drawn from both.

13. These were upset by the publication of the report of the Hilton Young Commission in January 1929. Thanks largely to the presence on the Commission of J. H. Oldham, the report did not confine itself to the economic effects of Closer Union, which was its brief. It reiterated the 1923 declaration of 'paramountcy' of native interests and looked, however distantly, to full

racial partnership 'on an equal franchise'. On the eve of the General Election Amery sent out Sir Samuel Wilson, Permanent Under-Secretary at the Colonial Office, in an eleventh-hour attempt to rescue his plan. The Labour Party, through Lord Olivier, said they would not feel bound by his report, and by the time he came to make it they had taken over the government.

14. Ross Diary, 1 August 1929: 'Grigg had made a very poor impression on Lord Passfield.' See Bennett, op. cit., pp. 64–76.

15. CO 533/384. Leys to Kenyatta, 31 July 1929. Kenyatta never received this as he was in Moscow. Leys forwarded it to Kangethe, 17 October 1929, which is how it fell into the hands of the police.

16. CO 533/384. Shiels to Grigg, 6 February 1930.

17. CO 533/395. Grigg to Shiels, 12 March 1930.

18. Ibid. Kenyatta to Shiels, 18 March 1930.

19. Ibid. CO to Kenyatta, 27 March 1930.

20. Ibid. Minute of 17 April 1930.

21. As a young man Ross had been interested in the history of his own family. Several of his ancestors were victims of the highland clearances in the nineteenth century and Ross evidently felt an instinctive sympathy for other people's sufferings.

22. *Correspondence between the Kikuyu Central Association and the Colonial Office 1929–1930.* Where the funds came from can only be guesswork. Ross, apparently, never asked, or gave no hint if he knew. He worked closely with Kenyatta on the proofs.

23. Ross to Bolton, 12 March 1930. Ross Papers, Colonial Project, Oxford.

24. H. O. Weller, *Kenya Without Prejudice* (1931) p. 84. Page 25 gave the information that 'shopping is done by visiting the shops'. Neville Chamberlain wrote the foreword.

25. *The Times* also published the letter on 26 March.

26. This phrase was cut out of the letter printed in *Suffering Without Bitterness,* p. 36. Kenyatta was by then President of an independent Kenya.

27. Hooper to Maxwell, 31 March 1930, CMS archives. Ross wrote to Kangethe on 6 February 1930, 'giving a good account of Kenyatta and asking that funds should be telegraphed to him to allow for Kenyatta's sailing back.' They worked out that Kenyatta was living on about £3 per week.

28. Barlow to Arthur, 4 August 1930, and Ross Diaries. Barlow took handwritten notes of his meeting with Ross, which are in the PCEA archives. Aided by Ross, Kenyatta had tried to fix an interview with the Moderator of the Church of Scotland in January, but the day appointed clashed with his interview with Shiels. Ross and the church leaders had a row over it. Barlow was dismayed to find how violently Ross expressed his views in front of Kenyatta. See correspondence in Church of Scotland archives and Barlow to Arthur, 4 August 1930.

29. Barlow to Arthur, 4 August 1930.

30. Barlow to Arthur, 23 September and 30 December 1930. Barlow also took handwritten notes of his meeting with John Cook, August 1930.

31. Less, presumably, the cost of the typewriter for which the bill went to Grigg and which Hooper had now pawned for Kenyatta. Kenyatta's various

IOUs are with the papers of the Anti-Slavery and Aborigines Protection Society, Rhodes House. When looking round for a means of returning to London in December 1930, Kenyatta appealed to these sources for his fare. The treasurer had to remind him that he had yet to repay the original loan. He did so on arrival in May 1931, presumably with the money collected for his trip.

32. Barlow to Arthur, 23 September 1930, quoting from Cook's letter to Barlow.

CHAPTER 11

1. In the Journal of the Royal Anthropological Institute, vol. LXI, 1931, L. S. B. Leakey suggested that a particular difficulty was the Kikuyu word used by the missionaries for the Virgin Mary, as it was the same as was applied by the Kikuyu to girls who had gone through the initiation ceremony and were awaiting marriage offers.

2. The latest revision of rules took place in 1928, when the public profession included the vow:

'Do you declare in truth that you have stopped all customs that do not agree with the Word of God, such as things pertaining to the worship of departed spirits, magic, witchcraft, lewdness, drunkenness, evil songs and dances and the circumcision of women?'

From Christmas 1928 many took this vow without objection.

3. PCEA Nairobi. ADC Fort Hall to DC, 5 November 1925.

4. The Governor's report in 1930 agreed that minor operations were very much the exception, less than one in a hundred.

5. Translation taken from Macpherson, op. cit., p. 108. Arthur took the view that the Tumutumu conference was 'the most direct cause' of the controversy, and Macpherson follows him. But the chain of cause and effect has not been established.

6. See the letter from Stevenson Githii, 'native office assistant' at the mission, in *Kikuyu News* no. 113 entitled 'An Appeal to the Mother Church'. It was written in his own English in a style reminiscent of seventeenth-century polemics.

7. CO 533/392, Governor's Dispatch no. 130, 12 October 1929.

8. CO 533/394, Cable, Grigg to Colonial Office, 22 January 1930. One verse ran: *'Ten thousand shillings were given for Harry; Now the same amount is offered for John.'* It referred to the money which was raised by KCA agents for Harry Thuku, of which he received not one cent. The same 'collections' were now being demanded for 'John' Kenyatta, and with the same empty result as far as he was concerned.

9. The best known was the rising of John Chilembwe in Nyasaland in 1915 which led to the deaths of some estate workers. Chilembwe cut off the estate manager's head and preached a sermon in his own church with the head on the pulpit in front of him.

10. 129 women signed a petition asking for government protection against female circumcision. Of these, 67 were themselves uncircumcized. But the counter

propaganda made skilful use of the word for signing—*Kirore*—which was the same as was used for the thumb printing on the hated *kipande* registration certificates, and the petition had to be dropped. As a result many girls who had stood out against the operation and were therefore beyond the requisite age submitted to it.

11. See Dutton to Shiels, 26 November 1929, in CO 533/384. One cannot fail to be struck by the similarities between this reaction and the reaction of Mitchell and his advisers on the eve of the Mau Mau Emergency. On 4 March 1930, the administrative officers spoke of the Kikuyu as being 'as contented now as they had ever been'. (CO 533/395) Dutton, however, went on to admit that officials were in danger of losing touch with the tribes due to their lack of knowledge of the language and their increasing use of motor transport which took them too fast through country districts. The official complacency also ignored other possible causes of unrest, for instance the laying-off of workers during the economic recession of the world slump, particularly in government services like the railway which reduced its African staff by over 7,000 in 1931 and 32. 1929 was a year of special hardship in East Africa, with drought, locusts and widespread famine. Mitchell was concerned about economic development, but it came too late to forestall the outbreak of the Emergency.

12. The Duchess of Atholl chaired a special Committee for the Protection of Coloured Women in the Crown Colonies which met at the House of Commons. Kenyatta attended this committee on 18 December 1929, and again on 14 May 1930. From December 1929 he was discussing female circumcision with Ross.

13. Ross Papers, Colonial Project, Oxford. This is the English draft. Ross was at work on this letter from early January 1930. He gave it to Kenyatta to translate on 20 January 1930, and then passed Kenyatta's version on to Hooper for checking. It went out some time before 12 March.

14. CO 533/394. Norman Leys, 18 February 1930, wrote to the Colonial Office condemning Philp's medical opinion as 'ridiculously and scandalously exaggerated . . . some people must have atrocities to wallow in in peace time.' Leys's words contrasted strangely with the joint letter he signed.

15. Two accounts of the meeting exist. The notes taken by the secretaries present were found to be full of blanks. From them the secretary of the Foreign Mission Committee produced one version which was largely taken up with the text of Kenyatta's petition which he had laid before them. Barlow found it 'very sketchy' so he produced his own version, which was much fuller, and sent it to Arthur on 8 August 1930. Kenyatta, as was his practice, asked for a record of the meeting and received, after some hesitation, the secretary's version.

16. PCEA Nairobi. Barlow was meant to bring the letter with him, but it was sent through the post instead. When he landed at Southampton, Barlow found Kenyatta waiting at the quayside. He assumed Kenyatta had come down to meet him and Kenyatta did not say otherwise. It turned out he had really come to meet Arthur Konye, a fellow Thogoto product, who was returning as valet to a wealthy Englishman. Konye brought papers for Kenyatta and, perhaps, some money.

17. Kenyatta admitted being present at a meeting in Nyeri in March 1928 when a deal was struck between the KCA and local tribesmen to run female circumcision as an issue in the forthcoming elections to the Local Native Council. Kikuyu loyal to the mission answered the KCA by forming their own Progressive Kikuyu Party and in the election their two nominees headed the poll. Kenyatta's comment on this affair was ambiguous, to the effect that 'no one belonging to the KCA said that the circumcision of women should continue except in the case of heathen; those who are Christian should follow the Christian law.'

18. Arthur to Barlow, 29 July 1930. It seems that the CID in Kenya used Canon Leakey, the CMS missionary at Kabete, as their translator, and that Leakey passed on information concerning Kenyatta to Arthur.

19. PCEA Nairobi, Arthur to MacLachlan, 15 October 1930.

20. Arthur to Barlow, 30 July 1930.

21. Grigg, op. cit., pp. 85 and 89.

22. PCEA Nairobi, Arthur to Kenyatta, 3 October 1930. Arthur wrote in his own hand, and in English.

23. Arthur to Barlow, 12 October 1930, and Arthur to MacLachlan, 15 October 1930.

24. PCEA Nairobi. The record of the meeting was incorporated with this document.

25. Arthur to MacLachlan, 26 February 1931.

26. Despite the Kenya government's attempt to forbid it them, the mission retained the right to include teaching against female circumcision as part of their preparation of catechumens. They could hardly do otherwise since the baptismal vow included the oath mentioned in note 2 above. This dispute with the government in Nairobi marked the parting of the ways between the missions and administration. It illustrates the totalitarian tendency of colonial rule and how the missionary church must ultimately challenge it.

27. KNA DC Kiambu to PC Nyeri, 29 October 1930. Minute of meeting between Director of Education and Kenyatta dated 13 December 1930. This, and Kenyatta's meeting with Arthur, were both against the wishes of the local administrative officer, DC to Arthur, 15 January 1931.

28. Arthur to Scott, 23 December 1930, with enclosures.

29. CO 533/512. Longhand note by H. S. Scott, written in 1939. In 1932 the LNC were authorized to make small grants to assist independent schools. A problem throughout was the land on which schools were built. Under existing legislation all land in the reserves was held in trust by the Crown. Recognition of individual land rights—the thing Kikuyu landowners were pressing for—raised the question of ownership of mission out-schools and other buildings. See Welbourne, op. cit., for the independent church and school movement.

30. 'Archbishop' Alexander of the Ethiopian Church. He arrived in November 1935 and stayed with James Beauttah in Mombasa. See Welbourne, op. cit., and Rosberg and Nottingham, op. cit., p. 129–30. The word *Karing'a* had made its appearance twelve months before the controversy broke out. See p. 125.

31. Arthur to MacLachlan, 26 February 1931.

32. Arthur mentioned that when Kenyatta first came to see him at the manse he was followed later in the day by an African policeman off duty at the mission who wanted to know on what business Kenyatta and his associates were engaged.

33. Through representations by the Colonial Office, Grigg was forced to ease these restrictions some months after making them; but this was not generally made known to Africans.

34. Memorandum from Acting Inspector of Schools to DC Fort Hall, 17 March 1931, Colonial Project, Oxford.

35. Kenyatta asked if he might photograph a school (he had already done so on arrival). Answer, No. Might he photograph the children? No. The Kikuyu, like most Africans, hate being asked direct questions. As for photographs! Anyone engaged in television work will recognize Kenyatta's problem in turning up uninvited with a camera.

36. CO 822/31.

37. Beecher to Hooper, 8 May 1931, CMS archives.

38. Ross used his native name in signing the cable, presumably to fool the police.

39. CO 822/33. Minute by A. C. C. Parkinson, 29 April 1931, and Moore to Parkinson, 2 May 1931.

40. Hooper to Pitt-Pitts, 7 May 1931, CMS archives.

CHAPTER 12

1. Was she a friend of Ross's? Her name appears among the guests at a tea-party at the Rosses which Kenyatta attended. Perhaps Ross put the Colonial Office in touch with her.

2. CO 822/33.

3. Charles Roden Buxton to Lord Onslow, 7 October 1931, 'Re. Appendix to E. A. Report'. The memorandum itself is in CO 822/30. It was dated 6 April 1931, and was the one Kenyatta prepared in Nairobi and sent to London for Ross's approval (see p. 174). As it 'whole heartedly supports the British Imperial Policy regarding Closer Union', it was not held to add anything to the official evidence given by Koinange.

4. Philip Mitchell, who was to be Governor of Kenya when Kenyatta eventually returned to Nairobi after the Second War, was also at this conference, and met Kenyatta. They did not, however, make any impression on each other.

5. CO 822/33.

6. CMS archives, Hooper to Pitt-Pitts, 4 September 1931, and 7 October 1931.

7. Horace Alexander and his wife, in particular.

8. Ross, too, corresponded with Gandhi, and a regular visitor to his home was the missionary C. F. Andrews, Gandhi's friend and biographer. Kenyatta often met Andrews out at Hampstead. Churchill's remarks were made in a speech to West Essex Conservatives in February 1931. He said how nauseating it was 'to see Mr Gandhi, a seditious Middle Temple lawyer, now

posing as a fakir of a type well-known in the East, striding half-naked up the steps of the vice-regal palace, while he is still organizing and conducting a defiant campaign of civil disobedience, to parley on equal terms with the representative of the King-Emperor.'

9. The DC, to whom Ross's enquiries eventually found their way, replied to his chief that the charges were 'fantastic lies'.

10. Ross to Kenyatta, 14 May 1932.

11. Ross found Carter 'somewhat unalert and with slight pro-settler sympathies'. He went to great trouble to prepare maps for him and put him on the track of other information. See CO 533/424 for Carter's change of plan. On 4 June 1932, he issued a notice in the Press inviting anyone wishing to give evidence in London and installed himself with a stenographer in a room at the East African Trade and Information Office in Cockspur Street.

12. *Kenya Land Commission: Evidence and Memoranda Vol. I* (Colonial No. 91) p. 422 et seq. The whole of this volume of evidence on the Kikuyu makes absorbing reading. Many of the first white men to live in Kenya, like Dr Boedeker, recorded their early experiences. Kikuyu, Masai and Wandorobo witnesses in Kenya vied with each other in their claims of what was their original land and in their accusations of lying by the others. Kenyatta's evidence was in keeping with the vast majority of Kikuyu witnesses and the map which he submitted, and which was included in the published evidence, appeared to be an enlarged section of the map which Harry Thuku also submitted. On this, the boundaries of old Kikuyuland allegedly extended far to the north and west of Mount Kenya and into the Athi Plain to take in Donyo Sabuk. A section from Kenyatta's memorandum to the Colonial Office of 24 February 1932 was also printed in the volume of evidence. It was forwarded to Kenya, Dispatch No. 210, 15 March 1932, and a reply from the Governor eventually reached the Colonial Office on 19 September. Kenyatta by then was with Padmore in Europe. See CO 533/422.

13. Kenyatta's name—Johnstone Kamau—was crossed off the Thogoto Register on 15 October 1931. Arthur later said he was 'excommunicated' and this phrase gave rise to the brief that Kenyatta was in some way formally anathematized by the Scottish missionaries because of the female circumcision controversy. This does not appear to have been the case. The deletion of his name, although with many others, was a routine matter of keeping the records up to date.

CHAPTER 13

1. Ford, in the pamphlet referred to below, note 2, asserted that the ITUC-NW originated in Moscow in 1928 at the Sixth World Congress of the Communist international after preliminary work by negro delegates to the RILU Congress held earlier in the year, also in Moscow. It is uncertain whether Padmore came to Moscow as early as 1928. When he was arrested by German police in February 1933, Padmore's passport showed that he left America on 26 November 1929. But it is impossible to say if this was a genuine passport. It was in his own name of Malcolm Ivan Nurse and had been issued in New York. It appears that he made at least one return trip to America after

visiting Europe and that he left finally without his wife and child. Britain's new Labour Government resumed diplomatic relations with Soviet Russia in October 1929.

2. See pamphlet *A Report of Proceedings and Decisions of the First International Conference of Negro Workers, Hamburg.* The date was July 7 and 8.

3. Hooker, op. cit., p. 18, who says that after the smashing of the German communists the house was taken over by a missionary society.

4. Another name listed was 'M. E. Burns, Transport Workers' Union, England, probably Emile Burns whose wife Elinor had been reported by the Special Branch to be in Kenyatta's company soon after his arrival in 1929.

5. *East Africa,* 18 June 1931, vol. 7, no. 352.

6. Ford was nominally the editor of the *Negro Worker* for its first issues. Padmore took over in the summer of 1931.

7. FO 372/2910. It is said that Padmore spent some months in a Nazi prison. It is likely that this is an exaggerated reference to the few days which followed his arrest when a suitable ship was awaited to take him to England.

8. See Kenya Police Report attached to Governor's letter of 4 April 1939, in CO 533/513.

9. Muggeridge, op. cit., p. 39.

10. *Suffering Without Bitterness,* p. 33.

11. *Manchester Guardian,* 4 July 1929, 'A Negro in Russia'. See *Sunday Worker,* 7 July 1929, for a rebuttal.

12. He told Negley Farson, *Last Chance in Africa,* p. 113, that he stayed at the Lux Hotel where all visiting Comintern members and students were housed.

13. Hooker, op. cit., pp. 31 et seq. Evidently the ITUC-NW was not disbanded at once, since its journal, the *Negro Worker,* published the attacks on Padmore in the summer of 1934. This remains one of the most obscure periods in Padmore's life—as in Kenyatta's.

14. See note 8 above.

15. All accounts agree that Kenyatta's approach was a narrow one and confined to his own people. This was his strength, though at the time others thought it made his perspectives too limited. For a fascinating discussion of what he calls 'The Fantasy of Black Nationalism' of American negroes, see an article by Theodore Draper in the American Jewish periodical *Commentary* for September 1969, vol. 48, no. 3. For violence as the only answer to the colonial experience, see, for example, Fanon's *The Wretched of the Earth* (*Les Damnés de la Terre*), first published in France in 1961 when Mau Mau was still fresh in people's minds.

16. For example, a talk by a 'member of the Board of Soviet African Friendship Association' on Moscow Radio's English for Africa service, 13 February 1960, and the article by Professor I. Potekhin, Director of Moscow's Africa Institute, dated 9 February 1961, in *Struggle for Release Jomo and His Colleagues,* p. 98. Neither says anything of interest.

17. C. L. R. James remembers Kenyatta with tears in his eyes after hearing on the BBC of the death of a famous Russian flyer (Lunachevsky?). But he also understood that Kenyatta quarrelled violently with the Russians over their cruel treatment of a South African negro who had come to Moscow illicitly and was at the Russians' mercy.

CHAPTER 14

1. *East African Standard* (Weekly Edition) , 27 May and 3 June 1933.
2. *Kenya Land Commission,* vol. 1, p. 221. The KCA in Nairobi also submitted a memorandum to the Carter Commission on 1 December 1932, signed by Harry Thuku as President and George K. Ndegwa as 'Hon General Secretary and Treasurer'. This was the same as the one Mockerie said he and Kenyetta had been deputed to carry to London on behalf of 'The Kikuyu Land Board Association'. Mockerie printed it as an Appendix to his book *An African Speaks for His People* because, he said, it was not published in the report of the joint select committee. But the memorandum which Kenyatta brought with him, dated 6 April 1931, was quite different. See note 3 to chapter 12. Kikuyu politics were in great confusion at this time. On 11 November 1932, Gideon Mugo asked the Carter Commissioners if Kenyatta had given evidence in London and was told he had. Evidently he did not pass this information along to the others. See also note 12 to chapter 12.
3. Thuku to Buxton, 10 March 1933. Note in pencil 'sent to M R'.
   Ironically, Thuku's name appeared in the pamphlet of the Hamburg Conference in July 1930, one of four 'Honorary members imprisoned or waiting conviction for activities connected with the struggles of Negro Toilers'. The addition of his name must have been Kenyatta's doing.
4. CMS archives. Hooper to Pitt-Pitts, 22 June and 1 August 1933. Other details concerning Mockerie's visit to London are also to be found in these archives. The Government appointed Mockerie a chief and he made no further contribution to Kikuyu politics.
5. CMS archives, Hooper to Pitt-Pitts, 12 September 1933.
6. Ibid.
7. CO 533/513, Governor's letter and enclosure, 4 April 1939.
8. CO 533/422.
9. KNA PC/CP 8/5/3/, PC (Horne) to DC Embu, 12 January 1934.
10. As note 7 above.
11. J. Kenyatta was shown as being a member of the editorial board of this issue of the *Negro Worker.*
12. *Labour Monthly,* November 1933, vol. 15, no. 11.
13. CO 533/437.
14. CO 533/446.

CHAPTER 15

1. See p. 149.
2. He was fortunate also in that in 1932 the University's School of Oriental Studies received a Rockefeller grant which enabled it to expand its study of African languages. The staff recruited were quick to seize on Kenyatta to help them. Kikuyu was a new and testing field for them. In 1935 the grant was extended and the name was changed to School of Oriental and African Studies.
3. *The Phonetic and Tonal Structure of Kikuyu* by Lilias E. Armstrong. It was published by Oxford University Press in 1940 for the International In-

stitute of African Languages and Cultures. Kenyatta was credited in a preface as 'an interested, patient, and critical native assistant' who 'discharged his duties excellently'.

4. Hooper papers. Kenyatta to Hooper, 7 December 1933. Hooper always spelt Kenyatta's name with an i, its original Kikuyu form, which is how Kenyatta signed himself when writing to him—J. Kinyatta.

5. Ross Papers, Colonial Project, Oxford. Mrs Hocken never received payment. Years later her husband recalled that Kenyatta finally left owing them about £200. After he had become President of Kenya, Mr Hocken wrote reminding him of this ancient debt. There was no reply.

6. She was Mary Trevelyan whose book, *From the Ends of the Earth* (London, 1942) provides the source for this account of the hostel.

7. *Sanders of the River,* p. 7. It was one of a series of books featuring Commissioner Sanders and Bosambo.

8. The film had its première at the Leicester Square Theatre on 2 April 1935.

9. *Paul Robeson* by Marie Seton (London, 1958), p. 81. On p. 97 Seton says that Robeson walked out of the opening night of the film. Others present do not corroborate this. See note 13 below.

10. *Paul Robeson* by Edwin P. Hoyt (London, 1968), p. 80. See also his account for Robeson's part in the film and visit to Russia.

11. Kenyatta would have enjoyed Robeson's famous song:

> On, on, into battle
> Make the war drums rattle
> Mow them down like cattle
> On, on, into battle
> Bring them into the dust, into the dust
> Charge, kill, shoot, spill
> Smash, smite, slash, bite
> And slay.

See also an interesting article by Robeson in *New Statesman and Nation* 8 August 1936, entitled 'Primitives', which discusses the African's vital creative processes. Africans ought to be able to take what they need of the West's technology while building on their own cultural traditions. It is an argument strikingly similar to the one Kenyatta was later to make himself.

12. To Dinah Stock.

13. Korda maintained the closest personal relations with Robeson all his life. After Korda's death his son found an unsigned letter on his desk which he had just written to congratulate Kenyatta on leading his country to independence. He forwarded the letter to Nairobi but received no acknowledgment.

14. According to Prince Peter of Greece. Kessie and Robeson's wife, Essie, were also members for a time.

15. *Punch,* 17 July 1963, article entitled 'Africana—Tribal Drums'.

CHAPTER 16

1. Many of these are incorporated in earlier chapters.

2. See p. 416, note 1 to chapter 11. Kenyatta's description of pre-marital sex

play between Kikuyu boys and girls, called *ngweko*, pp. 157–60, is taken directly from Leakey's article. Compare also p. 153 of *Facing Mount Kenya* with Leakey.

CHAPTER 17

1. *An Occupation for Gentlemen*, by Frederic Warburg (London, 1959), pp. 251–4. I am grateful to Mr Warburg for giving me this reference. The remaining 1,500 unsold copies, he writes, 'languished in our warehouse until destroyed by bombs in 1941'. But see p. 342 for 'present disaster' which became 'future success'.

   Ross reviewed it favourably in *The Friend*, September 1938. Isabel Ross was disappointed in it. Ross was declining in health. In 1940 he died of a brain tumour. Barlow's comment is in the Barlow Papers, Edinburgh University. Arthur's views are in a letter to Keigwin of the Lutterworth Press, 27 December 1939,

   'What I remember is the Kikuyu filth, physical and moral, which produced smallpox, and terribly yaws-sore bodies, periods of famine, a people bound by fear of evil spirits, degraded, with polygamy and all that that means in village life. All that is hidden in J.K.'s book under a veneer of an ideal African home life. It is untrue.'

2. The world of Kenya politics was a small one. Coincidentally, Ross's son Hugh was at Cambridge at this time and became friendly with Peter Mbiyu Koinange.

3. See Koinange's contribution to *Struggle for Release Jomo and His Colleagues*, compiled by Ambu H. Patel (Nairobi, 1963) for details of his meeting with Kenyatta. In the photograph which became the frontispiece of *Facing Mount Kenya*, Kenyatta is clearly holding a real spear. The idea evidently appealed to him, and Warburg tells how Kenyatta turned up at his door for dinner one night carrying it and wearing a leopard skin, somewhat to the surprise of his hostess.

4. James arrived in London in 1932 to report cricket for his Trinidad newspaper. He was an obvious candidate for Padmore's Moscow course, but the two men missed seeing each other then and Padmore recruited Kenyatta instead. But James was a follower of Trotsky.

5. Dinah Stock remembers Kenyatta half jestingly, half seriously, quizzing a distinguished aircraft designer—who happened to be a communist—on the most effective way of sabotaging an aeroplane on the ground with a spear.

6. The Emperor came via Jerusalem where he prayed at the Coptic Church for his restitution. It was a reminder to Africans of their historic ties with a Christian tradition that did not depend on the European 'mission'. It is worth recalling that precisely at this moment Archbishop Alexander of the African Orthodox Church was ordaining ministers to the independent church/schools in Kenya. See p. 171. See also Welbourne, op. cit., for this important religious element in the Pan-African movement.

7. Which was to have a happy sequel more than a quarter of a century later when Kenyatta welcomed Haile Selassie as the first Head of State to visit self-

governing Kenya. Kenyatta used to tell his African audiences that his cloak was a gift from the Emperor. See p. 271.

8. *Ethiopia: Liberation Silver Jubilee* (Addis Ababa, 1966), pp. 37 and 42.

9. An original IASB brochure, 'For the Defence of Africans and Peoples of African Descent', is in the Creech Jones papers, Colonial Project, Oxford, in a circular letter dated 17 June 1937. At one time or another Padmore engaged the interest of many of the future leaders of Britain's colonies as they passed through London: among them Dr Williams, a future Prime Minister of Trinidad and Tobago, Dr Azikiwe, a future President of Nigeria, and the economist, Arthur Lewis, then a junior lecturer at the London School of Economics.

10. As late as 28 July 1937, Kenyatta was still giving his address as 95 Cambridge Street. See letter from Creech Jones to Kenyatta, Colonial Project, London.

11. For these moves see CO 533/462, 533/466, 533/476, 533/487, 533/488. White Kenyans commonly referred to the Kikuyu as 'kukes'. At a *baraza* in May 1936 at the CMS mission near to Koinange's land the Carter proposals came under heavy attack from the Kikuyu. Why not call them the 'Black and White Highlands' they asked, and allow Africans to buy land there as well?

12. CO 533/502, letter of 7 May 1939, to Governor. See also letter of 9 November 1938, for joint protests from all sections of the Kikuyu, together with representatives of other tribes.

13. The Kamba were the first of the tribes to be formally limited to a reserve.

14. CO 533/492.

15. Creech Jones papers, Colonial Project, Oxford.

16. CO 533/487 and CO 533/501 contain the material on Kenyatta. The *New Statesman and Nation* letter was dated 25 June 1938. The civil servants assumed that 'Kenyatta is, of course, the mouthpiece of W. McGregor Ross'. The Archbishop of York was among those who wrote to the Colonial Office querying Kenyatta's activities.

17. CO 533/513, 'Kenya No. 49' of 4 April 1939. Among other unverifiable statements it referred to Kenyatta's being discharged from the Nairobi Corporation in April 1926 'owing to neglect of duties'. The City archives show no record of this, but they are incomplete. See p. 122 and note 15 to chapter 9.

18. Malcolm MacDonald, of course, was a member of National Labour and a supporter of his father, but he shared in the forward-looking ideas of men like Drummond Shiels. Baldwin brought him into the Cabinet.

19. CO 533/467.

20. CO 533/488, and CO 533/516, report by Wyn Harris, 17 June 1939.

21. See Hill, op. cit., p. 520, and, for example, the phrasing of the Kamba protest against Muindi's arrest: 'it makes persecution of Hitlerite Germany', CO 533/492. Grogan was one of the passengers on the inaugural flight of Imperial Airways in 1932. It took him eight days to fly from Cairo to the Cape. Beneath him, he wrote, lived people still 'the first step from apedom' (Wymer, op. cit., p. 210).

22. It is likely that Kenyatta discussed this with Paul Robeson after their experiences together in *Sanders of the River*.

23. CO 533/513. An unfortunate misprint on the new KCA writing paper gave their motto as 'Prey and Work', which caused mirth at the Colonial Office (CO 533/506).

24. Letter from C. W. Guillebaud, 15 March 1937, and minutes, CO 533/484. The Colonial Office analysis was perfectly correct. Yet in the *Kikuyu News* of March 1938, no. 143, the missionaries could write: 'Messrs. Mathu and Koinange, both old boys of Alliance High School, are keen Christians, who have a great future ahead of them in the uplift of their people.'

25. In July 1939 Creech Jones forwarded a letter from Koinange senior to the Colonial Office with the comment that it expressed 'feeling, apprehension, and a sense of grievance'. CO 533/502.

26. Letters in the possession of Miss Margaret Kenyatta dated 28 March, 8 May, 11 August, 1939. The letter of 8 May was from the Grand Hotel du Regent, Paris—'I'm staying about a fortnight in France—for talks.'

CHAPTER 18

1. Makhan Singh, op. cit., p. 95.
2. CO 533/506, CO 533/516, CO 533/518, cable dated 27 May 1940.
3. Kenyatta to Creech Jones, 25 August 1941, Creech Jones Papers, Colonial Project, Oxford.
4. *Bexhill Observer*, 18 October 1941, report of a speech by Kenyatta to the Heathfield Branch of the National Union of Public Employees.
5. *Hastings Evening Argus*, 18 May 1942, to another meeting of the National Union of Public Employees, this time in Horsham.
6. It was to be called 'White Man's Magic', and he gave chapter 1 the title of 'The Magical Arrow'. See p. 45.
7. Pp. 25–6 and 58. What Kenyatta attributed to Wangombe contrasts with John Boyes's account of the Kikuyu chief's attitude: 'Why all this humbug? The country is yours. What's the use of humbugging about like a woman' (Boyes, op. cit., pp. 202–3). See also Wangombe's son's evidence to the Carter Commission, Vol. 1 Evidence p. 92.

   The booklet was commissioned by the United Society for the Propagation of the Gospel as the first in a series by Africans about their own country. Unknown to Kenyatta, the editor of the series, Keigwin, consulted Arthur about his manuscript, whose views are interesting (Arthur to Keigwin, 27 December 1939. See note 1 to chapter 17). The booklet duly appeared in March 1942 and brought Kenyatta the grand total of £5. The correspondence over his contract showed that he intended using the material as part of his larger work on Kenya.

8. Elspeth Huxley's phrase.
9. Hooker, op. cit., p. 60.
10. Ibid., p. 66.
11. *Listener*, 26 August 1943.
12. Hooker, op. cit., p. 89.
13. See the pamphlet *History of the Pan-African Congress*, second edition 1963.
14. C. L. R. James assumed that Padmore wrote the whole pamphlet, as James and others had always taken a hand in composing Kenyatta's letters and writ-

ings for him. It is not without interest that Padmore's pamphlet *Hands Off the Protectorates* has sometimes been attributed to Kenyatta, and Kenyatta did not correct this when it occurred in the officially sponsored book *Suffering Without Bitterness*.

15. It has been said that Kenyatta's return was made possible through the intervention of Eliud Mathu on an official visit to the Colonial Office. It is as likely that Kenyatta himself stalled, and with the same objections as he put up in 1930—the fear that he would be arrested on arrival and exiled.

16. The tension this situation created drove Paul Robeson to Moscow, just as Padmore and Kenyatta were quitting international communism, and eventually into mental breakdown. Padmore later became Nkrumah's adviser on Pan-African affairs. Though distressed by the nature of Nkrumah's rule, he stuck it out until his death in 1959. Peter Abrahams lampooned Padmore in *A Wreath for Udomo* as Lanwood, 'a prosperous west end clubman', who turns out to be hopelessly at sea in colonial Africa. By remaining in America, James kept closer to the Black Power movement. He never forsook his Trotskyist belief in world revolution and felt a weary disillusion at what he considered the reactionary nature of Kenyatta's rule in independent Kenya. Abrahams retired to Jamaica.

17. She lost the baby.

CHAPTER 19

1. Hill, op. cit., p. 568.
2. Rosberg and Nottingham, op. cit., p. 196.
3. It was completed in 1933.
4. In November 1946 at the annual Caledonian Dinner on the subject 'The land we live in'.
5. To his son Peter Muigai, 1 September 1946.
6. Before the war about 60 per cent of African workers were engaged on European farms and able to maintain something of their traditional way of life. About 40 per cent worked in towns. By 1946 the proportions were reversed. The average wage in 1946 for an African in Nairobi was under ten shillings a week, on European farms under five shillings.
7. Boys at the Alliance High School were refused permission to line the road to welcome Kenyatta home, but the children from one of the independent schools—the one where Eliud Mathu had been headmaster—were out in force and sang a specially composed song of greeting.
8. But Peter Mbiyu Koinange signed a letter pledging loyalty to the British government in the war—see Thuku, op. cit., p. 64.
9. He was allowed to return secretly in 1960 for a brief visit while his father was dying.
10. Another Koinange son died during this period. Rumour suggested he was the victim of a Mau Mau sacrifice during some grim moonlit ceremony at Banana Hill. It is more likely he accidentally shot himself and was buried secretly to avoid trouble with the police. See Corfield, op. cit., p. 166.
11. For Kenyatta and Koinange, see the latter's contribution to *Struggle for Release Jomo and His Colleagues.*

12. Notably, *Mumenyereri,* edited by Henry Muoria, and pamphlets. The manifesto was dated 25 October 1946.

13. During the Mau Mau Emergency it was found that supporters of Mau Mau came in equal numbers from independent and mission schools. See Welbourne, op. cit., p. 160 et seq.

14. Farson, op. cit., p. 113. Chapter 11 throughout gives a good journalist's impression of Kenyatta's situation at this time.

15. They had already met in Geneva. See p. 178 and note.

16. It is not clear why the ban on the KCA was not lifted. Perhaps Kenyatta did not press for it, preferring something less overtly Kikuyu in inspiration. A document was produced at his trial which purported to show that in 1948 Kenyatta was in touch with KCA cells and still called himself their leader. These underground cells certainly continued throughout this period.

17. KAU's three formal resolutions condemned the restrictions placed upon Africans in the enjoyment of democratic rights; demanded the abolition of the *kipande;* and called for equal racial status for all 'citizens' of the colony. But the *East African Standard* headed its report of the meeting with the words: UNITED AFRICAN FRONT TO WIN FREEDOM FIGHT.

18. *East African Standard,* 6 October 1948.

19. Farson, op. cit., p. 115.

20. Odinga, op. cit., p. 98.

21. *East African Standard,* 16 June 1950.

22. KNA DC/KBU/1/38, Kiambu District Annual Report for 1947 by E. H. Windley, and KNA DC/KBU/1/40 for 1949 by N. F. Kennaway.

23. See Corfield, op. cit., p. 80. The missionary responsible for this interpretation was Revd Martin Capon. He passed it on to the Electors' Union (file in Murumbi archives). The phrase appears to have been taken from a pamphlet produced by Muoria under the auspices of *Mumenyereri* entitled *Kenyatta ri muigwithania witu* (Kenyatta is our Counciliator). In this Kenyatta is twice quoted as referring to weevils and corn, once to the Kamba at Machakos, and once to the Kikuyu at Nyeri. The word translated as 'Christianity' could also mean denominations or sects or religions *(Dini).*

24. *East African Standard,* 18 August 1948.

25. See Minutes of Electors' Union in Murumbi archive.

26. See, for example, *East African Standard,* 19 September 1947, for an emergency meeting called by Kenyatta to discuss illegal strike action.

27. Rosberg and Nottingham, op. cit., p. 246 et seq. Oaths of some kind also played a part in Chege Kibachia's strike activity.

28. In February 1947 he was elected President of the Kikuyu Age-Groups at Githunguri. At the time of his conviction he was chairman of the building committee of Githunguri.

29. Many different explanations have been given of the origin of the word *Mau Mau.* The most bizarre which has been brought to the notice of the author links the word with certain practices of South Sea Islanders which only Kenyatta could have picked up during his anthropological studies in London. The one in commonest currency in Kenya is derived from the Kikuyu habit of using code language, as in children's riddles, in which the letters of words are transposed out of their correct order. According to this theory, *Mau Mau*

was first used by a sentry at an oathing ceremony. When surprised by police and instead of shouting 'UMA UMA', meaning 'OUT OUT', he cried 'MAU MAU'. Far-fetched though this may seem to European readers, it is widely attested among the Kikuyu, and it illustrates the futility, in the author's view, of attributing too great a significance to the world itself.

30. See *Corfield Report,* p. 166, and L. S. B. Leakey, *Defeating Mau Mau* (London, 1954), p. 77. Leakey's book goes into considerable detail over the methods and organisation of Mau Mau and gives valuable translations of Kikuyu nationalist propaganda, including their 'hymns' etc. referred to below.

31. Makhan Singh, op. cit., p. 262.

32. Article by Kaggia in *Drum,* no. 237, January 1971.

33. It must be remembered that the administration relied heavily on African police and informers. This was what indirect rule meant.

34. 30 April 1952, according to Corfield, op. cit., p. 62.

35. Appendix F in Corfield gives the verbatim account of this Nyeri meeting as reported by Henderson, the European police inspector present. *Suffering Without Bitterness,* p. 50, adds the gloss on the meaning of the Kikuyu expression to 'know'.

36. Corfield, op. cit., p. 129.

37. *'Mau Mau' General* by Waruhiu Itote (General China) (Nairobi, 1967), p. 44 et seq.

38. See Itote, op. cit., pp. 49–80 for the beginnings of the forest bands and the forest oaths. His Appendix A, "The Meaning and Use of Oaths", gives further details. See also Kariuki, op. cit., p. 25 et seq. for another African account of oaths. See the *Corfield Report* and Leakey, *Defeating Mau Mau,* for the European interpretation.

39. A copy of a letter in which this phrase was used came into the hands of Murumbi who picked out the word 'liquidation' with a pen. In this form it was reproduced by Koinange in his booklet *The People of Kenya Speak for Themselves* published in America in 1955. The letter was dated 7 August 1952, and reputedly was signed by Kendall Ward, Executive Officer, and addressed to The Chairman, Elected Members' Organization. Koinange debated with Kendall Ward in London on 31 December 1953, at the Central Hall, Westminster, and produced the letter.

40. Members of Moral Rearmament (MRA) played a curious role. They were multi-racial in their approach but failed to make as much impact on Africans as did the East African Revival, which was authentically African in origin. Whereas the latter induced humility and a pietistic attitude towards political affairs, MRA was highly political and fanatically opposed to communism. Its European members tended to be at once starry-eyed about any Africans who came to Caux (and who could resist the offer of an expenses-paid flight to Europe?) and intolerant of those who refused. Mathu and some from the west coast of Africa fell into the former category, Kenyatta into the latter. Fred Kubai, curiously, accepted the offer to visit Caux at this time. At his trial he said he just wanted to see what went on there.

41. See Abraham's article in the *Listener,* 21 August 1952.

42. For this reason the meeting was well covered and many accounts exist of it.

There is no important discrepancy in the different reports. I have taken Koinange senior's speech from the version given by his son in *The People of Kenya Speak for Themselves.*

43. Corfield, op. cit., p. 153.

44. Ibid.

45. See Odinga, op. cit., pp. 100 et seq.

46. See press reports and Thuku, op. cit., p. 68 et seq. Waruhiu's last speech is quoted from another, private, source.

47. Through contacts in the telegraph service the Africans knew something was up. But Mathu, the African member of the Governor's Executive Council, or quasi-cabinet, was excluded from the meeting when the key decisions were taken. There was also a rumour that Kenyatta was to be assassinated at Waruhiu's funeral—presumably by Europeans. In a photograph of the graveside service he is standing beside a European who was allegedly a member of the Special Branch. But whether this man was present to watch Kenyatta's movements or to safeguard him from attack is not known. Nor has the truth of the rumour been established—it was one of several of a similar nature concerning Kenyatta.

48. There were 183 names on the list. Eight were already under arrest for other offences. 'By nightfall' of 21 October, ninety-nine had been accounted for. The decree authorising the arrests ran from midnight, but it seems that Kenyatta was actually detained before this. He referred to that night in a speech in Nairobi on its anniversary in 1967, when he mentioned the tip-off that he was going to be thrown from the aeroplane. (*Suffering Without Bitterness,* p. 340). It was a universal fear among the witnesses brought up to Kapenguria for his trial; it is possible the Italians resorted to this device for ridding themselves of prominent Ethiopians during their brief period of control in Addis Ababa, from whence it became one of the standard accusations levelled against all colonial regimes.

CHAPTER 20

1. At the trial the prosecution said that Kungu Karumba, one of the accused was also a member of KAU's executive, thus plainly indicating that the Emergency measures were aimed against the political leadership of KAU. But it seems Karumba was not on the national executive of the party.

2. It is important to remember here and elsewhere that the prosecution at Kenyatta's trial were unable to prove that there were any rites that were specifically Mau Mau.

3. *The Hunt for Kimathi* by Ian Henderson (London, 1958) with Philip Goodhart, a Conservative MP. Men who knew Kimathi in the forests thought he was a monomaniac.

4. A cousin of L. S. B. Leakey, Gray Leakey and his wife, were murdered by Mau Mau in October 1954. Gray Leakey's body was not found until some weeks later, when it was unearthed, head downwards. He was apparently buried alive and the nature of his death suggested that it was a placatory sacrifice of someone the Kikuyu loved.

5. Letter of 23 October 1952, in possession of Miss Margaret Wambui Kenyatta. Wambui was Kenyatta's mother's name. Following Kikuyu custom, the first daughter born to each of his wives was named after Wambui. As it happened he had three daughters by three wives. They were known respectively as Margaret Wambui, Jane Wambui and Christine Wambui.

6. The government had some difficulty in finding anyone to accept the post of resident magistrate to try the case. Several good lawyers 'begged to be excused', and finally it selected R. S. Thacker QC, who had recently retired from the Supreme Court of Kenya. He was a man committed to the colonialist philosophy.

7. It is not clear how Kenyatta got word out. Fenner Brockway paid Kenya a visit shortly after the Emergency was declared, to the fury of the settlers, and had to be provided with a guard against possible attack from them. But he was not allowed to see Kenyatta. It is possible he and others heard about the proposed trial by chance, or that Kenyatta smuggled a message out.

8. He sat in Parliament from 1935 to 1950. Pritt was expelled from the Labour Party in 1940 for his support of Russia's occupation of Finland. In the election of 1945 the official Labour candidate put up to oppose him lost his deposit.

9. The DC, Wilson, was one of the best types of colonial servants and he and Pritt got on well together, each helping the other when he could fairly do so. In this instance he must have been acting on direct orders from Nairobi. Pritt got him to remove the ten minute time restriction by threatening to get the foreign correspondents to 'headline' the matter in the British Press.

10. Somerhough was technically *Deputy* Public Prosecutor, but in reality he was the Public Prosecutor as the titular holder of the position was the Attorney-General.

11. The prosecution called an expert witness in the hope of proving that oaths described by Macharia were 'Mau Mau' oaths, but he honestly stated that all the oathing ceremonies described by the Kikuyu witnesses could not be distinguished from traditional Kikuyu forms. The expert witness was none other than Ian Henderson, the police officer in charge of the case. Henderson was born in Kenya and spoke Kikuyu fluently. He was able and tough and his diffidence over this key matter was noteworthy.

12. Counsel in cross-examination has to put to prosecution witnesses the substance of what his witnesses are going to say in contradiction of their evidence.

13. Kenyatta thought Leakey was adding statements of his own to what witnesses had said. The interpreter's oath—'I will interpret the evidence and to the court explain it'—might be held to lay an obligation on the interpreter to elucidate ambiguous evidence. Leakey was a member of one of the government teams investigating Mau Mau.

14. It was proved at Macharia's trial, out of the mouths of government servants, that all these payments had been made and these other services rendered to him. What was not proved, naturally, was how high up in the scale of authority it was known that the evidence was perjured and bought. The reaction of Kenya Europeans to Macharia's affidavit was to assume it was a propaganda stunt to boost the campaign of Mboya and others.

15. Curiously, no further light has been shed over this strange episode. In due course Macharia was forgiven by Kenyatta for his perjury, and he continues to live near to him at Gatundu.

16. It is only fair to point out that many Europeans deplored the extremism of the minority, and among them were men geniunely working for the future welfare of the Africans. But as always, in Kenya, the running was made by vocal backwoodsmen.

17. Tait took over from John Cook at Thogoto and was Kenyatta's instructor. A 'confidential note' by Tait is in the files of the *East African Standard* in Nairobi, dated May 1951. The Huxley article, headed 'A Small-Scale African Hitler' was a copy of a letter in the *Daily Telegraph* which was reprinted in *East Africa and Rhodesia* for 6 November 1952. Despite Pritt's complaint, the Crown declined to prosecute the Kenya paper for contempt of court. The only action taken was by the paper which sent a man to apologize in court.

18. Nuigai in transcript. Throughout, the transcribers spelt Kenyatta's baptismal name as Johnson.

19. But nearly all of the cross-examination was inadmissible in law, for the law of evidence in Kenya, as in Britain, confines the cross-examination of an accused person to matters tending to show that he is guilty of the offence charged. Somerhough broke this rule question by question for most of the seven days, and the magistrate supported him. Their observations suggested that neither of them understood the law of evidence.

CHAPTER 21

1. Kenyatta and the others were loaded into a lorry within five minutes of the end of the judgement and driven off as fast as the roads permitted. Not only did the police pack Pritt's bags for him, they also provided him with a car to take him to Nairobi.

2. Five, because Oneko had won his appeal to the Supreme Court and was not at Lokitaung. The letter was dated 8 October 1954.

3. Prison regulations in Kenya required Africans to eat the normal diet of the district in which they found themselves. At Lokitaung this meant a Turkana diet, which was unwholesome to a Kikuyu at the best of times, and particularly so for a man like Kenyatta who was accustomed to European food. See Itote, op. cit., p. 194 for Kenyatta being 'clean shaven'. A photograph between pp. 144 and 145 confirms it.

4. See Leakey, *Defeating Mau Mau* (London, 1954), p. 112.

5. Greaves, op. cit., p. 116–7. His chapter 5, '1952–1956 The Mau Mau Emergency', makes instructive reading for an idea of what Mau Mau was like seen from the fringes of Kikuyuland. Violence was less in evidence in the Kiambu district. According to Greaves, Carey's memorandum 'was never published but carried considerable weight behind the scenes'.

6. Kariuki, op. cit., p. 43.

7. The Emergency was officially declared at an end on 12 January 1960. In 1952 the number of African pupils enrolled in all schools was 254,593 boys and 79,960 girls. By 1957 the figures were 503,653 boys and 137,127

girls, and in 1959 671,999 boys and 199,732 girls. In the course of 1953 the government allowed 58 of the 188 independent schools which had been closed down at the beginning of the Emergency to reopen.

8. Fred Majdalaney, *State of Emergency* (London, 1962), p. 157.

9. Henderson, op. cit., p. 20.

10. Rosberg and Nottingham, op. cit., p. 304. The development of Kenya's agricultural potential was reflected in rising exports of coffee, tea, sisal etc. But at the same time the terms of trade were turning to the disadvantage of primary producers. Thus in the case of sisal, the total production in 1959 showed a rise of almost half as much again on the figure for 1952, but its export earning power actually *fell* by £1 million.

11. The Order 'will remain in force indefinitely' were the words used. It followed from Thacker's sentence at Kapenguria, and similar restriction orders were passed against the other prisoners at Lokitaung. Baring gave the news at a *baraza* of Kikuyu tribesmen a few miles out of Nairobi.

12. *The Psychology of Mau Mau,* by Dr J. C. Carothers (Kenya Government Publication, 1954). See also *Defeating Mau Mau,* by L. S. B. Leakey (London, 1954), For a detailed criticism of the philosophy of rehabilitation see Chapter 9 of Rosberg and Nottingham's *The Myth of 'Mau Mau',* from which the title of the book itself is taken.

13. Blundell, op. cit., p. 198–9. Quoting the commandant of the camp. Blundell himself, it is only fair to say, was sceptical of the psychological and quasi-religious arguments about Mau Mau and took the more balanced view that the key factor was the 'old and characteristic division among the Kikuyu themselves' (ibid., p. 106).

14. See Itote, op. cit., pp. 195 et seq. for these and following details.

15. By 1959 sales of the second edition were already over the 8,000 mark (Warburg, op. cit., p. 253). Kenyatta wrote to Dinah Stock, 5 March 1958: 'I entirely agree with you that the money should be used to help Magana with his education. I will certainly make the necessary arrangements with the people concerned.' Dinah Stock forwarded the letter on to Edna, but no money, in fact, ever arrived.

16. Kenyatta to Husbands, 19 December 1956.

17. Letters dated 14 February and 30 April 1956.

18. Letter dated 17 January 1957.

19. The prisoners were required to write in Swahili or English. Kenyatta succeeded in smuggling some letters out through sympathetic *askaris,* and he wrote these in Kikuyu. But there was always a danger they might fall into police hands and he said nothing in them that he could not have written openly. Normally he wrote to Margaret in Swahili.

20. Letter dated 22 February 1957.

21. Letter to Margaret dated 25 May, and to Husbands, 10 August 1957.

22. Letter dated 22 February 1957.

23. Letter to Edna Kenyatta dated 4 January 1958, and to Husbands, 5 March 1958.

24. To Margaret Kenyatta, 4 September 1958.

25. Letter to Dinah Stock, 6 June 1955.

26. *Mzee* is a Swahili word which in its simplest meaning is applied to one who

has born children. Thus it comes to have a subtle combination of ideas: 1. a person advanced in years, 2. a village elder, and, 3. parents or 'elders and betters'. The use of it as a title for Kenyatta, when he became President, therefore approaches the thought of 'Father' in the sense of 'Father of the People', somewhat like the way the Kikuyu thought of their tribal Adam, Gikuyu. In the same way, President Nyerere, in neighbouring Tanzania, uses the title *Baba wa taifa,* 'Father of the Nation' or 'Teacher'.

27. It is not impossible the colonial government hoped that by putting Kenyatta up for trial alongside the others, these tensions might be inflamed and give the prosecution the lead they so badly needed. Kenyatta's noteworthy restraint at Kapenguria could be interpreted either as fear of, or as a desire to shield, colleagues like Kaggia of whose activities in eliminating informers he could hardly have been unaware. They were all surprised to find how little the government appeared to have uncovered of their secret activities.

28. Revival Christians were apt to speak of Kenyatta's 'conversion' while at Lokitaung. Only in this way have they been able to reconcile in their minds Kenyatta's utterances since leaving detention and what they firmly believed was his role in managing Mau Mau. Yet Kenyatta had always acknowledged that he was a Christian; he had refused, only, to be drawn to any strict denominational loyalty. Also, it is clear from his letters to Margaret that his sense of supernatural guidance was always strong, and remained unaffected by Kariuki's visit. The author does not feel competent to discuss the theological implications of Kenyatta's words about 'Almighty God' in whatever language he might be using. One point, however, may be made: Kenyatta never referred to the person of Jesus Christ in a manner that would be meaningful to Revival Christians.

29. The *Observer* letter caused a rumpus and the following week the paper printed the full text of the Chief Secretary's statement. (*Observer,* 15 June 1958). On 22 June it also published a letter from an ex-inspector of the Kenya Police which lifted the lid slightly on conditions in 'the real concentration camps' where Mau Mau suspects were sent, and called for an independent commission of enquiry into the way they were being run. Eventually the Hola Camp tragedy was to prove that the general charge of irregularities was not unfounded. See page 357.

30. See Odinga, op. cit., chapter 9.

31. Letter dated 4 September 1958.

32. Ibid., continued on 9 September.

CHAPTER 22

1. It is not clear whether he was released at this moment because he had earned remission or because of a developing sense of guilt at some levels of official thinking at his treatment. China remained at Lokitaung until November that year.

2. Aware that the siting of the runway and its proximity to Uganda, the Sudan and Ethiopia, made it a simple matter to effect, the British government prepared an elaborate, secret, plan which they called Operation Leg-Bye to meet any attempt 'by a foreign power' to rescue Kenyatta. Determined com-

mandoes would have had no difficulty giving Operation Leg-Bye the slip, but no one called for a run! The runway, of course, was out of bounds to Kenyatta.

3. 20 March 1964. Quoted by Rosberg and Nottingham, op. cit., p. 347.

4. Blundell was welcomed at Nairobi airport on his return from London by a settler who threw thirty pieces of silver at his feet. Derek Erskine, an open supporter of Kenyatta, carried pistols to protect himself against European extremists.

5. Did Renison mean to imply by this parenthesis that Kenyatta could have been hanged had he been arrested and tried under later Emergency laws? There were some Europeans who thought Baring's advisers had moved prematurely against Kenyatta, and that if they had stayed their hand a bit longer, Kenyatta would have become more deeply implicated in Mau Mau. In view of the Macharia case it is not impossible they had some kind of frame-up in mind.

6. The Corfield Report is a puzzling and controversial document which has been banned in independent Kenya. Its references to official and secret papers from the critical years leading up to Kenyatta's arrest make it an important— perhaps unique—source. What is not clear is how much Corfield left out. As it is, there is much that bears a different interpretation from the one drawn by Corfield. Corfield's premiss, as has been shown, was false. From the start Kapenguria was a rigged trial. No further evidence has ever been produced to support the Crown's view, as expressed in the trial and as assumed in the report. Those who purport still to have secret and positive proof of Kenyatta's so-called guilt have yet to come forward with it. Meanwhile the Corfield Report has damaged not Kenyatta but the reputation of the colonial government.

Corfield was writing of the period before 1952, but his mind was overshadowed by the Mau Mau terror which had followed Kenyatta's arrest and the declaration of the Emergency. Government counter-terror, of course, did not enter the picture. Instead Corfield drew on the more sensational aspects of Mau Mau to colour everything he said about African politics, on that realm of menstrual blood and 'unheard of bestialities' which took him back in mind to the 'black magic of the Middle Ages'. In Corfield's clear prose many outside Kenya read for the first time that Mau Mau supporters in the forests were made to 'suck the dismembered penis of some unfortunate victim of Mau Mau.' Whether true or imagined, whether general or an isolated case, such stories had little to do with Kenyatta's activities before 1952 and nothing after the date of his arrest. Corfield did great violence to any sense of historical detachment, but, like Somerhough's prosecution at Kapenguria, it was powerful propaganda.

Readers should remind themselves that Ian Henderson, the prosecution expert witness on Kikuyu customs and on Mau Mau at Kapenguria was unable to distinguish any peculiarity in the rites which at that time appeared to accompany Mau Mau oathing ceremonies. The idea that Mau Mau was predominantly a psychological or quasi-religious problem and must be treated accordingly came later.

7. Renison, it must be remembered, flew straight from seeing Macleod to the

press conference where he used the phrase 'leader to darkness and death'. It is inconceivable he did not clear this with Macleod before leaving London. One of his arguments against releasing Kenyatta was that no one knew what was in his mind. But it was not until August 1960 that Coutts, the Chief Secretary, flew up to Lodwar to see Kenyatta.

8. But it is worth noting that Harry Thuku, op. cit., p. 71, believed his own life was spared on orders of Kenyatta 'from detention'. Readers should consider the implications of Thuku's repeating the story in the context under discussion.

9. It may be significant to this view that Corfield provided an Appendix with the names of Africans and others who had supplied him with information. This was omitted when the report was published.

10. Two accounts were: 1. the warders at Lokitaung were given spirits to give to Kenyatta; 2. the warders were given the spirits to give to Kenyatta but consumed it themselves. MacDonald, op. cit., believed Kenyatta drank heavily at Lodwar. No doubt the climate made him very thirsty and he suffered from severe pain in his teeth but where could he have bought spirits?

11. Blundell, op. cit., p. 296.

12. He was also given back a tape-recorder. But the ton and a half of documents which were removed in October 1952 were not returned. Their fate remains a mystery.

13. See MacDonald, op. cit., for Kenyatta before and after the election and the politics of independence.

14. Son of Ramsay MacDonald. Baldwin brought him into the Cabinet in June 1935 as Colonial Secretary and he moved between that office and Dominions Secretary until 1940 when Churchill offered him the Ministry of Health. In 1941 he became British High Commissioner in Canada which started him on his distinguished diplomatic career. It was somewhat ironic that his previous experience of Kenyatta had been through the files of the Colonial Office and the secret Police report of 1939. See chapter 17.

CHAPTER 23

1. Odinga, op. cit., p. 100.

2. Odinga deported Henderson when Kenyatta was out of the country in mid-1964; but according to Odinga this was at Kenyatta's request (op. cit., p. 277). Whitehouse was still active as a magistrate at Kitale in 1971. If he met him at a function Kenyatta would introduce him to his guests as 'my old gaoler'.

3. In 1965 MacDonald became Britain's Special Commissioner in Africa with wider responsibilities than Kenya alone. But he continued to make Nairobi his main base and hence the main base of British policy in Africa. He retired, in theory, in 1969.

4. See Kenyatta in *Suffering Without Bitterness*, especially statement on 'A One-Party System' of August 1964, pp. 226 et seq., and for a more down-to-earth denunciation of Odinga's recently formed opposition party his broadcast in April 1966 on 'Dissident Activity', pp. 302 et seq. See also Mboya,

op. cit., and Odinga, op. cit., for the role of the party as *the alternative government* to the colonial regime during the freedom struggle. See also Kenneth Kaunda's *A Humanist in Africa,* pp. 82 et seq., for the role of the leader. Kaunda sees urbanization as the key factor in breaking down traditional loyalties and creating a new allegiance to independent national institutions, an interesting comment on Livingstone's idea of 'commerce and Christianity'.

5. See, for example, 'The Prayers of Waiyaki' (*Mahoya ma Waiyaki* by Mgugua Njama, Nairobi, 1952) for the explicit idea of Kenyatta as 'resurrected' Waiyaki. A translation by James Ngugi is included as an appendix to Brian McIntosh's unpublished thesis 'The Scottish Mission in Kenya, 1891–1923' in Edinburgh University Library.

6. After the independence of India and Pakistan it became customary to describe 'Indians' as Asians. White men are now referred to as 'expatriates'.

7. Odinga called his autobiography *Not Yet Uhuru.* It was published in 1967 with a foreword by the exiled Nkrumah. Its final chapter was entitled 'Obstacles to Uhuru'.

8. See *Sunday Nation,* 26 October, and *East African Standard,* 27 October, 1969, for accounts of the Kisumu incident, and *Target,* no. 67, November 1969, for a comment on it.

9. See, for instance, article by David Martin in *The Guardian,* 13 August 1971.

10. British television viewers saw him dominate a discussion between a group of Commonwealth Prime Ministers sitting in a London studio. They included Sir Alec Douglas-Home, Ayub Khan of Pakistan and Dr Williams of Trinidad and Tobago. It was on this visit, too, that Kenyatta was attacked by British racists outside his London hotel.

11. But after Nkrumah's fall in Ghana in 1966 Kenyatta refused to recognize the new regime until his old friend T. R. Makonnen, who had been working with Nkrumah, was released from custody. Kenyatta found work for Makonnen in Nairobi.

12. *Suffering Without Bitterness,* foreword p. xi.

13. Ibid., vi.

14. Ibid., v.

INDEX